Palestinians

Palestinians

THE MAKING OF A PEOPLE

Baruch Kimmerling
Joel S. Migdal

Harvard University Press
Cambridge, Massachusetts

This edition is reprinted by arrangement with The Free Press, a
division of Macmillan, Inc.

First Harvard University Press paperback edition, 1994

Library of Congress Cataloging-in-Publication Data
Kimmerling, Baruch.
    Palestinians : the making of a people / Baruch Kimmerling and
    Joel S. Migdal.
        p.   cm.
    Includes bibliographical references and index.
    ISBN 0-674-65223-1 (pbk.)
        1. Palestinian Arabs—History.   2. Jewish-Arab relations.
    I. Migdal, Joel S.   II. Title.
DS119.7.K4943   1993
956.94'0049274—dc20   92-25208
                                                    CIP

In memory of Ted L. Stein and Adam Kimerling

Contents

Maps

Preface

When Yasser Arafat strode onto the White House lawn on September 13, 1993, he basked not only in Washington's late-summer sun but also in the triumph of world recognition that he and the Palestine Liberation Organization had sought through more than a quarter-century of struggle. With the Israeli Prime Minister Yitzhak Rabin's hand grasped firmly in his own and President Bill Clinton's arm around him, Arafat stood as a symbol of how a small and displaced people could bend the will of even their bitterest enemies. When he and Rabin signed the Declaration of Principles outlining a resolution of the century-long conflict between Jews and Arabs in Palestine, Arafat offered to his people the hope, if not the explicit promise, of their own independent state.

But Arafat's triumph was bittersweet. The agreement fell far short of what the PLO had promised its people. Initially its pledge had been for a democratic, secular state, within the territorial framework of all of Mandate Palestine. That plan was pared down five years before the signing of the Declaration of Principles; in 1988, after more than a decade of internal debate, the PLO had recognized Israel's right to exist and accepted the idea of an independent Palestinian state in the West Bank (including Jerusalem) and the Gaza Strip. In 1993, the Palestinians would have to accept, for the time being at least, only the unruly Gaza Strip and the sleepy town of Jericho, where the PLO would set up autonomous rule under the watchful eyes of the Israelis.

The decision to enter into secret negotiations with the Israelis in Oslo, Norway, and finally to sign the Declaration of Principles came not from a string of PLO successes or a vindication of its policy of armed struggle but from the increasing weakness of both Arafat and the organization he headed. If there was any consolation in this weakness, it was that Israel, too, came to the bargaining table exhausted by the effort to suppress the Intifada, the Palestinian uprising in the West Bank and Gaza Strip, and fearful of waning United States support in the aftermath of the Cold War.

Arafat's address to the United Nations General Assembly in 1974 was arguably the pinnacle of PLO prestige. Twenty years later, he and his followers were much more beleaguered. A decade and a half of civil war in Lebanon had left the PLO deeply divided and relocated its headquarters far from the battlefield with Israel. By the end of that war, the organization's strongest supporter, the Soviet Union, was on the brink of disintegration, uninterested in the fate of the Palestinians. The PLO's support of Saddam Hussein in the Gulf War only compounded these problems, leaving it politically isolated and financially ruined.

Even more ominous were the direct and indirect challenges from among the Palestinian people. The growth of powerful Islamic political organizations in the Gaza Strip and the West Bank, especially Hamas, cast serious doubt on the PLO's claim to be the legitimate representative of all the Palestinian people. Islamic militants disputed the PLO's right to bargain away parts of Palestine and offered a very different picture of the future Palestinian state and society. A much more subdued but just as disquieting challenge to the PLO came from the Palestinian civil society that emerged during Israeli occupation of the West Bank and Gaza Strip. While paying homage to both Arafat and the PLO, many Palestinians in the occupied territories felt that the outside leadership was too distant—physically and politically— to understand and respond to the travails of daily life under Israeli rule.

At first, the Declaration of Principles seemed to sweep all the naysaying and doubt away. Some polls showed nearly 75 percent of Palestinians supporting the agreement. But the rigors and length of the negotiations between Israel and the PLO that followed the signing allowed the challenges to Arafat and his organization to resurface in an even more focused way. Decades of dispersal and exile have broadened and deepened Palestinian identity, but they have also created a complex social structure, not easily guided by a single leadership. After a century-long process of creating a Palestinian people, the widely scattered Palestinians and their leaders face the biggest challenge of all: knitting that people into a functioning, politically unified society.

February 1994

Acknowledgments

Albert Hourani wrote in his grand new book, *A History of the Arab Peoples*, "It will be clear to specialists that, in a book with so large a scope, much of what I say is based upon the research of others. I have tried to give the essential facts and to interpret them in the light of what others have written." Of course, this book does not have the scope of Professor Hourani's, but the two centuries we do cover are far more than any pair of scholars could explore exclusively through their own primary research. Our effort was only possible because of many original works on the Palestinians appearing in recent years.

Special thanks go to a number of colleagues who read all or parts of the manuscript. They include Resat Kasaba, Joshua Teitelbaum, Zachary Lockman, Ellis Goldberg, Aaron Klieman, Shibley Telhami, Jere Bacharach, Penina Glazer, and Myron Glazer. Students and faculty in Israel, the United States, and Russia, who participated in several seminar presentations on various chapters, gave many helpful comments. Special thanks are due to Nabil al-Salah, who assisted with Arabic language materials. Also lending important support were Jolanta Lawska, Merlyn Goeschl, Ann Glazer, and Jane Meyerding. We would like to acknowledge, too, the Eshkol Research Center of the Hebrew University and its director Michael Shalev for spiritual and material support, as well as the Henry M. Jackson School of International Studies at the University of Washington. The Shein Center of Social Research at the Hebrew University, then directed by Moshe Lissak, also provided a portion of the resources that made the writing of this volume possible. Our acknowledgments would not be complete without a tip of the hat to Bitnet, which made our transoceanic collaboration feasible. Finally, we owe a special debt of gratitude to our families, who suffered the hogging of the family computer and other indignities so that this book could be written. We have dedicated this book to the memory of Baruch Kimmerling's brother, Adam Kimerling, and of Joel Migdal's friend Ted Stein, whose budding academic career in international law was premised on the ability to resolve disputes civilly.

A Note on Transliteration

In the transliteration of Arabic terms and names, we have decided to leave out diacritical marks; ayin and hamza are not designated. In other cases, transliteration is in keeping with scholarly convention, except in a few cases where there is a commonly accepted English spelling (thus, Gamal Abdul Nasser instead of Jamal 'Abd al-Nasir; Hussein and Husseini instead of Husayn and Husayni; *sheikh* instead of *shaykh*; *fellaheen* instead of *fallahin*). Such a system, we believe, will make the Arabic equivalent quite clear to the specialist, without burdening the general reader with the sometimes cumbersome transliteration conventions of the academy.

Introduction

Towards the end of the eighteenth century, powerful economic and political forces at work in Europe began to affect everyday life in the Middle East, eventually impelling its peoples to redefine both their communities and their vision. Such change did not come without great struggle, continuing in one form or another until the present. Social boundaries—those factors defining insiders and outsiders and what binds the insiders together—have been as much a source of the struggle as the political boundaries of the new Middle Eastern states. In the case of the Palestinians, the process of redefinition has been obscured, and even transformed, by the ongoing conflict with the Jews.

The creation of a nation involves a melding of values and myths, of people's imaginations and their identities. It demands leadership, but also a social foundation empowering the leaders and establishing the limits of what they can achieve. In this book, we are less interested in protocols and diplomacy than in the dynamics and beliefs of peasants, urban workers, merchants, and landowners, and their relationships to the leaders. For particularly with *al-Nakba*—the catastrophic shattering of the Palestinian community in the 1948 war with the Jews[1]—we find the content of what it means to be Palestinian shaped as much by this foundation as by the old, established leadership. The Palestinian people were not mere victims, as so many accounts have presented them (although, to be sure, fate has not treated them kindly), but were active participants in the creation of their people's collective character.

We hope to write against the grain of the sort of history that has been written as part and parcel of mythmaking national projects. In different ways, Palestinians have suffered a great deal from such mythmaking. The historiographical debate has been an integral part of the conflict between Palestinians and Jews. Note the account of one national historian:

> The Palestinians' claim is predicated on the right of ownership evidenced by uninterrupted possession and occupation since the dawn of recorded history. They lived in the country when the Hebrews (of whom the Jews claim descent) came and lived there for a comparatively short period. They continued to live there during the Hebrew (and Jewish) occupation. They remained there after the last Hebrew or Jew left the country nearly two thousand years ago. . . . The people today called Palestinians or Palestinian Arabs, who have been fighting the Zionists and State of Israel which Zionism created in 1948, are largely the descendants of the Canaanites, the Edomites, and the Philistines who lived in Palestine when it was invaded by the Hebrews in ancient times. But the Hebrews finally left or were driven out two thousand years ago.[2]

The search for connection with the past has sometimes transformed history into a handmaiden of those seeking to give the nation a proper pedigree—an effort that involves denigrating the adversary's experience of the past. This exercise has been as evident on the part of Jews as Palestinian advocates. Historians sympathetic with Israel have frequently shared Golda Meir's perspective: "There was no such thing as Palestinians. When was there an independent Palestinian people with a Palestinian state? . . . It was not as though there was a Palestinian people in Palestine considering itself as a Palestinian people and we came and threw them out and took their country from them. They did not exist."[3]

One of the best-known expressions of such a viewpoint has been Joan Peters' *From Time Immemorial: The Origins of the Arab-Jewish Conflict over Palestine*, heavily documented and, apparently, a serious work of scholarship. Its basic argument is that most of Palestine's Arab population was not indigenous. Rather it consisted of migrants, attracted by opportunities offered by Jewish settlement, who came from disparate streams and certainly did not (do not) constitute a people. "The 'Palestinians' ' claim," Peters explains, "is avowedly based upon 'history' and their goal is the dissolution of another state. Their alleged right of 'self-determination' is based upon the erroneous alleged '90% majority of Arabs' in 1917 on the Jewish-settled areas that became Israel in 1948."[4] But as numerous sober historians have shown,[5] Peters' tendentiousness is not, in fact, supported by the historical record, being based on materials out of context, and on distorted evidence.

Almost nothing was shared willingly between Jews and Arabs in the historiographical battle, which began in the reincarnated Palestine of the interwar years. Even the appropriation of the term "Palestinian" became a source for controversy, as seen in Golda Meir's and Joan Peters' protests. The term eventually became attached to the Arabs living in Palestine prior to British withdrawal, as well as to their descendants, while the Jews discarded it in 1948 in favor of "Israelis." For the Arabs, the term indicated not only a land of origin, but also an increasing sense of a shared past and future. In the following pages, for convenience we will refer to Palestinian Arabs as Palestinians, and to the country as Palestine, even when applied to periods in which such usage is anachronistic—when the Arabs' sense of participating in a common history had not yet evolved, and when the territory was administratively fragmented. But our use of the term for the nineteenth or early twentieth centuries should not obscure our main point, the one that has so often been missed on both sides of the historiographical divide: a Palestinian national identity, like those of other modern nations, has been created—invented and elaborated—over the course of the last two centuries.

In some ways, the Jewish national movement has shaped the Palestinian people almost as much as it did the Jews themselves. Had it not been for the pressures exerted on the Arabs of Palestine by the Zionist movement, the very concept of a Palestinian people would not have developed; and Palestinians quite accurately understand their society's essential, existential status as the direct result of Jewish political rejuvenation and settlement. They see their own lives as reflections of a catastrophe, with Zionism—as Palestinian writer Fawaz Turki has put it—"having its day and the Palestinian [movement] its eclipse," individual Palestinians ending up in "the world of the exile. The world of the occupied. The world of the refugee. The world of the ghetto. The world of the stateless."[6] Nevertheless, focusing our attention exclusively on the Palestinian Arab conflict with the Jews would obscure other important factors, particularly the extension of the world market into Palestine and the imposition of politically and administratively capable states, both beginning in the nineteenth century. Until quite recently, Palestinian writers paid scant attention to the contours of their own society, preoccupied as they were with the other, the Jews—the key to unlocking the secrets of those forces that turned their world upside down. For their part, the Zionists have been absorbed in a nationalist project rendering the Palestinians almost incidental. In the process, they have failed to grasp the extent to which their own society has been shaped by its ongoing encounter with the Palestinians. Perhaps doing so would involve too painful an encounter with Zionism's political counterpart—what we might call "Palestinism": the belief that the Arab population originating in the area of the Palestine mandate is distinct from other Arab groups, with a right to its own nation-state in that territory.[7]

As young academics, the authors of this book joined a handful of Jewish social scientists beginning, in the wake of the 1967 war, to view the Palestinians, not as anthropological curiosities, but as a social group deeply affecting the future of the Jews. In addition to its 2.4 million Jews, Israel then governed almost 1.5 million Arabs, including around 400,000 citizens of Israel, 665,000 in the West Bank and East Jerusalem, and 356,000 in the Gaza Strip. We both came to know many Palestinians, mostly in West Bank villages and on the campus of the Hebrew University. Kimmerling wrote about Jewish and Palestinian interdependence in the half century since World War I, while Migdal focused on the long-standing impact of different rulers, including the Israelis, on Palestinian society. Hovering behind all this work has been an awareness that mutual Jewish-Palestinian denial will disappear slowly, if ever. Still, recent events have made one thing quite clear: The Palestinian dream of self-determination will likely be realized only with the assent of a secure, cohesive Israel, and the Israeli dream of acceptance throughout the Middle East will likely need Palestinian approval.

As much as any people in the world, the Palestinians have suffered from media stereotypes: "terrorists" and "freedom fighters," "murderers" and "victims." At times, the Palestinian leadership has reinforced such images by insisting on a national consensus denying the rifts in their society. In the following pages, we intend to satisfy neither the demonic nor idyllic vision of the Palestinian Arab. Rather, we will describe the contours of a people at the center of one of the most volatile conflicts of our time.

PART ONE

FROM REVOLT TO REVOLT
The Encounter with the European
World and Zionism

The Revolt of 1834 and the Making of Modern Palestine

Palestine is the crossroads of three continents. It is a land of shifting boundaries: a political entity that vanished, only to re-emerge like a phoenix. The home of the great monotheistic religions—Judaism, Christianity, and Islam—it has been the object of countless bitter wars and struggles through nearly four millennia. It is a land of pitifully few resources and starkly beautiful terrain.

While Palestine's borders have always been vague and changing, its center has never been uncertain. Nestled in the hills of Jabal al-Quds, or the Judean Mountains, Jerusalem (in Arabic, *al-Quds*) is synonymous for most people with the Holy Land. King David and his son Solomon established the city three thousand years ago as their capital. The site of the Jewish Temple, of Jesus's last preaching and crucifixion, and of the Prophet Muhammad's ascension to heaven, it still holds the remnant of the Temple's outer courtyard wall—the Western or Wailing Wall—which is also the outer fence of the Haram al-Sharif, Islam's third holiest site. In the nineteenth and early twentieth century, it became the center for the new leadership of Arab notables.

Palestine's four natural regions surround Jerusalem. The hilly, most barren region in the eastern part of the country was the center of ancient Jewish civilization, known as Samaria and Judea and today commonly referred to as the West Bank. Its largest center remains Nablus, a town dating back to biblical times that was the heart of early nineteenth century Arabic village society. The southern Negev, starting in the town of Beersheba, long served as the home and transit route for nomadic Bedouins. For the most part, this harsh desert has remained sparsely populated through the centuries, those who did try to settle it facing the enmity of the nomads. The third region, the narrow strip forming the coastal plain, extends from Gaza in the south through Haifa's bay in the north and past the mountainous Carmel up to Lebanon. The ancient maritime civilizations—some stemming from the Phoenicians—were settled here, as well as the great cities of Palestine—Gaza, Jaffa, Haifa, Acre, and, in this century, Tel-Aviv. (By the early nineteenth century, the coastal plain was a neglected remnant of its former glory.) Finally, fertile valleys and breathtaking hills dominate the country's northern section, including the region from Acre to the hills of al-Jalil (the biblical Galilee), the Valley of Marj Ibn Amir (the Jezreel Valley), and the Baysan.

For a country of 10,500 square miles (about the size of Maryland), Palestine encompasses a remarkably varied physical environment. About half the land has been entirely uncultivable, while large portions of the other half have been rocky, sandy, or swampy, with a low and unstable amount of rainfall. But, for all the scarcity of rich soil and the inadequate irrigation, Palestine has always been a country of farmers. Archaeologists have discovered the remains of agricultural sites near Jericho, northwest of the Dead Sea, stemming from the earliest phase of human culture—approximately 8000 B.C.E.

Traditionally, these farmers have coexisted (albeit often uneasily) with the country's nomadic Bedouins. Having long laid claim, through their ties to real or fictive common ancestors, to being parts of the early Islamic nomadic communities, the Bedouins have assumed the title of the "original Arabs." According to local lore, these ancestors swept out of Arabia under the leadership of the second caliph, Umar ibn Abd al-Khattab, in the first half of the seventh century. The caliph's warriors gave an Islamic and Arab stamp lasting until now to all of Syria (including Palestine), the Fertile Crescent, and much of North Africa.

Over the centuries, Bedouin men maintained their identity as warriors while looking after grasslands, water resources, and livestock—as well as occasionally engaging in smuggling and robbery. Women reared the children, cooked and cleaned, and lent a hand in the fields or with the livestock. The strongest Bedouin loyalties were to their families and larger kinship groups, but they were quick to enter into alliances with almost any force offering material or political benefit. Their nemesis was the state, or any other central authority wishing to settle or disarm them and force acceptance of its political boundaries. Sometimes Bedouins have triumphed over such authority. At other times, the state has had its way, and at yet others, the Bedouins have assumed the leading role in the state. This took place, for example, in twentieth century Transjordan, where the Hashemite dynasty, claiming direct descent from the Prophet Muhammad, absorbed local Bedouin groups into the top echelons of the state and its army, the Arab Legion.

Starting with the dawn of Romanticism, the image of the Bedouin warriors, wild and noble, dominated both Orientalist literature and the general Western concept of Palestine.[1] But as enticing as the image was, it was only peripheral to the history of Palestinian society, which begins with the settled agriculturalists—the *fellaheen* or peasants—and their ties to the powerful landowning families that dominated rural economic and social life. It was peasants and landowners who put their indelible stamp on day-to-day life in Palestine and who were at the center of the bloody battles punctuating the last several centuries. For this reason, while the Bedouins will have their role in the story that follows, our primary focus will be on the peasants: on how the economic and administrative forces of the last two centuries have remolded them into a multilayered society, the basis for the eventual emerging of a coherent and self-conscious people.

Of all the violent struggles in Palestine, three revolts have defined the modern history of the country's Arabs. The first revolt in 1834, was a bloody attempt to stave off the momentous changes instituted by Egyptian empire builders, who ruled the country through most of the 1830s. Its suppression confirmed that the parameters of peasant society would be redrawn. While a good many Palestinians bitterly resisted the changes, the ensuing transformation laid the basis for a much more complex society. The second revolt, from 1936 to 1939, came in the context of Britain's imperial rule and was the first real effort to demonstrate decisively this fledgling nation's political will. The third is the Intifada, which began in 1987; its goal, like the rebellion in 1936, has been to lay the foundation for political

independence, but now in the difficult circumstances of the powerful rule of its rival for the soil of the country, Israel.

THE FIRST PALESTINIAN REVOLT:
ORIGINS, PROGRESSION, AND OUTCOME

The seeds of Palestinian rebellion were planted with the country's conquest in the 1830s. The Ottomans, exhausted from trying to restore more direct rule in a number of provinces and from
the draining Greek war, lost control of Syria and Palestine between 1831 and 1840. A vassal of the Ottomans, Egypt's upstart
governor Muhammad Ali, overran portions of the Empire right
into Anatolia and occupied them under the leadership of his son,
Ibrahim Pasha.[2] In time, much of the Palestinian population,
especially its Muslim majority, turned against the occupation.
The total population was probably under a quarter of a million,
several tens of thousands of Jews and, of the rest, about 20 percent Christian. Nothing alienated the local Arabs as much as
Ibrahim's demands for conscripts. Peasants were well aware that
conscription was little more than a death sentence: The term of
service was frequently for life and, given the sanitary conditions
and military technology of the day, there was little chance parents would ever see their sons again.

Despite his unpopularity, Ibrahim Pasha did manage to enforce security in a country that had been battered by extreme
lawlessness. The new security enabled farmers to venture into
previously uncultivated areas, merchants to forge ties to the
European market from safer coastal enclaves, and pilgrims to
visit the country in unprecedented numbers. With the Egyptian
administration initiating new farming techniques and helping to
prepare previously uncultivated lands for farming,[3] local trade
expanded, and foreign trade, while still quite small, showed
some new signs of life. For the Egyptians, Syria and Palestine
were to be Levantine breadbaskets, as well as a source of fresh
conscripts and additional revenues for the inevitable next battle
against the Ottomans. Corresponding to Muhammad Ali's push
for industrial growth and cotton production in Egypt itself, Ibrahim Pasha's attention to agriculture and trade in Syria and Palestine involved an effort to establish the basis for specialized
crop production, meant eventually to supply Egypt with the raw

materials it needed. To speed the process, Ibrahim allowed Christians to trade in grain and livestock—activities that the Ottomans had previously banned.[4]

The tough rule and the new reforms led to the 1834 revolt's outbreak in the heart of the country, uniting dispersed Bedouin, rural sheikhs, urban notables, mountain fellaheen, and Jerusalem religious figures[5] against a common enemy. It was these groups who would later constitute the Palestinian people.

The revolt was centered in the key town of Nablus and, to a lesser degree, in Jerusalem, with uprisings in other towns, too; but the backbone of the fighting forces was the peasantry.[6] Nablus lay in the heart of the hilly agricultural area that, in the 1830s, was the most populated and productive part of the country. Starting as an oversized village, it had developed into a town of 10,000 inhabitants, with a surrounding area that included some 200 villages with roughly another 100,000 people. From their bases in Nablus, notable family groupings associated with the longstanding Arab cleavage of Qays and Yaman dominated the entire region.[7] The revolt would eventually forge an alliance between these coalitions.

Jerusalem, a town of 15,000–20,000 people, was the religious seat of the region and enjoyed an unusual amount of autonomy in the Ottoman Empire. The Ottomans appointed both its religious leader, the Mufti, and its chief judge, the Grand Qadi; they exercised strong influence throughout the country, imposing levies and taxes on the city's non-Muslim inhabitants and on Jewish and Christian pilgrims, and— most importantly—controlling appointments to religious offices, schools, and the Waqf (religious endowments). Inside the city, two powerful families ruled—the Husseinis and Khalidis. In the 120 surrounding villages, the Abu Ghush clan dominated (with opposition, to be sure), partly through its control of access to Jerusalem along the strategic road from Jaffa.

The revolt's first signs came on May 19, 1834, when a number of important families and sheikhs from Nablus, Jerusalem, and Hebron informed Ibrahim's civil and military governors they could not supply the quotas of conscripts for military service demanded of them: The peasants—so went the claim—had simply fled from their villages into the difficult, mountainous terrain to the east. Since Ibrahim was already facing similar resistance in northern Syria, in the area east of the Jordan River, and in the Arabian peninsula's Hejaz (where his forces had suffered some heavy casualties), the notables' declaration would not have been totally unexpected. His response was to postpone conscription in these other areas, but to maintain strict enforcement of the policy in Palestine.

His decision turned out costly. Riots first broke out in the Hebron region. When Egyptian troops arrived, fellaheen from the village of Sair, supported by Bedouins, killed about twenty-five soldiers, and Hebronites overcame the town's small garrison, arresting Ibrahim's governor. Some local peasants began to move towards Jerusalem. In the nearby Nablus region, the Egyptians had gained the support of an important clan, the Abd al-Hadis, but that insurance policy turned out far from adequate. The Abd al-Hadis' main rivals, the Qasims, declared a general revolt against the Egyptians, refusing to supply conscripts or pay taxes. Gathering most of the country's notable families in their home village, the Qasims urged opposition to the Abd al-Hadis and Egyptian rule, at the same time mounting an unsuccessful attempt to capture Nablus.

While their storming of that city failed, their call to rid Jerusalem of the Egyptians had greater success. Hundreds of peasants from all over the hilly eastern portion of Palestine joined those marching from Hebron to lay siege to the walls of Jerusalem. When the Abu Ghush clan, with their control of the Jaffa-Jerusalem road, joined the rebel forces, the noose was drawn tight: With two thousand men carrying rifles and the support of most of the country's clans (as well as much of the Muslim population inside the besieged city), the rebellion had produced an astoundingly powerful and broad coalition of local groups.

By the end of May, Ibrahim's situation appeared desperate. The attempt by his regiment from Jaffa to relieve the Jerusalem forces ended in a disastrous ambush. The flush of rebel success broke the Abd al-Hadis' hold on Nablus which—with the Qasims now reigning—also joined the revolt, turning into the center of opposition to the Egyptians. On the last day of the month, Muslims in Jerusalem managed to open the gates, allowing the rebels to take over the city everywhere but the citadel, where the Egyptian forces took refuge. Ibrahim's foothold in Palestine had shrunk, essentially, to the four coastal towns of Gaza, Jaffa, Haifa, and Acre. In Jerusalem, the peasants set upon the local Jewish and Christian populations, looting houses and raping women. Even the local Muslim population, especially the notable families, came under the onslaught. As in the two twentieth century revolts, a deep populist strain seemed to underlie this rebellion.

Although in June Ibrahim mounted a number of counterattacks inflicting heavy artillery damage, the revolt continued to spread, his military suffering thousands of casualties at the hands of the numerically superior rebel forces. He did manage to retake Jerusalem that same month. But along with some smaller coastal towns, Haifa came under siege, and Tiberias and Safad fell in the north. In Tiberias, Muslims launched fierce attacks upon both the town's Jewish population and a number of Christian families.

Both the rebels' fury and the breadth of the revolt stemmed from Ibrahim's uncanny ability to institute change alienating almost all Muslims. Only the minorities and selected notable families had found their positions enhanced by Egyptian rule. Complementing the personal tragedy it inflicted, the dreaded conscription threatened families and whole villages with an inadequate labor supply. Notables had found the basis of their autonomy shattered. Ibrahim Pasha's centralization of tax collection had taken from the *ayan*, the notables, their most important lever of control, especially over the minority religions. The Egyptians had targeted the Bedouins, as well. Nomads no longer could impose road tolls or protection levies, and they found Ibrahim maneuvering to settle them permanently.

Ibrahim also speeded up an integration process that may have resulted, ironically, in it becoming that much easier to struggle against him. The process had already begun at the turn of the nineteenth century, when Ahmad Pasha al-Jazzar brought Palestine under single rule and administration for the first time in centuries (see chapter 2). That feat was repeated shortly before the Egyptian invasion by another Ottoman vassal, Abdallah Pasha. Based first in Sidon (now in Lebanon) and later in Acre, Abdallah established his rule in the subdistrict of Nablus and the administratively autonomous Jerusalem. While maintaining the local power of the notable families, he had brought the entire province of Sidon under his control by the eve of Muhammad Ali's conquest. These earlier efforts, as well as those fostered by local sheikhs, had resulted in some changes in peasant crop production, taking advantage of new European markets. But Ibrahim's own rule differed significantly from that of the earlier rulers in his refusal to respect the autonomy of the local notables. His radical measures of direct governance and taxation made many people, especially among the powerful ayan, feel that the social, religious, and economic fabric of the society was at risk. At the same time, those same measures, particularly ones stressing the primacy of the state over equal subjects, battered the society's previously rigid hierarchical barriers.

The Peasant Revolt in Syria, as contemporary sources and historians labelled the revolt of 1834, threatened not only the flow of conscripts and material resources to Egypt but Muhammad Ali's entire plan for its renewal. Palestine was turning into a graveyard for his dreams as well as for his soldiers. His response, not surprisingly, was rather clever. First, through deception and rumor, he convinced his foes that his reinforcements were a much bigger force than the 15,000 men and 40 cannons he actually had available (mostly in Jaffa). Next, he worked to break the coalition of notables, his most impressive achievement in this regard being to open the Jerusalem road by offering the Abu Ghush clan everything from guaranteed amnesty to positions in the Egyptian administration. Finally, he promised the harshest consequences for those who continued to defy him. Ibrahim Pasha carried out the last part of the plan. On July 4, 1834, he directed a military expedition at the heart of Qasim-led rebel forces in the Nablus region. The Egyptian soldiers reduced 16 villages to ash on their route, including those dominated by major rebel leaders. After a bloody battle, the Egyptians routed the fellaheen, publicly decapitating their leaders; they took Nablus on July 15. The final battle occurred in Hebron on August 4: The Egyptian victory there was complete and included levelling of the city, rape of the women, mass killing and conscription of the men, the furnishing of 120 adolescents to Egyptian officers to do with as they wanted.

Throughout the country, the rebels were cruelly handled. About 10,000 fellaheen were recruited and shipped to Egypt. Sections of entire towns, including the Muslim quarter of Bethlehem, were destroyed, and their inhabitants expelled or killed. And, in a measure that struck very hard, even given all the other atrocities those in Palestine faced, the Egyptians disarmed the population: For Muslim men, the rifle had become part of their identity, a symbol of honor and freedom; in the insecure conditions of the nineteenth century, it had also been seen as a necessary safeguard for one's family. Ibrahim's action was, in effect, the announcement of a new order, one in which the state would monopolize the use of violence.

That new order confronted a largely agricultural society that, while continuing to be so until well into the twentieth century, would be subject to increasingly rapid rates of change.[8] The period following the Egyptian conquest and Muhammad Ali's withdrawal at the end of the decade (with considerable European help, the Ottomans would manage to oust him) saw a change in where and how the peasants farmed, the crops they grew and the markets they were grown for, their legal relationship to the land, and their ties to the powerful social forces above them. Three forces converged to spearhead the changes, two of them increasing their impact considerably under Ibrahim Pasha's stern hand: the Europe-dominated world market, which was deepening its penetration of the Middle East and, for that matter, of peasant societies all over the world by the last part of the nineteenth century,[9] and the new, much more intense role of government in local affairs. From midcentury on, revived Ottoman control of Palestine included a spate of reforms affecting both landholding (directly) and land use (indirectly). The third and in some ways most momentous force was Zionism and Jewish settlement.

Zionism, of course, did not exist during Muhammad Ali's era. Still, the Egyptian reforms seemed to energize the Jews as they gained new rights. Accompanying the emergence of various forms of proto-Zionism, immigration to Palestine increased and the Jewish population began to grow substantially. With Zionism's much clearer impact on the country in the 1880s and after, the Jewish presence intersected with Arab agricultural life at any number of points, and a good part of Arab-Jewish frictions focused on the issues of land, water, and agricultural labor.[10]

To the naive observer, the process emerging during Ibrahim's brief tenure seemed to involve taking the agriculture of a miserably poor, technologically backward peasantry and transforming it into one increasingly marked by cash crops, technological sophistication, and higher production. John Pinkerton's *Modern Geography*, written in 1802, captures how a Westerner saw the state of the fellaheen before this wave of change. "The peasants," he wrote, "are in the most miserable situation; and although not sold with the soil, like those of Poland, are, if possible, yet more oppressed; barley, bread, onions and water constituting their constant fare."[11]

There is no denying the misery of early nineteenth century peasants, but they may have had far more autonomy and rights than Polish serfs of the time. More to the point, an oversimplified view of agricultural progress as a straight line from a set of dire conditions to the paradise of cash crops (especially citrus fruit) in the twentieth century obscures not only the dynamics of the earlier period but a much less sanguine side of rural change: the decreasing viability of agriculture as an economic bedrock for the vast majority of the Palestinian population. Palestinian peasants faced a no-win situation. When wealthier Arabs adopted new technologies they reduced overall agricultural employment and when peasants managed to hold onto their lands they found themselves uncompetitive with more modern Jewish and Arab farming. To understand the effect of this double-bind on Palestinian society, we need to look more closely at the three major forces of the world market, government intervention, and Zionism that helped transform the country's agriculture, starting with the "Peasant Revolt in Syria" and ending with al-Nakba, the Palestinian Disaster of 1948.

THE WORLD MARKET

The Ottoman reappearance in 1840 left some of Ibrahim's changes in place. Local Arab Christians, for example, continued playing a disproportionately large role in the country's economic life. Renewed Ottoman control also brought with it an influx of outsiders—consuls and missionaries—who spearheaded a permanent European presence in Palestine. Not far behind were European merchants, who, while mostly based in the coastal towns, carried auguries of change to rural areas.

The towns served as conduits for wheat grown in Palestine to consumers in England, Ireland, and elsewhere. Small peasants rarely had any face-to-face contact with the Europeans, but increasing numbers of Palestinian Christian merchants began to settle in the coastal towns.[12] Together with a number of Muslim landlords and tax farmers, who collected their due from the peasants in kind, they managed to establish ties with Europeans whose ships docked in the ports. A renewed wave of insecurity in the 1850s, when notable Palestinian families led a destructive round of intervillage violence, disrupted agriculture, but rural life was resuscitated with the increasing social and political order of the 1860s. The Ottoman forces, freed from participation in the Crimean War, turned their attention to establishing order in the country, especially the potentially rich coastal plain and northern valleys, and the resulting changes signalled the beginning of the end for subsistence peasant agriculture.

Palestinian farming now moved towards deep, inextricable involvement with the world market. Rising world prices in the 1860s and 1870s made ties to the European economy ever more attractive to merchants and large landowners. Much of the southern coastal land around Gaza, for example, was devoted to growing wheat, barley, and maize, which were all increasingly in demand in Europe.[13] Specialty crops also rose in popularity, with sesame, cotton, oranges, olives (for oil), and grapes (for wine) leading the way. Crops such as olives and sesame had long been Palestinian staples, but widespread cultivation of cotton, and an intensive planting of new orange orchards to take advantage of the high profits citrus fruits offered, represented a major innovation. In the 1870s, Arabs exported most of their oranges to Egypt and Turkey; by the early years of the twentieth century, Britain had become the biggest customer for high-quality oranges from Jaffa.[14]

Both overall farming output and the proportion of cash crops grew considerably. After a long stagnation, cultivation of the coastal plain and northern valleys showed a dramatic increase, many of the cash crops being concentrated in these areas. Some of the new output was a response to need, the Arab population alone expanding by about 70 percent between 1870 and World War I.[15] But a sizeable portion went to exports. Distant wars—first the Crimean and then the United States' Civil War—propelled world agricultural prices upward in the 1850s and 1860s, as did growing British and Continental affluence, which also led to greater demand.[16]

It took major changes in landholding and even local warfare around midcentury to put some groups in a position to react flexibly and quickly to new world-market opportunities.[17] Together with rising land prices—paving the way for a new Arab leadership that would stay in power until the creation of the state of Israel[18]—these changes had deep, long-term effects on the Palestinian Arabs, even before the Zionists arrived on the scene.

THE NEW ROLE OF GOVERNMENT

Once the Ottomans expelled Muhammad Ali's forces, they were none too eager to return to the type of loose rule they had previously exercised in Syria and Palestine. The Egyptian method of direct administration seemed both more secure and more lucrative; Ottoman authorities now viewed the possibility of a similar approach on their part as a way to break the rebellious independence of the notables and sheikhs once and for all. One Ottoman official told recalcitrant sheikhs, "Formerly the Turkish Government was weak in Syria and we could not compel you always to obey us, but now we are strong and if you are insubordinate I will . . . throw you into the sea."[19] Nevertheless, the Ottomans achieved only some of their aims and, indeed, unintentionally paved the way for changes that subverted some of their most important goals. Their historic use of the notables to rule the Arab provinces injected an ambivalence into policies designed to sweep away the notables' political power and adopt some form of direct rule.

First, in the Ottomans' efforts to oust the Egyptians, they armed local forces—led of course by the ayan and the sheikhs—and made tempting promises about both short-term exemption from taxes and their long-term reduction, which ended up tying the hands of Ottoman revenue collectors.[20] After the end of the Egyptian occupation in 1840, they then proceeded to neglect the country for several years, giving the notables ample opportunity to reestablish themselves; by the time the Ottomans attempted to reassert direct control in 1844–45, it was too late. Ibrahim Pasha was reported to have warned a Turkish general, "You with the assistance of the English have expelled me; you have again put arms into the hands of the mountaineers [the sheikhs]; it cost me nine years and ninety thousand men to disarm them. You will yet invite me back to govern them."[21] Ibrahim was not invited back, and the sheikhs were subjugated; but talk of tossing them into the Mediterranean notwithstanding, the Ottomans never did destroy or even bypass the town notables. (They did have some success against the rural sheikhs.) In fact, the reforms following the reconquest of Syria and Palestine expanded the reach of the ayan's power considerably beyond their own sleepy towns and subject villages,[22] their position in the country being shored up firmly by the end of the Ottoman period.[23] What did occur as the Ottomans spattered out reforms throughout the century was a change in the basis of the notables' power and control.

The larger context of this process was the Ottoman *Tanzimat*: the great push in the middle decades of the nineteenth century to salvage the decaying empire through legal and administrative changes. Ottoman authorities, attempting now to govern domains over which they had previously exercised control in name only, focused on taxation, land ownership, town government, and general administration. Their aim was to insinuate the government into the daily routine of the Empire's subjects, enhancing its ability to mobilize both people and revenues. The most important of the Ottoman reforms for Palestinian rural life involved land tenure, beginning with the land law of 1858. The land reform was one of a number of the initiatives unintentionally bolstering the ambitious ayan—and helping to create new agrarian and national relations among the Palestinians that would carry over to the middle of the next century.[24]

In this respect, a pivotal innovation was the requirement of *Tapu*: a title of ownership for all land, which, in turn demanded a centralized land register for all holdings in Palestine.[25] Previously, ownership had been demonstrated simply by cultivation; the new law allowed unoccupied land to be registered. Town notables quickly realized the tremendous potential of such land, especially as government control increased in the most fertile parts of the country. By the mid-1870s, the Ottomans had subdued Bedouin marauders, and the ayan used the new law to take possession of large estates in the valleys and plains. Here the tastes of far off Europeans began to shape a new cash-sensitive agriculture. And these estates, stretching well beyond the small towns where the notable families actually lived, became the foundation for the ayan's role as the dominant and dominating Arab class in Palestine.

At times, the notables bought lands only to turn a quick profit through resale. Later, the Zionists would become ready customers for large tracts, driving up the price of land generally. Some

Arab landowners converted their estates into farms, with orchards and fields producing cash crops. The notables' ability to marshal investment capital put them in a competitively superior position to the fellaheen: Continuing to farm with traditional methods, the peasants grew in numbers in the country's far less fertile, central and eastern mountain regions and provided a pool of ready hands to undertake the work of cultivation. Many urban landowners, especially those uninvolved in the new citrus sector or who lived outside the country, showed little interest in the day-to-day working of their estates beyond collecting their due. It was the tenants on the newly reclaimed lands, drifting down from the east, who provided the muscle—and often the technical innovations—to create profit-making agricultural enterprises.

Migration westward was certainly not novel for the mountain fellaheen. Traditionally, in times of greater security some farmers would move into the frontier zone of the valleys and plains, where they built temporary extensions of their villages—the *khirba*. Now, in the latter part of the nineteenth century, the khirbas and their independent farmers reappeared, but they were dwarfed by the larger estates.[26] The movement did not come to a halt until 1948, when the flow was first reversed as refugees fled to the hills and then was choked off entirely as new boundaries came into existence.

Migrants to the coastal plain and valleys in the 1860s and 1870s were still a minority of the population, still settled mostly in 800–900 mountain villages where the rocky land afforded some insulation from both marauding bands or armies and government authorities. So did the construction of the villages themselves. Sociologist Rosemary Sayigh has noted that

> Unlike many villages in the Mediterranean area, those of Palestine were not walled, but the clustering of their solid, stone-built houses in close formation, with walls almost a metre thick and flat rooftops from which lookout could be kept and stones hurled, made them a formidable obstacle to most attackers.[27]

In the hills, the central institution was *musha*, a co-ownership system that acted as an equalizing force in village life by periodically redividing land among the village clans.[28] The musha system worked to sustain the extended family (which tilled the divided parcels) as the basic social unit. It typically consisted of the father, mother, and unmarried children as well as married sons and their wives and children. Clans, too, remained important, linking extended families, often through the marriage of first cousins.[29] Given the often violent environment, the clan helped protect villagers from the ravages of war, marauding Bedouins, and *fidya* (a form of collective retribution in blood feuds).[30]

Inequalities abounded in village life. Within families, older males tended to dominate, although women exerted considerable influence through their critical role in maintaining the household.[31] With designation as an elder stemming as much from status as from chronological age, the elders' redivision of land gave them significant power within the clan, often leading to inequalities among its various family groups and sometimes to serious abuses. Inequities persisted among the clans as well, since during the land redivision process consideration was often given to those having more sons, cattle, oxen, and donkeys. Thus land division to some extent reinforced the positions of those already possessing wealth by assigning them the largest and most fertile parcels. Often, the power of a clan could be discerned by the lavishness of its *madafa*, the guest house always open to strangers or outside authorities.[32]

Although the system did not entirely equalize households and clans, it often prevented huge disparities, maintained a sense of cooperation and identity, and avoided the loss of village lands to outsiders through personal sales (which were forbidden). Later, both the British and the Zionists saw the fellaheen's inability to sell and purchase land freely as a major impediment to the progress of agriculture and of Arab villages generally.[33] They also believed that the regular redivision of the land removed incentives to improve it.[34] It is not surprising, then, that by the end of British rule, musha lands had diminished to less than a quarter of all Arab holdings.[35]

The new land law, with its official registry and proliferation of deeds, opened the way to much easier transfer of ownership, largely in the newly cultivated coastal plain and northern valleys. An unintended result of the reform was to confirm the central and eastern mountain region as a bastion of a Palestinian social and agricultural life remarkably different from that emerging in the country's western portion. The hilly region sheltered determined small freeholders who had to cope with infertile soil, overpopulation, and competition from much more advanced agriculture in the valleys and plains. With its rapid rise of population, it also served as a source of labor, first for the large agricultural estates in the latter region, and then for other enterprises starting to emerge along the coast.

Along with irreversibly altering landholding patterns and village and clan relations, the dismantlement of the musha system involved the imposition of tax after tax upon the peasantry, who found themselves—in an experience shared with peasants almost everywhere in Asia and Africa—sinking deeper and deeper into debt.[36] While urban moneylenders served as a bridge between the mountain and the plain, these moneylenders were often the same notables gobbling up land under the new reforms. In this manner they engendered a dependency upon themselves by way of cash loans, often repossessing land when peasants went deeply into arrears.[37]

The key figures in the reforms were the *mukhtars,* a new government designation for chiefs of the village.[38] Unlike the powerful village sheikhs who had preceded them and who had paid little heed to government dictates, the mukhtars were officials of the state. Once the Ottomans rid the countryside of the sheikhs and their incessant local warfare, the mukhtars emerged as important local figures—unpaid go-betweens, representing the government to the peasants and, less frequently, the peasants to the government. Their roles included recording information on births, deaths, and marriages, and local responsibility for the land registry.

But the mukhtars' most important function was to keep order: Any village watchmen or guards were under their direct supervision. The Ottoman authorities had also hoped to use them as key personnel in a more centralized tax system, but the general failure of the tax reforms meant a repeated recourse to tax-farming—an inefficient system in which the state auctioned off its revenue-collecting rights to individuals.[39]

The mukhtars were an odd mixture of powerful local figures—akin to their predecessors, the sheikhs—and mere links on the far end of the government's bureaucratic chain. Supposedly chosen by the village's male population, they often came to their positions as local strongmen or as protégés of other powerful figures. At the same time, at least in theory, they were completely subservient to the district governor, who also had a say in their selection. Unlike the sheikhs before them, they did not serve as village arbitrators and judges, instead finding themselves preoccupied with a host of petty bureaucratic tasks.

In some ways, the mukhtar lent a new unity to the village, defining its place within a more tight-knit empire. His role was intertwined with an emerging new self-definition for the local rural community: much less autonomous, more a distinct unit within a larger whole that impinged constantly on rural life. In other ways, the role simply reinforced some of the old divisions in village life, with large villages (3,000–5,000 people as opposed to the average 700–800) frequently having a number of mukhtars, each representing a major clan. Here, the tensions among these chiefs often mirrored continuing divisions in the village itself.

Village life still had a distinct pace, even in the last phase of Ottoman rule, and the mukhtars played pivotal roles in negotiating how outside pressures would be assimilated. Nevertheless, the mukhtar did not have a monopoly of control over the economic and political forces drawing Palestine's isolated villages into a widening world. Different groups in the village (or, in the plains and valleys, absentee landlords) derived considerable power from varying degrees of direct contact with outside authorities and enterprises.[40] Teachers or village preachers, for example, began reading city newspapers aloud and interpreting them to eager villagers by the start of the twentieth century.[41] A very few villages contained families that—at least by local standards—were very rich, owning a hundred or more acres of land. These families established branches in some of the urban centers and were the first to educate their sons in Western schools. Below them were a larger number of families, often farming with the help of hired seasonal hands or tenants, who would sometimes also send their sons to study in a missionary school in town. Such contacts enabled both groups to play important leadership roles inside the village and, for the most powerful, in an even wider domain.

A third group consisted of those with land supporting them

but absorbing all their labor. Below them were peasant families
that also owned land but whose members had to seek additional
income as tenants or hired hands. Often sending sons to become
tenants on the new estates in the lowlands, or even to work in
the bustling coastal towns, such families—while subservient to
the large landowners—did maintain an important standing in
village life.

That sort of status did not exist for the poorest village groups—
the tenants and hired workers with no land of their own, considered "strangers" or nonmembers of the village community.
Many of them even lacked the economic leeway to send a son
from the hilly region to the coastal plain. As was also true a
century later, when rising oil prices created new opportunities
for Palestinians in the Persian Gulf, migrants came largely from
selected groups within the village. And even the positions they
assumed outside would depend on their group of local origin.

Sons travelling to nearby towns or more distant ports on the
coast did not always leave the village permanently—many returned not only with important resources for raising their families in the village hierarchy, but also with the new habits and
ideas starting to influence the Palestinian Arabs. As time went
on, more and more of these imported ideas concerned the growing Jewish presence in the country, a phenomenon that was so
far affecting villagers in the mountainous region only vaguely
and indirectly.

ZIONISM DURING OTTOMAN RULE

In the period after the 1834 revolt, even before Jews gave birth to
an organized Zionist political movement in Eastern and Central
Europe, there were some signs of change in the Jewish community of Palestine. The end of Egyptian rule and the Ottoman
reestablishment in 1840 served as a kind of benchmark for its
increased security, the Jewish population more than doubling in
the four decades between the end of the Egyptian occupation and
the beginning of what is called the First Aliyah (the initial wave
of Jewish immigration) in 1882.[42] But while young Jews began to
establish settlements outside the existing centers of Jewish
life—that is, Jerusalem and, to a lesser degree, Tiberias and Safad[43]—the community still subsisted largely through donations

from other Jews abroad, and for protection they looked to the European consuls who had established themselves in Palestine after the ouster of Muhammad Ali. Only in the twenty-odd years leading up to the 1880s did some Palestinian Jews show even the remotest inclination for serious agricultural projects.

With Jews in Eastern Europe confronting increasingly hostile conditions, emigration to the West stepped up considerably in the 1880s. Palestine attracted a small fraction of that emigration, a younger and more enterprising Jewish population, sharing little with its predecessors in the Holy Land. The interest of some Jewish organizations in resettling emigrants there coincided with the Russian emergence of the *Hovevei-Zion* (Lovers of Zion), a cluster of groups dedicated to Jewish social and cultural rejuvenation.[44] Those members now making their way to Palestine argued for the flowering of the Hebrew language and for the creation of Jewish agricultural settlements, independently worked by Jewish farm laborers.

The actual agricultural enterprises of the 1880s and 1890s turned out to be tenuous ventures. If Palestine was more politically inviting than Russia, it was less than hospitable economically or in terms of public health. The arduous journey itself (not to speak of winter in the forlorn Palestinian landscape) could break the resolve of many Jews intent on reclaiming the Land of Israel. For instance, Bilu, the group often credited with ushering in the new period of immigration called *aliyah*, started in Kharkov with about 300 members in 1881; about 100 actually left to sail from Odessa and of these, about 40 reached port in Istanbul; finally, 16 stalwarts arrived in Palestine to set up an agricultural working group.[45] In one of the very first settlements, Petah Tikvah, the Jews had to abandon the enterprise temporarily because of malaria, returning only several years later. In the mid-1880s, the new agricultural settlers probably did not total more than 1,000. By the century's end, merely 21 Jewish settlements with about 4,500 inhabitants—two thirds working in agriculture—had been established.

These numbers were hardly large enough to have any serious impact on Arab agriculture. The Jews were even less likely to have an effect on Arab village life as a whole—they established their settlements on the coastal plain and in the valleys, where the peasant population was sparse, sometimes negligible, and where the Muslim town notables were then establishing their own new agricultural enterprises. In the early 1880s, the Jews could not have been perceived as very different from the Templars, a marginal group of evangelical Germans who settled in Palestine at about the same time in the belief that they were the new chosen people destined to inherit the Holy Land.[46] Most of the country's rural Arab population was simply unaware of either group's existence; those who did come into contact with them fretted over their appropriation of potentially rich land, but relations remained mostly nonviolent, if uneasy.

At times, uneasiness would give way to coexistence, even cooperation. Nevertheless, Jewish land buying, mostly of state-owned or notable-owned tracts, did affect the local peasants and resulted in numerous land disputes, especially because the fellaheen were far from reconciled to the new property rules emphasizing deed ownership rather than cultivation. Serious tension arose, for example, from 1899 to 1902, when Jews bought up considerable tracts around Tiberias.[47] The new Jewish settlements absorbed some of the local peasants as laborers (much to the distress of later, more ideological Zionists, who feared that the Jews would become an exploitative class), with most settlements using from five to ten times as many Arab workers as Jewish ones. If the Arabs were not hired, they were displaced by Jewish purchases—an issue of nearly unsurpassed importance half a century later.[48]

When the Jews, and for that matter the Templars, did have an impact on Arab agriculture, it was mostly indirect. The Templars brought a new aesthetic into the country, demonstrating to neighboring Arabs what a model settlement could be. Both Jews and Templars also introduced new farming technology. The Templars imported the scythe; along with the Jews they unsuccessfully attempted to adapt the sod-turning plough to local conditions, in order to replace the more primitive single nail plough. More success came with the "Jewish plough," an iron nail plough later elaborated into a plough with two and then three nails. Jews also developed a more sophisticated thresher and changed from human and ox to horse and donkey power, and finally to mechanical power by the end of the century.[49] Those who employed the new techniques gained a hard-edged efficiency enabling them to take advantage of both the rising world prices and the deepening penetration of the world market.[50]

A technological leapfrogging in agriculture started to take

place. Arab farmers also began to adopt new methods and tools. Growing demand for oranges in England and elsewhere was stretching citrus agriculture to its limits, and existing methods of pumping water—through the use of a mule—were proving inadequate for the expanding plantations. Only the internal combustion engine's introduction would allow orchard growers to overcome the problem of pumping sufficient water from the necessary depths for a qualitative leap in citrus-devoted acreage.

Although the mountain fellaheen did not sense these innovations very strongly at first, some indirect benefits did make their way to the hill country. The clearing of long-neglected land by Jews and others, followed by the adoption of the new innovations, made the coastal plain a more attractive resource for expanding population of the hills. New jobs proliferated on the coast—not only in orchards depending on mechanically pumped water, but in flour mills and other enterprises using steam and internal combustion engines.

Rather more ominously, the mountain fellaheen were not contestants in the leapfrogging game. Their agriculture—dependent on human, not mechanical power and in many cases not even using animals—was inexorably putting them at a great disadvantage. True, they had little direct contact with the world market, but its steady nineteenth century penetration into Palestine did not bode well for those whose agriculture was coming to be viewed as backward within their own country.[51] As the economic and social links between the coast and the hills grew over time, peasants in the hinterland found themselves relegated to a dependent role in the economy, supplying cheap, unskilled labor or maintaining an increasingly uncompetitive agriculture.

The paucity of contacts between the Jews and most fellaheen was not for lack of grandiose Jewish ideas. A Zionist settlement plan of 1919 included all of the eastern portions of the country plus a good part of what was to become Transjordan, which the British did not separate from Palestine until 1922.[52] But actual settlement proved much slower and more regionally concentrated than Zionist leaders had hoped. Although the numbers of immigrant Jews did begin to swell in the final stretch of Ottoman rule (the first eight years of the new century saw a more than doubling of the number of Jewish workers, mostly farmers, to about ten thousand), concentrations in the mountainous region were negligible. Only the small number of fellaheen contiguous to the new settlements felt an unmediated Jewish presence.

But even if the scope of Jewish land purchases was limited, they did shape future Jewish-Arab relations. The Jews were establishing an economy based largely on the exclusion of Arabs from land they farmed and from the Jewish labor market. Slowly, the most fertile lands in the northern valleys and in the coastal plain passed to Jewish hands, with jobs and higher wages going to the Jewish newcomers. The logical conclusion of this process was the separate development of the Arab and Jewish economies and, eventually, the creation of two separate nationalist movements.[53]

While some Jews and Arabs managed to cooperate, relations between many, even then, were rocky.[54] As soon as one dispute between a Jewish settlement and neighboring Arab tenants or smallholders seemed settled, another would erupt. In the Tiberias district between 1899 and 1902, for example, Jewish land-buying aroused bitter opposition from a local district officer. And in Petah Tikvah, where the Jews bought peasant land that had been forfeited to Arab moneylenders and the state, the fellaheen felt the land was still rightfully theirs. In 1886, local Arab disgruntlement finally led to the settlement's ransacking and the death of a Jewish woman. Still, within a short time there, Arabs and Jews reestablished working, if mutually suspicious, relations.[55]

In the years immediately prior to World War I, Zionism acquired more ominous overtones for many Arabs. The Jews were taking ever-bolder steps to build a Palestinian beachhead, creating the Palestine Land Development Company in 1908 to train workers in farming and develop cooperative groups to settle newly purchased land. Jewish numbers rose to 85,000, about 10 percent of the country's population. From 1908 to 1913, the Jewish National Fund bought over 10,000 acres of farmland and stood to buy 35,000 more just as war broke out in Europe. These were still negligible amounts in terms of the country as a whole, but they did represent a major advance for the Jews. Before the war, they had even established a new city, Tel-Aviv, which threatened to overshadow Jaffa as a capital of the coastal plain. In addition, the years from 1904 to 1914 brought what the Zionists have since called the Second Aliyah, a wave of immigrants including a core of committed socialists. These Jews, mostly from Russia, became the central leadership of Palestinian Jewry, and later of Israel. The Arab community would have to confront their vision and their skills over the next half century.

Palestine on the eve of the Great War scarcely resembled the country of a century earlier. It was now a land connected to Europe by railroads, shipping lines, and a telegraph network. It joined Europe, too, through the increased number of Europeans living in Palestine, both Jews and gentiles, now appearing on the docks almost daily; by the cinema; and by the European plays that began to be staged in 1911. More and more, the notable Arab families sent their children to foreign schools in the country, or even abroad. Life in Jaffa, Haifa, and Gaza resembled that in other Mediterranean cities—Marseille, Athens, Beirut, and Alexandria—more than the towns of the Palestinian hinterland.

True, it was mainly the ayan who profited from these drastic changes, transforming their way of life and widening the social gap between them and the Arab majority. But the fellaheen by no means could avoid the effects of the European market and the Ottoman reforms, nor for that matter the Zionist presence. For one thing, they found their resources stretched to the limit as the new conditions precipitated the beginnings of a meteoric rise in the Palestinian population, tripling from the start of the nineteenth century until World War I from about a quarter to nearly three-quarters of a million.[56] Migration of some family members to the coast, and the continual shuttling of people and resources back and forth between the mountain and the plain, became as regular as the agricultural cycle itself. And, as elsewhere, the impoverished peasantry was forced to finance many of the new changes through enhanced revenue collection by the government.

The increased connections of Palestinian agriculture to the coast and to distant markets brought a change in the fellaheen's position. With the European influx and the rise of the ayan, they simultaneously gained a more central social role and became socially more marginal. They simply could not fend off the political and economic changes drawing them like a vortex—as

debtors, taxpayers, titleholders, and migrants—into urban life.
At the same time, they were becoming more distant from the
classes above them, and were lagging technologically. Palestinian Arab society was forming two quite different branches.

AFTER THE GREAT WAR

The last seventy-five years of Ottoman rule were tumultuous for
the Empire. But they passed without catastrophic changes in the
daily life of Palestine—no wars in the country, no major revolts,
and even internal violence fell off dramatically. The most concerted violence facing Palestinians was probably the Crimean
War, which drew fellaheen conscripts far from their homes.
Within the country, changes were incremental, sometimes insidious: people did not observe them from one day to the next,
nor from year to year for the most part.

After 1914, things were very different. Embedded in a series of
earthquakes and aftershocks, the only period approaching "normal" was that from 1922 to 1935—years also having their share
of violence (the most memorable in 1929) and a rapid pace of
social and economic change. Their relative tranquility was followed by the Arab Revolt, World War II, and the 1948 war.

World War I, the "war to end all wars," must have seemed
nearly as apocalyptic to those in Palestine as to subjects of the
European frontline states. Palestine suffered unspeakable damage; some of it, such as the denuded landscape, is still evident
today.[57] Seeking fuel and fodder in their last gasp, the Ottomans
cut down the country's trees and commandeered farm animals
and grain. As always, the peasants took the brunt of the onslaught. After suppressing all foreign financial agencies and pro
hibiting the import of any capital from enemy countries at the
war's inception, the Ottomans drafted thousands of fellaheen for
the imperial army's lost cause, so that, as one Arab observer
remarked, the country seemed to consist only of the elderly,
women, and children.[58] But the peasants were not the only ones
who suffered in the Great War: Links to the European world
dissolved as missionaries, consuls, and others left the country,
along with a large number of Jews. With the cash economy's
crumbling, this emigration caused a near collapse of the way of

life the ayan had fashioned in the coastal towns. By the time of British General Edmund Allenby's triumphal march into Jerusalem in 1918, the economy was in ruins.

If Jews and Arabs both suffered from the war's economic effects, the Jews fared far better on the diplomatic side of the ledger. Initially split between the two major blocs, European Jews slowly shifted support to the British. On November 2, 1917, they were granted the crucial Balfour Declaration—celebrated by Jews and condemned by Arabs to this day—which pledged Britain's support in the establishment of a Jewish national home in Palestine.[59]

For Palestine's fellaheen, the Declaration passed unnoticed, the rigors of the war being of far more immediate concern. Once the war ended, it was the new British mandate that primarily absorbed their attention, the years of British rule witnessing an economic transformation in Palestine beyond what any nineteenth century inhabitant could have imagined. Trade quickly surpassed its prewar level, restoring links to the world market. The British built a modern port at Haifa that included a refinery and facilities to export British oil pumped in Iraq. They also expanded Jaffa's port facilities and added new airports, roads, and railroads.[60]

Imports skyrocketed. The value of imported goods quadrupled in a dozen years, and with growing imports came increasing trade deficits. This negative trade balance was offset by an influx of Jewish capital, especially during the 1930s, which dwarfed the earlier Zionist efforts.

Agriculture played a central role in the new economic growth as production expanded rapidly in vegetables and other crops.[61] Even more important, citrus orchards continued expanding after the Great War, rising sevenfold in twenty years.[62] Citrus growing—most notably of the desirable Jaffa orange—so dominated the economy that Palestine was in danger of becoming a monocrop society, dependent on one dominant buyer, Great Britain.[63]

For the small Arab farmers of Palestine, much of the boom brought bitter results. Cash crops lay at its heart, farming as an exclusive source of income thus now becoming simply unviable for most smallholding subsistence peasants and their families.[64] Many Arab peasants seemed on a treadmill. Even as some devoted a portion of their acreage to truck crops, such as vegetables, they found themselves falling farther and farther behind the Jews and the most advanced Arab sector.[65] Unlike cereal production, the more profitable cultivation of citrus fruit and vegetables demanded intensive irrigation and fertilization of the soil, hence considerable investment and new skills. New orchards required about five years of investment before the fruit could be marketed. All this was beyond the capabilities and resources of most small farmers.

The peasantry also had to fight against other powerful forces. More and more, it was becoming difficult for village families, even in the mountainous regions, to hold onto land. The profitability of the newer sectors and the shortage of additional unused land in the plains and valleys made peasants' tracts increasingly desirable, which compounded the high land prices already resulting from active Jewish landbuying.[66]

If all this were not enough to batter Palestinian Arab village society, the village population grew by over 40 percent between 1922 and 1936. The Arab population as a whole expanded two to three percent yearly in this period—one of the fastest rates in the world. Although there was a significant movement from the distant hill settlements into the maritime cities, many hill villages continued to grow quite rapidly. A British survey indicated that more than half of Arab households did not have enough land for subsistence.[67] The fellaheen, for the most part, were unable to cover their expenses or keep up payments on their debts, which had reached alarming proportions—the average total debt was more than three times the average annual household income.

The boom years of the mandate, then, brought increasing desperation to Palestine's peasants. Whole families abandoned their villages for opportunities in Jewish ventures (at least until the mid-1930s), British public works projects, or new Arab enterprises. Others sent their sons to large agricultural estates or the port towns of Haifa and Jaffa, or went themselves, leaving wives and children behind. Cities swelled with peasants from the mountains. During World War II, British use of Palestine as a rearguard base created tremendous economic activity in the urban areas, particularly striking because it came in the wake of the Arab Revolt, which had temporarily driven many laborers back to their villages in the late 1930s.

BRITAIN'S FAILURE AMONG THE PEASANTRY

Through the thirty years of British rule over Palestine, mandate officials were well aware of the battering of village life. The Palestinian high commissioner received report after report decrying the effects of the restructured Palestinian economy on the Arab population. Various British commissions collected direct testimony and other evidence demonstrating the competitive squeeze on peasant agriculture and land as well as the formidable pressures working to create a landless underclass of Palestinians. For all their concern—and even their good intentions—British officials did little to ameliorate the situation. In the end their policies simply hastened the crumbling of the oldest sector of Palestinian life.[68]

The mandate turned out to be full of contradictions. Governing in a period of unsurpassed economic growth following the already momentous Ottoman transformation, the British tried to clamp a lid on social change, taking a markedly conservative stance regarding the question of Palestinian leadership. From the beginning, they aimed to win over and work through the major families of the ayan, and despite all the conflicts eventually developing between them (see chapters 3 and 4), the result would be to crown this group officially—with its Jerusalem branches at the head—as leader of the Arabs. This leadership extended beyond the Arab nationalist institutions that proliferated during the mandate; the ayan's participation in the mandatory state itself, for all their opposition to its purposes, offered a useful platform for boosting their power. The British rulers handpicked members of important Arab families, for example, to form a small corps of prestigious district officers for the government.[69] The British were frustrated at the disproportionate number of Christian Arabs ending up in such positions, despite the care they gave to such appointments. Still, those district officers who did come from important Muslim families further cemented their dominance over the rural population.

The group thus used both British support and, ironically, its opposition to the British to consolidate its position at the top of Palestinian society. At times, the notables took on the cause of villagers struggling with the mandate authorities and the Zionists; at other times, the split between peasants and the ayan led to violent clashes within Palestinian society, especially during the Arab Revolt of the late 1930s.

British rule also affected the peasantry more directly. The mandate's goals regarding village society were often the same as those of the Ottomans. In fact, the British openly adopted nineteenth century Ottoman legal precedent—specifically, the Ottoman Vilayet Law of 1913—as its benchmark for governing Palestine. Like the Turks, they sought more tax revenue, a more efficient land registration system, a breakup of co-owned musha land, enhancement of the mukhtar as the official arm of government in the village, and more productive agriculture generally.[70]

What differed was the greater British efficiency in carrying out its rule. To be sure, there were gaping holes in the administration that allowed peasants—who by necessity were experts in such matters—to circumvent rules and regulations. But compared to what the fellaheen had known previously, the British bureaucracy they encountered in the 1920s quite fully penetrated village life. In Ottoman times, the execution of law at the village level was often a haphazard affair and sometimes nearly nonexistent. Also, the Turkish hand stretched over provinces on three continents while the British mandatory state was a small, tight affair.

Reflecting their wider state policy, the British aimed for three often clashing goals within the village. First, they sought to be as nonintrusive as possible, preserving Ottoman laws where they could, respecting village custom, and working through established leadership. Second, like governments everywhere, they tried to increase their revenues. In practice, peasants faced demands for endless tithes and taxes that only accentuated their indebtedness, which had already begun to expand in the Ottoman period. Much of the growing rural debt was owed to urban moneylenders, who were usually charging 30 percent per year.

Finally, while anti-British sentiment did grow substantially during the course of the mandate, the ill feelings did not result from total disinterest by the authorities in the plight of the villagers. The British made efforts to improve their situation, and to ensure that the nearly uncontrolled economic growth did not claim them as its victims. Unfortunately, genuine British dismay failed to produce a comprehensive economic plan. Instead, British officials created programs piecemeal—cooperative societies, small loans, seed loans, and so forth—that together lacked the strength and coherence necessary to protect the fellaheen.[71]

In effect, British mandate rule pulled hard in separate directions. The mandate tried to strengthen the village leadership, but through active economic intervention reduced its importance instead. British officials worried that peasant debt would create an army of landless laborers displaced by Jews and Arab notables, but its tax policy seemed only to add to the peasants' woes. While the Department of Education created a generation of literate men in the villages (the expansion of education for rural Muslim girls was much slower),[72] government officials held to the delusion that this would have a negligible influence on day-to-day life. Mandate officials wished to keep the peasants on the land and prevent the creation of huge numbers of landless laborers; but at the same time—especially during World War II—they sank significant sums into public works in Palestine's western section, drawing thousands of peasants from their homes in the eastern, hilly regions. Given such a confusing mix of policy, it is not surprising that the peasantry became an important hub of activity and agitation during the Arab Revolt of 1936–39, which temporarily crippled the British administration in the rural areas (see chapter 4).

In addition, the ferocious pace of change had jarred even the remotest villages out of whatever autonomy they had managed to preserve during the Ottoman period. As their horizons changed from the village—and beyond that from local and even regional markets—to a larger market system and a growing national movement, the peasants looked for more government action to address their special circumstances. Instead, they found a British-run state neglecting their need to make progress in their agriculture.[73] The fellaheen did prosper momentarily from the rise in construction opportunities and agricultural prices during World War II.[74] Many were even able to pay off their onerous debts. At the same time, their farming was becoming less competitive, and those who abandoned it for the cities were relegated to the lowest-paying, unskilled jobs. Government schools had been established by the British in about half of Palestine's villages, and rural illiteracy had declined from 90 percent to 70 percent of the male population. Still, these numbers indicate that the bulk of the villagers were woefully unprepared to deal with the demands of the new life on the coast, or even the changed life in their villages, as they encountered the increasingly sophisticated agriculture of the country, except on the very lowest rungs of the social ladder.

THE GAINING MOMENTUM OF ZIONISM

If Zionism was a mild curiosity for most Palestinian fellaheen at the end of World War I, it changed in the 1920s and 1930s into a force affecting crucial aspects of their lives. Jewish plans were more ambitious than ever. In talks with Arab political leaders, the Zionists spoke openly of their hope to bring 4–5 million Jews to Palestine.[75] The alarm these statements caused remained the motivating force behind the Arab political agenda until 1948. From World War I on, then, one of the central political issues in Palestine was whether or not the Jews would have unrestricted immigration and landbuying rights. The land issue served as an important bridge between Arab notable leaders, who were eager to build a broad constituency, and the fellaheen, who were growing fearful about the implications of huge numbers of Jews buying land in the country.

Like almost every other question concerning Jews and Arabs, there are two radically different interpretations of the Zionists' effect on the fellaheen during the mandate. It is difficult to sort out the evidence, which was mostly provided by the interested parties (including the British authorities). The Jews, who devoted much more effort to data collection than the Arabs, certainly did not deny that they were precipitating a deep transformation in Arab village society, but they tended to emphasize its beneficial character. Zionist spokesmen noted how Jewish agriculture had helped enable peasants to free themselves from debilitating "feudal" relations, which had ground them down in poverty and debt.[76] The Zionists also pointed to their introduction of new practical techniques—irrigation, growing fodder for animals, new seed varieties—for the improvement of peasant farming.[77] In contrast, Arab spokesmen (and increasingly, British authorities) dwelt on Arab displacement from land and the growing Jewish control over scarce cultivable soil. All sides tended to underplay the deleterious socioeconomic and political factors considered in this chapter. In all likelihood, the Jewish impact on the fellaheen was not nearly significant enough to cause all the beneficial results the Zionists touted; at the same time, the farmers displaced by Jewish landbuying were not a large enough group to have a great impact on the overall Arab economy.[78]

Many Arabs were attracted to the coastal areas where Jewish activity was most intense. But while between 1922 and 1944, the rural population around hill towns such as Hebron, Nablus, Ramallah, and Jenin fell significantly as a percentage of the total Arab population, the absolute numbers still rose. In fact, the rural population did not dip much below two-thirds of the total. In a bit more than two decades the number of Arabs doubled from 570,000 to 1.14 million, while the rural figures alone went from about 375,000 to nearly 734,000.[79]

The result of this stupendous increase was that farm holdings were growing smaller through continuing subdivision—this shrinkage of plot size not being offset by any great improvement in the smallholders' agricultural methods and tools. Nor had the government or any private agency materialized as a source of investment capital. The peasants still relied on moneylenders, although now more often merchants than large landowners. Some increases in production and some adoption of new crops (such as potatoes) were evident, but few smallholders could afford the risks involved in substantially changing their agricultural practices.

Jewish landbuying contributed to this malaise by shrinking the pool of cultivable Arab-owned land, about ten percent of it passing into Jewish hands by 1948. With time, an increasing share of purchases was coming from the ayan, rather than absentee owners in Lebanon or elsewhere, and from local peasants seeking to extricate themselves from debt. Already by the 1940s, few small farmers could survive without some supplementary income from the thriving nonagricultural sectors, especially construction. The combination of Jewish capital investment on the coast (producing jobs taken up by former Arab villagers) and Jewish land purchases only helped further dissolve the differences between village society and its urban counterpart.

A CENTURY OF CHANGE IN VILLAGE LIFE

The image of an extended peasant family eking out its living from subsistence crops, with perhaps some olive oil going to local and regional markets, was a distant memory by the mid-1940s. Cash crops and nonagricultural supplementary income were now its staples. If in the Ottoman period the Palestinian villagers seemed to be ambling toward novel habits and routines, during the mandate years they appeared to be racing into an unknown future. Since 1948 so uprooted Palestinian society, we can never really know what that future would have held. It is nonetheless clear that the village was becoming ever more marginal to that society, villagers and ex-villagers alike now constituting part of a national movement and a broader economy whose centers lay in Jerusalem, and in Haifa and Jaffa.[80]

Displacement of tenants from land bought by Jews from absentee landlords and others accentuated the new mobility. Peasants moved from the purchased land, often with monetary compensation in hand, to another village or to the city. A Zionist movement that had been resuscitated by the Balfour Declaration and the terms of the mandate added further weight to the pressures of a growing peasant population on a fixed or shrinking share of the country's cultivable land. Meanwhile, without sufficient capital and consolidated plots, small farmers found much of the new agriculture beyond their reach.

After World War I, Arab peasants faced new state officials who clucked their tongues about these trends but did little more than tighten the tax noose, so that peasants had to pay 25 to 50 percent of their income to the government.[81] While this was occurring, Jewish landbuying stepped up considerably: In the decade starting in 1933, for example, Jews bought over eighty thousand acres of Arab land. The Zionists never did have all the capital they needed for the purpose, and objectively the number of fellaheen thus alienated from the land was not very large relative to the total population (just over one thousand households between 1939 and 1945).[82] This was, nevertheless, a substantial increase over the Ottoman period, and it gains importance from the way the matter was perceived by the Palestinian community.[83]

Zionism's main impact came in different realms. The Jewish influence on the Palestinian economy as a whole left the fellaheen even farther behind the country's more privileged population. They also perceived the mandate itself as linked to Zionism, since it had legitimated the conception of a Jewish national home in Palestine. Finally, the threat from Jewish inroads cemented their ties to the town notables, who had taken the lead in opposing Zionism (as we shall see in chapters 3 and 4). That cement was crucial in the formation of a Palestinian national movement. But the future of Palestinian Arab society, and the place in it of both hill-village fellaheen and migrants to the coast, rested on more than resistance to Zionism. Notables and merchant groups, struggling among themselves to set the tone of the culture, economics, and politics that would define the Palestinian national consciousness, created institutions to which the fellaheen responded and against which they reacted. Let us now turn back to the nineteenth century in order to consider these notables and merchants more closely, and their efforts to put a firm stamp on Palestinian Arab society.

The City:
Between Nablus and Jaffa

At the beginning of the nineteenth century, the towns up and down Palestine's coast were mere shells of their former selves, the grandeur and vibrancy of the biblical, Roman, or Arabic eras having been eroded by prolonged misery and neglect. It is true that Acre and, to a lesser extent, Haifa, had a moment of renown outside Palestine around then. In 1799, its Turkish governor, Ahmad Pasha—sometimes known as al-Jazzar—turned back the advancing, but weary and plague-weakened, French revolutionary army.[1] (Napoleon had wanted to use Palestine as a beachhead for a drive to the Euphrates.[2]) Ahmad Pasha's mix of skill, determination, and luck offered a brief respite to coastal Palestine's lethargy. After a lengthy siege, he forced Jaffa's Ottoman governor to flee the city. Like other local strongmen in the Empire, he had gained considerable advantage from the Industrial Revolution's inception on the Continent, trading Palestinian raw materials—cotton and grain—for firearms, which he used to equip the mercenaries under his command. As "master of Palestine,"[3] he succeeded in transcending the Ottoman administrative divisions of *sanjaks* and *vilayets* that had carved the country into districts including parts of today's Jordan, Lebanon, and Syria (see map 1). Ahmad Pasha now diminished the administrative role of Damascus and Sidon, enhancing that of Haifa—and exalting Acre, even over the religious influence of Jerusalem.[4] For a brief moment Palestine became as important

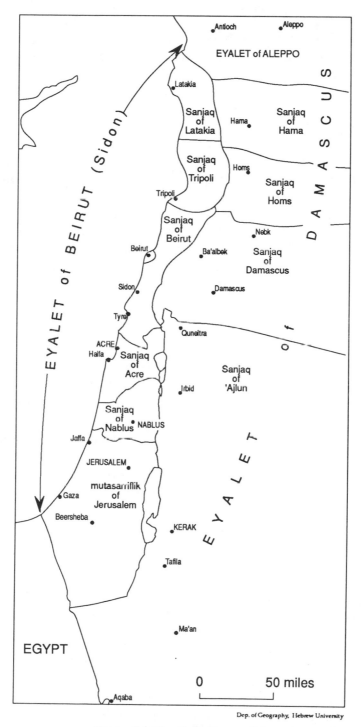

Map 1. Palestine Under Ottoman Rule

as the key Syrian towns. Nevertheless, in making Acre the base of a personal satrap eventually reaching across the country, Jazzar had in fact turned his strength against the local population, exacting higher taxes and generally impoverishing the surrounding villages. Almost from the moment he left Acre, the town regressed to the typical sorry state of Palestine's other ports.

For most of the early decades of the nineteenth century, along the entire coast and in the maritime plain, the Ottomans could do little more than hope for some percentage of the collected taxes to find its way to the Sublime Porte.[5] Various strongmen—whether Ottoman governors or local sheikhs—enriched themselves at the expense of the population and neglected the area's infrastructure. The ships making their way to the eastern Mediterranean from Great Britain, the center of world trade, followed routes far from the run-down ports of Palestine.

British ships did not begin docking anywhere near Jaffa—little more than an overgrown village—until the late 1840s. At the century's turn, around 2,500 people lived there, mostly within the walled city. Some risked traveling outside the walls to cultivate surrounding fields, retreating at dusk to the town. A single gate in the wall looked away from the sea, and it was locked every night. Jaffa's total area—about 25 acres—was 7 percent of what it would become by the end of World War I.[6]

Visitors described Jaffa as having a ravaged look: Napoleon's armies, local sheikhs, Ottoman governors, had left their mark, drying up the traffic that had been its lifeline.[7] Jerusalem's merchants sent most of their trade (especially their locally produced soap and olive oil) through Damascus.[8] No doubt, in choosing Jerusalem as the site of their most important consuls,[9] the European powers desired to gain influence with sympathetic Christian sects tied to the Christian holy places, especially the Holy Sepulchre; but they were reflecting, as well, the reality of Palestine's political and economic center of gravity: To the degree there was urban control, Jerusalem and Nablus dominated the mountain region, where population and production were concentrated.[10]

THE INLAND TOWNS

In contrast to Jerusalem—with its chaos of religious and administrative offices, diverse ethnic makeup, and countless sects—

Nablus, Hebron, and Ramallah were extensions of village society. Farmers moved out daily to work on their plots; those with a little more land rented fields to tenants or worked alongside *harraths*, hired workers.

These inland towns were cultural and economic centers for the farming villages. Each had its own character—deeply Bedouin and Islamic Hebron, relatively cosmopolitan Christian Ramallah—serving as a source of identity for village peasants. The attachment was not nearly as strong as the existential identity set by clan or religion, but still significant in defining the outer boundaries of their lives. Peasants from different villages would meet there, holding festivals and joining cults that formed around the tombs of holy men. Just as importantly, farmers with a surplus would trade there: in produce and livestock, for crops like rice or sugar, and for processed goods, including soap and fabrics.

These towns also contained workshops, the variety and amounts of their products expanding into the twentieth century. With each town surrounded by mountain villages dotted with ancient olive trees, the olive was one of the mainstays of this industry.[11] For example, by the 1920s, there were fifty soap factories in Nablus. Made from the area's aromatic olives, the soap not only met the entire country's needs, but penetrated other Middle Eastern markets (particularly Egypt) and those in Europe. This foreign trade was in any case much more the exception than the rule. The soap factories were simple affairs, with no more than five to eight workers along with the owner's family. Especially in the nineteenth century, workers were paid in kind, and in turn they became peddlers, exchanging soap for grain and other agricultural products.

All the towns likewise incorporated one or more commercial olive oil presses, and most at least one flour mill. In fact, they must have appeared startlingly alike in some ways, the economic and social life inevitably revolving around these mills. But the towns did have different economic specialties. For Nablus it was olives; Hebron produced grapes, along with blown glassware, waterbags, and candies.[12]

Nothing added more to a town's distinctiveness than its rulers—leading families continuing to dominate well into the twentieth century, even after the British established formal governing procedures and sponsored elections for mayors and municipal

councils. In most instances, these were the same families of
ayan and ulama—landowners and religious notables—who had
directed life in the region since the early nineteenth century.
Some went as far back as the seventeenth, when chiefs who had
fled or were banished from other regions of the Ottoman Empire
established themselves as strongmen, at the expense of the decaying central authority.

The rugged mountain landscape provided just the sort of insularity these men wanted. But this insularity was not the same
as simple distance from Istanbul, many developing complex,
ambiguous relations with the Ottoman authorities. At the same
time that they built autonomous bailiwicks, they served as government representatives or tax-farmers. Their aim was to garner
the benefits of office without the burdens of supervision and
control from above, and while their stature in many ways derived from their connection to the empire, much of their energy
went into subverting its efforts to rule effectively. Once the
Porte instituted the Tanzimat reforms starting in 1832, official
positions became all the more important to the strongmen, if for
no other reason than to protect their domains from the onslaught
of the new legislation.

These strongmen were responsible to a great extent for molding an assortment of villages scattered over difficult terrain into
a unified distinctive region. Through their tax collection and—
even more important—their protection, ruling families developed networks of lieutenants, and with them fear, influence, and
occasionally even loyalty. While the coastal plain was even more
dangerous than the hills, hill families did insure their positions
through the ability to organize violence, their members serving
as small militias and enforcers. In difficult circumstances,
strongmen recruited workers, tenants, and small farmers from
their villages for pitched battles. Most villagers owned an anti-
quated firearm.

Various coalitions among the leading families formed and reformed, occasionally based on the two, old Fertile Crescent factions mentioned in chapter 1—Qays and Yaman—occasionally
on another real or imagined division. Although protracted stand-
offs came to define particular towns or regions, they were never
totally free of the Ottoman factor: Officials reacted when violence spread, linking disparate feuds into fighting alliances.
While most battles were entirely local—against other families or

invading Bedouin—at times they involved the Ottoman authorities themselves, supporting a government drive or (occasionally) even opposing the designs of a governor.

As in military matters, so in politics. Even at its most tenuous, the Ottoman rule would leave its mark on local affairs. Ottoman officials played on the bickering of the families, who toyed in turn with the officials by manipulating their administrative jealousies. Some families drew their strength from their Turkish ties, others from fending off the Porte's representatives. The eight or nine families dominating the Nablus region at the start of the nineteenth century struggled with one another to gain lucrative tax-farming concessions from the Ottoman authorities.

The Tuqans, emerging as leaders of one of the poles of power, were the first clan in the region to ally themselves with the Ottoman authorities, using their connections as the foundation for far-reaching controls.[13] Hafiz Tuqan began as a tax collector in the village of Tubas and used the capital from that position to build a lucrative soap factory in Nablus. His family came to dominate the Yaman faction, while the Abd al-Hadis (who like the Tuqans transferred their power from the countryside to the town) grew in importance in the Qays coalition.[14] (The Abd al-Hadis, it may be remembered, were the notables who allied themselves with the Egyptian administration at the outbreak of the 1834 revolt.)

On a daily basis, the families were at the center of affairs in towns such as Nablus. Senior Ottoman officials did influence the struggle over which would rise to the top, but their impact generally came from behind the scene. Once a year, governors would come to the mountains to garner taxes, and to confirm a respectful, if uneasy, relationship with the central government.

To some extent, during much of the eighteenth century, a struggle for control of Nablus between the Ottoman governors in Damascus and those in Sidon offered the leading families a way to neutralize the designs of both. Even after Ahmad Pasha became the Damascus governor and began his drive for Palestinian unity, the Nablus region bent less to his will than any other part of the country. After his death in 1804, no governor of Sidon or Damascus was able to gain full control over the families despite several major military drives into the mountains. While in the 1820s Abdallah Pasha had achieved some semblance of unity, the relationship between central and local au-

thorities changed dramatically only starting in late 1831, when
Muhammad Ali began the drive through Palestine that would
sweep away the Ottoman administration altogether.[15] Historian
Shimon Shamir goes so far as to say that the Egyptian conquest
signified "the first application to Palestine of the concept of
territorial state. . . . This was the inception of the [country's]
modern history."[16]

In the first few years of the occupation, it must have come as
a surprise to the leading families of Nablus that Egyptian rule
would undercut their hard-earned autonomy. At first, all but the
Tuqans saw Muhammad Ali's son, Ibrahim, as a governor who
would enhance their strength. They were to be disillusioned.
Only the Abd al-Hadis, the Tuqans' great rivals, managed to
maintain close relations with him, and even they found their
status transformed from independent chiefs to links on the Egyptian administrative chain.[17]

As has been suggested in chapter 1, Muhammad Ali's conception of administration was not of a distant sovereign negotiating
from weakness with powerful local lords but of a streamlined
bureaucracy penetrating into the domain's remotest parts. Both
the ayan and the ulama found the new bureaucracy cutting into
their prerogatives and discretionary power: a rude shock to be
repeated several decades later with the Ottoman introduction of
the Tanzimat reforms.

The ayan's eventual response to this government penetration
—adapting the tools necessary for the new conditions—was reflected both in starting to supply their sons with formal education[18] and in a move from their villages into the towns (in a
number of important cases, the establishment of family
branches in one or several towns). A clear sign that the old order
was dead and new skills were needed came in the 1850s, when
after a period of remarkably destructive interfamilial fighting,
the Turks attacked. A direct assault on the Abd al-Hadis led to
their complete submission.[19] The ayan learned their lesson.
Even as they became more attentive to Ottoman rule, they increased the gap between themselves and the mass of the population, the peasantry.

Among the ways in which the new skills were useful was in
coping with one of the Turkish pillars of the Tanzimat: their
effort to transform town government. Traditionally, such government reflected power struggles among a number of forces,

only one of which was the official Ottoman authority. In fact, there were cases where local forces so overwhelmed a town's Ottoman official that he was forced to leave altogether, as occurred in uprisings in Jerusalem in 1808 and 1826.

Turkish soldiers had gone to the trouble of attacking the Abd al-Hadis and other strongmen in Palestine's remote mountains precisely with the goal of preventing such chaos. The Tanzimat legislation was the logical follow-up to the expeditions, establishing the basis for permanent central control of the empire's cities. And indeed, the notables had to adapt to the bureaucracy's expansion and the establishment of town councils—the main tools of the empire's control. But as with so much of the Tanzimat, actual administration of the reforms led to a quite different effect on town and village life from what had been intended. In effect, the Ottoman tools became springboards for local forces to reassert a new sort of limited autonomy. Since the ayan and the ulama—the town's religious elite—dominated membership on the councils, they were able to shape control of municipal life.

While Ibrahim Pasha had used similar public bodies as a vehicle to appoint deputies representing various social classes and religious groups, the Ottomans found their councils overwhelmed by prominent Muslim civic and religious notables. And while Ibrahim had given the councils little more than an advisory role, the Ottomans turned over almost all areas of administration, finance, and judicial affairs, thus "reinforc[ing] their political position and . . . further[ing] their private interests."[20] They did so, as well, by taking a variety of posts in the expanded bureaucracy and using legal machinations to acquire large tracts of land.

Even with the new roles of the ayan, they could not prevent the decline of the hilly regions relative to the coastal towns. Although the rebellion against Ibrahim in 1834 had been centered in Nablus,[21] improvement in the coast's status was already evident. The population of Jaffa had nearly doubled by the 1840s (to close to five thousand people). Construction—including a protective sea wall—was evident everywhere, and exports had begun the slow climb that would gain momentum in the decades leading up to World War I.[22]

The complex relationship between Palestinian coastal city and inland town was mirrored in some other Mediterranean societies, most notably in Lebanon.[23] It involved a growing economic dependency on the port, a widening disparity in ways of life and standards of living, and, at the same time, increasing elements of social integration between town and country. In Arab Palestine, this process would be reversed only with the catastrophe of 1948.[24]

THE RISE OF THE COASTAL TOWNS

By the 1930s, the two most important Palestinian coastal cities, Jaffa and Haifa, had come to represent the new face of Palestinian Arab society, taking second place to Jerusalem only in the realms of politics and religion. Jaffa had the country's largest Arab concentration, with Haifa not far behind, comprising—in a country that was still largely centered on the village—more than 10 percent of the Arab population between them. Muslim and Christian merchants, bankers, displaced villagers, wage laborers, shantytown dwellers, orchard owners, all met in a cosmopolitanism distantly evoking the urban centers of classical Arab history.

Jaffa's fortunes, which began to shift in the mid-nineteenth century as trade and agriculture revived on the coast, also benefited from Jerusalem's growth and from Western fascination with the holy city. It was the port with the most direct link to Jerusalem, and in 1869 the Ottomans built a new connecting road, due at least partly to the pressure of uncomfortable Western travellers. With the pacification of the countryside by Ottoman forces in the 1850s, Jaffa also began to develop its own outer area of agricultural villages, much like Nablus and the other inland towns. The surrounding land was fertile and had plenty of water.

These villages soon developed different traits from their inland counterparts. Rising world grain prices in the 1860s and 1870s forced landowners near the port to plant cash rather than subsistence crops, or to find tenants who would. The value of exports out of Jaffa—mostly grains, and later oranges—skyrocketed, more than doubling on average between the late 1850s and the early 1880s.[25] Coastal landowners and tenants resembled the hill farmers less and less as they became tied to a network of relations with merchants, shippers, bankers, insurance agents, and others seeing to it that crops made their way to Great Britain and other countries.

Of course, changes in the coastal towns matched those of the outlying villages, as they became the basic link between Palestinian growers and European consumers. Haifa, for example, which was little more than a fishing village (less than 1,000 people; some estimates are as low as 200) in 1830, had a population of 3000 by 1850. As the century progressed so did the pace of change; by the Great War, the population was over 20,000. Not weighed down by the conservative presence of old-time notable families, Haifa became a center of regional innovation. It absorbed a new railroad and port, a growing Jewish and entrepreneurial Christian population, a Templar and Carmelite presence along with that of a considerable foreign community, and a large network of schools (many of them Catholic). Germany, in particular, singled out Haifa as a conduit for its influence in the Holy Land.[26]

In Jaffa, the original 25 walled acres grew to nearly 400, and the population of 5,000 (already double what it had been at the beginning of the nineteenth century) swelled to 50,000. Construction continued to change Jaffa's face as well. From 1880 to 1910, merchants opened 400 shops, corresponding to a heavy investment in private housing, public buildings, mosques, and commerical buildings.[27]

While there was considerable growth in the city's industry and tourism (especially Christian pilgrims from the West), the engine of change was trade. Growth rates for both exports and imports were extraordinary, surpassing even as dynamic a port as Beirut, and outperforming Tripoli and Sidon combined.[28] Wheat, sesame, and soap were all shipped through Jaffa, and oranges became the premier export. It was, in fact, oranges that made Jaffa the second largest Palestinian city by the end of the Ottoman period.[29] Imports, largely from Great Britain, fueled the growing consumption in the city and supplied both Jaffa and Jerusalem with construction material. A new train line linked the two cities in the 1890s. Surprisingly, this enormous growth in trade occurred in a hopelessly inadequate harbor. Not only was it unable to accommodate the late nineteenth century's new steamships with direct loading facilities, but it proved downright dangerous to smaller ships. When, in the mandate period, the British finally undertook port modernization, they ended up bypassing Jaffa altogether and investing in Haifa.

Such economic dynamism was not limited to these two cities. From 1880 until 1918, the population of the six leading Palestinian cities jumped by an average of 3 percent a year. Shipping dramatically expanded everywhere, once steamships took up regular routes to the eastern Mediterranean at the century's close, solidifying the value of the ports. The changes helped establish those Palestinians acting as middlemen between the European consumers and local growers, and those reorganizing agriculture to provide produce for export.

The new economic networks were making it increasingly difficult for independent peasants in the plain and in the valleys. Around Jaffa, people with sufficient resources, including bankers, were grabbing fertile land, either to invest in profitable citrus groves or in the hope that others would later pay exorbitant prices for the land. The groves did pay handsome dividends, but only after a considerable investment and waiting period—a system of credit excluding the smallholder and enhancing the position of the ayan. Wealthy landowners used both their own capital and depended on the willingness of European merchants to offer an advance purchase of crops.

The boom in the coastal plain, along with a worrisome population rise in the inland areas, precipitated a flood of migration towards the area bounded by Jaffa and Haifa: by 1922, 200,000 people—almost a quarter of the country—lived there. The definitive eclipse of the inland towns took place under the mandate. In an outdoing of the earlier, already dramatic increases, between 1922 and 1944 (the dates of Britain's first census and last population survey), the Arab population of Jaffa and Haifa nearly tripled, at a time when the entire Arab population was nearly doubling. The figure for Haifa was 342 percent.

For the Arab migrant, the coastal cities offered a few glimpses of familiar social terrain. For instance, as in the world they came from, notable families often dominated municipal and social affairs—the Saids, Dajanis, and Bitars of Jaffa; the Shukris, Tahas, Khayats, Khalils, and Mahadis of Haifa (although the Haifa families certainly lacked the clout of those in Jaffa). But on the whole, the new urban setting—the sights and sounds, the people on the street—must have seemed much more distant than the thirty or forty miles actually involved.

For one, the typical Muslim migrant was much more likely to meet Christian Arabs, who by the end of the mandate were overwhelmingly urban (80 percent as opposed to only 27 percent of the Muslims). They also could not miss the growing numbers of Christian missionaries and travelers. Certainly, encounters between Muslims and Christians had never been unknown. In the early years of the twentieth century, the proportion of Christians among the Arab population hovered around a formidable 15 percent—a figure that was to drop gradually in subsequent years because of the higher Muslim rate of natural increase. Nevertheless, the homogeneity of many villages, and even of towns, such as Hebron, meant that until Muslims began to encounter the new social mix on the coast, many would never have come face to face with a Christian.

Both Jaffa and Haifa also had growing Jewish populations during the mandate. Even before the 1920s, Arabs in the coastal towns (and in Jerusalem, where there was actually a Jewish majority) could not avoid the Zionist project. Jaffa had already spawned a Jewish twin, Tel-Aviv, founded by Zionists on the sand dunes north of Jaffa in 1909. At the start of the nineteenth century, there had been no Jews at all in Jaffa; by the Great War, the figure was 30 percent of the city's population of fifty thousand. Trying to establish a new way of life, the Zionists concentrated their new institutions in Jaffa before the war, avoiding the more parochial setting of Jerusalem. And in Haifa, despite the Arab population's tripling between 1922 and 1944, its total in the city dropped from 74 to 48 percent as Jewish immigrants became more and more prominent.

All sorts of other Europeans could be found on the streets of Jaffa and Haifa, especially after the war—British security forces and civil servants, merchants, pilgrims, members of Christian religious orders. Migrants quickly found signs, as well, of a new Arab society: labor unions, banks, women's associations, and political parties, along with pharmacists, clinics, and a display of photographers' studios, restaurants, and shops full of Western goods. There were now private cars on the narrow roads, and British and Jewish influence—as well as Egypt's cultural impact—led to a sudden interest in scouting, camping, and sports.

Jaffa, for example, fielded a well known soccer team of the Governmental Secondary Boys' School.

These institutional artifacts symbolized the lure—and decadence—of the coastal towns. First was the bicycle epitomizing a new, lower middle-class mobility and freedom. Second was the coffee house. In the inland towns, men would spend endless hours playing backgammon and smoking the nargila; here in the urban coffee houses they would both listen endlessly to oriental music (recorded or broadcast) and gain a much greater sense of contact with national and international events. Third was the cinema: a great seduction to new city dwellers, which was looked on with intense suspicion by those staying in the hills.[30]

Located in the city's central square, the modern city hall helped to furnish a sense of coherence and distinctive character to the big, open, and heterogeneous city, slicing into the old, strict controls that had governed people's daily lives. (The destruction of Jaffa's central municipal building, the Grand Sarai, by Jews early in the 1948 War thus held a special poignancy for the city's Arabs.) The new city dwellers often most intensely experienced the unsettling diversity of their social setting in the workplace. By the mandate's end half of Palestine's Arabs were already working outside agriculture, with about a third of the urban population being active in industry, craft workshops, and construction. Sizeable proportions also worked in commerce and transportation; others were bureaucrats and professionals or provided services. Coping with an utterly new milieu, they were engaged in a typical struggle to define who were the insiders, representing various levels of intimacy and trust, and the outsiders, to be feared or opposed. In the process, they collectively began to define the new social boundaries of Arab society.

In no circumstances is the reshaping of social demarcations an easy process; in the Palestine of the mandate period, it was further complicated by the fits and starts of the economy emerging along the coast. The cities plunged into depression in the late 1920s, and even more severely for a brief period beginning in 1935, forcing many recent migrants back to their home villages. In any event, throughout the mandate, a number of groups competed, none with terribly much success, in helping Arab workers cope with urban life.

At first, the Zionists tried to organize the Arabs. Undoubtedly, their motivations were mixed. Unionized Arab workers could demand higher wages, reducing some of the intense competition their Jewish counterparts faced from cheap Arab labor. On another level, some Zionists—both idealists and pragmatists—struggled to transcend the issue of wage competition, to influence the very identities of Muslim and Christian urban Arabs.

The Zionists discussed three ideas for furthering the organization effort: Jewish and Arab unions, separate unions under a central agency, parallel organizations. Only the Union of Railway, Post and Telegraph Workers, established in 1924, included both Jewish and Arab members, and that was a rather short-lived experiment. Nevertheless, despite a chorus of protests to the effect that the movement was spending too much time on the Arab question, some Zionists hoped that mixed unions would help break down divisions pitting Arabs and Jews against each other.[31]

For the most part, Zionist labor union activity was exclusive. The Histadrut—the General Federation of Jewish Workers in Palestine—remained totally Jewish for nearly four decades after its founding in 1920.[32] At the same time, its leaders preached the "liberation of the Arab working people from the bondage of its oppressors and exploiters, the ruling landowners and property holders."[33] On a practical level, this policy was largely limited to supporting Arab unions engaged in strikes, and to an Arabic-language newspaper it published for a while. Its major achievement was the creation of the Palestine Labor League: an agency encompassing both the Histadrut and Arab unions. The League did eventually manage to draw about a thousand Arab workers into its ranks.

But these were limited successes, most coming earlier rather than later in the mandate. Counteracting Jewish pressure on Arabs to leave the Union of Railway, Post and Telegraph Workers and the exclusion of Arabs from the Histadrut itself reinforced a two-tiered Palestinian labor system evident to this very day: Jewish enterprises could draw on the skills of higher paid Jewish workers and, when needed, recruit poorly paid Arab labor for low-skill tasks.[34]

Many of these enterprises also faced pressure to participate in the social transformation of the Jews into productive workers by hiring only Jewish workers. In the absence of success, and with growing Arab hostility, the Zionists paid increasingly more attention to bolstering their own defenses. And in a vicious cycle, their growing disinterest, and the miserable Arab pay and working conditions, nourished a propensity of urban Arab workers to define themselves in opposition to both Jewish workers and Jews in general.

With the Zionists thus preoccupied, in the 1930s, with forging a Jewish working class, notable Arab families took their own initiatives. For example, Rashid al-Haj Ibrahim established a workmen's organization in Haifa, but like other such efforts, it did not prove lasting. The notables' primary tool to gain leverage among the Arab population had always been the judicious distribution of patronage, particularly to peasant tenants and hired farm workers;[35] it turned out much more difficult to provide adequate rewards to migrants in the tumultuous city economy. Many of the new jobs were in Jewish enterprises and, especially after the outbreak of World War II, in British projects and agencies—both clearly outside the control of the ayan. They also faced difficulties simply because they lacked the same commitment to rising wages held by the people they wished to organize.

Communists, intellectuals, and those drawn directly from the workers' ranks also took up the challenge of labor organization.[36] The Palestine Arab Workers Society, founded in 1925, was the first such far-reaching, independent effort. Splinters of that group formed afterwards, along with similar societies, but none succeeded in meeting the wide-ranging needs of the new Arab working class, such as higher wages, job security, and protection against inflation.

There was some progress: A labor-movement congress was held in Haifa in 1930,[37] and in both the 30s and 40s unions managed to call some strikes, occasionally together with the Histadrut, whose ideology and tactics influenced Arab labor leaders even when there was no direct collaboration. In the latter decade, union leaders also negotiated a linkage of workers' wages to the cost-of-living index. A large influx of villagers into the city, taking advantage of work opportunities among the mobilized British armed forces, led to several new attempts at labor organization,[38] especially on the part of the Communist party early in World War II.

Most of these labor activities did not amount to much. Significant union-organizing progress only started to take place in the 1940s, with the flood of Arab workers entering into wage-paying, nonagricultural labor, and with the creation by the British of a responsive Labor Department.[39] In 1945, the seventeen branches of the Palestine Arab Workers Society had fifteen thousand paid members. But even the rise of union organizing during the Second World War left the Arabs with one-tenth the Jewish union membership, for a population more than twice as large.

Perhaps the labor scene was still too chaotic for any organization to do better. The working class remained a jumble: wage earners with permanent jobs, itinerant laborers (often with one foot still in the village), daily laborers assigned work by labor contractors, workers in small family workshops, employees of large enterprises, the unemployed. For most, the coast's prosperity contrasted sharply with their own economic desperation and need to scratch out a living.

A GROWING PALESTINIAN IDENTITY

The uncertainty and tenuousness of life in the city became evident—the rapid swings of the economic cycle, the consignment of Arab labor to low-skill and Jewish labor to more lucrative, high-skill positions, the precariousness of the wartime hiring rise, the predicament of workers bouncing from job to job. As one researcher describes it, it was "to a great extent . . . the continuing vitality of the village community that enabled the migrants to resist the splintering . . . and the new urban associations helped in turn to preserve the village foundations of the migrants' identity."[40] Villages became important in a practical sense, too. Resources flowed back and forth in divided clans or families. Relatives often gave emigrants a stake to establish themselves in the city, and they in turn, sent wages back to the village. Some migrants returned at every opportunity to land and houses they had managed to retain, and to their families.[41] Those who ended up moving permanently built social circles, even whole neighborhoods, around old village or regional ties. Even permanent migrants could use their home villages for security and refuge, as in the politically and economically difficult days of the late 1930s, when many Palestinians abandoned the city, at least temporarily.

Rather than engendering a comprehensive framework for ongoing urban interactions, and a viable reproduction of what had been before, the urban migrant's attachment to the village was to a mythic good life. The myth portrayed an idyllic past—centered on the primacy of family and personal ties of loyalty, rather than the impersonal relations of the marketplace or even the contrived ties created in social clubs—that continues suffusing Palestinian culture today.[42] For the most part, this ideal was a feeble lure back to the village. Facing the test of the reduced economic opportunities immediately following World War II, former villagers proved reluctant to return to their roots. They could think of the villages as home, and use old village ties as an anchor, but in the end recreating the old social boundaries proved impossible in a labyrinth of new social experience.

What other structure might have worked is unclear. The period of rapid urban growth may simply have been too short for Arab workers to resolve the issues of trust and loyalty, and more research may be needed to determine what sorts of groups did manage to coalesce. Many migrants existed on the city's margins scratching for work and living in rundown, temporary shacks. Both official and unofficial accounts of the time documented their experiences much less fully than those of more educated and successful urban Arabs. In any event, it seems that even poorer migrants had contact with supportive institutions catering primarily to them: religious organizations, political parties, youth groups, women's associations, sports clubs, and so forth. Although the number of such Jewish and Zionist institutions appearing on the scene dwarfed their Arab counterparts, to some extent hiding them from history, they were crucially important in at least one respect: the drawing of Palestinian Arabs into a single social grouping, set off both from non-Arabs in the country and from other Arabs outside the country.

One of the most important institutions was the set of organizations known as the Muslim-Christian Associations, first emerging in Jerusalem and Jaffa following the Great War and then spreading to other municipalities. The existence of the organizations was in itself remarkable, because religious tensions between Christians and Muslims had reached new heights in the decade leading up to the war. Religious identity was of course a cornerstone of Arab society, and this was reinforced by British mandate policy, which, in a number of cases, treated the different religions as distinct administrative entities. Countless incidents put one group on guard against the other; the outnumbered

Christians, in particular, viewed many of the Islamic overtones in the growing national movement with apprehension. In 1931, for example, they expressed uneasiness over an international Muslim conference held in Jerusalem.

Despite this internal Arab division, in the 1920s the Muslim-Christian Associations succeeded in drawing established members of leading Muslim and Christian urban families into the struggle against Zionism. The road to such concerted action—examined in the following chapter—was a rocky one, political factionalism plaguing the Palestinians throughout the mandate. It would be a mistake to overstate the depth of national sentiment at its start. In Jaffa, a Muslim-Christian unity emerging with the Associations in 1918 crumbled in 1923 over the issue of the city's acceptance of electrical power from a Jewish-built power plant. The rift was patched up by the decade's end, at least partly because of violent anti-Zionist outbreaks in 1929. In Haifa, where relations between Christians and Muslims had deteriorated badly towards the end of the Ottoman period, a single association did not coalesce until the 1930s; nevertheless, cooperative anti-Zionist Muslim and Christian activity began earlier.

The Muslim-Christian Associations did not initially define themselves as part of an explicitly political organization.[43] But as with other similar groups—such as the Literary Club and the Arab Club, which both catered to younger members of the leading urban families—their central principles were Palestinism and anti-Zionism. Palestinism meant the assertion of Palestine as a common homeland at a time when political boundaries were new and still quite uncertain. After a brief flirtation with the notion of their incorporation into Syria, the new organizations began to proclaim emphatically the existence of a distinct Arab people in Palestine. Even when some adopted pan-Arab programs, they took care to distinguish Palestine's Arabs from those outside the country and, of course, from the Jews and British within.

The scores of Palestinian clubs and other social groups that followed the Muslim-Christian Associations after they began to disintegrate in the 1930s reasserted this fundamental distinction. While their members most often came from the more privileged sectors of Arab urban society, the clubs hammered out social demarcations—a Palestinian profile—that also became increasingly appealing to ordinary workers facing the quandaries of urban life. Eventually, Palestinian villagers, caught between the Zionist/ayan land squeeze and their own rapidly growing numbers, would begin to adopt the same profile.

The upper classes, the workers, and the fellaheen came to the new Palestinian demarcation through very different routes. Each group faced a unique set of challenges, humiliations, and opportunities in the rapidly changing politics and economics of the interwar years, resulting in a different sense of social boundaries regarding Jews, the British, and other Arabs. The Arab Revolt of 1936–39 brought these differences to the surface, erupting at times in mutual recriminations and even violence among the Palestinians.[44] Such factionalism, however, should not obscure the extent to which a social boundary encompassing all Palestinian Arabs began to establish itself in a few hectic decades following World War I.

One of the key elements in the emerging Palestinian profile was the growing intelligentsia. Although neither universal nor compulsory, education generally became more available during the mandate, with one-third of school-age children in schools by 1946.[45] Members of the ayan and other upper-class families were increasingly sending their sons to universities in Cairo, Beirut, and sometimes Europe.[46] They represented a remarkable increase over the handful of Arabs, mostly Greek Orthodox and Catholic, who had attended universities in the nineteenth century.

Both Jews and Arabs established institutions of higher learning in this period. The Jews founded the Hebrew University; the Arabs built the Arab College, also in Jerusalem, whose curriculum emphasized Western liberal and classical themes as well as the Islamic-Arab tradition.[47] In the late nineteenth century, a university education had served as an entrée into the newly reformed Ottoman administration. A similar mobility for men existed during the mandate, as young Palestinians became magistrates, commissioners, and other upper- and middle-level figures in the British administration. Additional avenues were opening, especially in the free professions (lawyers, teachers). This intelligentsia would play a central role in furnishing the shared aesthetic and intellectual material for a concrete expression of the new Palestinism—a cultural glue helping to keep the society together. The principal medium was the printing press, producing textbooks, fiction, history, political tracts, translations, and more. But no form seemed to capture the Palestinian imagination more than poetry.

Palestinian authors—including, for the first time, women writers—worked under the long shadow of the late nineteenth-century Arab cultural renaissance, along with that cast by contemporary Egyptian culture. Twentieth century Palestinian writers have long suffered from comparison to the creative pre–World War I generation,[48] and to Egyptian writers whose magazines, books, and newspapers inundated Palestine. Nevertheless, the mandate-period Palestinian output was considerable. In 1945, Dr. Ishaq Musa al-Husseini surveyed the publications of local authors.[49] He found fifty-four Arabic titles, published between 1919 and 1932 (several more appeared in English and French); from 1933 to 1944, the figure almost tripled.

The contemporary historian Tarif Khalidi speaks of the passionate intensity characterizing Palestinian writing of the mandate years—the intelligentsia's reaction to social violence suffered in face of the British and the Zionists: "Little wonder, then, that this frantic commitment to the cause of Palestine should produce a pervasive cultural tone of anguish and disgust, of resentment, resistance, rebellion and death."[50] Poets fused deep feelings for the soil—they must have resonated among urban migrants now holding an idealized image of the village—to the conception of a people, collectively besieged and victimized within their social boundaries. Note the words of one poet:

> This is Palestine; transformed into a sacred
> shrine,
> So kiss its soil, wet with dew.[51]

Another Palestinian wrote the following before his death in the Arab Revolt,

> Do not think I weep from fear,
> My tears are for my country
> and for a bunch of unfledged kids
> Hungry at home
> Without their father[52]

For many intellectuals, commitment spilled into direct political activity, some becoming prominent figures in the struggle against Jewish settlement and British rule. As one critic puts it, "When the . . . society arrives at historical crossroads as it gropes for a viable definition of its identity and destination, the serious writer can ill afford to remain uninvolved and merely watch history march by from his aesthetic ivory tower."[53] The power of their pens, however, may have been more considerable than that of such activity. The British Royal Commission reported in 1937, "No less than fourteen Arabic newspapers are published in Palestine and in almost every village there is someone who reads from the papers to gatherings of those villagers who are illiterate"[54] (illiteracy among peasants and workers remained over 90 percent).

The notion of a cohesive society with a unique history, its members facing common threats and a shared future, gained ever-broader acceptance among Palestine's Arabs in the interwar years. The disproportionately influential urban intellectuals eventually succeeded in drawing a broad section of the population into active opposition to the Zionists and the British. But beyond that emerging consensus, the question of what that society should ultimately be like produced much less agreement, with stiff resistance building in parts of the country to the idea of the city as a model for the future.

Opposition surfaced on the part of several groups, both from inland areas such as Nablus and from cities on the coast where many found the new economy disorienting and alienating. Such opposition tended to focus on the port towns—seen as an insidious representation of the dislocation brought by the West—on the open embrace of European manners and dress, and on an all-too-eager acceptance of by-products of the Enlightenment and the Western scientific revolution.

This amounted to a rejection of everything British, including the technological basis for the new society; in some ways, it was unexceptional. In Central and Eastern Europe and elsewhere, similar sentiments were being articulated in the 1930s. A socioeconomic system based on mass production and international high finance was in deep crisis, and those whose ways of life had been hurt at its rise seized the opportunity to pierce the arrogance of its carriers. To be sure, Palestinian industry paled in comparison to that of Manchester—or even Prague or Warsaw.[55] Jewish factories overshadowed the Arab efforts—which in 1942–43 accounted for about 13.5 percent of total production.

Along with many other impediments—insufficient invest-ment capital, a largely unskilled work force, the inconsistency of the world economy—the Arabs faced a British rule largely inhospitable to industrialization efforts. While European states built formidable tariff walls during the 1930s, the League of Nations required the Palestinian mandate government not to discriminate in its trading policy against any other state. At the same time, the British denied Palestine those preferences it granted to its colonies in access to markets. Such disadvantages made industrial growth all the more difficult in a period in which a formidable depression shook manufacturing worldwide.

As might be expected, Arab manufacturing in Palestine was still in an embryonic state following World War II. The disloca-tions of peasants stemming from the Arab Revolt of 1936–39, the huge employment increases in services and public works during the war, and Zionist purchase of land, all acted to create a labor force now pried loose from agriculture, but still largely incapable of absorption into the nascent Arab industrial sector. In 1939, the government had estimated the number of workers in this sector at less than 5,000 out of an Arab wage labor force eventually peaking at 100,000.

Nevertheless, for all its limitations, the growth in industry represented a radical departure for Arab society and a message to Palestinians about the future. Arab manufacturers were drawing increasing numbers of workers into their enterprises, adding to the pull of British and Jewish economic activity on the coast and the push of the land squeeze and rising population in the rural areas. Although most of the Arab factories were still little more than workshops, employing 5 or 6 workers including the owner and his family, there were already by the mid-1940s about 30–35 Arab industries engaging over 30 workers each.[56] And while many industries manufactured longstanding products (that is, soap and olive oil), others now manufactured cement, shoes, matches, metals, processed food, tobacco products, textiles, and so on.[57] This signaled a fundamental challenge to a society rest-ing on the foundations of an independent smallholding peas-antry and of a Muslim notable class drawing its strength from its relationship to tenant farmers.

The terms of the challenge were also established by rapidly expanding trade and commerce. From the 1930s to the 1940s, there was a 25 percent increase in the numbers of Arabs engaged in these activities, which like industry were not entirely new to Palestinian Arab society. For centuries, peasants had supplemented their incomes in hard times by peddling crafts and farm surpluses; some moved permanently to the cities to try full-time door-to-door selling or work in the bazaars. By 1900, such commerce was as indigenous as the desert sands.

Once the Great War ended, Palestinian commerce picked up its pace, thanks in no small part to a spate of improvements in roads, ports, and communications facilities in the twenty years before the war. During the mandate, Arab-owned shops proliferated much faster than the population grew. In 12 Arab towns, the number of bakeries increased sixfold from 1921 to 1939 (to nearly one thousand), and the pace was even faster in Jerusalem and Jaffa.

The mandate's new material culture was reflected in the appearance of ice cream and motorized transportation, with gas stations and garages to follow. There was a fivefold increase in cafés, and cutting hair became an established profession. Arab co-ops made their debut in the 1940s. Imports began to suffuse daily life; in a sharp reversal from what had been the norm, the Arab sector built a chronic deficit in its trade balance despite the continuing growth of citrus exports. Almost all segments of the Arab population joined the cash economy to some degree, even the peasants selling about 20 percent of their gross production.[58] By the 1940s, there were specialized marketing companies buying peasant produce directly in the villages for eventual consumption in the cities. But the impact of the capitalist economy was felt differently by various groups and regions. While some prospered in the new environment, embracing the new technology and ways of life, others suffered badly or found themselves marginalized by the changes.

Businesses demanding considerable investment also became essential parts of the Palestinian Arab economy. The large commercial enterprises tended to be in the hands of notable families or well-to-do Christians, many of them specializing in foreign trade.[59] While early in the mandate, they specialized in grains, citrus products, and food, starting in the 1930s, some began to compete with Jewish traders in merchandise such as textiles and machinery.[60]

For both poorer city dwellers and the fellaheen, the new commercial culture was problematic, offering glimpses of a life that could not be shared, bringing dislocation and distress along with ice-cream. Large farmers and exporters, for example, warmly greeted a free-trade agreement with Syria opening major markets for Palestinian watermelon and soap. But peasants found the pact opening Palestine to a flood of Syrian grain, depressing the price of their major product. There was an astounding 200 percent increase in national income from 1939 to 1943[61]—but the cash economy benefited Arab social groups very selectively.

This fact is particularly striking in regard to Palestinian Arab transactions with Jews. By the mid-1940s, Jewish buyers had acquired nearly 10 percent of the cultivable land, including nearly half of the most fertile tracts used for citrus groves. At the same time that these land purchases displaced tenant farmers and menaced smallholders by driving up land prices, Arabs who did the selling gained handsomely—a source of ongoing tension among Arabs. There were other important transactions of this nature. Repeated efforts by Zionist leaders to convince the Jews of the Yishuv to develop an autarchic economy accomplished much less than the Arab enforcement of economic separation between the two communities, starting in the general strike of 1936. Before that, 8 to 10 percent of Arab agricultural produce— vegetables, eggs, meat, and olives (between one-quarter and one-third of all cash crops)—was purchased by Jews, mostly from merchants ensconced comfortably in the country's developing commercial orbit.[62] In this manner, many considered powerful Arabs in the coastal cities as little more than collaborators with the Jews and the British injecting a hated new commercialism into the country. That unfortunate association placed great obstacles in the path of a common vision, grounded as it was in the experience of the dominant classes.

The world of finance, like that of commerce, was not new to twentieth century Palestinian society. Traditionally, Arab notables and other large landholders would tide peasants over with loans, a credit system surviving into the 1940s.[63] The new economy demanded more complex financial arrangements, seen to by a number of banks established with foreign capital, both before and after the Great War. Crédit Lyonnais set up the first bank in 1892, like others that followed, building branches in Jaffa and Jerusalem. The most prominent of the foreign banks was Barclays, already having branches in Acre, Haifa, Jaffa, Jerusalem, Nazareth, and Tel-Aviv in 1930.

In the late 1920s, Palestinian Arabs tried but failed to establish their own bank with the help of Egyptian capital. In 1930, a Palestinian returning from America, Abd al-Hamid Shuman, started up a small family-owned bank in Jerusalem. Shuman's enterprise, the Arab Bank, achieved remarkable success in a very short time—even by capturing a relatively small proportion of Arab savings, its deposits rocketed.[64] Its branches first opened in Jaffa and Haifa and extended later to Amman, Damascus, Beirut, Baghdad, and Cairo.

The Arab Bank served as a key element in the Palestinian nationalist vision, offering a basis for long-term investment and economic growth, the hope of confronting the Zionists on an equal economic footing—and even of engaging in economic warfare against them. In the rural areas, it could provide fellaheen the credit needed to avoid taking local loans at usurious rates, which had too often led to repossession of their land and, ultimately, sale of their plots to the Jews.

Seeking to cast a net far beyond the urban centers of Palestine's new economy, the new finance was thus bound to challenge existing rural patterns: the personal loan and the power relations tied up with it. In 1933, the Arab Bank spun off a subsidiary, the Arab Agricultural Bank;[65] in the 1940s—now as the independent Bank of the Arab Nation—about half its loans in fact went into agriculture. But as has been the case with so many banks established to help peasants in this century, credit found its way to the wealthiest peasants and the large landowners, rather than to their more needy compatriots. And even among people with money, new Arab-controlled financial institutions elicited as much ambivalence as the vision they symbolized: Together, the two banks attracted only 10–12 percent of total Palestinian Arab deposits, the great majority of depositors continuing to use the more familiar foreign banks. (Many others still preferred to stash their assets under the mattress.)

For those profiting from the industrial, commercial, and financial sectors of this emerging civic society, their enterprises involved an adoption of "Jewish techniques" to stave off Jewish domination.[66] But to those whose power was challenged by the reach of the new economy or who found themselves battered by it—the groups represented by Nablus rather than Jaffa—life in the coastal cities seemed less to produce weapons against Zionism than collusion with it.

In Arabic, the term *shabab* refers to young men. At times, it also refers to members of a gang. In the context of the tension between Nablus and Jaffa, it took on another meaning: those set adrift from their moorings, no longer bound by family or clan loyalties and responsibilities. For Palestinians most threatened by the new social life along the coast, the shabab represented a road not to be taken.

The condemnation of city life by those still in the hilly region, however, masked the underlying similarities between the urban shabab and the fellaheen. The shabab came mostly from families of transplanted peasants, both groups now finding themselves made marginal by changes wrought by prosperous, established Arabs. There clearly existed a potential to forge an alliance of the urban underclass with that still in the rural, eastern part of the country, and a figure who was to become a Palestinian legend, Sheikh Izz al-Din al-Qassam, managed to do so, thereby challenging the more westernized Arabs' vision of the future.

Qassam, a graduate of the Islamic al-Azhar University in Cairo, became a preacher in a Haifa mosque after he fled his native Syria in the wake of the French occupation of the country and their defeat of the Arab nationalist regime there. He began gathering supporters from nearby rural areas and the most marginal groups in the city, later using a religious court position to do the same in the northern villages. His aim was an eventual uprising of these slum-dwellers and fellaheen.

One researcher has noted that "Al-Qassam's Weltanschauung was wholly rooted in Islam, which constituted the nexus of all his ideas and deeds. [He sought to defend] Islam internally against infidelity and heresy; and politically against external enemies, namely the West—with which Islam was in political and ideological conflict—and the Zionist enterprise."[67] But, as was occurring in Egypt, Islam was now conceived in much more directly political and national terms in the face of European domination. His was not a lone voice in Palestine in building a national movement on an Islamic foundation: Along with the disintegration of the Muslim-Christian Associations, the 1930s witnessed the rise of the Young Men's Muslim Associations and other Islamic groupings.

According to contemporary memories, the sheikh would

preach with a gun or sword in hand, urging "the bootblack to exchange his shoebrush for a revolver and to shoot the Englishmen rather than polish their shoes."[68]

In the early 1930s, his preaching built the foundation for a formidable underground organization with the ominous name of the Black Hand, which he used as a springboard for a call to *jihad* and attacks against Jewish settlers.[69] By 1935, he had recruited several hundred followers, in cells of no more than five men each. Other clandestine groups organized by Muslim leaders appeared on the scene, fueling Islamic-nationalist militancy in the shantytowns of Acre, the Jerusalem-Ramallah area, and elsewhere. The Green Hand—consisting of veterans of the 1929 outbreak—directed its actions mostly against the Jews and had more resemblance to bandit gangs of the past. A group led by Abd al-Qadir al-Husseini, the son of Musa Kazim al-Husseini, mostly relied on Boy Scout commanders, members of his clan, and followers from the Jerusalem area, but did not get beyond a very preliminary conspiratorial stage. (His major role came in the 1936 revolt and in 1948.) Spurned by the mainstream nationalist leadership, Qassam and a small armed band of followers (estimates run from fifteen to fifty men) set out from Haifa in the fall of 1935 only months before the outbreak of the Arab Revolt using a village near the inland town of Jenin as a base to spark and lead a peasant uprising. The British almost immediately stifled this initiative, but Qassam's death at their hands occasioned a tremendous outcry at his funeral.

Qassam's organization and revolt were too brief and surreptitious to draw definitive conclusions about what they mirrored in Palestinian society. It is in any event clear that while he struck a responsive chord among Palestine's urban underclass and the fellaheen, not only members of the secular Palestinian intelligentsia, but established Muslim leaders, found his anti-Western message extremely unsettling.[70] It conflicted with principles prevalent in Haifa and the other coastal cities, based on an appropriation of Western and Zionist techniques, if only to resist domination. These leaders, too, often had a stake in calm relations with the British—either because of British salaries to them and their relatives or because of other sorts of British patronage.

This was not the only discordant note among the Arabs. One member of a leading Nablus family, Awni Abd al-Hadi, made a strong claim before the British Royal Commission of 1937 that there was "too much [Arab] industry in the country." His cries and those of Qassam and other Muslim militants were not mere echoes from a fading past. They represented living sentiments that, while strengthening the opposition to the Zionists and the British, also signalled a tension within the Arabs' new social boundaries that would weaken the national movement and lead, in the Arab Revolt, to mutual recriminations and violence.

3

Jerusalem:
Notables and Nationalism

JERUSALEM OF DREAMS AND REALITY

Jerusalem . . . When I mention the name, I see the white Jerusalem of summer when the brightness is blinding and the nearly
cruel light is thrown at you from every stone. I see Jerusalem in
the rays of twilight—neither orange nor pink nor purple—which
embrace the surrounding mountains and caress its houses of
stone . . . It is hard to describe Jerusalem in words. One has got to
feel it. Jerusalem is the source. It is the heart and the spirit, the
soul and the oversoul.[1]

These words could have come from Christian, Muslim, or Jew,
Jerusalem being, like the Holy Land itself, so deeply evocative to
all three faiths. "There is no other city like it," exclaims F. E.
Peters, "so solemn yet modest, so attractive and so intelligible;
so earthly, even provincial, and yet somehow spiritual and universal."[2] Of course, the city's significance does not really lie in
the hues of its twilight or in its solemnity and modesty, but in
something much closer to the heart of cultural myth. Note the
reaction of François René Chateaubriand, catching his first
glimpse of Jerusalem in 1806:

Suddenly, at the end of this plain I saw a line of gothic walls
flanked with square towers and behind them rose the peaks of

buildings. At the foot of this wall appeared a camp of Turkish cavalry, in all its oriental splendor. The guide cried out: "Al-Quds! The Holy City," and went off at a great gallop. . . . If I were to live a thousand years, never would I forget this wilderness which still seems to breathe with the grandeur of Jehovah and the terrors of death.[3]

More than half a century later, Mark Twain echoed this shudder of recognition: "I think there was no individual in the party whose brain was not teeming with thoughts and images and memories invoked by the grand history of the venerable city that lay before us. . . . The thoughts Jerusalem suggests are full of poetry, sublimity, and more than all, dignity."[4]

The mythology associated with Jerusalem has not been static, the constant struggle among Muslim, Jewish, and Christian factions for control of the city adding layers of meaning to existing beliefs. After the Crusaders' conquest, for example, both oblique references to al-Quds in the Quran (it is explicitly mentioned neither there nor in the Pentateuch) and the accounts linking Muhammad's personal experiences to the city took on growing importance. The result was its increased sanctification in the Islamic tradition, despite some resistance on the grounds that Mecca's special place was being diminished.

The stream of foreign Christian pilgrims and growing Jewish presence during the nineteenth and early twentieth centuries similarly renewed the Muslim attachment to Jerusalem (as did the Israeli conquest of the walled part of the city in 1967), the struggle with the Jews, in particular, validating and strengthening its religious importance. At the same time, the political and administrative changes after the revolt of 1834 gave Jerusalem's ruling elites an opportunity to place their own stamp on the entire country. This chapter recounts the rise of these elites, including their central role in the new nationalist politics after World War I—played out, ironically, quite apart from the two most important centers of Palestinian Arab society, Jaffa and Nablus.

In the early 1800s, the real Jerusalem—as opposed to the Jerusalem of dreams—was small and rundown,[5] covering less than a square kilometer and housing fewer than ten thousand people.

With a clear Arab majority, Muslims outnumbering Christians and another 20–25 percent being Jews, it was less a unified city than an accumulation of fairly autonomous sections—the Muslim, Christian, Armenian, and Jewish quarters and the Mughrabi neighborhood. Jerusalem, as a Jewish chronicler somewhat exaggeratedly put it, was "strictly confined within her high, dark wall, like a lizard in his skin," then adding that "a kind of perpetual mourning enveloped the city."[6]

Donations from abroad sustained most of Jerusalem's Jews and foreign Christians. While some people supported themselves through agriculture, farming did not hold much promise in a city more suited to being a fortress than a center for landlords and peasants. Embraced by treacherous ravines, it was largely cut off from the surrounding plains. A handful of residents worked in the usual small-scale industries (soap, textiles, leather, pottery, and Christian souvenirs),[7] but the city had always basically failed to establish a sound productive foundation for its population.

The plan of the city went back to Roman times, with its main streets modelled on the great thoroughfares of antiquity, the Cardo and the Decumanus. Much of the rest was a maze of winding alleys and courtyards. Even many of the churches, mosques, and synagogues that today seem a timeless part of the landscape were not built until the middle and end of the nineteenth century. The dominant structures, in addition to the Dome of the Rock and the nearby al-Aqsa mosque, were the Church of the Holy Sepulchre and the Armenian monastery and church.

Beyond their splendor stood dilapidated houses, muddy and unlit streets, and the filth of animal and human waste. As in antiquity, with no natural water sources of its own, the city faced chronic shortages for drinking and bathing—the Ottoman authorities paid little care to the development of water pools and aqueducts, and private cisterns often remained in disrepair. Cholera and plague descended on the city regularly through the middle of the century.

In dispirited yet melodramatic fashion, one traveller offered a typical view of Al-Quds' plight in the 1830s:

> The glory of Jerusalem has indeed departed. From her ancient high estate, as the splendid metropolis of the Jewish common-

wealth and of the whole Christian world, the beloved of nations and the "joy of the whole earth," she has sunk into the neglected capital of a petty Turkish province; and where of old many hundreds of thousands thronged her streets and temple, we now find a population of scarcely as many single thousands dwelling sparsely within her walls. The cup of wrath and desolation from the Almighty has been poured out upon her to the dregs; and she sits sad and solitary in darkness and in the dust.[8]

Later, in *The Innocents Abroad*, Mark Twain would voice related sentiments: "Lepers, cripples, the blind, and the idiotic, assail you on every hand, and they know but one word of but one language apparently—the eternal 'buckshcesh'. . . . Jerusalem is mournful, and dreary, and lifeless. I would not desire to live here."[9]

Despite Twain's own gloominess, Jerusalem was in fact already in the midst of a remarkable renascence, its population growing to over seventy thousand by the Great War's outbreak. Both Arabs and Jews began to move outside the walls starting in the 1850s, with new neighborhoods forming in all directions. The city's total acreage increased nearly sixfold in the seventy-five years prior to the war, the great majority of the growth being outside the walls. Construction of churches, mosques, synagogues, and private houses was continuous, and land prices rose astronomically.[10] The number of water cisterns increased with the population, new roads connected the city to neighboring towns, and the railroad linked it to Jaffa and the sea. The nineteenth century thus saw an end to Jerusalem's three-hundred year stagnation. By the time the city was made ready for the visit of the German Kaiser in 1898, it had been transformed into the largest and politically most important urban region in Palestine—a far cry from the town Napoleon had bypassed, in favor of more strategic places such as Acre, only a century before.

THE METAMORPHOSIS OF JERUSALEM, 1830–1914

As elsewhere in Palestine, the fortunes of Jerusalem, and especially of its Christian and Jewish inhabitants, began to improve dramatically during the time of the Egyptian occupation. The Egyptian innovations, however, were not greeted with universal approval—for instance, by the hill-area rebels who, in the Nablus-centered revolt of 1834, poured into Jerusalem and briefly took control with the embrace of the city's Muslims. But, unlike previous Muslim uprisings (1808 and 1826), which succeeded in both driving out the city's ruler and preserving the autonomy of the powerful families, that of 1834 was a last hurrah for those who imagined they could bypass outside governing authorities.

The Egyptian ouster of the rebels signalled not only immediate, bloody retribution by Ibrahim Pasha but a long-term shift in the city's delicate social and political balance. Christians (and Jews to a lesser extent) benefited as Ibrahim opened economic activities to them, especially in commerce, as well as positions in his administration. Even with the return of Ottoman rule in 1840, the Jews and Christians kept their enhanced status, despite Muslim murmuring about revenge against them for their complicity with the Egyptians. While the number of Jerusalem's Muslims grew slowly and steadily—from about 4,000 in 1800 to approximately 12,000 prior to World War I—the Christian population exploded from less than 3,000 to almost 15,000.[11]

Even more remarkable was the rise in Jewish population, from slightly over 2,000 in 1800 to approximately half the city's 22,000 in 1870, a decade before any Zionist immigration began. By the start of the Great War, Jews constituted more than 45,000 of the 70,000 total. In the course of the century, then, Muslims slipped from being the largest of the three groups to the smallest.

Jerusalem continued to be altered after the Sublime Porte's ouster of the Egyptians, through a slow elevation of its role as an administrative unit within the overall scheme of the empire. To be sure, other towns had not been on a truly equal footing with Jerusalem before the reforms. As a religious seat, it was furnished with a religious officer, the Hanafi Qadi, who could appoint deputies for the other towns and collect taxes for the ulama of Jerusalem.[12] Even so, its status was that of a backwater provincial center in the early nineteenth century. From this low point, it was gradually transformed into the ruling center for almost all of southern and central Palestine. In 1887, it became the capital of a sanjak, or district, no longer accountable to a provincial governor, such as the one in Damascus, but reporting directly to Istanbul.[13] About three-quarters of present-day Palestinians are descended from those who lived in the Jerusalem sanjak. Jerusalem's autonomous status, notes Abu-Manneh, "was of tremendous importance for the emergence of Palestine" later, after the end of Ottoman rule, and helped provide the grounding for a separate Palestinian identity.[14]

Towards the century's close, the new administrative links enabled the empire to increase both the absolute sum of revenues garnered from the district and the percentage of total income transferred to Istanbul. With Jerusalem as their base, the Ottomans extended their control outwards to towns such as Gaza, Hebron, Jaffa, and even Beersheba (where the Bedouin were now suppressed) and, not as successfully, to villages surrounding these towns. In the city itself, while it would have taken considerable time to be felt, by 1860 a more centralized rule modeled on Ibrahim Pasha's administration had undermined the autonomous power of Jerusalem's Muslim notable clans. Most consisted of ten to fifteen families: the most prominent names were Alami, Dajani, Husseini, and Khalidi.

Another important source of this shift in power was the rapid expansion of Jerusalem's foreign communities. As a local center, Jerusalem had few natural endowments to recommend it above other towns, and if it came to be fawned upon in the nineteenth century, it was because of a renewed international interest,[15] grounded to a considerable degree in its significance for Christians. A number of foreign powers developed a significant religious presence in the city, none greater than the Russian Orthodox Church. This followed Russia's defeat in the Crimean War and the inauguration of a regular shipping route between Odessa and Jaffa. The construction of the Russian compound, starting in 1860, at the site of a majestic viewpoint outside the walls, was an aptly symbolic gesture. In any case, from 1839 to 1854, almost every Western state, including the United States, opened a consulate there. And powerful consuls such as Britain's James Finn (his books *Byways in Palestine* and *Stirring Times* provide some of the most vivid portraits of the milieu) further cut into the influence and prerogatives of the notables. Several leading families continued to hold impressive agricultural estates in the country; some owned whole villages. But as a group Jerusalem's ayan were removed from Palestine's farming heartland and thus lacked both the strong ties to agriculture and the sorts of patron-client ties undergirding their power in towns such as Nablus.

Jerusalem's great Muslim families also lacked the commercial wealth of their counterparts in Jaffa and Haifa. They needed something else to maintain their preeminence, which turned out to be offices, both political and religious. The Ottoman creation of the municipality of Jerusalem as a corporate legal body probably occurred in 1863. The body's new institutions, such as the civil service and municipal council and those, a bit later, of the enhanced sanjak, became a haven and training ground for the families, even as the demography and character of the city changed around them. By the 1880s, the council had numerous responsibilities, from maintaining roads and water systems—along with an edict that banned tossing waste in public areas, this helped relieve the city's stench—to establishing fire and police departments, tax collection, and the like. Offices to supervise these activities proliferated. Control of key political, administrative, and religious posts both in the city proper and in the wider sanjak came to be the foundation of the notables' authority, eventually not only in Jerusalem but throughout Palestine. Younger, less established family members would often start their careers elsewhere in the Ottoman bureaucracy.

Manning such posts was not entirely new to Jerusalem's ayan and ulama. Prominent figures had long administered both the public *waqfs* (religious trusts) and private family funds. Their social prestige had put them in line to run the waqfs, which in turn, had reinforced their social and political power.[16] Some administrative positions related to the waqfs were hereditary; others could be sold, but often only to another clan member.

The ayan thus inconspicuously slipped from mostly religious offices at the beginning of the nineteenth century to largely political-administrative offices at its end, although some connection with the religious sphere continued to be important for maintaining status. The highest levels of the sanjak were occupied by Turkish Ottoman officials, but increasing numbers of Jerusalem Arabs, particularly Muslims, were making their way into the lower ranks. There were even some examples of Muslims being appointed at a level just below the governor himself, exercising authority in one part of the district or another. An Alami, for example, served as inspector of harvests for Gaza, Jaffa, and Beersheba. "These and similar cases," Haim Gerber comments, "are particularly interesting because they enabled the Jerusalem élite to lay the foundation for their later influence in other parts of the country."[17] The Ottomans at times engaged in what today would be called a privatization of government. Their method was to auction the performance of public functions, from collecting taxes to providing interurban mail service, to well placed, private contractors.

The Jerusalem ayan thus moved along a number of different routes in attempting to maintain their preeminence in the face of Ottoman power and demographic reality. As the proportion of Muslims in the city shrank, they kept a solid majority on the council. In the last council prior to the demise of Ottoman rule, six of the ten members were Muslim, two Christian, and two Jewish.[18] Part of the reason for this involved a series of Ottoman precedents resulting in Muslim overrepresentation. At the same time, the Muslims attached great importance to the new field of public service, in contrast to the Jews and Christians, whose interests rarely extended beyond their own communal groups.[19]

Prominent members of the Khalidi and Alami clans, for example, held council positions, as did those of the Nashashibis, one of the ranking clans at the end of the nineteenth century. The Ottomans guarded against any single family gaining too much power, the governor in one instance stripping the Husseinis of key posts in favor of the Khalidis, with this in mind. Nevertheless, on the whole, the notables were remarkably well-behaved subjects, especially given their proclivity to autonomy and rebellion before the 1850s. As indicated, the Jerusalem leadership's social power was grounded in neither agriculture nor commerce—thus denying it the sort of leverage available to the families of Nablus and Jaffa—but in offices created by the Ottomans, desperately attempting to shore up a dying empire.

For the notables, such a power base naturally meant severe dependency on the empire, and few Muslims opposed it until the twentieth century. The first hints of such opposition came several years after the 1908 Young Turk revolt, when anti-Ottoman feelings stirred outside Anatolia, followed by more serious resistance in World War I. Until then, the notables had shared sentiments of both Ottomanism and, in the Palestinian arena, noblesse oblige. In this regard, the very nature of Jerusalem supplied valuable experience for their later rise to the top of the Palestinian Arab nationalist struggle. It is important to recall that while in many parts of the country the Sunni Muslim majority and assorted Christian minorities had little to do with one another (towns such as Hebron barely had a Christian population), the situation in Jerusalem, as in other mixed cities, was very different. It was nearly impossible for Muslim notables holding local offices not to deal regularly with Christian Arabs, and this interaction became a cornerstone of Arab organization for confronting the British and Zionists after World War I. Similarly, the renewed foreign interest in Jerusalem and the influx of Jews offered important exposure to those who would end up ruling there for most of the next century.

At the same time, Jerusalem's new importance strengthened a sense in the ayan that they were somehow at the center of things, and this would have an important effect on their own sense of destiny in the embryonic nationalist movement. In the nineteenth century (later, as well) it also added fuel to the conflicts among the important families, wrangling for Ottoman administrative offices and for the governor's support.

Occasionally, such conflicts were intimately linked to others that were more longstanding. That between the Khalidis and the Husseinis, for example, incorporated the enduring feud between the leagues of Qays and Yaman, which had divided Arabs for centuries. The Khalidis had benefited handsomely from the Ottoman reforms at the expense of the Husseinis,[20] and in the resulting fray the Khalidis drew on the Qays as allies, while the Husseinis lined up supporters among the Yamani. As the Palestinian sociologist Salim Tamari notes, these alignments "cut across the village/city dichotomies and often united [even] Christian and Muslim families."[21] In this manner, prominent clans succeeded in fortifying wide-ranging networks as they reached out for allied families in other towns and, of course, for the non-Jerusalem branches of their own clans.

Some key notables from outside Jerusalem—the Tuqan, Abd al-Hadi, and Nimr families of Nablus, for instance—steadfastly resisted the vortex drawing them to side with one or another of the prominent Jerusalem clans. In fact, at times they sought the same sort of countrywide prominence that the Jerusalem ayan were so assiduously cultivating for themselves. But these efforts did not get very far. By the twentieth century, the clans of Nablus and other local centers could serve as little more than adjuncts, and sometimes counterpoints, to the struggles in the holy city.

BRITISH CONQUEST AND ZIONIST AMBITIONS: THE NOTABLES' RESPONSE

The events during and immediately after the Great War confronted the Jerusalem notables with the need for many changes, none more difficult to contemplate, perhaps, than the shift from Muslim to Christian rule. Before the war, the Muslims of Palestine, like all Muslims in the Ottoman Empire, had tacitly accepted their place within an Islamic domain.[22] The war now cut them off from their political and religious center—it left them somewhat adrift in a sea of religious and ethnic groups, all vying with one another within the new British military administration.

For the notables, the administration was a mixed blessing. On the one hand, it now unified Palestine into a separate country, with Jerusalem its official center. On the other hand, the new reign brought with it, alarmingly, the Balfour Declaration of 1917:

> His Majesty's Government view with favour the establishment in Palestine of a national home for the Jewish people, and will use their best endeavours to facilitate the achievement of this object, it being clearly understood that nothing shall be done which might prejudice the civil and religious rights of existing non-Jewish communities in Palestine, or the rights and political status enjoyed by Jews in any other country.[23]

Today, roughly seventy-five years after the Declaration's issue, there is a tendency to paint Arab-Jewish relations in Palestine before World War I in idyllic colors. Palestinian author Sami Hadawi reminisces about his Jerusalem boyhood:

> I remember how we children looked forward to the yearly community festivities. In the Spring, Moslem, Christian and Jew alike took part in the Moslem Pilgrimage to the tomb of the prophet Moses and watched with delight and excitement the dance of the *dervishes* to the chanting of heroic songs and banner waving. In the summer, Moslem, Christian and Jew flocked to the Valley to take part in the Jewish celebrations at the tomb of Sadik Shameon. And in the Autumn Moslem, Christian and Jew alike picnicked in the gardens around the tomb of the Holy Virgin Mary, near Gethsemane, where the Christian community spent a day and a

night rejoicing. . . . Ours was indeed a Holy City, a city of peace, love and brotherhood, where the stranger could find shelter, the pilgrim loving care and the faithful salvation.[24]

Unfortunately, in the Holy City as elsewhere, things were often much less harmonious. The Balfour Declaration was not the Jerusalem leadership's first unwelcome exposure to Zionism, which in any case had only intensified the already unsettling nineteenth century demographic changes there. In light of the city's continuing Jewish population surge in the 1880s—the period of the first wave of Zionist immigration—the Ottoman governor had made some passes at enforcing restrictions on Jewish settlement. Approximately two years after his removal in 1889, leading Jerusalem Muslims and perhaps some Christians made their first protest on June 24, 1891, by sending a telegram to the Porte asking that Russian Jews be prohibited from entering or buying land in Palestine.[25]

While at least at the political level, the ayan's anti-Zionism did not crystallize before the twentieth century, anxiety was surfacing time and again. Merchants, in particular, expressed the fear to Jerusalem officials that Jewish immigration would lead to their eventual control of Palestine's business economy. Following the century's turn, newspapers in the city increasingly covered the Zionist movement, often critically. Here as elsewhere, the Arab response was not always condemnation. Landowners appeared less troubled than merchants since they were already watching the price of land climb rapidly. And a report written in 1899 indicated that Jerusalem notables were prepared for Jewish settlement, provided that the Jews became Ottoman citizens and did not retain their foreign status. Still, after the Young Turk Revolution of 1908, which fanned local patriotism and incipient nationalism throughout the Empire, the notables came to view Zionism less through the lens of their Ottoman loyalties and more through that of the threat it posed to the Arabs of Palestine. In fact, for the first time they now began to refer to themselves as Palestinians.[26] While some worked to come to an agreement with the Zionists before the war, others called for action, including violence, against the Jews. A number of Palestinian Christians, among them several publishers, joined in the call for a new anti-Zionist consciousness that would blur the line between Christians and Muslims.

While his overall position and influence is of some question, Negib Azouri was one such intellectual, propounding "Arabism," a vague sort of Arab nationalism, as the answer to the Zionist challenge. In a pamphlet written in Paris in 1905, he prophesied darkly about the future of Jews and Arabs:

> Two important phenomena, of the same nature but opposed, are emerging at this moment in Asiatic Turkey. They are the awakening of the Arab nation and the latent effort of the Jews to reconstitute on a very large scale the ancient kingdom of Israel. These two movements are destined to confront each other continuously, until one prevails over the other. The final outcome of this struggle, between two peoples that represent two contradictory principles, may shape the destiny of the whole world.[27]

With such a political and ideological backdrop, the period after the issuing of the Balfour Declaration clearly did not find the Jerusalem notables totally unprepared for a struggle against Zionism. But they were stunned at how British intervention now became the framework for prolonged rule and for large-scale Jewish colonization of the land. They, along with other Arabs, believed that their abandonment of the Ottomans in World War I, along with Sharif Hussein's important revolt against the Ottomans during the war, should have led the British to grant them Arab independence. The revolt, in fact, had come in the wake of an agreement with the British—the McMahon-Hussein correspondence—promising independence for the Arab lands and reestablishment of an Arab Caliphate. It was ambiguous whether or not Palestine was included. Now they faced the replacement of the Ottomans by the British—and by the French in nearby Syria—and by the near-euphoria of the Jews, standing ready to govern the country along with the British. In the wake of General Allenby's conquest of Palestine in 1917 and 1918, some of the fears of the ayan began to be realized, and European rule to seem a transparent ruse to hand the country over to the Zionists. Jews argued for the official use of Hebrew either instead or alongside of Arabic, an allocation of seats on municipal councils, official recognition from the British of their special status and autonomy; and they spoke openly of creating a Jewish majority.

A chain of events served to fan these fears.[28] On the first anniversary of the Balfour Declaration, the Zionist Commission, headed by Chaim Weizmann, organized a parade. As the first public show of Jewish political power, it unsettled the Arab leaders, who petitioned Great Britain to "put a stop to the Zionists' cry." A month later, in December, 1918, a conference representing all the Jews in Palestine drew up national demands to present to the Paris Peace Conference. The result was a "Plan for the Provisional Government of Palestine," which urged largely Zionist and European control of the country, with a fairly inconsequential role for the Arabs. Zionist leaders now spoke of forming a future commonwealth—a bolder notion than that of a national home but not quite as bold as of a state, which was suggested by a number of participants, including David Ben-Gurion.

Following their conference, the Zionists met in Paris with Faysal, son of Sharif Hussein (now king of the Hejaz), and himself a key figure in the revolt against the Ottomans. Faysal, as we shall see momentarily, was to play a critical, if indirect role in the development of Palestinian nationalism; he had already met twice and established a cordial relationship with Weizmann. On January 4, 1919 in Paris, he and the Zionists signed an agreement appearing to support both the Jews' aspirations and his hopes of establishing an independent Arab regime, although the exact political disposition of Palestine was left unclear. Faysal, declaring that Palestine should have its own guaranteed status as a Jewish enclave, was unequivocal in his acceptance of unfettered Jewish immigration as long as he received his promised independent state. Shortly after the agreement was signed, the Zionists offered the Arabs a free zone at Haifa and a joint Arab-Jewish free port on the Gulf of Aqaba. The agreement, we will see, did not last long,[29] but when word of Faysal's concessions leaked out, the Palestinian notables were horrified, declaring they would "not agree to be sacrificed on the altar of independence."[30]

The dealings of European statesmen also heightened their alarm, as the Great Powers held conferences and dispatched commissions to dispose of the Great War's spoils. In July, 1920, the San Remo Conference took up the division of the territories of the Middle East, and several months later the British replaced their military administration in Palestine with a civilian one. The first British high commissioner was Herbert Samuel, whose origins led other Jews (before their later disillusionment) to dub him their "king," and an offspring of the Davidic dynasty. Within months of his appointment, leading Palestinian Arabs complained loudly about Samuel's partiality to the Zionists.

Next in the array of international conferences was the Cairo Conference of 1921, in which Winston Churchill, the new British colonial secretary, laid out his ambitions for Britain's role in the Arab world for the next generation.[31] In 1922, the League of Nations ratified the mandate for Palestine. Coming into effect in the fall of 1923 with the Balfour Declaration as the preamble to its principal articles, it called for the establishment of a Jewish Agency to assist in the governance of the country.

The new, assertive Jewish nationalism, with its strong British backing and its colonization of the land, played out against this backdrop of international conferences and decisions, spurred the Jerusalem ayan to begin building an Arab national movement. This symbiosis parallels the struggles among emerging nationalism in the Balkans and other territories ruled by the Austro-Hungarian and Ottoman empires during the period leading up to World War I.

Within months of the British conquest of Palestine in 1917, Palestinian notables already began organizing their response to what they—and some British officials—called "Zionist provocations." The response was not limited to creating new organizations such as the Muslim-Christian Associations. The first blows in a communal war lasting until this day occurred when Arabs attacked two northern settlements, Tel Hai and Metullah, in February, 1920, providing the Jews in Palestine with their first martyrs and military heroes. Less than two months later (April 4–5, 1920), more violence was unleashed at the annual Muslim Nabi Musa pilgrimage to the traditional grave of Moses. Until then mainly a local popular religious meeting, this now became a first, nationwide Arab-Palestinian festival, and would be celebrated as such in years to come. Musa Kazim al-Husseini, the mayor of Jerusalem, invited delegates from many parts of Palestine to the celebration. Haj Amin al-Husseini, the eventual leader of the nationalist movement, returned from Damascus, where he worked in support of Faysal's short-lived kingdom. He made his first public appearance with a speech arguing that the British eventually would support Faysal's rule over Palestine.

The agitated mob attacked the old Jewish quarter of Jerusalem; five Jews were killed and about 200 wounded, and when the British intervened, four Arabs killed and 32 wounded were added to the toll.[32]

More agitation followed, the source of all these outbreaks lying in political events that would have great influence both on who would emerge as the leading Arab notables and on the ultimate course of Palestinian history. At the center of the events stood Faysal—for whom the 1919 peace conference and the agreement with the Zionists were but sideshows to the establishment of an independent Arab state in Syria, with him as monarch. By "Syria," Faysal meant today's Syria and Lebanon, as well as Transjordan and Palestine (often referred to as Greater Syria). For politically aware Palestinian Arabs, the notion of such a state seemed the best route to escape both Zionism and British rule.

In January, 1919, the leading Palestinian families organized a Palestinian Arab conference under the auspices of the Jaffa and Jerusalem Muslim-Christian Associations. Despite some sentiment for Palestinian autonomy under British guidance, including that of Jerusalem's Arif al-Dajani, who presided over the proceedings, a consensus emerged to support Faysal's ambition. Zionism was strongly rejected; Palestine would remain an Arab country as part of a federated, Faysal-led Syria.[33] With Faysal's army in place in Damascus since October, 1918, and the British at first well disposed towards his desires, the prospects seemed reasonable for his emergence as a truly independent Arab ruler, capable of staving off the Zionists.

A coterie of young Arabs full of passionate intensity from towns all across the Fertile Crescent clustered around Faysal. Many—such as Iraq's Nuri al-Said—would become the outstanding Arab nationalists of their generation. Those from Jerusalem established a Damascus offshoot of their Arab Club to collaborate with Faysal's political organization, while a contingent from Nablus—a strong center of Pan-Arab and Islamic sentiments, and always a competitor to Jerusalem's dominance—both set up their own club and participated actively in Faysal's army.[34] For his part, Faysal courted the support of the Palestinians. He disowned his earlier agreement with the Zionists by supporting anti-Zionist resolutions at the Second General Syrian Congress, which elected him king in March, 1920 (the first Congress had taken place the previous July). But he had his differences with the Palestinians as well, courting the British for protection of his fragile political organization and vulnerable army. One view of the British held by politically active Palestinians was as little more than a Zionist vanguard.

Events in Damascus spilled over into agitation in Palestine. Intimations of Arab rebellion were in the air.[35] The Muslim-Christian Associations organized demonstrations supporting the Syrian scheme and lambasting Zionism (one slogan was "Palestine is our land and the Jews are our dogs"). In ways reminiscent of the great families' mobilization of peasants in the revolt of 1834, the notable-dominated Associations managed to organize events involving a broad cross-section of Arab society, but now including a much larger Arab urban sector. In the major towns, both upper and lower classes sent the strident message that the country's future was as part of a unified Arab state, with its center in Damascus; the Jews' presence would be at the sufferance of the Arabs. It was in this context that violence erupted in 1920.

Neither the stridency nor the violence ended up being of much help to Faysal or his Palestinian allies—whose support was in any case a mixed blessing. The Palestinian-dominated Arab Club turned out to be the most coherent of supporting organizations, but it also maneuvered him, unavoidably, into positions he probably would have preferred not to take, including a declaration of independence and renunciation of cooperation with the French. In response to the violent turn of events, and from fear of the French advantages in a unified Syria, the British swept in to thwart the Palestinian aspirations. They arrested some young notables and sent others—including Haj Amin al-Husseini—into flight from the country. They also removed Musa Kazim al-Husseini from the mayoralty of Jerusalem and installed a member of the family that was emerging as the major rival to the Husseinis, the Nashashibis—thus opening wider an already serious fissure among the Jerusalem notables. It was at this point that Britain confirmed its hold over Palestine at the San Remo Conference and established its civilian government under Samuel.

Faysal's fall in July—the French took military action to force him into exile—simply underscored what had already become obvious since April to many Palestinian political activists: the idea of Palestine within a Syrian Arab state was dead. The framework upon which many of the notables had pinned their hopes for building fervent loyalties and a workable political identity collapsed into rubble. At the very moment that the country's future was being decided by the British and other Europeans, the Palestinians had no workable vision of the future.

In the 1930s, George Antonius, the most famous Palestinian historian and an active nationalist, reflected on events that, with time's passage, the Palestinians have largely forgotten:

> What with the decisions of the San Remo conference, the occupation of the whole of Syria by the French, the consolidation of British control in Iraq on a basis which denied even the outward forms of self-government, and emergence of a policy of intensive Zionist development in Palestine, the year 1920 has an evil name in Arab annals.[36]

Long before 1948 came to be identified with the term, it was 1920, as Antonius noted, that was spoken of as *Am al-nakba*, the year of catastrophe or disaster. The disaster hit both individuals and the community. With Faysal's ouster from Syria, Palestinians in Damascus scattered in various directions. A number ended up in Transjordan, some being assimilated permanently into that newly formed country's politics. Others, including the founders of the Istiqlal Party, which would later play an important role in Palestine, faced eventual expulsion. Those who fled to Palestine itself, native Palestinians as well as Syrians who would settle there, found a dispirited Arab leadership in Jerusalem and Jaffa.

For the community as a whole, the new permanent boundaries in the Middle East after World War I demanded a reorientation. Some sects, such as the Druze of northern Palestine, Lebanon, and Syria, found their communities fractured. The European powers now demanded passports and visas for previously uncontrolled routes. Different currencies, customs regulations, and trade patterns forced financial and commercial restructuring in Palestine.

The new boundaries also made the Palestinians' political prospects seem bleak, particularly when compared to neighboring countries. In Iraq, the British gave Faysal a sort of booby prize, establishing him as the soon-to-be king. They did much the same for Faysal's brother, Abdallah, by setting off part of the territory planned for the Palestine mandate to be a separate country, Transjordan, under his rule. This must have been especially galling, since many of the non-Bedouin Arabs of Transjordan were practically indistinguishable from those of Palestine, branches of Palestinian families having moved east of the Jordan River in the nineteenth century to become, in effect, the country's settled population. And Syria, as well, had its political future laid out by the French, with prospects for the independent states of Syria and Lebanon.

Responding to the fiasco of Faysal's Syrian defeat, the notables began developing alternative goals and strategies. At the Third Arab Congress, held in Haifa in December, 1920, they revived the plan that Arif al-Dajani and some of the other older notables had proposed in the country-wide conference of January, 1919. That plan had stressed the autonomy of the Palestinian Arabs and their unique circumstances. The emphasis on the continuity with the congresses held in Damascus in July 1919 and March 1920 contained considerable irony, since the concept of a Greater Syria, so confidently trumpeted there, was here nowhere in evidence. Musa Kazim al-Husseini commented, "Now, after the recent events in Damascus, we have to effect a complete change in our plans here. Southern Syria no longer exists. We must defend Palestine."[37]

The new strategy focused exclusively on Palestine, and that meant addressing the threat that Zionism posed, which became a conceptual linchpin. The platform drawn up in Haifa would change little over the next few decades. It contained the following six elements: the first public recognition of Palestine, as it would be constituted by the mandate, as a distinct political entity for the people living there (although there was no legitimacy afforded to the mandate itself); a total rejection of any political or moral right of the Jews over Palestine; a declaration of unity among the Palestinian Arabs to supersede any other loyalties, such as those to religion, region, and clan; a call to the new administration to halt any transfers of Arab or state lands to Jewish control; the demand to close Palestine to further Jewish immigration; a call to recognize the Arab Executive Committee (popularly known simply as the Arab Executive) as the legiti-

mate representative of the population before the British authorities (with a status similar to that defined for the Jewish
Agency).[38] And in the fall of 1921, a Muslim-Christian delegation to London submitted an even more elaborate set of conditions, including the demand for the creation of a "national
government" whose parliament would be democratically elected
by the country's Muslims, Christians, and Jews, and a call for
the nullification of the promise for a Jewish national home.[39]

More comprehensive Arab unity (as in the plan for a Greater
Syria) was never totally done away with in the Palestinian Arabs'
political agenda. In one guise or another, it reappeared throughout the 1920s and in subsequent decades, although in each of its
incarnations Palestinians were often frustrated that other Arabs
did not share their degree of alarm about Zionist ambitions.
Still, Faysal's fall marked an important turning point. From then
until 1948, Palestinian politics and loyalties were determined by
the idea of an independent Palestine.

THE FACE OF THE NEW PALESTINIAN LEADERSHIP

The notion of Palestinian autonomy, however vague as the basis
for either a long-term vision or a concrete strategy, did signal
several important trends in the social composition of the emerging political leadership. In the first place, as Britain's administrative headquarters, emerging from the shadow of Damascus
and a Greater Syria, Jerusalem moved strongly centerstage on
questions of Palestine's political future. It was not an accident
that at the Haifa congress, both the head and deputy head of the
Arab Executive elected by the country-wide delegates of the
Muslim-Christian Associations, Musa Kazim al-Husseini and
Arif al-Dajani, were members of prominent Jerusalem families.
Husseini, who had nurtured his career in the Ottoman bureaucracy, had been mayor of Jerusalem until he was unceremoni-
ously removed by the British following the violence in the city
that spring; Dajani was president of the Jerusalem Muslim-
Christian Association.

A marked ambivalence toward the British on the part of this
Jerusalem-dominated leadership emerged at the congress. After
all, Jerusalem's debt to British rule was clear enough. At the
same time, there was no escaping Britain's role in promoting

Zionism through the Balfour Declaration. The delegates trod delicately through that problem, calling for British rule, but in a context very different from what the Declaration implied: that of Palestinian Arab self-rule under British aegis. The immediate task was to rid Great Britain of the ignorance, as Jamal al-Husseini put it, that had brought it to its pro-Zionist stance and created the framework for the Jews' quickening colonization of the land.

There was one other reason for the present leadership choosing a British connection. Husseini domination of the congress resulted in near-total exclusion of the Nashashibi clan, which recently had moved to become the Husseini's most significant rival for power in Jerusalem. The Nashashibis had been closer to the French than the British in the past few years' turmoil, and an underlying Husseini calculation may have been that a British-leaning Arab policy would leave them at a disadvantage. In any event, the Nashashibis soon recovered well enough to displace the Husseinis in British favor.

Accompanying Jerusalem's emerging dominance was a shift from a younger to an older generation of ayan. Musa Kazim al-Husseini was already in his seventies, and the others on the new Arab Executive were largely middle-aged or older. A number of them had established their credentials as officials in the Ottoman Empire's Jerusalem sanjak. Their careers flourished in the context of working with an existing ruling power, whether Ottoman or British, that gave political legitimacy to a Jerusalem-based administration. In light of the Balfour Declaration, they were unequivocal in refusing to work officially for the mandate. But as members of the most representative, though never formally recognized, Arab institution, the Arab Executive, they found themselves the objects of repeated British efforts to lure them into some such cooperation.

For its part, the Executive drew increasing criticism from younger, more militant figures. Reflected in its almost ceaseless, occasionally spirited, communications with the British over nearly fifteen years was a basic stance of polite negotiation, and its role, as the contemporary Palestinian social scientist Taysir Nashif has put it, was "largely passive."[40] The country's notables continued holding congresses—the seventh and last in 1928—which in turn elected the Executive; it dissolved in 1934 upon the death of Musa Kazim al-Husseini.

While it did not displace the older leadership, a potentially far more dynamic factor in the interplay among Arabs, Jews, and the British was the emergence of Islam as a powerful political force in postwar Palestine. This was the case despite a carefully cultivated Muslim-Christian consensus, and the Muslim-Christian Associations' offering the Jerusalem notables dominance over a countrywide organizational network.

The defeat of the Ottoman Empire and the imposition of British boundaries left Palestine's Muslims without the central religious institutions that had answered to the sultan in Istanbul. A significant amount of Palestinian political action during the mandate period took place within the framework of new institutions established to fill the void. While it was the British, above all, who made them possible, they soon took on a character quite unanticipated by the mandate officials.[41]

Despite Jerusalem's exalted status as the third holiest site in Islam, under the Ottomans the status of the nonjudicial religious leaders, the muftis, was roughly equivalent to that of their colleagues in other provincial centers. The Hanafi Qadi, in contrast, was based solely in the city, selected by Istanbul and with the power to appoint deputies for other Palestinian towns. Now, finding a compliant Kamil al-Husseini as the city's Mufti and chairman of the Central Waqf Committee, the British sought to enhance his role and extend his religious authority over all Islamic Palestine. Thus, when the British appointed him as Jerusalem's first Grand Mufti (a newly established religious title) and qadi, or judge, of the main Islamic law court in Jerusalem, they succeeded in creating a new Palestinian Islamic hierarchy.

Kamil al-Husseini's untimely death in March, 1921, brought into the open the vicious squabbling among Jerusalem's Muslim notables, led by the Husseinis and Nashashibis already gnawing away at the hope of Arab unity. With a pardon from High Commissioner Herbert Samuel in hand, Haj Amin al-Husseini had returned to Palestine from his refuge among the Bedouin of Transjordan and now presented himself as the Husseini candidate to replace his brother.[42] But the opposition was intense, first from within the Husseini clan by those fearing Amin's youth and impetuousness, and later from both the Nashashibis and the Khalidis, and the struggle increasingly bitter. On one occasion, wall posters appeared in Jerusalem warning that the Jews sought to promote someone, presumably the Nashashibi candidate who would accept Zionism, squelch the Palestinian movement, sell Waqf property near the Wailing Wall (*al-Buraq*), and cede the Haram al-Sharif so that they could rebuild their Temple.[43]

In the midst of such political turmoil, more Arab-Jewish violence erupted in 1921, this time in Jaffa, in the wake of a May Day parade by Jewish leftists. A jittery Samuel was confronting a ticklish problem: "Here was a Christian mandatory power [with a Jewish high commissioner], committed to establishment of a Jewish National Home, controlling a Muslim majority in a country considered holy to the three main monotheistic religions."[44] Apparently hoping to diminish a growing Arab sense of alienation from his government, he took steps to strengthen the Islamic community's role as a cohesive force in Palestinian affairs. Using some questionable procedures, he appointed al-Husseini Mufti (queasiness over his past role in the Nabi Musa violence of April, 1920, led Samuel to drop the newly developed title, Grand Mufti, but Kamil's authority also accrued to his brother). Samuel also shepherded the new mufti into the position of president of another newly created body, the Supreme Muslim Council, formed in January, 1922.[45]

Samuel gave the Council far-ranging authority, affording a significant degree of self-rule for the Muslims. The Council's president (i.e., Haj Amin) would gain considerable patronage, especially through his control of the waqf and his power to appoint and dismiss almost all Islamic officials in the country. Soon after his appointment, Amin offered the highly controversial, never-settled claim that the presidency had lifelong tenure.

Using these posts of Mufti and president of the Supreme Muslim Council, Haj Amin would determine the character of the emerging Palestinian political framework. He set about placing Palestine, and the ever-simmering struggle against Zionism, at the center of universal Islamic concerns, first through an international campaign to refurbish the two revered mosques on Haram al-Sharif, al-Aqsa and the Dome of the Rock, and then through the convening of an ambitious international Muslim conference in Jerusalem in 1931. These two events propelled him into the top ranks of the Islamic world and established him as the most important leader in Palestinian history, at least until Yasser Arafat.

With a solid base for solidifying power, Amin built a countrywide network fueled by patronage and curricular control in Islamic schools. In one example of this process, he neutralized opposition in Nablus by appointing a rival nationalist leader and intellectual, Izzat Darwaza, as General Director of the Waqf endowment. Darwaza's influence would subsequently extend far beyond the Waqf, into the turbulent waters of Palestinian nationalist politics.

Although it was the British who gave Amin such wide latitude, they later were quite ambivalent about this. Often, they worried about his abuses of influence and funds and looked, as one high commissioner put it, for ways to clip his wings. At the same time, enthusiasm for doing so was dampened by what the British considered his role, in much of the 1920s and the early 1930s, in preventing what they called the religious cry from being raised—the type of violence that had broken out during the Nabi Musa celebration in 1920. The country was, in fact, relatively free of communal violence from the time Amin assumed his power until the Arab Revolt of 1936.[46]

The one, not insignificant exception to this tranquility reinforced British suspicions that without the Mufti religious mayhem would erupt in Palestine. On the holy day of Yom Kippur, 1928, Jews modified the status quo by erecting a divider between men and women praying at the Western Wall—the Jews' holiest site and an abutment to the Muslims' Haram al-Sharif. Any issue involving holy places would promptly mobilize the Supreme Muslim Council, rather than the Arab Executive, and from that point on, the Council engaged both the British and the Zionists in a running controversy over how much autonomy the Jews should have over the wall and the adjacent area. This thrust the Supreme Muslim Council into the role of Arab political spokesman to the British against the Zionists—just as the series of Arab congresses promoted by the Muslim-Christian Association were sputtering to an end. The violence took place after a decade of intermittent Zionist immigration. Barely a trickle in the early part of the decade (this had made talk of a Jewish majority seem somewhat fanciful), it had increased at a rate quite alarming to the Arabs in the few years before the riots.

The Supreme Muslim Council's refurbishing of the Haram al-Sharif with funds raised through Haj Amin's international campaign was also at issue. The Jews argued that the reconstruction was having adverse effects on the wall and their ability to pray there. In the end, the gathering storm of nationalist and communal conflict between the Zionists and the Palestinian Arabs burst over religious rites and symbols. It did so, after a summer of almost incessant wrangling, in August, 1929, as a religious melee between Jews and Muslims. Muslims called for a holy war against the Jews and eventually against the British colonial power.[47] With rallying cries of protecting the al-Aqsa Mosque, Muslims battled Jews, and then British troops, in a number of places in the country. The riots left nearly 250 Arabs and Jews dead and more than 500 wounded—the worst episode of bloodletting until that time in Jewish-Arab relations.[48]

The peak of these events occurred on Friday, August 23. Following rumors that the Jews were planning an attack on Haram al-Sharif, Arabs attacked Jewish quarters in Jerusalem, Safad, Tiberias, and Hebron, cities mainly populated by Orthodox anti-Zionist Jews. The locus of the horror was in Hebron, where 64 Jews—men, women, and children—were massacred, and the core of the old Jewish community of Hebron ceased to exist. The massacre of Hebron was a traumatic event in Arab-Jewish relations that exacerbated suspicions, mutual anxieties, and stereotypes.

Islam's rise in the emerging national movement was not lost on Palestinian Christians.[49] In part, they responded by joining in acts whose origins lay in Islam but that came to be reinterpreted as national events—the development of a kind of civil religion. The celebration of the Nabi Musa pilgrimage, into which the Supreme Muslim Council had poured considerable effort and funds, is probably the best example. Some Christians even began to speak of Islam as a national Arab culture that they, too, could embrace.

Many others harbored grave doubts. They noted the calls in the Arabic press for Christian conversion; they worried that religious slurs against Jews at demonstrations could be turned against them too; and they fretted about the Mufti's international Islamic actions, including his leading role against a Christian missionary conference in Palestine and his convening of the worldwide Muslim conference in Jerusalem. Even the pilgrimage was cause for worry, the Mufti having converted its format into a sort of teach-in, what in Arabic was called *tanwirat*. While part of it focused on the threats Zionism posed to the Arab nation—such as transfer of fellaheen land to the Jews—other parts focused on specific threats to Muslim society. The peril was to the holy mosques, through putative Zionist plans to re-build their Temple. It was also to the moral state of Muslim society, through the corrupting practices brought to the country by the Jews, by the socialism and communism that many of the Zionists espoused, and by Western culture.

Even with the Islamic turn of Palestinian politics, some Christians, such as George Antonius, remained in the forefront of the new nationalist movement. The two leading newspapers, Haifa's *al-Karmil* and Jaffa's *Filastin*, were Christian founded, run, and written. *Filastin* was founded in 1911 by Isa al Isa, who adopted a strong anti-Zionist and nationalist editorial stance. The newspaper's reappearance after World War I and Isa's return from Damascus, along with counterparts such as *al-Karmil*, pushed the urban population towards a more nationalist perspective in the 1920s. In the 1930s, it would have a similar effect on the fellaheen. Greek Orthodox Christians, seeking support in their own struggle to Arabize the Patriarchate of Jerusalem, remained closely wedded to the Muslim nationalist leadership. Nonetheless, many Christians seemed to be resigned to the impossibility of building a secular nationalist politics among the Arabs of Palestine. Khalil al-Sakakini, a prominent Christian active in the various congresses, despaired of his role in the national movement in a letter to his son. "As long as I am not a Moslem," he wrote, "I am nought."[50]

To be sure, the expansion of Islam in Palestine did not signify the death of a national self-consciousness nurtured by the Muslim-Christian Associations.[51] Instead, what seemed to emerge was a Palestinian community, groping towards its own distinct identity, that coexisted, often uneasily, with other established, parochial identities. Tensions between clans, religious groups, city dwellers, and fellaheen remained prominent and worrisome elements of the social structure. The leadership, itself caught up deeply in these tensions, was unable to move Palestinian society beyond them—even as Zionist immigration gained increasing momentum.

CHALLENGES TO THE NOTABLES' LEADERSHIP

For the Mufti, the events of 1929 were a turning point. Just before the Western Wall upheaval, the Nashashibi-led opposition (apparently financed in part by Zionists) had made some gains against Amin al-Husseini.[52] Their success in the 1927 municipal elections was linked to intimations that the Husseinis had blown the Zionist threat out of proportion. In the upheaval's wake, they slipped to a much more marginal position. Until then, Amin had left diplomacy and the political affairs of the Palestinians to the Arab Executive. Afterwards, he moved ever more closely towards the political spotlight. The following year he was already negotiating with the British in London. As Philip Mattar has put it, he "emerged from the political violence both famous and infamous"—famous among the Arabs and infamous among the Jews.[53]

For the Palestinian community as a whole, 1929 meant a rapid political mobilization, with all sorts of new figures entering the political arena, from Jaffa professionals to Nablus peasants. Such figures, representing a new generation of 1930s activists, were for the most part based outside Jerusalem. Sheikh Izz al-Din al-Qassam, the initiator of the Palestinians' first guerrilla force, had settled in Haifa and drew his strength from the northern districts, where Jerusalem's influence had always been lowest. The leader of the Youth Congress, organized in 1932, came from the Ramleh district and looked to the surrounding coastal plain as a first source of support. In 1931, a conference of 300 young activists demanding a more anti-British position by the Arab Executive took place in Nablus.

The impact of such activity varied tremendously, but together it eroded the ayan's oligopoly of power—a process that was double-edged. While unleashing tremendous sociopolitical forces—what Ann Lesch has called "mobilization from below" —the new participants in a formerly exclusive political process also made it increasingly difficult for the Palestinians to speak in a single voice.

At least part of the problem for the notables in the 1930s arose from their leadership styles. The Jerusalem-based ayan were largely cut off from the dynamic of Jaffa, Haifa, or the villages, doing little to incorporate new urban or rural groups into political life or take account of the changing day-to-day issues confronting the entire society. The fellaheen ironically and derogatorily referred to the ayan as *effendiat al-quds,* the Masters of Jerusalem. Peasants muttered about their collaboration with the British leading to Zionist-induced displacements of tenants from the land and to high taxes.

The notables eventually did establish political parties in the 1930s, but these were closer to being social clubs for particular clans than mobilizing agents for the society at large. The Palestine Arab Party was the creation of the Husseinis, the National Defense Party of the Nashashibis, and the Reform Party of the Khalidis. Although the attitude of noblesse oblige the notables had taken with them from the Ottoman period into the mandate led them to speak for the Palestinian population, wider political involvement certainly would not have taken place within such a framework. Salim Tamari has alluded to the limited leadership role of the ayan, attributing it, at least in part, to the character of the new mandate:

> The colonial state apparatus after the First World War strengthened the role of the "leading families" of Palestine since alternative institutional mechanisms of "intermediate" power were absent. They became the mediators between the state and the rural masses and the urban poor as well as the representatives (or rather, the clemencers) of the latter towards the central authorities.[54]

From time to time, the ayan transcended this mediating role to call upon the population for popular demonstrations, but the farthest any went in social organization was the construction of patronage systems and of family networks.

Of all the leaders, Amin al-Husseini was most intent on going beyond this old way of doing things. But the very terms of his effort revealed the same weaknesses plaguing the other notables. From his position as president of the Supreme Muslim Council, Amin operated within two distinct circles. The inner circle consisted of a group holding the most powerful Islamic appointments in the country, and in order to insure loyalty as best he could, he fell back on his own clan. Husseinis held a disproportionate number of the appointments as well as of other high positions in the mandate administration, obviously furnishing good connections to British officials. The outer circle included hundreds of appointments in mosques, courts, and schools throughout the country, and his need to continuously allocate offices and honors—that is, his role at the center of a vast patronage network depending on nepotism and parochial politics—only further deepened the cleavages in Palestinian society. While his rhetoric freely incorporated a unifying imagery of an Arab, all-Palestinian community, his actions revealed a much more limited vision.

In short, the foundations of al-Husseini's power—the patronage, his call to religious sentiments, familism, and proper relations with the British administration—prevented him from leading an all-embracing national movement. In the end, the Mufti represented merely one faction, albeit the largest, to participate in that movement. To be sure, some of the new mobilization around him reinforced the predominance of the Jerusalem-led ayan. For example, in October 1929, an Arab Women's Congress drew over 200 delegates, mostly the wives of active notables.[55] Its chair was the wife of Musa Kazim al-Husseini, the head of the Arab Executive, and, predictably, its resolutions closely mirrored that group's positions. Other such activity was much less reassuring and eventually transformed British-Palestinian relations, first into acrimonious exchanges, then into full-scale violence.

Much anti-British agitation came in the aftermath of the Wailing Wall riots. A report in 1930 stemming from the riots, the Passfield White Paper, seemed to vindicate the Arab Executive's patience, promising severe restrictions on Jewish land purchases and immigration, two of the Arabs' key planks.[56] But, before the old leadership could savor its apparent victory, a letter by Prime Minister Ramsey MacDonald to Chaim Weizmann in 1931 reversed the White Paper.[57] The MacDonald letter, which the Arabs acerbically called the Black Paper, shocked the Palestinian community, with young Palestinians at a Nablus conference pressuring the Arab Executive into a much more anti-British stance. This marked the first occasion that outsiders succeeded in forcing such changes on the ayan.

Practically all the new activism had a militant, anti-imperialist tone, directed at the British, without exception viewing Zionism as a foreboding menace. But there the unanimity stopped, as different organizations pulled Palestinian society in contending directions. They divided on means. Some, including most Christians, largely stayed within the bounds of respectable diplomacy; others—among them, Istiqlal Party members and participants in the Youth Congress of 1932—participated in illegal demonstrations. Clandestine guerrilla groups such as that organized by Sheikh al-Qassam prepared for armed assault.

The activists also differed in their visions of the future. Some, such as those in the Istiqlal Party, moved towards greater pan-Arabism. "Palestine is an Arab country and natural part of Syria," read the party's *Manifesto to the Arab World* in December, 1931. Others, such as organizers of the Young Men's Muslim Association, were narrowly sectarian and markedly anti-Christian. Both stances frayed the edges of the notables' vision of a united, autonomous Palestinian nation, their answer to the failure of the Faysal-led Syria plan. Still others sought to give the old strategy an even more explicitly nationalist flavor. In 1931, Izzat Darwaza of Nablus, for instance, convinced his town's Muslim-Christian Association to change its name to the Patriotic Arab Association. Often these varying ideas were not recognized as clashing. Darwaza at the same time supported pan-Arabism, Islamicism, and an increased dedication to the Palestinian nationalist ideal.

By the mid-1930s, the Palestinians had generated the clear beginnings of a popular movement—one with significant intellectual ferment and diverse notions of its future. The ability of the Jerusalem notables to impose their will on that movement and restore its coherence had eroded badly. In a statement to the high commissioner before a demonstration in Jaffa, the members of the Arab Executive noted, "In the past, the leaders were able to appease the people, but now they have lost their influence."[58]

Among the new groups seeking to put their stamp on the movement, none stood out more prominently in the early 1930s than the Istiqlal.[59] After disappointments in Syria in 1920 (where Izzat Darwaza had been one of the party's founders) and in Transjordan a decade later, the Istiqlal reassembled in Palestine in 1932. Its rallying call consisted of two simple themes: the old, "lethargic" notable leadership had failed the Palestinian people and only British imperialism had made the Zionist threat viable, even menacing. The party coaxed Palestinians towards more defiant tactics—demonstrations and political and social boycotts. Even when, in 1935, the high commissioner convinced all five other Palestinian political parties to meet with him, at a time when Jewish-Arab relations were moving towards unbridled violence, the Istiqlal refused to join in the negotiations.

The party typified the mood of the 1930s, through both its introduction of novel political ideas and methods, and its recruitment of until then politically inactive Palestinians. It drew its leadership from the north of the country, and from Nablus and Jaffa—but not from Jerusalem. Young professionals filled its ranks. So did the ragged shabab. The zeal of both social groups deeply frightened the notable leadership, especially Amin al-Husseini.

The Istiqlal had a brief, but powerful, moment in the sun, its major impact coming in the two years after its Palestinian debut. But already by 1935, the Mufti had succeeded in discrediting its leaders and sabotaging its efforts. For the rest of the decade—the period that determined the direction of the Palestinian movement and included the bloody Arab Revolt—it was reduced to impotence. It would reemerge in the 1940s with the old leadership in disarray, as the major opposition to the Husseinis' Palestine Arab Party.

Such shifts in fortune on the part of various alternative movements should not obscure the fact that Palestinian Arab political leadership during the mandate was the province of the Jerusalem ayan. Their achievements were impressive. They grasped the political situation quickly and accurately after the demise of Ottoman rule, adapting readily to the British administration—which they understood needed them to maintain law and order in the country. Even their command of English—many had been trained in French—came quickly.

Of their accomplishments, none rivalled their ability to fashion a popular national movement out of a rapidly changing Arab population. They succeeded in establishing Jerusalem as a national center, from which they exerted their control. In today's terms, that control would be considered weak. Despite their leverage, they did not pay sufficient attention to the evolving civil society around them. Their own interests as landowners and as officeholders dependent on the British led them to suppress or ignore other emerging groups. They did manage to prevent the rise of rival groups that might have supplanted their leadership, and they pushed competing centers, such as Nablus and Jaffa, into limited regional roles. Even with the ayan itself badly fractured, they were thus able to command broad enough—if not particularly deep—authority, across the various segments of Palestinian Arab society, to fortify it against the Zionists. Years later, after they had passed from the political scene, their program for dealing with that challenge remained deeply influential.

HEADING TOWARDS COMMUNAL WARFARE

The discord manifest in the Palestinian national movement in the mid-1930s could not obscure the essence of their common struggle: Who would eventually control Palestine? The calls to pan-Arab or Islamic sentiments notwithstanding the land—as defined by the League of Nations mandate—stood at the center of the hopes and concerns of both Arabs and Jews, bestowing an increasing legitimacy on the idea of a state, even as they both became exasperated with British rule over it.

By the mid- to late 1930s, most illusions, such as reconstructing the Caliphate or establishing a pan-Arab federation linked to a Palestine with a Jewish majority, had been largely abandoned by Jews and Arabs for the harsh reality of an impending struggle.[60] In that sense, we can speak of a conflict at this point between two national movements, even if the leaders were still trying to instill a sense of national consciousness in their communities. The conflict took a variety of forms on each side, from incessant diplomatic pleadings in Jerusalem and London to organizing for future violent clashes.

A rich range of issues became arenas for battle—for instance, over how the name of the country should appear on its postage stamps. The British proposed printing the name *Palestine* in the country's three official languages, English, Arabic, and Hebrew. Quite understandably, Arab leaders strenuously argued against the inclusion of Hebrew (as they had against Hebrew programs on the Palestine broadcasting service). Equally understandably, Zionists first insisted on the term *Eretz Yisrael* in the three languages, relenting later in order to argue for at least *Palestine—The Land of Israel*. The upshot was stamps with the inscription *Palestine* in the three languages, with the addition of an almost invisible two-letter Hebrew abbreviation of *Eretz Yisrael*. The pictures on the stamps were also controversial. Interpreting the stamps of the Tomb of Rachel as part of a process of

Judification of the country,[61] the Arabs insisted on representations of the Dome of the Rock—and demanded, as well, that the Arabic *Palestine* appear in larger letters. By 1938, the national movement was issuing its own stamps, to be affixed to all letters, carrying the slogan "Palestine for the Arabs."

Some private attempts were made to bridge the gap between Zionist and Arab aspirations. In the mid-1930s, Musa Alami, Awni Abd al-Hadi (one of the founders of the Istiqlal), and George Antonius held discussions with Zionist leader David Ben-Gurion, to little avail. Ben-Gurion's proposal was for an exchange of Jewish agreement to a pan-Arab federation linked to Palestine for Arab agreement to unrestricted Jewish immigration into Palestine and Transjordan, leading to an independent state with a Jewish majority. Some Arabs showed interest in the scheme, but the idea of an Arab federation linked to a Jewish state did not get far. Alarmed by every Jewish gain, most Palestinian Arab leaders saw few prospects for a settlement.

These gains appeared to be snowballing in the 1930s, with Jewish immigrants seeming to arrive in droves after the MacDonald letter. In 1932, approximately 12,500 arrived, and the number rose to 66,000 in 1935. In the decade's first half, the total Jewish population more than doubled, and the rise of Nazism precipitated a tidal wave of central European emigration, the greatest share of it ending up in Palestine.

The Arab population was itself by no means stagnant. Fewer than 500,000 Palestinian Arabs at the beginning of the century grew to close to a million by the middle of the 1930s. But this growth was not reassuring to Arab political leaders. They watched the Jewish expansion with horror. In their own backyard of Jerusalem, the numbers of Jews grew from 53,000 to 70,000 in the four years between 1931 and 1935.

Even more distressing was that this influx was taking place just as Palestinian unity seemed to unravel, the new voices and classes reducing the old leadership to ineffectual self-absorption. At the height of Zionist successes, Musa Kazim al-Husseini died, and the Jerusalem notables entered into a bout of mutual recrimination. The ayan seemed on the brink of political bankruptcy. When the need for resolute leadership appeared greatest, the Arab Executive simply passed from the scene.

The Arab Revolt, 1936–1939

The Great Arab Revolt in Palestine, as Arabs have called it,[1] was sparked by the murder of two Jews on April 15, 1936. Although there were some claims that the act was purely criminal, it was probably engineered for political purposes by a disciple of Sheikh Izz al-Din al-Qassam.[2] In any event, Jewish retaliation followed swiftly, leaving two Arabs dead as well. Within a few days, beatings and additional murders inaugurated a period of horrifying violence in the country. In a short time, the violence was transformed into a major Arab upheaval.

As the first sustained violent uprising of the Palestinian national movement, and the first major episode of this sort since 1834, perhaps no event has been more momentous in Palestinian history than the Great Arab Revolt. It mobilized thousands of Arabs from every stratum of society, all over the country, heralding the emergence of a national movement in ways that isolated incidents and formal delegations simply could not accomplish. It also provoked unprecedented countermobilization. Astonished by its tenacity—as were the Palestinians themselves—the British poured tens of thousands of troops into Palestine on the eve of World War II. And the Zionists embarked upon a militarization of their own national movement—nearly 15,000 Jews were under arms by the Revolt's end. Inaugurating an increasingly militarist Jewish political culture,[3] it contributed in the 1940s to a decision by Ben-Gurion and other Zionist leaders to prepare for military struggle against the Arabs rather than against the British, a change in strategy instrumental in their ultimate triumph.

Just as significant as the revolt's intercommunal and international outcomes were the social changes that followed in its wake. It highlighted Palestine's transformation from a fairly self-sufficient and homogeneous peasant society into one incorporated into world markets and politics, distinguished by division and disharmony constantly sapping the prospects of achieving common goals. Despite shared belief about the threat of Zionism and actions in pursuit of a common cause, the distance between the old leadership and the peasants became unbreachable. Much Palestinian fury came, in fact, to be directed at the most privileged Arab groups in the country. In 1937, when the ayan lost its key asset, its special ties to the British rulers, it rapidly faded. In its place came two new sorts of leadership, with characteristics marking Palestinian leaders even today: those whose influence was confined to specific regions, and those who, claiming to speak for the national movement as a whole, were based outside the country.

The social distance of the ayan from the people now became the physical distance suffered by the new national leadership. Some of its members—most prominently, Haj Amin al-Husseini—were familiar faces or came from the same families supplying Arab leaders since the Ottoman period. But on the whole it was younger, more militant, and necessarily much more inclusive, absorbing compatriots from the newly mobilized segments of society. Inversely, the Arab population found itself worn down at the revolt's end, and disarmed by British forces. When the Zionists began their own rebellion against the British following World War II, "the Palestinian Arabs," notes W. F. Abboushi, "proved too exhausted by the effort of rebellion between 1936 and 1939 to be in any condition to match it."[4]

In any event, while the Arabs' concerted opposition would not in the end bring about the demise of Zionism, they did appear, for the moment, to have the advantage. The result impelled the British to reverse their policy in support of a Jewish national home, first set out in the Balfour Declaration two decades earlier. The extensive Arab mobilization and the intensity of their activity demanded unprecedented British attention to the Palestinian position, and Palestinians somehow seemed to have developed the social and political cohesion necessary to make their point forcefully and unambiguously.

If the events between 1936 and 1939 added up to something unique in Palestinian history, some of the tactics used in the revolt and its social character grew out of the fundamental changes in Palestinian society and the growing challenge posed by the Zionists in the five preceding years. While responding to the transformation of their society in different ways, across the social spectrum, Palestinians applauded the creation of a national movement, sharing an ideology that totally negated any Jewish political right over the country. The mandate's history did not simply consist of periods of calm punctuated by unusual bursts of violence on the part of Arabs, as many accounts of the period imply. Rather, the violence was the sign of this steadily unfolding national movement and the unanimity among Palestinian Arabs about the Zionist threat.

PORTENTS OF REBELLION

Prime Minister Ramsey MacDonald's refusal to suppress the Zionists, as the Passfield Report had recommended following the violent outbreaks of 1929, caused great disappointment among the Palestinian Arabs in the early 1930s. At the same time, their leaders used the plight of the Arab victims of the 1929 riots to enhance the sense of a shared fate among the Arab population. They established aid committees for families of those arrested and killed and made the three Arabs hanged by the British into national martyrs. The deep resentment caused by both the hangings and the later MacDonald letter sent a surge of solidarity through the Arab community that had considerable impact on the Palestinian national movement—not least in a shift in hostility away from the Jews alone and towards two new targets: the British and, what at the time seemed far more remarkable, other Palestinians.

The 1936 general strike thus came only after half a decade of shifts in stance and actions vis-à-vis the British. It emerged as a shared sense that imperialism could only thwart Palestinian Arab aspirations. By the early 1930s, Palestinians were already reinterpreting the violent clashes at the Wailing Wall in 1928 and 1929 in light of this new anti-imperial stance.

That day was a day of honor, splendour and glory in the annals of Palestinian-Arab history. We attacked Western conquest and the Mandate and the Zionists upon our land. The Jews had coveted our endowments and yearned to take over our holy places. Silence they had seen as weakness. Therefore, there was no more room in our hearts for patience and peace. . . . The Arabs stood up, checked the oppression, and sacrificed their pure and noble souls on the sacred altar of nationalism.[5]

To be sure, there had been bloody encounters with the British at the time, but almost exclusively in the context of violence directed at the Jews. Yet here Emil al-Ghawri, later the secretary of the Arab Higher Committee, refers to the riots as motivated by nationalism more than religion and directed as much against the British as the Zionists.

The new anti-mandate activism was designed not only to force the British away from their support of Zionism but also to rid the country entirely of imperial rule. Young nationalists now argued that British support of Zionism was not simply a delusion, to be corrected. Rather, Zionism was part and parcel of Western imperialism in the Middle East, and only the eradication of the latter could halt the advance of the former.

The mandate government's decision, following the 1929 turmoil, to release 587 rifles previously kept in sealed armories to isolated Jewish settlements naturally aggravated Arab anti-British sentiment. But beyond any such direct British decisions, the strongest force affecting Palestinian Arab opinion, transforming the British into a prime target of Arab wrath and political action, was the appearance of new Arab militants, most prominently during the brief flourishing of the Istiqlal Party. The Istiqlal's demand for noncooperation, like Gandhi's doctrine of disobedience, struck a highly responsive chord among the Arab population at large.[6] A portion of the old ayan—members of the Husseini and Nashashibi clans and their allies, as opposed to some of the Nablus leadership, who embraced the new anti-British tone—represented a sole exception. Fearful of losing essential support for their own positions, they tempered the Istiqlal's enthusiasm for open resistance. Nevertheless, even these notables adopted a measure in the early 1930s to boycott official British events.

Anticipating the tone and tactics of the Arab Revolt, a group of nationalists sympathetic to pan-Arabism—most of them young, many Nablus based, and chafing under the Jerusalem-dominated leadership—called a national meeting for July 13, 1931. The delegates now thrust the British problem to center-stage, calling for a general strike in August. The shutdown occurred peacefully in most towns, but in Nablus itself, women and teenagers engaged in a rock-throwing melée with the British police.

That year, a series of general strikes, political demonstrations, and violent exchanges with the police followed. While some public protests were called by the established leadership (Musa Kazim al-Husseini himself led an October general strike in Jerusalem), the new activism was clearly in the hands of a younger generation. It was expressed in the new political role of the shabab, and in the formal constitution of the Istiqlal Party in 1932. The party was forthright in proclaiming that the British, not the Jews, should be the primary targets of action—in some cases, Palestinians even organized contingents of guards to protect Jews and their property during demonstrations.[7] In fact, during this period, while the British were firing at Arab demonstrators and breaking into offices of the Muslim-Christian Associations, not a single Jew was attacked in urban protests.

In the first half of the 1930s, internecine verbal sniping and occasional violence among the Palestinians, like the tactics being used against the British, presaged a motif of the 1936–39 revolt. Among the Jerusalem ayan, factional fighting grew to unprecedented levels, certainly slowing (without destroying) the momentum towards political unity. Late in 1929, Jerusalem's mayor Raghib al-Nashashibi commented privately that his opposition to Haj Amin al-Husseini was ten times stronger than the aversion of the Jews to the Mufti.[8] In a 1933 meeting in Jaffa, a member of the Nashashibi clan suggested that as an act of noncooperation with the British both Raghib al-Nashashibi and the Mufti resign their positions. But the tactic was little more than a ploy to remove Haj Amin from the source of his patronage and power. When it was exposed as such, it did little for either its supporters (the Nashashibi-led opposition—the *Muarada*, who declined dramatically in the following years) or for the doctrine of noncooperation.

Mudslinging and political maneuvering reached a new pitch of intensity. Defying clan loyalty, Musa Kazim al-Husseini forged an alliance with Raghib al-Nashashibi against Haj Amin. The Mufti's opponents accused him of misusing funds, and he brandished the charge that his enemies assisted the Jews in their landbuying. Substantive differences also existed. Some of the Nashashibis, at least, were much more inclined than the Mufti to grant the legitimacy of Jewish rights in Palestine and to seek some accommodation with the Zionists.

More significant than this continuing factionalism, with its intemperate charges and countercharges, was a surge of opposition to the ayan as a whole. This was initiated by the Istiqlal with others quickly joining—the radicalized urban political activists, who organized the Young Men's Muslim Association, literary groups, sports clubs, and so forth. Such organizations were of course not unique to the Arabs. Palestinians had the young, brown- and black-shirted European fascists to emulate, and even the very active local Jewish movements. In particular, the Zionist right-wing Betar and left-wing Hashomer HaZa'ir presented models of youth militancy in service of a national cause.

By the 1930s, youth groups increasingly focused their attention both on stepped up, direct political action and on the inadequacies of the national leadership. Sharp criticism was levelled both at the Arab Executive and the entire tenor of Jerusalem-dominated politics. The first national Congress of Arab Youth met in January, 1932, pointedly not in Jerusalem but in Jaffa. Establishing its main headquarters there, delegates criticized the ayan's "controlled protest" policy. The attacks escalated through the early 1930s. In part, Amin al-Husseini's collaboration furnished a platform for such denunciations. The Mufti wished to transcend the sectarian soapbox that the presidency of the Supreme Muslim Council afforded him, in favor of a more encompassing national one. At least until 1932, he was quite pleased to join in condemning the Arab Executive's old guard as "frail ghosts," unsuited for national leadership.[9]

As the decade wore on, the Istiqlal and the youth groups continued their strident criticism, but the Mufti drew back. After the signing, in 1932, of an agreement supplying the Supreme Muslim Council with new British funds, he was much less eager to criticize either the old leaders or British. Until 1936, he publicly urged the Arabs to target the Jews, not the British, although deflecting the Istiqlal's criticism had him occasionally advocating an antigovernment stance. For their part, reacting against the pretensions of the ayan, with their "feudal" titles such as pasha, bey, and effendi,[10] Istiqlal members did not hesitate to single out the Mufti, along with others, as collaborators with the imperialists. Directed against Haj Amin, this sort of criticism was enough to prompt a frenzied counterattack, which led to the rapid decline of the Istiqlal Party.

Even after it began to fade, many youth groups maintained their militancy. Boy Scouts turned out to be among the most dedicated new nationalists, "already at this stage . . . instrumental in forcing the shopkeepers and merchants to take part in nationalist strikes or as the vanguard in nationalist processions. . . ."[11] They aimed their fury at the British, the Jews—patrolling beaches in search of illegal Jewish immigrants and forming fighting groups during the revolt—and again, at other Palestinians. Like the internal bickering, such pressure tactics foreshadowed patterns that would dominate the Arab Revolt itself.

Serious religious tensions were also appearing in the Palestinian nationalist movement. These tensions were deeply grounded, merely exacerbated by both Haj Amin's base of power in the Supreme Muslim Council and the British propensity to differentiate between the Muslim and Christian communities. Muslims resented the over-representation of Christian Arabs in the bureaucracy, and the presence of foreign Christian missionaries in the country. This resentment interacted with the exclusivist Islamic component of Palestinian militancy, and the question of what role Islam would play in the emerging national identity. While most of the leadership, both the ayan and its opponents, officially set a secular independent Arab state as its goal—a concept that has since been maintained and embellished—popular feelings about the role of religion in politics were difficult to quell. There were even some scattered attacks on Arab Christians by Muslim gangs.

It is important to recall that the political evolution of Palestinian nationalism—the mass demonstrations and militant political parties, the use of mosques as bases for popular mobilization—took place against a backdrop of ever-increasing Jewish immigration, growing social dislocation, and Arab urbanization.

It was in the early 1930s that the dispossessed Arab farmer became a poignant symbol of the simmering conflict between the two peoples. Perhaps no other subject had its capacity to prompt the charges and countercharges, the presentation of evidence and counterevidence to British commissions. Likewise, Arabs living in the city observed the higher wages paid Jewish workers and the call for exclusively Jewish labor in Jewish enterprises. In this context, the delegations to London, the rising Zionist tide, the periodic communal and religious violence, and the never-ending stream of British decisions were not distant echoes for ordinary Palestinians, but ever-more central daily concerns, nurturing a sharpened political consciousness. The process was furthered by the British-imposed educational system, which while surely inadequate, both drew young men, usually with strong nationalist views, back into the village as schoolteachers and fostered increasing levels of general literacy. The growing number of schools produced new consumers for the nationalism promulgated in the Arabic newspapers.

In October, 1933, thousands of Palestinians took to the streets in an anti-British demonstration in Jaffa. By the end of the day, a dozen demonstrators had been killed along with one policeman. The "Jaffa Massacre" touched off further violent demonstrations in other cities, the occupation of several towns by British troops, and an Arab general strike. One of the most respected Arab officials in the mandate government, Musa Alami, commented that "the program of the Arab youth is based only on the use of force and violence.... The youth prefer an open war.... The prevailing feeling is that if all that can be expected from the present policy is a slow death, it is better to be killed in an attempt to free ourselves of our enemies than to suffer a long and protracted demise."[12]

The rural resistance that would play such a critical role in the 1936–39 revolt was also foreshadowed by preceding events. Following the Jaffa massacre, Sheikh Izz al-Din al-Qassam, who had allegedly contemplated building a military organization from his earliest days in Haifa in the 1920s, stepped up his organizing in northern Arab villages. Combined with his Haifa sermons, he thus laid the basis for the guerrilla actions he hoped to mount against the British authorities. Although once his group was destroyed, the government labelled it a band of thieves, Qassam instantly gained a reputation among Palestinians as an important symbol of armed resistance to imperial rule, especially outside the cities. While his posthumous influence was strongest immediately following his death, that is, during the Arab Revolt, it would extend to the concerted attack by the fedayeen on the state of Israel after 1948.[13]

THE URBAN REVOLT

Reflecting a widely shared Palestinian sentiment, the Arab Revolt was in many ways more a product of the people at the base of society, in the villages and poor urban neighborhoods, than it was of those at the top, trying to put their own stamp on the evolving national movement.[14] Indeed, recent writings have celebrated the revolutionary spirit of workers and peasants during the revolt. They have suggested that the lower classes were the true backbone of the movement and have cast doubts on the basic motives of the notable leadership.[15]

With the outbreak of violence in April, 1936, the government quickly declared a state of emergency. Jaffa became both the center for attacks by the shabab on Jews and for the initial Palestinian political responses to the attacks. Reflecting gathering anger at the British, Arab leaders called for their first general strike. Immediately, prominent notables from Nablus seconded this move by creating a National Committee, appealing to leaders of other towns to join the protest. In a matter of days, almost each one had its own National Committee.

By April 25, ten days after the first violence, the Jerusalem-based leadership created a new countrywide coordinating body, the Arab Higher Committee, to pursue the general strike and deal with the British. Led by Amin al-Husseini, it succeeded in extending the strike until October 1936.[16] Its demands did not differ substantially from those voiced before the revolt by the much tamer Arab Executive or by other Palestinians: an end to Jewish immigration, the banning of land sales to Jews, and national independence.

The first rioters, even before the calling of the local strikes, were led by the shabab. In some ways, the Arab Revolt was the shabab's debut; this product of Palestine's rapid urbanization would appear again on the national scene, most notably in the Intifada. But both the urban working class and cosmopolitan, Western-educated Palestinian Arabs played their part. The Arab Car Owners and Drivers Association, for example, imposed a shutdown of all Arab transport, and a nearly unknown Jerusalem physician named Dr. Khalil al-Budayri led intellectuals in calling for Gandhi-style, peaceful non-cooperation with the British. Inspired by the recent 45-day strike begun in February by Syrian Arabs against the French, which deeply impressed the Palestinian community, those who had been in the Istiqlal Party and others formed the National Committees and pushed for a general strike.

Quickly, the strike embraced the merchants, small shopkeepers, city workers, and Arab agricultural laborers in Jewish settlements. The shabab created local youth guard units to enforce compliance. With the paralysis of the Jaffa port and the diminished agricultural market, the strike created shortages for the Jews and British—and untold hardship for the Arabs, especially the poorer Arabs, who had difficulty gaining access to food.[17] The Arab leadership decided to raise "taxes," allowing the National Committees to create strike funds, particularly for the crucial transport workers and longshoremen. Merchants paid a levy, citrus growers 1 percent of their sales, wealthy women a portion of their jewelry. Poor families paid a one-piaster coin.

Popular revolt both offered the ayan significant new human and material resources for waging their national campaign and imposed new constraints. They found themselves saddled with the shabab, which aggressively collected the new levies but in the process began to drive wealthy Palestinians into Lebanon and Egypt. They faced demands that they and their relatives in government posts join the strike—an act threatening to erode their power bases. Their compromise was to leave government workers on the job, but to demand at least 10 percent of their wages for the strike.

A cartoon in the July 12, 1936, edition of the newspaper *Filastin* shows a startled Chaim Weizmann looking at Amin al-Husseini and Raghib al-Nashashibi, the two longstanding rivals and representatives of the two leading notable families, shaking hands beneath the spirit of Sheikh Qassam, now a symbol of the resistance. But this impressive unity was a fragile one. The varying costs that different segments of the population were paying, the hidden benefits that some were receiving, the differences in capacity to bear the pain of the strike, all served to undermine its foundations.

The sustained use of violence also frightened many notables and other wealthy Palestinians. Although mostly unorganized and poorly coordinated, it represented a repudiation of the gentlemanly diplomatic discourse they had long conducted with the British. For the time being, it was directed mostly at Jews—about eighty were killed in this initial stage—with some additional attacks on British forces and installations. Among other targets, Arabs destroyed forests planted by the Jewish National Fund, a prime symbol of Jewish settlement to both sides,[18] and repeatedly hit the railroads, a symbol of imperial rule. But the possibility existed of uncontrolled violence turning against Arabs, and this was a further source of alarm among the privileged.

A major deployment of British troops brought a respite from the urban strike and the rural violence that had accompanied it. But this lasted only until the summer of 1937 and the publication of the report by the Royal Commission (popularly known as the Peel Commission),[19] which the British had dispatched to investigate the events of 1936—and which recommended partitioning the country between Arabs and Jews.

In September, 1937, Arabs in Nazareth assassinated Lewis A. Andrews, an acting British commissioner who was sympathetic to the Zionists. The killing has been attributed both to followers of Sheikh Qassam and to the Mufti. Whatever the precise circumstances, the mandate authorities reacted strongly, proclaiming martial law within forty-eight hours and dissolving the short-lived Arab Higher Committee, as well as other Arab national agencies. Two hundred Arabs were arrested, decimating the movement's leadership. Among them were officials of the Supreme Muslim Council, the Arab Higher Committee, the local National Committees, and the activist youth organizations. The mandate authorities issued numerous arrest warrants, including those aimed at Muslim religious leaders.

Their biggest target was Amin al-Husseini, in whom they had placed so much of their faith over the last decade. Stripped of the presidency of the Supreme Muslim Council, he was hunted in the sanctuary of the Haram al-Sharif, where he was known to have taken refuge earlier. Apparently alerted to British intentions, the Mufti succeeded in disguising himself and fleeing to Lebanon, where the French placed him under house arrest.

He never again set foot on the soil of a unified Palestine. Rather, he twice returned briefly to what formerly was part of the country. The first was for ten days to the Gaza Strip, that sliver conquered by the Egyptians in 1948. And the second was to Jerusalem, the home denied him by both his blood enemies, the Israelis and the Jordanians, until a brief visit permitted by the latter shortly before it lost any control of the city in 1967. His exile, however, would not put an end to the strong influence he exerted over events in Palestine.

Besides the arrests, the mandate officials denied reentry to leaders outside the country at the time, such as Izzat Darwaza, the former head of the Istiqlal. Some Palestinian political figures managed to flee the country; others faced deportation. In Damascus, Darwaza and a number of others established the Central Committee of the National Jihad in Palestine (*Al-Lajnah al-MarKaziyya lil-Jihad*). Echoing Sheikh Qassam's repeated call for holy war, this is one example among many of the Palestinian nationalist movement's assimilation of Islamic religious terms into its vocabulary.[20] The Committee's official head was Darwaza, but it worked closely with the Mufti in Lebanon to garner support and supplies for the revolt and, as much as possible, to supervise the rebels still in Palestine.

But for the most part, the Palestinian elite could not continue to play an effective leadership role in the revolt. Not much of it (9 percent) participated, and only an additional 5 percent directed military operations.[21] With the demise of the urban leadership in 1937, the revolt shifted to rural Palestine, meeting with astonishing success in the hill country. Then—in a notable reversal of direction of influence that had prevailed in Palestine—it moved from the countryside to the cities. Inland towns, including Nablus, Hebron, Bethlehem, and Ramallah, were taken over by the rural rebels, who expanded their reach at the revolt's height in August and September, 1938. In Jaffa, they wrested control from the British authorities for several months, and—echoing events of the revolt of 1834—they even managed to occupy the walled portion of Jerusalem for five days. Rebel soldiers slipped into Tiberias on September 5 and killed a large number of the town's Jewish population. On September 9, they occupied Ramallah and Beersheba and in the process released prisoners from British jails.

In most towns, the breakdown of order forced the closing of banks and post offices—frequent targets of rebels seeking cash to sustain the uprising. For a period, British rule in these areas was nominal.[22] The revolt now took on a very different tenor from that of its inauguration by workers and merchants in Jaffa in April, 1936. The urban centers became as much its victims as its perpetrators. Urban agitation had already lost steam with the drastic British countermeasures of 1937. By the revolt's second and third years, much of the urban populace seemed to tire of the prolonged turmoil. The shabab, suffering from the alarming rates of Arab unemployment and thinned by migration back to villages, struggled to keep it alive but only intermittently succeeded. The focus of events had clearly shifted to rural Palestine.

THE RURAL REVOLT

In the charged political climate of Arab Palestine, the events of April, 1936, seemed to touch the countryside directly. By May, rural national committees called for withholding taxes from the government. More dramatically, both in the Galilean hills and in the east, spurred by members of the Istiqlal, followers of Qassam and other militant Muslim preachers, peasants were organizing into guerrilla bands, taking aim at Jewish settlements and at British installations with hit-and-run tactics.

Operating from mountain caves or other hideouts, the rebels went so far as to sabotage the Iraq Petroleum Company oil pipeline to Haifa. After the Arab Higher Committee called off the general strike in October, 1936, enabling its members to ship out their prized citrus crop and peasants to attend to their harvest, agitation continued in the villages. Many peasants bought weapons and prepared for continued fighting.

By 1938, they carried the uprising on their backs. Thousands—some estimate as high as 15,000—now joined the revolt, up to 10 percent becoming permanently active fighters.[23] Most groups were purely local, operating in very circumscribed areas, with fighters continuing as best they could to farm during the day. Their diffuseness—as well as their sheer numbers—would eventually overwhelm British administrative capacity.

Alongside such bands there emerged others that were larger and more established—sometimes even clusters of allied forces fighting across broad swaths of territory. Single commanders organized as many as several hundred men into subsidiary bands, each having its own lieutenants, with authority over some thirty to sixty men, to carry the brunt of the hit-and-run fighting.[24] One commander who would later establish an indelible imprint on Palestinian history was Abd al-Qadir al-Husseini. It took some time for these complex structures to form, and the process was certainly not a smooth one. Lieutenants flouted their commanders, bands struck against one another. But, by 1938–39, they were by far the Palestinians' most effective fighting forces. In August, 1938 rebel leaders in the hills created the High Council of Command.

The biggest barrier to forming a true national fighting force—one that could be distinguished from the rural criminal gangs that had previously dotted the countryside—was the absence of a hierarchical system of command and control for the various guerrilla groups, especially the larger and more permanent ones. The effort to forge such a system began close to the revolt's onset, in the spring of 1936. It continued in the summer with the entry into Palestine of an outsider, Fawzi al-Din al-Qa'uqji, who drew the immediate attention of both local peasants and the Arab Higher Committee. He brought with him a group of two hundred experienced *mujahidin*, or holy warriors, gathered from Transjordan, Syria, and Iraq.

Like Abd al-Qadir al-Husseini, Qa'uqji's name would frequently emerge in a Palestinian context through 1948, although he lacked Husseini's national pedigree. Born in Syria, he had been trained by the French military and, in 1925, had led a Druze revolt against French rule. After that revolt's collapse, he had served as a military adviser to King Ibn Saud, the founder of Saudi Arabia. With the support of the rebel leaders of five cooperative local bands, he now declared himself the commander of what he called the General Arab Revolt in Southern Syria—a geographic term scarcely heard since Faysal's failure at the start of the 1920s. Qa'uqji's choice for a name underscored his pan-Arab approach to the uprising, diminishing the importance of the more narrowly defined Palestinian national effort and relegating the Palestinians to one among several Arab players. Although some accounts attribute Qa'uqji's mandate to lead the rebellion to the Mufti,[25] his actions seem to have reflected a refusal to subordinate his pan-Arab vision to any local political control such as the Arab Higher Committee.

Carving out an administrative structure that could incorporate the existing rebel groups in the hills, he relegated the Palestinians to one of four main military companies. The others were Iraqi, Syrian, and Lebanese Druze.[26] He appointed Fakhri Abd al-Hadi—a man who would later play an important role in subduing the revolt—as deputy commander-in-chief. He also formed an intelligence unit to collect information (mainly from local Arab policemen and civil servants), and created a Revolutionary Court composed of local rebel leaders, who meted out severe sentences.[27] But Qa'uqji's command dissolved soon after his arrival in Palestine. In an ambush of a British military convoy and a subsequent pitched battle, the Palestinian company abandoned him, suspicious of his motives and his attempts to choke off their autonomy. Mutual recriminations and accusations followed—one even had Qa'uqji as a British agent—but the real effect was to frustrate any sense of coordination to the revolt. After the general strike, the British managed for a time to rout Qa'uqji from the country altogether, pushing him into Transjordan.

Nearly two years later, in the summer of 1938, the now exiled Haj Amin al-Husseini initiated an effort to use his followers in Damascus—the Central Committee of the National Jihad in Palestine—as a basis to gain control of the guerrilla groups. Doing so from abroad—a geographic dislocation that has come to characterize the Palestinian nationalist leadership—proved as costly and difficult then as it has since, despite Amin's increasing popularity.

The Central Committee contacted a number of people to serve as the revolt's supreme commander. After receiving several refusals, it unsuccessfully turned again to Qa'uqji. As at other times during the revolt, in the end the ayan's initiatives could do little more than confirm what already existed on the ground—in this case, a loose coordination among the largest fighting forces. For example, once Abd al-Qadir al-Husseini became commander of the Jerusalem area, he considered himself head of the entire revolt, appointing his own commander for the Hebron region and maintaining direct ties to Damascus, instead of going through the local council of rebel chiefs—actions obviously generating great resentment. Using a variety of names for the command council, including the Bureau of the Arab Revolt in Palestine and the Council of Rebellion (*Diwan al-Thawra*), the Central Committee tried to institutionalize this coordination into an official joint rebel command in 1938. But in the face of rapidly proliferating numbers of rural bands, with mutually suspicious leaders deeply distrustful of the old urban leadership, striving for individual autonomy of action, and pulling the revolt in different directions, any real central command and control remained quixotic.

Nevertheless, the rural forces succeeded in confusing the British by striking at their logistical and communications systems, as well as other targets. By the summer of 1937, there were hundreds of peasant bands undertaking near-daily acts of sabotage. With weapons pilfered or captured from the British or old surplus rifles smuggled in from neighboring countries, they wreaked havoc on the countryside. "Telephone and telegraph communications were cut, the oil pipeline from Iraq to Haifa was severed, police stations attacked, rail lines blown up, roads mined and bridges destroyed." For more than eighteen months the country's interior was controlled by the rebels.

After the harvest in June and July of 1938, the rebel units recruited thousands of peasants and opened their most effective offensive. In the face of extreme measures by British troops and the hanging of Sheikh Farhan al-Saadi—the disciple of Sheikh Qassam who probably touched off the revolt with the murders of April, 1936—they paralyzed British and Jewish movement on the inland roads.[28] In most of the villages, the green, red, and black Arab Palestinian flag waved in the summer breeze, and rebel chiefs declared many of the rural areas liberated zones.

With the exception of the Tiberias massacre of September, 1938, and several similar episodes, the Jews managed to defend themselves fairly well during the upheaval. Their settlements remained intact, transportation between them continuing with convoys. The British were the primary Arab target, in any case. Over 40 percent of the approximately 1,800 major rebel attacks in 1938 were directly on the military or else involved sabotage to telephones, railways, roads, the pipeline, and other government property. A bit less than a quarter of the strikes were against Jews (about 1,300 cases of sniper fire) and their property.[29]

The effect of the onslaught in late 1938 was that the British lost control of most of the Arab population for months. City and countryside now came under rebel command. In the most active regions, the so-called dangerous triangle bounded by Tulkarm, Jenin, and Nablus, this had a significant effect on Arab rural life, especially in 1938 and 1939. An anthropologist depicts the transformation of the countryside:

> The various bands [in the most active regions] set up their own court system, administrative offices, and intelligence networks. While peasants and ex-peasant migrants to the towns composed the vast majority of band leaders and fighters, young urban militants played important roles as commanders, advisers, arms transporters, instructors, and judges. Qassamites were particularly well represented at the leadership level. By taxing the peasantry, levying volunteers, and acquiring arms through the agency of experienced smugglers, the bands were able to operate autonomously from the rebel headquarters-in-exile set up by the notable leadership at Damascus.[30]

This transformation entailed a muted cultural revolution, reflected in the appeal by the revolt's leaders for city Arabs to discard the fez or tarbush—the rounded hat commonly found among middle- and upper-class men in urban areas—in favor of the kafiya—the distinctive head wrap popular among the peasants. The order included urban Christians, who had never before worn the kafiya, and Arab lawyers appearing before British courts. While this innovation eased the rebels' ability to blend into the towns when they entered them, its symbolic meaning was that a head wrapping previously the mark of the underclass was now imposed, through a specific order, on the upper classes. In 1938, one educated Palestinian noted that "the fellahin do not conceal their delight at seeing their 'uppers,' the effendis, come down a peg and look like them in the matter of head dress. They feel proud having raised themselves in the social scale."[31] Once the rebellion was over, the urban population quickly discarded the kafiya and did not take it up again until the 1960s.

Both Muslim and Christian women in the cities were also ordered to veil themselves during the revolt. There is some irony at work here, since traditionally the veiling of women had been much more an urban Muslim than village custom. But now it was the rural commanders, along with the Mufti (he had always been adamant on the issue), who demanded the use of the veil, now a cultural symbol as it was in the later, Algerian struggle against the French.[32] Along with the kafiya, it became a symbolic protest against urban assimilation. Rural fighters had come to regard the urban culture that had dominated from the late Ottoman period as tainted by its proximity to the imperialists and Zionists.

The shift of influence from Jaffa and Jerusalem to the hinterland came in the wake of two extraordinary processes. The first, already described, was the rapid decimation of the ayan by the British. Possibly because the national movement's painstakingly built institutions, from the literary clubs to the Muslim-Christian Associations, had included such a narrow segment of Palestinian society, they proved extremely vulnerable in the wave of British arrests. The second process, continuing for the revolt's duration, was the new reverse migration—thousands of new and temporary city dwellers now moving, with the revolt's toll on the urban economy, back to the hills and the security of their old villages. Using Palestine as a forward outpost, the British would draw the villagers back to the coastal towns during World War II.

The shift would take on the quality of class struggle. Peasant bands demanded funding from wealthy merchants and citrus growers. They also declared a moratorium on paying debts to landowners and cancelled rents.[33] In some cases, urban landowners and creditors were barred from setting foot in villages. All of this continued the repudiation of the ayan begun in the early 1930s. The peasant bands directed the uprising against the notables as well as the British and the Jews. Increasingly, popular culture romanticized the lower classes, especially the peasantry, interpreting the revolt as a struggle against the collusion of oppressive forces, the Zionists, the British, and the ayan. It is not surprising that some upper-class Palestinians saw the rebellion's endgame as performed by thugs.

After the British finally eradicated the guerrilla groups, many peasants placed blame on the corrupt leadership. Salih Baransi, who was a boy in the village of al-Tayyiba during the revolt, remembers how "the people endured without a murmur and gave without wearying or complaining, while the leaderships showed such weakness and squandered all the fruits of the people's sacrifice." His memory is of the unselfish "role played by the peasants—their ungrudging sacrifices and generosity."[34] Another villager states that "people paid to the revolt, and they were willing to pay. Willing! As for the zu'ama' [chiefs], they never behaved properly. . . ."[35]

Writing from the heart of the turmoil, the Palestinian historian George Antonius took note of the social-revolutionary undertones to the surface anger vented on the British and the Jews:

> One of the most prevalent misconceptions is that the trouble in Palestine is the result of an engineered agitation. It is variously attributed to the intrigues of the effendi class, to the political ambitions of the Grand Mufti. . . . The rebellion to-day is, to a greater extent than ever before, a revolt of villagers. . . . The moving spirits in the revolt are not the nationalist institute leaders, most of whom are now in exile, but men of the working and agricultural classes. . . . Far from its being engineered by the leaders, the revolt is in a very marked way a challenge to their authority and an indictment of their methods.[36]

In some very important senses, the break in the social patterns that had evolved over the last century became permanent, perhaps briefly dissolving, on occasion, in the frenzied decade between the revolt and the Zionist victory in 1948: Already battered by the effects of Palestine's incorporation into the world market, the bond between the ayan and the lower classes disintegrated, with a new leadership languishing due to its physical separation from the land and from most of the people. Jaffa and Haifa would enjoy only a brief resurgence as centers of Arab activity after 1940. And perhaps most ominously, the latter stages of the revolt seemed to revive the old lines so long dividing the Palestinians—religious tensions festered, along with those of kinship:

> This gradual killing off of the leaders was having its effect. More and more, the Rebellion was tending to degenerate from a national movement into squabbles between rival rebel bands. Beir Zeit, like many another village, was now little better than a hornet's nest of long-standing family feuds, stirred up afresh in the hope of getting some advantage through the help of this or that party of rebels.[37]

This statement is from a British school teacher in a mostly Christian village, offering her impressions of March, 1939, when the British offensive against the rural guerrillas was in full swing.

It was not simply that the breakdown of order, or of the discipline of coordinated action, opened the door to the airing of more mundane concerns. Rather, the petty feuds came to be caught up in the cycle of Arab attacks and British retribution. Even villagers attempting to stay clear of the revolt found themselves taxed by the rural bands and subject to both their collective punishment and that of the British, meted out for failing to inform on their neighbors. The British exploited religious and other factional differences, while the rebels abducted and killed a sizeable number of village chiefs—mukhtars, who were on the British payroll. They also assassinated others suspected of collaboration or against whom grudges were held, creating all sorts of new grievances on the part of their kin. Swedenburg, for example, cites the account of a former chief of a village in the Qalqilya district. A doctor had told a local band that a member of the leading al-Zaban clan was a British agent. The denounced man was killed by the rebels. In retribution the al-Zaban clan divulged the band's location to the British, which led to the death of several rebels, including the one who had carried out the execution. (The charge eventually turned out not true.) The al-Zaban clan also fired on the car of the doctor, killing his father. Similarly, we have the account of Sheikh Rabbah al-Awad—the leader of a small rebel band—concerning the assassination, in the waning days of the revolt, of a man from a notable family. He had recruited Sheikh Rabbah into the rebellion, and his father had been an old rival of the Mufti. In 1939, the sheikh assumed it was the Mufti's men who had committed the murder; at the urging of the victim's son, Rabbah and his band crossed over to the British side to help avenge the death.[38] Resentments over such issues have remained intact until this day.[39]

Such pressures and manipulations greatly exacerbated already existing village divisions. As the revolt wore on, no authority, British or rebel, was powerful enough to control the local disputes. Once the rebels were defeated, and with the victorious British discredited, the result "was the alienation of dislocated villagers from all existing forms of authority."[40]

THE REVOLT TURNED UPSIDE DOWN

Complementing the tensions of religion and kinship and the longstanding feuds between villages was a growing violence between rural and urban Palestinians. At first, demands on the latter were directed at the wealthy notables and merchants, each rebel unit, sometimes several units, determining the rate of "taxes" the wealthy would pay to sustain the revolt. When notables or merchants resisted paying, they were beaten or murdered. The violence then spread to people defined as collaborators or traitors, the problem being that the definitions were highly arbitrary. Some Arabs used "collaboration" as a way of satisfying vendettas and old grievances, thus injecting more uncertainty and lawlessness into Palestinian society.[41] The first targets were allies of the Nashashibis—the Muarada (opposition). In this way, Hassan Sidqi al-Dajani—the head of one of the most important Jerusalem families—met his death.[42]

But the civil strife went beyond the notables. As the mayor of Haifa—traditionally a city with some of the most cooperative Jewish-Arab relations—Hasan Shukri was assassinated because of alleged pro-Jewish views. Communist or labor union leaders such as Sami Taha and Michel Mitri met the same fate. A leaflet distributed by the rebels in Haifa and Jaffa warned against the use of electricity because it came from a "Jewish-British" plant. Many residents interpreted this as an effort to reduce the cities to the same level as the villages.

The Druze and Christian religious communities became targets of the rural bands, the latter being particularly singled out, in part because many wealthy merchants were Christians but also because of the uprising's strong Islamic component. In 1936, a leaflet signed by the followers of Sheikh Qassam had called for a boycott of the Christians because of the "crimes they committed against the national movement." In a march through a Christian village, one band changed its chant from "We are going to kill the British [or Jews]" to "We are going to kill the Christians." The strong intervention of Amin al-Husseini, through the preachers in the mosques, staved off any attacks on the Christian community, but many individual Christians were killed during the revolt. In the fall of 1937 and the winter of 1938, Druze villages on Mount Carmel also faced systematic attacks.

As their successes in 1938 emboldened the rebels, their decrees became more radical. They followed the moratorium on payment of fellaheen debts with death threats against loan collectors. Once they abolished rents for city tenants, they warned tenants not to rent from Jews or the British. They declared a compulsory draft for males between the ages of nineteen and twenty-three, and one commander in the Southern District, Yusuf Abu Durra, even announced the creation of a free Arab government.[43]

Many Arab city dwellers with connections and resources neither resisted the rebels nor risked their wrath, simply fleeing the country. But by the Revolt's end, nearly 500 others were dead, nearly the same as the number of Jews, creating widespread fear. After being deposed as mayor of Haifa by the British in 1938, for supporting the revolt, W. F. Abboushi's father

> went to Beirut because the revolution had deteriorated and Arabs were assassinating Arabs. Life had become insecure for the urban "aristocracy" of Palestine, and consequently, Beirut acquired a new community of political refugees made up of well-to-do Palestinians.[44]

With the dead and self-exiled added to those deported from Palestine or barred reentry by the British, the Palestinians found themselves—at a time when the course of British policies and decisions would carry as much import as at any point since the Balfour Declaration—without the groups that had reshaped their society, molded the national movement, and furnished their domestic and international spokesmen. The leadership had begun an exile continuing to this day.

Ties between the villages and the cities had existed before the revolt, through the British civil administration, Arabic language newspapers, the Arab school teachers, migration, and markets. But the revolt robbed the national movement of a symbiosis between its growing urban organization and its reservoir of rural Palestinians ready for violent action. The withdrawal and flight of large parts of the urban population, along with the weak coordination offered by an exiled leadership, resulted in bands that appeared more like traditional rural gangs. What Qa'uqji had feared and tried to prevent right at the revolt's beginning—the anarchy of fighting forces he had witnessed in the rebellion of Syrian Arabs—threatened to undo the rebel gains.

In this regard, it is important to recall that the rural Palestinians had not created the same rural sorts of organizations giving shape to life in the cities—the Boy Scouts, Young Men's Muslim Associations, the labor unions, and the like. Their uprising mirrored the structure of life in the villages, consisting of loosely organized groups, usually relatives or people who knew and trusted each other, jealously guarding their autonomy. Formal training and a hierarchical military structure barely existed. It is not surprising that the tactics and traits of traditional rural banditry often surfaced, especially when any semblance of central coordination disappeared.[45]

In the wake of the rebels' 1938 summer offensive, the situation of Palestinians in the country deteriorated badly. With the rebels stepping up their demands, many city dwellers, already exhausted by the general strike of 1936, now felt under economic and mental siege. Newly dispatched British troops offered relief: They ousted the rebel bands from the towns, relentlessly pursuing them in the villages and hills. Jewish retaliation, often coordinated with British actions, also took an increasing toll. By the end of the revolt, the Zionists' military activism differed markedly from the policy of *havlagah*, or self-restraint, the mainstream Labor Zionists (but not the Irgun), had adopted at the outset, when they had relied heavily on the British to reestablish law and order. On the Arab side, the Damascus leadership failed to supply the weapons and financial support the rebels desperately needed; as a result, the rebels made ever stiffer demands upon the foundation of their strength, the fellaheen. One peasant protested that "we . . . are falling between the devil and the deep blue sea. . . . The rebels come to our villages, take our money, food, and sometimes kill some of us. . . . [Then] the Police come to our villages following these rebels with their dogs."[46]

Like popular renegades everywhere, the rural fighters were thus assuming dual identities in the eyes of the peasants: rebels fighting foreign occupation and little more than bandits. Many peasants were thus decidedly ambivalent about the rebels. The British and Zionists naturally emphasized their criminality— many Israeli histories still use the word "gang" to describe the rebel bands and identify the revolt as the "disturbances," in this way denying its political essence. But among the Palestinian population during the mandate, even some truly criminal gangs, such as that headed by Abu Jilda, had achieved a quasi-heroic notoriety. Jilda's gang had robbed and killed English, Arabs, and Jews, but its success in embarrassing the authorities made it an object of delight and popularity.

At the revolt's apogee, its fighters were often referred to as mujahidin—a term with strong Islamic overtones. Originally it meant warriors defending the faith; in its new context, freedom fighters. One of the first national groups to define themselves in this way was the popular Green Hand, operating in the north for about four months in 1929–30 and participating in a slaughter of Jews. But by the revolt's end, such popularity had worn thin. Opposition to the bands spread by late 1938 from the cities to the countryside, ultimately leading to civil war among the Palestinians.[47]

Some villages, especially those aligned with the Nashashibi opposition rather than the Mufti, established self-defense units (at times with British encouragement and funds). A number of such units, called "peace bands," participated in the uprising or at least professed dedication to the national cause. The one organized by Sheikh Naif al-Zubi actually took part in attacks against the petroleum pipeline running from Iraq to Haifa. In reality, however, their main task was to defend their villages. Some of the Nashashibis tried to raise money for the peace bands, apparently even from the Jews and British.[48]

In certain respects, the split between the rebels and the Arabs fighting them simply reflected irreconcilable differences between those loyal to Amin al-Husseini and those siding with the Nashashibis. But by the late fall of 1938 and the winter of 1939, it was clear that what was at stake was more than a dispute among notable families.[49] Fakhri Abd al-Hadi, who had fought alongside Qa'uqji, flip-flopped several times between the rebels and their opponents before finally spearheading a large Arab force against the former. In December, 1938, notables and three thousand villagers gathered in a village near Hebron in the presence of the British regional military commander to condemn the terror of the rebels and to pledge to fight against them. The actions of these Arab anti-rebel forces helped the British quash the last stage of the revolt in 1939.

A TRANSFORMED POLITICAL STAGE

In the years between the 1929 Wailing Wall riots, which had shaken the Zionist leadership's complacent faith in eventual Arab acceptance of the Zionist enterprise,[50] and the outbreak of the Arab Revolt, informal negotiations took place between Ben-Gurion and Musa Alami. But various acute differences blocked any serious progress. In particular, the rapid rise in the Jewish population prompted George Antonius and other Arabs to underscore that no agreement could come in the absence of immigration restrictions. The Arab demand flew in the face of deeply held Zionist convictions—although a number of Zionist leaders, including Ben-Gurion, refused to confront seriously the significance of Arab adamancy. In any case, until the start of the revolt, those leaders believed they could reach all their goals, whether there was agreement with the Arabs or not.

The Zionists misread the revolt from its beginning, attributing the general strike to the small class of privileged notables and failing to grasp its popular basis—at least in public. In fact, following his talks with Antonius in the midst of the Arab general strike, Ben-Gurion seemed to come to a more sober understanding of the Arab position: "There is a conflict, a great conflict. There is a fundamental conflict. We and they want the same thing: We both want Palestine. And that is the fundamental conflict."[51] And in one private meeting, he remarked that "the Arabs fight with arms, strike, terror, sabotage, murder and destruction of government property. . . . What else must they do for their acts to be worthy of the name 'revolt?' "[52]

The Zionists' essential response to the revolt was to move in two policy directions. The first was to shore up a self-sufficient Jewish economy, independent of Arab labor and markets. Although the general strike had initially caused serious dislocations in the Jewish sector, with the Jewish population now nearly 30 percent of the country's total, they were able to mobilize effectively. The second was to strengthen their illegal armed forces considerably—the policy they defined as havlagah, restraint based on defending settlements without reprisals or outside pursuit. As the revolt moved into 1937 and 1938, havlagah prevailed only intermittently. Surprise night attacks, increased military preparations, direct reprisals, all reflected a more militant, embattled outlook. By the revolt's last stages (from May, 1938 on), the Zionists collaborated closely with the British in its suppression.[53]

Some writers have claimed that before the onset of real social chaos, the British were not firm or consistent enough in securing public order.[54] In any case, from the general strike on, they showed a perfect willingness to make amends for the past failing, initiating a number of severe measures including the Palestine Defence Order-in-Council and the Emergency Regulations. Later, when unable to maintain control of Jaffa, they levelled a good portion of the walled city by creating a wide road through its center. By then they had arrested 2,600 strikers. At the end of the general strike in 1936, they had registered 145 Arabs as killed, but the actual number was probably on the order of 1,000.

With time, the British resorted to ever-heavier doses of brutal force. With the rebel occupation of the walled part of Jerusalem on October 17, 1938, they suspended civil rule and imposed military government throughout the country, using harsh and illiberal methods to break the revolt's back. Among the methods were collective fines, the demolition of houses, the use of prisoners as human minesweepers, hangings, and far-ranging military sweeps. Even while grappling with the fearful prospect of war with Germany, they committed themselves to crushing the rebellion completely. Upon signing the Munich pact, they poured new troops into Palestine, increasing their garrison to nearly twenty-five thousand men.[55] After suppressing the urban uprising at the end of 1938, they built roads into the remote hills where rebel bands were taking refuge, isolated and collectively punished collaborating villages, and built the Tegart Wall—a barbed wire barrier between Palestine and Syria—to disrupt communications and supplies.

Aside from the Gandhi-led agitation they confronted in India, the British faced no more formidable opposition to their imperial rule than that of Palestinians. This militancy induced not only a military but also a political response, with diplomatic maneuvering feverishly proceeding, and several important shifts in political policy, carrying with them a long-term impact on Palestine's Arabs. First of all, the locus of British policy-making shifted from Jerusalem to London and, within London, from the Colonial Office to the Foreign Office.[56] This freed the British from the constant, direct pressure of the Zionist and Palestinian Arab leadership and made them more responsive to the regional repercussions of Palestinian events. Next, the British ceased negotiating with Palestinian leaders, in favor of the heads of surrounding newly independent Arab states. In other words, the leadership vacuum developing among the Palestinian Arabs came to be filled by non-Palestinian Arabs. This process was actually inaugurated by the Mufti, who used the Arab heads of state to call for an end to the general strike, thus helping to extricate the Palestinian leaders from their self-inflicted dilemmas.

Finally Britain abandoned the policy line dictated by the Balfour Declaration, acceding, in good part, to the Arab demands. The revolt had begun in the wake of the failure of one British policy initiative, the scheme for a Legislative Council, and it ended on the eve of another initiative, the White Paper of 1939. The Legislative Council's purpose was to incorporate both Jews and Arabs into self-governing institutions. It foundered mostly because of Jewish insistence on communal parity, and partly because of the Arab demand for a majority rule invalidating the thrust of the Balfour Declaration.

After the general strike, the Colonial Office attempted to maintain control of the Palestinian situation by dispatching the Royal Commission headed by Lord Peel to the country. Even in its collection of evidence, the Peel Commission's presence was humiliating to the Palestinian leadership. The Arab Higher Committee's decision to boycott the commission had to be reversed in the face of stiff pressure by Arab heads of state. In the end, the commission's recommendation to partition Palestine— the last flicker of the Balfour Declaration's spirit—led to the resumption of the revolt in 1937.

For the Arabs, the 1939 White Paper had an ironic aura. Its acceptance of their demand for majoritarian national independence (in ten years' time), a strict prohibition on Jewish immigration, and a banning of land sales to Jews came just as the British finished them militarily and destroyed their national leadership. A more drastic irony was the contemptuous rejection by the exiled leadership—most notably the Mufti—of the White Paper. Perhaps nothing else was possible with the Palestinian community in a state of civil war. Perhaps an exiled leadership removed from the pressures faced by Palestine's Arab population (5,000 dead, 15,000 wounded, 5,600 detained in the revolt;[57] up to a quarter of the casualties inflicted by other Arabs) could not recognize the opportunity. Perhaps, as the Mufti's biographer suggests, Amin acted out of personal pique at the way the British had treated him.[58]

The revolt and the rejection of the White Paper thus left the Palestinian national movement in an abyss. As the fighting waned, the British killed one major rebel leader and his band dissolved; another surrendered with his band to the French in Syria; the Transjordanians extradited yet another, who was then hanged by the British. The Palestinian Arabs were exhausted and fractured, shorn of basic trust between leaders (often exiled) and followers. Paradoxically, the revolt was a distinct watershed, crystallizing the Palestinian national identity as nothing before. It offered new heroes and martyrs—most prominently, Sheikh Qassam—and a popular culture to eulogize them;[59] it constituted an unequivocal declaration that, whatever their social status, Palestinians unalterably opposed the Zionist program. To be sure, this nationalism reflected what one writer has termed the various local idioms of Palestinian nationalism.[60] But the diverse circumstances and motives should not obscure the fact that the revolt helped to create a nation—even while crippling its social and political basis.

PART TWO

DISPERSAL

5

The Meaning of Disaster

Between the last month of 1947 and the first four and a half months of 1948, the Palestinian Arab community would cease to exist as a social and political entity: a process that neither Jew nor Arab foresaw in the tumultuous years of World War II. More than 350 villages would vanish,[1] urban life would all but evaporate—war and exodus reducing Jaffa's population from 70,000–80,000 Palestinians to a remnant of 3,000–4,000—and 500,000 to 1,000,000 Palestinians would become refugees. Looking back at the situation in 1956, poet Mu'in Basisu described it in these words:

> And after the flood none was left of this people
>   This land, but a rope and a pole
> None but bare bodies floating on mires
>   Leavings of kin and a child
> None but swelled bodies
>   Their numbers unknown
> Here wreckage, here death, here drowned in deep waters
>   Scraps of a bread loaf still clasped in my hand
> Here quivering dead eyes
>   Here lips crying vengeance
> Scraps of my people and country
>   Some weeping, some crazed, some in tremor,
> Scraps of my people, my father, my mother
>   There's nobody left in the tents

Here Children? you ask and she'll scream
   And the torrent is jeering, she never gave birth
How to these people, black tents,
   On pale sands
      Drowned have they been forever.[2]

Accompanying this cataclysm was a drastic weakening of both axes molding the special character of the Palestinians over the previous century: (1) the tension between Nablus and Jaffa—between the more self-contained, agriculturally centered life of the inland towns and the European-facing coastal cities; and (2) the fragile structural balance achieved between the notable leadership and the society around them. With the disintegration of the country's urban backbone in 1948, the center of Palestinian life would return to the hill country in the east. At the same time, the catastrophe of 1948 and the ignominious role of the notables in it destroyed the remnants of the leadership.

In place of a familiarly constructed society, and the sense of self-worth that accompanies it, Palestinians would grasp the belief that they were the victims of an immense conspiracy and of a monumental injustice. They would see their plight as representing a breach of the cosmic order. They would seethe in anger, not only against the hated Zionists, but also against their putative allies—their Arab brothers from neighboring countries—and against a wider world that could allow such an injustice. As Fawaz Turki (born in the small town of Balad al-Sheikh, near Haifa) would note in *The Disinherited*,

> The Western world, which had long tormented and abused the Jewish people, hastened to bless an event that saw an end to their victims' suffering. A debt was to be paid. Who was to pay it and where it was to be paid were not seen as of the essence, so long as it was not paid by Europeans in Europe.[3]

The experience of exile—of a tragedy perceived as both personal and national—would overshadow all else for this generation of disaster (the *jil al-Nakba*) creating both a sense of ennui and ironically, a new form of cultural ferment, largely literary in nature. (Cf. Fadwa Tuqan's explanation that "In 1948, my father died and Palestine was lost . . . These events enabled me to write the nationalist poetry my father had always wished that I would write."[4])

A folk culture conveyed by songs and ballads, poetry and narrative would form around three motifs: the praise and memory of the lost paradise from which the Palestinians were expelled, the bitter lament of the present, and the depiction of the imagined triumphant return. In the wake of the demise of the political leadership, writers such as Tuqan and Ghassan Kanafani would use these motifs to maintain and rebuild the Palestinian national identity. This chapter recounts the factors leading to the very emergence of such a challenge, starting with the defeat of the Arab Revolt and ending with the Palestinian war against the Jews.

BETWEEN REVOLT AND DISASTER

Emerging from the revolt's long ordeal—with its accompanying drastic economic contraction—at the onset of World War II, Palestine faced the prospect of scant respite from upheaval. The country did manage to escape the war's direct impact, but the proximity of the North African campaign reverberated. Using Palestine as an important rear base, the British invested there heavily, the ensuing economic growth being accompanied by even further erosion of peasant life and a more severe physical and psychological dislocation.[5] It took place at a time when "there were no political institutions in the country capable of carrying the banner of the nationalist movement."[6]

The revolt had not resulted in a closing of the economic gap between Jews and Arabs. While both communities suffered, the fragile Arab urban economy was ravaged, with wage-earners fleeing back to already strained villages, and Arab merchants and importers—many of whom had controlled both Jewish and Arab markets before 1936—now facing ruin. With wealthier Arabs heading for more tranquil shores, thousands of urban migrants fled back to their home villages, leaving the urban economy without its most important human resource.[7]

During World War II, the most obvious economic hardship thus came in the early years, real wages falling through 1940 and into 1941. The shipping crisis in the Mediterranean hit the ports very hard, bringing citrus exports to a halt—in 1943, they amounted to less than 10 percent of what they had been in 1938,[8] and nearly twenty thousand Arab orange-plantation workers returned to their already crowded villages.[9] These villages, accustomed to both supplemental income earned on the plantations and (prior to the revolt) on employment outside agriculture, were now forced to rely on their own land, while accommodating a sizeable proportion of an expanded Arab population.

With the British mobilization, the economic situation changed so dramatically that it threatened to destroy the old social institutions—the family, the village, even the national movement. From 1940 to 1945, the Arab economy grew by nearly 9 percent a year (compared to a 13 percent rate for the Jewish economy, which seemed to get a head start at the beginning of the war). In the two years after the war's end, the Arab sector equalled the Jewish, growing at an average rate of over 12 percent.[10] By that time, Palestine far outdistanced neighboring Arab countries on almost every economic indicator.[11]

The mobilization meant a 400 percent increase of British military investment, and vastly expanded construction.[12] The numbers of garrisoned troops increased from 90,000 (an already considerable figure) to 280,000. The mobilization required labor for everything from building barracks and roads to producing weapons and ammunition. The primary British strategy for meeting the requirement was to offer wages high enough—in the context of drastically elevated world agricultural prices—to lure fellaheen from the land. Unemployment gave way to a severe labor shortage, leading the government, as a second part of its strategy, to import thousands of workers from neighboring Arab countries. (Some of these laborers eventually returned to their home countries.)

While construction jobs in rural areas often enabled Palestinian men to stay in their villages, those in the urban work force would typically leave, for half a year at first. As the war dragged on, the stream of men, and of entire families, leaving for the coast, permanently, had become a flood. Women were left behind to manage the farms—an arrangement bringing them into a more public realm and widening their roles as household managers.

Such changes in the rural social structure interacted with others, such as the discrediting of numerous village leaders who had cooperated with the British during the revolt, and an elimination, finally, of peasant indebtedness: a problem that had haunted the fellaheen, as well as British officials concerned with the viability of village life. Rural communities managed to raise their living standard considerably, taking advantage of both a growing need for their produce in the absence of imported competition with their crops and British efforts to help them raise productivity.[13] Agricultural yields rose, in fact, by 20 percent during the war—without any significant increase in the amount of land under cultivation,[14] and while the male agricultural work force was plummeting.

For men now working in the cities, the change was even greater than for the village fellaheen. As we have seen in chapter 2, labor unions—a hapless undertaking in the years before the war—now became significant urban institutions. In part, this reflected new government policies, in part new conditions promoting an ideology of unionism—that is, the existence of a separate Arab working class supported a distinctive organization to demand its rights.[15] The new circumstances in the city often increased the individual mobility of the worker and his affinity to a larger, more impersonal Palestinian working class. In turn, both these circumstances and union encouragement of the expression of class interests ran against the grain of parochial clan, village, and religious ties—and also of the ayan's demands for national solidarity.

Radicalization of the working class through left-leaning unions proved worrisome both to the British and to the ayan, prompting conservative counter-organizing efforts by the latter.[16] Arab unionism thus became an odd amalgam, nonetheless attracting about twenty thousand workers (approximately 20 percent of all wage-earners) by the end of the war.[17] Even the British and Jews found themselves responding to the new Arab wage-laboring class. Mandate officials established arbitration boards to deal with the increasing disputes in small and large Arab factories, and the powerful Jewish labor federation, the Histadrut, once again hazarded an effort at Arab labor organizing.

Some Arab workers found themselves caught painfully between their attempts to improve the lot of workers as a class (which meant solidarity with Jewish laborers) and their deep antipathy to Zionism. Difficulties between Arab and Jewish workers stemmed both from such antipathy and from Arab resentment over being largely concentrated in the unskilled jobs.

In fact, the major collaborative Arab-Jewish effort, a strike of junior civil servants against the government in April 1946, came precisely in the absence of that status gap.

With the resurgence of Palestinian nationalism in 1944, and especially with the return of Jamal al-Husseini to the country in 1946, organized labor activity among the Palestinians began to wane. But through their own experiences, and through the observation of Jewish laborers, they had glimpsed possibilities for organizing their society quite different from the ideal put forth by the notables, or even by other nationalists. A historian of Arab labor during the mandate outlines the dilemma:

> As [the unions] stressed the need for the definition and recognition of a separate working class, they began to suggest alternative principles of social integration to the thousands of workers who supported them. In their efforts to provide a positive culture to Arab workers, however, Arab unions came into real conflict with existing elites by challenging their legitimacy. The consequences of this collision of interests were made the more complex by the deep entanglement of the labor movement with family and clan concerns and by labor's commitment to the nationalist cause. Arab workers, caught between these contrary orientations, were placed in a confusing situation. Moreover, the weakness and the eventual eclipse of the labor movement in 1947 and 1948 finally deprived them of any effective leadership.[18]

The debacle of 1947–48 thus found the Palestinians united in their opposition to Zionism, yet dislocated and disorganized. Prosperity during the war had had its costs in a complex, physical and sociocultural displacement. (Even Palestinian women— that seemingly insular segment of society—found their lives substantially changed, assimilating the changes, within the family, "in a more intensified and personal way than men."[19])

As suggested in the above citation, the "confusing situation" of the Palestinians was exacerbated by the absence of the national leadership that had played such a prominent role in the previous two decades. Until the defeat of Rommel's army in North Africa in 1942, the British had banned political activity. Afterwards, Palestinians found that earlier arrests, deportations, and flight had done their damage. To some degree labor leaders, professionals, and Arabs working in the middle and higher echelons of the government emerged as community spokesmen during the war. But for a people who had been among the most politically violent and nettlesome in the vast British Empire, the Palestinians remained remarkably quiescent and pacified in its immediate aftermath.

In the latter half of the war, the British permitted the return of some of the old political leaders, including members of the disbanded Arab Higher Committee, but with the firm provision that these figures would not participate in any political activity. Nevertheless, there were some significant diplomatic forays: In the summer of 1940, Colonel Stewart F. Newcombe, a British representative in the service of Lord Lloyd, arrived in Baghdad and, under the auspices of the Iraqi foreign minister, Nuri al-Said, tried to reach an agreement with Jamal al-Husseini and Musa Alami. The Iraqis agreed to send troops to the western desert, and in exchange the British were to agree to the establishment of an autonomous government in Palestine and gradually to pass power and authority to local Palestinian representatives. Apparently, Winston Churchill vetoed the agreement when it came for cabinet ratification.[20] In any case, as with the mainstream Zionists, there was genuine sympathy among many Palestinians for Britain during the war, which in practice translated into a respite from harassment for the government. Leaders such as Fakhri al-Nashashibi encouraged enlistment for British army service. About nine thousand signed up directly, and another fourteen thousand joined the Transjordanian Arab Legion, a fighting force linked to the Allied deployment.[21]

Even those Palestinians who followed the lead of the exiled Mufti and pinned their hopes on a Nazi victory turned out not to pose much of a political challenge. The anti-British and anti-Jewish themes sounded by the Germans and Italians—Axis plans called for a sphere of Italian influence in the Mediterranean[22]— certainly had some appeal. Nazi propagandists attempted to present Haj Amin as a pan-Islamic figure, "der Grossmufti," and let him broadcast on Radio Berlin to the entire Middle East, North Africa, and even India, calling the faithful to jihad against the godless British-Zionist-Bolshevik forces.[23] A small Arab unit became part of the Wehrmacht, fighting on the Russian front in 1942. But the Mufti failed to rally the Arabs of Palestine to support the Germans—no organized pro-Nazi movement developed inside the country, as occurred in several other Arab lands.

In 1943, some figures banded together under the prodding of a former Istiqlal leader to renew the Fund of the Arab Nation. Its goal was to prevent the sale of Arab-owned land to Jews, who continued to acquire tracts even with the restrictions imposed on them by the 1939 White Paper. In one case, the Fund managed to raise £P100,000 for 2,500 acres of land about to be purchased by the Jewish National Fund. It also initiated a series of trials to prevent title transfers and, once again, put the issue of land on the Palestinian community's agenda.[24]

Various figures (again including some former Istiqlal heads) made efforts during the war to revive the Arab Higher Committee and to reconstitute the Istiqlal itself, along with other political parties.[25] Heads of the National Bloc party, for instance, proclaimed it the vanguard of the national movement, with Nablus as its center. That city would always tend to claim control of the national movement when Jerusalem, Jaffa, and Haifa, more closely tied to European currents, were faltering.

But such activity merely underscored the general political quiescence, resulting, perhaps, from a growing confidence after the White Paper that Britain would eventually grant Arab independence in Palestine. Many Arabs interpreted the 1944 Zionist revolt against the British authorities, spearheaded by the Irgun, as a sign of anxiety and weakness.[26] All they needed to do was bide their time.

That position, of course, turned out fraught with illusions. With the war's end and the revelations of Nazi horrors, the future of Palestine reemerged as an international issue, prompting Harry Truman, shortly after Japan's defeat, to back a proposal that the mandate accept 100,000 Jewish refugees. Within a year, the Anglo-American Committee of Inquiry made a similar proposal, and also that Britain remove the White Paper's restrictions.

Although Britain's response was rejection, the Palestinians were now alarmed—and discovered new constraints on their political activity. Since their call to end the general strike of 1936, and their participation in the Round Table Conference of 1939,[27] the independent Arab states, in fact, had begun to define the contours of Palestinian politics. In 1944, they held a conference to explore political union among themselves; when the Palestinians could not agree on the makeup of their observer delegation, the prime ministers of Iraq and Egypt did it for them. They chose the highly respected Musa Alami, perceived as generally neutral and acceptable to all Palestinians.

Between 1946 and 1948, the Husseinis had consolidated their position. Despite the war, they had succeeded in nullifying any attempts to resurrect the Istiqlal or—to the great disappointment of some Zionist leaders, who felt there still was hope for accommodation with the Palestinian opposition—to reestablish the Nashashibis: Fakhri al-Nashashibi was assassinated in late 1941, possibly as a result of orders from the Mufti. But their various efforts to gain autonomy and to reestablish an official Palestinian body on the model of the old Arab Higher Committee were thwarted by the newly formed League of Arab Nations (or Arab League). The League sent a clear message that it, not the Mufti and his associates, would be paramount. It appointed the Arab Higher Executive for Palestine, soon reverting in 1946 to the name of the Arab Higher Committee. Eventually, it included a fairly broad spectrum of Palestinian leaders, but with a decidedly Husseini stamp.[28]

Complex Arab rivalries surrounded the League's main issue—some sort of political unity versus a looser confederation or even simple cooperation among the Arab states. These states' interests in Palestine were thus in many ways inimical to the perspective of the Palestinian leaders, who in the end, were relegated to the sidelines, robbed of any possibility of autonomous action.[29] One writer has termed the process "the political and military neutering of the Palestinian Arabs."[30] Long after the Arab defeat in the 1948 war, Amin al-Husseini would suggest that the Arab states' invasion of Israel was never intended to liberate Palestine, but was a result of their own territorial ambitions.[31] The Mufti's opposition to that invasion demonstrated his feeling of powerlessness in controlling events.

In some ways, Palestinian acceptance of the reconstituted committee, with its chairmanship left open for the still exiled Husseini, made perfect sense. Back in Cairo, the Mufti was invoking the Zionist menace to build the military and financial nucleus for a government-in-exile. On the critical issue that he personified, unrelenting opposition to Zionism and to British partition of the country between Jews and Arabs, there was near unanimity. As Walid Khalidi has noted, he was still "unquestionably the paramount Palestinian leader."[32]

In other ways, the committee, full of familiar names from the old dominating families and under the long shadow of Haj Amin, left the Palestinian community in a highly vulnerable position, unwittingly confirming their powerlessness in what would be the most important few years of their history. For one, key international players harbored deep mistrust for the Mufti. The British still held him personally responsible for the Arab Revolt and refused to allow him to return to Palestine, the Iraqis had not forgiven his involvement in a coup d'état in Baghdad in 1941, and the Transjordan government saw him as an obstacle to its own territorial ambitions. At the same time, the Mufti was very distant from Palestinian events, having last been in the country a traumatic decade before.

In this respect, his situation was not much different from that of the other notables, removed more than ever before from daily Palestinian travails. By 1947, when tensions among the Jews, Arabs, and British had become extreme, thousands of wealthier Arabs fled the country, leaving little intact of the old ayan class—or even of the rudimentary leadership that had grown in the country during the war years. The workers and fellaheen who stayed behind, "leaderless and confused . . . fell easy prey to rumor and to the alarm which soon overcame all parts of the Arab population."[33]

In one or another manner, many observers have attributed the failure of the Palestinians in 1948 to their being "backward, disunited and often apathetic, a community only just entering the modern age politically and administratively."[34] The contrast with the political skill and unity of the Zionists in such accounts is always at least implicit. In fact, Jewish political prowess and unity has been vastly exaggerated—the Zionists suffered from repeated incidents of infighting and political failure. And the thesis of Palestinian political immaturity is misleading.

As we saw in chapter 4, the early 1930s witnessed a virtual explosion of new political institutions and of increased political participation, contentious though it was. But in 1948 the Palestinians were still suffering from the British military and political assaults, during the Arab Revolt, against the leadership and political institutions that had emerged in the 1930s. In the circumstances of World War II and the new constraints imposed by the Arab states, they never managed to recapture these political foundations, nor adapt politically to the vast social changes overtaking their community.

FACE TO FACE IN COMMUNAL WAR

The British mandate in Palestine did not so much draw to a close as collapse.[35] From 1946 on, domestic turmoil recalled the previous decade's most violent period, 1936–39—but now it was Jews who were in revolt. Attacks, kidnappings, and assassinations by the Irgun prompted one government step after another: evacuation of some British civilians from the country in January, 1947, construction of secure compounds for mandate officials, martial law in parts of the country. The fact that the Haganah briefly aided government forces against the Irgun in an action called the *Saison*, or hunting season, was of little consolation to the British, and of little interest to the Palestinians: the violence had become intolerable. By the summer of 1947, both the British administrators in Palestine and weary officials in London concluded that the cost of imposing a solution on Arabs and Jews—in terms of material resources, world public opinion, and the sentiment of Arab state leaders—was simply too high. The growing role of the United States in the Palestine affair— what London officials considered sabotage—especially the repeated personal interventions of President Truman, had corroded their resolve,[36] as had the constant, demoralizing effort of trying to curb mounting illegal Jewish immigration of Holocaust survivors. In July, key British officials in His Majesty's Government made the decision to withdraw.[37]

Some time before this (on February 18, 1947) the British had referred the Palestine problem to the United Nations, and the Special Committee on Palestine (UNSCOP) was well advanced in its own combative deliberations on the country's future; having spent five weeks in Palestine in June and July, at the end of August it issued its report. It proposed a solution that the Mufti had long dreaded, partition of the country between Jews and Palestinians,[38] along with a termination of the mandate and a prompt granting of independence.

Britain's reaction to the proposal was the hardening of its resolve to quit Palestine as fast as possible. London feared jeopardizing its position with the new Arab states if it supported partition, and it wanted no part in controlling the strife that it was certain would engulf the country if a partition plan was implemented. The effect of this hands-off policy was free play for the multiplying clashes and spreading violence that began in December, 1947.

UNSCOP's recommendations made their way to the United Nations in the form of the famous resolution advocating—along with partition—the internationalization of Jerusalem and its environs, including Bethlehem (see maps 2 and 3). Partition was

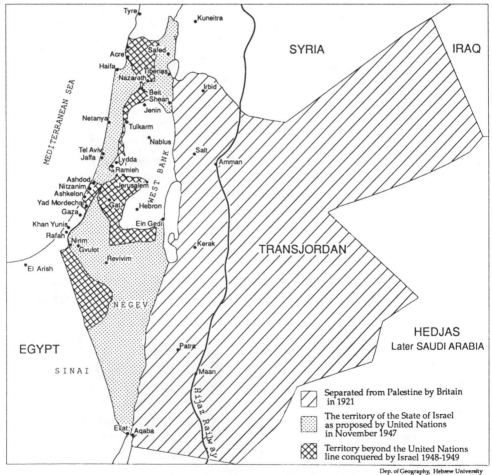

Dep. of Geography, Hebrew University

Map 2.   Two Partitions of Palestine (1921, 1949)

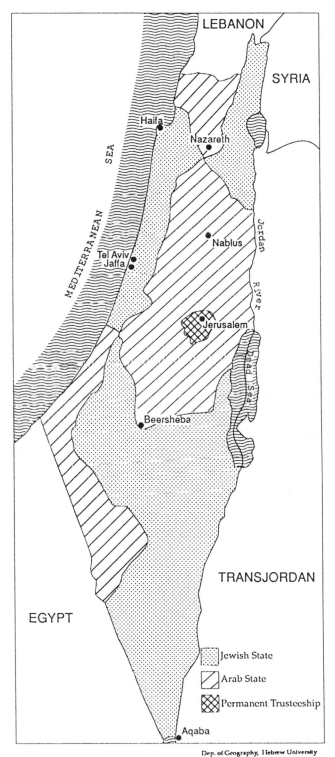

LEBANON

SYRIA

MEDITERRANEAN SEA

Haifa

Nazareth

Jordan River

Nablus

Tel Aviv
Jaffa

Jerusalem

Dead Sea

Beersheba

TRANSJORDAN

EGYPT

Jewish State

Arab State

Permanent Trusteeship

Aqaba

Dep. of Geography, Hebrew University

Map 3. United Nations Recommendation for Two-States Solution in Palestine (1947)

the fashionable diplomatic solution of the period for a host of seemingly intractable situations, including those in Germany, India, and Korea. None of these other cases managed to forestall international war or repeated diplomatic crises, and Palestine was no exception in this regard.[39] The crazy-quilt pattern of suggested borders for the two proposed states, and the high concentration of Arabs in the proposed Jewish state (over 40 percent of the projected total population) seemed to doom the idea from the beginning.[40] Nonetheless, supported by both the Americans and Soviets, with no other solution in sight and with the mandate power having thrown up its hands in exasperation, the General Assembly passed Resolution 181 on November 29, 1947, in one of its moments of high drama. The vote was 33 to 13, with 10 abstentions.

Lobbying furiously, both Jews and Arabs had, of course, awaited the vote's outcome rather tensely. Once the UN acted, the Arab Higher Committee responded politically on February 6, 1948, declaring that it would never recognize the validity of partition, nor the UN's authority to implement it. This communique also emphasized that any attempt by the Jews to establish a state would be seen as bald aggression and would be resisted by force, as an act of Arab self-defense.[41] For its part, the World Zionist Organization responded by accepting the resolution, with some qualifications. The mainstream Zionists had decided in the summer of 1947, although not without significant internal dissent, to support a partial partition plan.[42]

The UN vote shattered two illusions shared by Jews and Arabs: that a resolution to the question of Palestine's future would not be quick and that the colonial power would pass its authority on to its successor in an orderly fashion. In the weeks that followed the vote, British administration all but disintegrated. Concerned primarily with protecting and enhancing their positions to the utmost in the face of implacable opposition, the two communities—for the first time in their history face to face without intermediaries or third-party protectors—prepared for violent confrontation.

Communal war began consuming the fabric of normalcy the day after the UN vote, with an Arab attack on a Jewish bus near the town of Lydda. The Palestinians seemed to have the upper hand, at least in numbers—their population of 1.3 million was more than double that of the 620,000 Jews. But such figures are deceptive: Jewish immigration had created a society with a disproportionate share of young men of army age—one and a half times the Arab figure.[43] And even though few Jewish women engaged in direct combat, they did have auxiliary roles closed to women in traditional Islamic societies.

The conflict's opening looked as if it had been rehearsed by the earlier Arab Revolt. Two days after the UN vote, the Arab Higher Committee called a general strike. Although key figures of the Committee assured the British that it would be peaceful, Jerusalem was wracked by violence, and the Jewish commercial sector was set ablaze. National committees, like those during the earlier revolt, coordinated Palestinian activity in various localities, and Arab leaders created a sort of home guard, modelled after efforts in Great Britain during World War II.

But two key differences marked this wave of violence: The Jews, not the British, were the primary target, and this time around the Zionists eschewed havlagah, meeting Arab attacks with a fury of their own. By the conflict's latter stages, the Jews had organized for a total war the Arabs were ill-prepared to fight.

The first week of the fighting was chaotic, setting the stage for the next four months. Skirmishes occurred around the country, Arabs expressing their anger and Jews trying to consolidate a major diplomatic triumph. Although the skirmishes stretched their forces thinly, the Jews found an advantage in the lack of coordination, sometimes even downright animosity, among the Palestinian fighting groups. Over and over again, Haganah leaders would put this to their advantage until the communal warfare's transformation into an international war in May, 1948. In any case, for the time, it was Palestinian initiative that established the pace and style of warfare.[44]

The week after the vote introduced another motif that would become familiar—the migration of Palestinians from their homes to what they hoped would be safer ground. Arabs from neighborhoods in Haifa and Jaffa spearheaded the migration. The second day of fighting, a Haganah intelligence source reported on events in Jaffa's northern suburbs: "Empty carts are seen entering and, afterwards, carts loaded with belongings are seen leaving."[45] Although Benny Morris notes that "Abandoning one's home, and thus breaking a major psychological barrier, paved the way for eventual abandonment of village or town and, ultimately, of country,"[46] such psychological barriers may in

fact not have prevailed at all. As we have seen in the events of
1936–39, Palestinians had created a highly mobile society, reflecting frequent communal and economic crises. Movement to
a symbolic high ground, particularly home villages away from
areas of dense Jewish settlement, was an established pattern of
self-defense for workers in the cities and on the citrus plantations, matching the ayan's and merchants' habit of taking refuge
in more tranquil spots outside the country.[47]

In early December, 1947, the Palestinian national movement
was struggling to forestall the disintegration of the Arab community and thwart the Zionists, and the Jews were still not
properly prepared for combat. Haj Amin al-Husseini moved from
Cairo to Lebanon to direct the combat and, as in the early stages
of the Arab Revolt, many of the shabab became its backbone.

With the Jewish forces caught offguard by the early outbreak
of hostilities, the Palestinians scored some impressive military
triumphs. Starting on December 8, they managed to capture
isolated Jewish neighborhoods and settlements. In the following
weeks, their guerrilla forces attacked oil refineries in Haifa,
Jewish targets in downtown Jerusalem and neighborhoods of Tel-
Aviv, and transportation convoys trying to maintain communications between Jewish settlements. From their commanding
positions in the hills surrounding Jerusalem, they mounted repeated attacks on Jewish traffic, almost breaking the fragile links
between the coastal plain and the capital. They even managed a
frontal assault in January on a concentration of Jewish settlements between Jerusalem and Hebron—the Etzion Bloc, finally
destroyed by Palestinian forces, reinforced by Transjordan's Arab
Legion, in the last days of the war's communal stage. That loss
left a scar in Jewish memory. Confidence soared among the Palestinians, while the morale of the Jews and their backers wavered. In March, the United States withdrew its support for
partition. From the Zionists' perspective, the situation in March,
1948, looked grim, with Jerusalem cut off, the Etzion Bloc and
other settlements under siege and the Arab states poised for
invasion upon the departure of the British.

But such Palestinian successes were camouflage for deep political and military weakness. What Antonio Gramsci has referred to as political society—organizations linking leaders and
followers, ranging in Palestine from the Muslim-Christian Associations to labor unions to relatively broad political parties,

such as the Istiqlal—mostly had not survived the decade of turmoil beginning in 1936. Haj Amin's handmaiden, the Arab Higher Committee, while committed to the same immediate political goals, did not create firm institutional ties to the population, nor could it count on the old leverage held by the nineteenth century notables. For all his popularity, Amin was thus in no position to impose the planning and coordination on Palestinian forces that the Zionist leadership was able to achieve for the Jewish forces. The logistics of war—assured supplies, access to weapons and ammunition, communications and planning among units, regular methods of recruitment and mobilization, the means to concentrate forces—were largely absent.

The leadership found itself hamstrung as much by its allies as by its enemies. Once the issue of the future of Palestine had been appropriated by the United Nations, King Abdallah of Transjordan, rekindling his father's Hashemite ambitions, came to the conclusion that he should acquire the Arab part of Palestine and merge it with his own country.[48] Beyond such designs, the Arab League itself constantly thwarted the Mufti's political plans: It stood in the way of his determination to create a temporary Palestinian government once the British had left; it blocked a loan to establish an Arab administration in the country; and—what was most irksome—it overlooked the Arab Higher Committee whenever critical decisions had to be made.[49]

Nowhere were such cross-purposes more evident than on the battlefield. Both the Palestinians and the Arab League fielded military forces, and throughout the communal war, rivalries and friction marked relations between them. At the outset, Palestinian forces consisted of two main groups that could mobilize fighters: a youth company of several hundred young men called *al-Futuwwa*, associated with the Husseinis, and *al-Najada*, a unit of 2,000 or 3,000 men associated with opposition notable families, mainly from Jaffa—as well as a scattering of smaller bands. With the Haganah fielding over 35,000 mostly part-time fighters, the challenge for the Palestinian leadership was immense. A number of those soldiers had benefited from British military training in World War II or cooperation with the British in counterinsurgency attacks during the latter stages of the Arab Revolt. The Arab Higher Committee tried to meet the challenge by turning to Abd al-Qadir al-Husseini—the son of Musa Kazim al-Husseini—to head these Palestinian units and mobilize an overall coordinated army. As noted in chapter 4, Abd al-Qadir had gained notoriety during the Arab Revolt by heading a major fighting band in the Jerusalem district and had considered himself the revolt's chief military leader; later, he gained additional military experience in the Wehrmacht. Now he succeeded in raising a volunteer force of 5,000 men to fight for control over the central area of Palestine.[50]

The Arab League established its own volunteer force, the Liberation Army (*Jaysh al-Inqadh*), consisting of almost 4,000 men—largely Syrian volunteers. Its leader was Fawzi al-Qa'uqji, the controversial military commander who first came to the country in the 1936 uprising, from then on constituting a thorn in the side of Amin al-Husseini. Qa'uqji represented a pan-Arab solution to the challenge of Zionism, implicitly downplaying the significance of the Palestinian national movement, its institutions and leaders, in favor of a vision reflecting his own rich experiences in Syria, Saudi Arabia, and Iraq. The Mufti protested the Arab Liberation Army's role and Qa'uqji's designation as supreme military commander for Palestinian operations. And when Qa'uqji and his army marched across the Allenby Bridge into the country in March, 1948, the Arab Higher Committee published a communique warning that all who cooperated with "strangers" would be considered traitors and subject to expulsion from the country.

Pronouncements of that sort did little to alter the leadership's weakness. At a time of rising anxiety, Haj Amin's distance from the country once again was proving troublesome. It hindered the sort of mobilization that could have overcome factionalism, presenting a serious counterweight to Abdallah and the Arab League. In the end, the Palestinian hopes rested, not with national leaders, but with the dispersed, popular National Committees and scattered fighting units of young men, both tied closely to their specific locales. Even the minimal coordination that had existed in the Arab Revolt was now often absent.

In the context of both sides' initial military strategy, these problems were not glaring. The fighting, fought largely in intermittent and dispersed encounters, had two faces, the war of the cities and the war of the roads. The war of the cities, most intense at the very outset of the communal fighting, involved occasional sniping, mutual urban terror (mostly bomb attacks), and bloody retaliation. Among the most notorious incidents was the retaliatory raid by the Jews against the town of Balad al-Sheikh, killing sixty Arabs, in response to an attack on Haifa oil refinery workers and the Arabs' booby-trap bombing of three trucks in Jerusalem, killing fifty Jews. The war of the roads was largely initiated by Arab forces; their main success came in the almost total sealing off of Jerusalem from Jewish reinforcements and supplies by March, 1948.

Often holding the upper hand at the end of 1947 and the beginning of 1948, and with the promise of an invasion by the Arab states, the Palestinians' fortunes seemed to be rising. But as the Zionist forces began to improvise, the Arab inability to fight an all-out war became apparent. Even early on, the war of the cities had resulted in an Arab flight out of the urban areas—a process the Mufti attempted to stem by shifting to more hit-and-run attacks in the countryside. With the Haganah's increasing reliance on full-time soldiers, Palestinian forces found themselves at still greater disadvantage, and the Palestinian population came under attack through severe Jewish retaliatory acts. The Arab League's Liberation Army proved incapable of altering the situation, engaged as it was in a series of running quarrels with leaders of the Palestinian units. Despite the quarrels, efforts to field effective military forces were sabotaged most of all by a general absence of a firm political foundation. The following personal account by Qa'uqji of his lament to the inspector-general of his army could have been written, with some small differences, by Palestinian commanders:

> I strongly criticized the method of choosing officers and men, and the grave lack of military competence evinced by many of them in battle—some of the men could not even load a rifle properly. I also said that among the officers there were some elements so corrupt that I did not know how the Inspectorate-General could have agreed to their being attached to units of the Liberation Army. I told him frankly that, but for a group of loyal and energetic officers who had dedicated their lives to the great Arab cause, and but for the enthusiasm, courage and disciplined conduct of some of the companies, we should not have been able to stand up to the enemy for a single day.
>
> I told him of the scandalous lack of arms, ammunition, rations, clothing, health services and means of communication, and of the delays in giving the men their pay to send to their families.[51]

By the first months of 1948, the Zionist leadership had managed to mobilize a regular army of fifteen thousand full-time soldiers. In addition, in April Jewish units switched from reacting to Arab initiatives—a strategy termed active defense—to going on the offensive. More and more Jewish forces took advantage of divisions among Palestinian units, reflected in events such as what occurred in April in the Haifa district: a refusal by Husseini loyalists of arms, ammunition, and fighters to allies of the notable opposition.

Also in April, Abd al-Qadir al-Husseini died in battle, thus joining al-Qassam in the ranks of Palestinian national martyrs. Abd al-Qadir's death was a serious blow. With total war now being fought by regular armies, it became more and more difficult to hide the Palestinian political and military shortcomings. The British command had privately predicted in December that "in the long run the Jews would not be able to cope with the Arabs," but in February it predicted that they would, indeed, hold onto at least part of their designated state.[52] By the end of April, the turnaround was even more pronounced. Here is the appraisal of the American consul in a cable to Secretary of State George Marshall:

> Palestinian [mandate] government has generally ceased to function and central public services no longer exit. In Jewish areas Jews have taken effective control and are maintaining public services within those areas. Preparations for establishment Jewish state after termination of Mandate are well advanced. . . . In Arab areas only municipal administration continues without any central authority. . . . Morale following Jewish military successes low with thousands Arabs fleeing country. Last remaining hope is in entry Arab regular armies, spearheaded by Arab Legion.[53]

THE SHATTERING OF THE PALESTINIAN COMMUNITY

The entry of the Arab regular armies after the declaration of Israel's independence on May 14, 1948, did not, of course, bring the hoped for salvation. By the time all the fighting had ended in early 1949, the peasant communities in the north and the coastal plain had suffered severe damage, with peasant life remaining intact in areas far from Jewish settlement—particularly in the east. On the other end of the social spectrum, the notable leadership had seemed to vaporize into thin air. In its place emerged an entirely new stratum of Palestinian society, the refugees dispersed among five separate countries (see map 4). No one can say precisely how many of the 1.3 million Palestinians became refugees, the reckoning—like so much else in Palestine's legacy—becoming a constituent part of the Arab-Israeli conflict. Arab estimates varied between 750,000 and 1,000,000. The Israelis proposed 520,000, and the British between 600,000 and 760,000.[54]

Map 5 gives a sense of the new refugee society's *Ghurba*, exile. Flight of Palestinians from their homes began in December, 1947, as a fairly marginal event. As militiamen on both sides attempted to improve their positions, the fringes of neighborhoods and isolated settlements came under heavy attack. Palestinians caught in the cross fire began to seek refuge, as did Arabs living in largely Jewish neighborhoods. The result was two waves of movement. Many wealthy merchants and others with money, including leading notables, took refuge outside the country. Fleeing from the most beleaguered cities, densely populated with Jews—Jaffa-Tel-Aviv, Haifa, and Jerusalem—they landed mostly in Lebanon, Egypt, and Transjordan. This group included a disproportionate number of Christians—rekindling Muslim suspicions that they were not as committed to the national struggle. The second wave consisted of more of the upper and middle classes, as well as numerous villagers from the Jerusalem area and the coastal plain, who ended up in their home villages, or in all-Arab towns such as Nazareth and Nablus.

By February–March, 1948, the number of displaced Palestinians had reached between thirty thousand and seventy-five thousand, 2 to 6 percent of the Arab population.[55] Frightened Palestinians abandoned several entire towns and villages. Those who stayed put in cities such as Jaffa faced flying bullets, lack of food, and soaring prices; those who fled experienced the agony of displacement; and those who received them took on the burden of an exploding population.

Some villages managed to conclude "peace agreements" or nonbelligerency pacts with their Jewish neighbors, and others expelled Arab fighting forces so as to avoid Jewish retaliation, but such insurance policies often failed to hold up. Palestinian flight was the reaction to the risks and insecurities of a brutal,

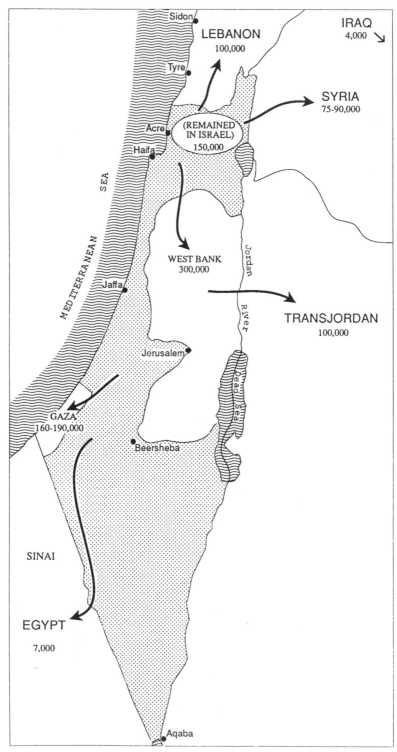

Map 4.   The Exodus of the Palestinians (1948)

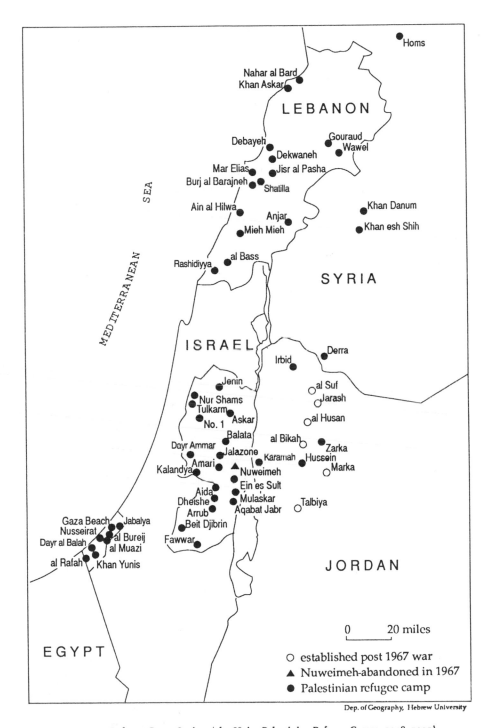

Map 5. A Refugee Camp Society (the Major Palestinian Refugee Camps, 1948–1991)

Within the map:

Homs

Nahar al Bard
Khan Askar

LEBANON

Debayeh
Dekwaneh
Gouraud
Wawel
Mar Elias
Jisr al Pasha
Burj al Barajneh
Shatilla
Ain al Hilwa
Anjar
Mieh Mieh
Khan Danum
Khan esh Shih

SEA

al Bass
Rashidiyya

SYRIA

MEDITERRANEAN

ISRAEL

Derra
Irbid

Jenin
al Suf
Jarash
Nur Shams
Tulkarm
No. 1
Askar
al Husan
Balata
al Bikah
Zarka
Dayr Ammar
Jalazone
Karamah
Hussein
Amari
Nuweimeh
Marka
Kalandya
Ein 'es Sult
Aida
Dheishe
Mulaskar
Talbiya
Arrub
'Aqabat Jabr
Gaza Beach
Jabalya
Beit Djibrin
Nusseirat
al Bureij
Dayr al Balah
al Muazi
Fawwar
al Rafah
Khan Yunis

JORDAN

EGYPT

0   20 miles

○ established post 1967 war
▲ Nuweimeh-abandoned in 1967
● Palestinian refugee camp

Dep. of Geography, Hebrew University

increasingly unavoidable war between two communities, under the aegis of a power desiring nothing more, at this point, than to protect itself. A mass exodus of entire Arab families continued, despite the opposition—temporary evacuation of women, elderly men, and children excepted—of the remnants of the Palestinian leadership. It continued in the absence, at this point, of a Zionist policy to forcibly expel or evacuate Arabs—though instances of intimidation of local villages seemed to hasten the process, and isolated, ominous evictions had begun in March.[56]

In May and June of 1948, the intensity of the fighting, from scattered guerrilla-like encounters to conventional warfare, went far towards dismantling the Palestinian Arab community. As the British evacuated areas of the country, the Haganah implemented the core of its new strategic thinking, what it called Plan Dalet.

> The essence of the plan was the clearing of hostile and potentially hostile forces out of the interior of the prospective territory of the Jewish State, establishing territorial continuity between the major concentrations of Jewish population and securing the Jewish State's future borders before, and in anticipation of, the Arab invasion. As the Arab irregulars were based and quartered in the villages, and as the militias of many villages were participating in the anti-Yishuv hostilities, the Haganah regarded most of the villages as actively or potentially hostile.[57]

While Plan Dalet did not directly call for the eviction of Palestinians from their homes, it did give free reign to Haganah officers "to clear out and destroy the clusters of hostile or potentially hostile Arab villages dominating vital axes."[58] But it was not that element of the Plan that unleashed the massive exodus in April, May, and June—most Arabs had fled the chaos and insecurity rampant in areas of intense fighting before Haganah commanders had to make such decisions.[59]

At the same time that Jewish forces were pressing the Arab villages, they were winning the war of the cities. The fall of Jaffa on April 22 and of Haifa on May 13—on the eve of Israel's declaration of independence and of the invasion of the Arab armies—marked the end of urban, coastal Palestinian society. The terror of the fighting and the possibility of Jewish rule and revenge, coupled with mistreatment and intimidation by Palestinian and Liberation Army forces,[60] prompted a massive exodus. Tens of thousands left even before the two cities fell, and tens of thousands of others fled once the Jews gained total control. In all, an additional 200,000–300,000 refugees fled their villages and cities between April and June. There was a sad irony to this death-knell: Palestinian military plans had rested on the presumption that Jewish urban society would collapse in the hellish street-to-street fighting.

Perhaps a quarter of the entire Arab population was now displaced, but in the coastal cities the depopulation was nearly total. In Haifa, for example, the Arabs had been caught between a Jewish municipal leadership that had urged them not to flee and Haganah officers who had begun to see the opportunities presented by Arab evacuation. By the end of the communal war, only 3,000–4,000 of its 70,000 Palestinians remained.[61]

It is impossible to discuss this pivotal period without reference to Dayr Yasin, which would become the war's symbol for the Palestinians. The village was one of several attacked by Jewish forces in April in an attempt to clear the besieged roads leading to Jerusalem. That offensive was important in itself, since it marked the first time Jewish forces fought with the strategic goal of permanently ridding an area of Arab villages in order to insure the viability of their own settlements.

The sequence of events in Dayr Yasin is now scarcely disputed. The village's nonbelligerency pact with local Jewish forces did not spare it being swept into the Jewish offensive to break the Arab stranglehold on Jerusalem. Following an intense battle between Palestinian militiamen and Irgun forces with some Haganah mortar support, Palestinian forces departed and the Irgun entered the village on April 9. In brutal acts of revenge for their losses, the Jewish fighters killed many of the remaining men, women, and children and raped and mutilated others. Those not killed immediately were ignominiously paraded through Jerusalem and then sent to the city's Arab sector.

For their own purposes, both Israeli and Arab sources later inflated the number of those killed to approximately 250. A recent study by a team of researchers at Bir Zeit University found that the figure probably did not exceed 120.[62] But that does not diminish the depth of the atrocity or its short- and long-run effects. In the immediate aftermath, the massacre became the subject of intense public concern. Despite their active participation in the early stages of the battle for the village, which itself left numerous local families decimated, the Haganah commanders and central Jewish leadership distanced themselves from what had taken place and condemned it. The Arab media used Dayr Yasin as the focus of their claim that Zionism was innately wicked, and to rally Arabs behind the impending Arab invasion. Broadcasts and newspaper stories prompted popular mass demonstrations in Damascus, Baghdad, Cairo, and Tripoli, including attacks on the local Jewish communities.

The stories had the effect of catalyzing rumors and striking further fear into the Palestinians, speeding the pace with which they ran for their lives, from other villages and even from large cities such as Haifa.[63] Exaggeratedly or not, the Irgun, in fact, stressed the degree to which this one incident had turned the tide in assuring that the new Jewish state would not have a disabling proportion of Arabs. Later in the year, when Israel went on the offensive that finally defeated the invading Arab armies, the image of Dayr Yasin created an expectation of similar Jewish acts. Combined with the real determination of Israeli commanders to create Arab-free regions, this precipitated another shattering wave of exodus.[64]

In the longer term, the events at Dayr Yasin hardened the demonic images each side was developing of the other. For the Jews, the 1929 massacre in Hebron, and to a lesser extent the events in Tiberias and Safad, had fostered the idea of a murderous Arab culture.[65] And aware of this Jewish reaction, Palestinians fully expected retribution should the Jews have the opportunity—all manners of cruelty were to be expected from them. Once the fighting ended, Dayr Yasin became a key element in the Palestinian transformation of the events of 1947–49 into a cosmic injustice—the enemy was not simply a party with antithetical interests, but a pure representation of evil in a world in which the forces of fate, for the moment at least, had lined up against the Arabs.

The final decimation of Palestinian Arab society during the war involved a mass expulsion by Israelis from within the boundaries of what was to become their new state. In one ten-day period in July, 1948, Israeli commanders sometimes nudged, sometimes drove, over 100,000 Arabs into parts of Palestine held by the Transjordanians, the Egyptians, and the Liberation Army, as well as into Lebanon. At times, Muslims were expelled while Druze and Christians were allowed to remain. In the Israeli offensive in October, 1948, which routed the Liberation Army and the Egyptians, another 100,000–150,000 Arabs became refugees.

Was there, indeed, a Zionist master plan to expel the Palestinians? Walid Khalidi, among others, cites Zionist talk, even before the fighting, of population transfer, as well as other pieces of evidence that support the existence of such a plan. He derided those who view "the Palestinian exodus in an historical vacuum" or who see expulsion "only as an afterthought, an extemporized innovation, a lightning brainwave with no ideological, attitudinal, motivational, or strategic antecedents."[66]

The evidence is far more equivocal than Khalidi suggests. Plan Dalet itself was full of inner contradictions, referring to both expulsion of Arabs and their administration in secured areas. Israeli leaders were aware that mass expulsions, population exchanges, and huge movements of people had long been recognized practices during and after international wars. In fact, they cited cases such as the transfer of the Greeks from Turkey. But such abstract musing was not responsible for the shattering of the Palestinian community. The tragedy resulted from a convergence of emotions: the Jewish fear, in the aftermath of the Holocaust and with the mounting attacks in Arab countries against Jews, of what the Arabs would do if they prevailed, and of not being able to sustain a state with a vanquished and disloyal Arab population (a third or more of the state); the anxiety of Jewish commanders at having a hostile population behind their advancing lines during the fighting; the Israeli sense of what could be accomplished with abandoned Arab property; and, not least, the Palestinians' own image of what the Jews would do to them if Israel prevailed and they were left in its territory.

In general the idea of expulsion does seem to have grown along with Jewish confidence in victory. During the dark days at the end of 1947 and in the first months of 1948, the central concern was simply hanging on; later, in the wake of an Arab flight that had significantly eased their burden, the new Israeli rulers began a deliberate effort to evacuate Arabs from specific parts of their state.[67] There is no doubt that in the latter stages of the war, Israel explicitly created refugees by driving Arabs from areas it ruled. Israel attempted to create Arab-free zones in some regions, such as those around Gaza and Lydda (Lod). In other regions such as Galilee, an uneven pattern emerged in which the Israelis evicted some Arabs, others fled on their own, and others remained in their communities. One Christian village whose residents showed tenacity was Miilya, in the Upper Galilee. Historian Elias Shoufani, then a boy of 14, has recalled some of the events surrounding its final fall in October.[68] Humiliation of the villagers had begun even before the Jews broke through their lines. They had reluctantly quartered a Yemeni contingent of the Liberation Army, and Shoufani's aunt drowned herself to escape molestation by a drunken soldier.

While some residents, including Shoufani's brother, developed a sense of camaraderie with the Yemenis, who after all were fighting alongside them, many felt they had simply commandeered the village. With the breakdown of government services, particularly police protection, the fellaheen had left old feuds behind and showed a cooperative spirit in administering the village themselves. Under the threat of Jewish attack, they purchased rifles from gunrunners working both sides of the Lebanese border, thus deterring local Arab threats as well. They also used this newfound unity to forcibly prevent any family from leaving the village for Lebanon, as so many from neighboring villages were now doing.

Unable to ship their cash crop, tobacco, through the coastal ports, Miilya's fellaheen smuggled it into Lebanon in small packets to sell to local Lebanese peasants. By May, 1948, the village was facing the burden of fields captured by Jewish forces, leading to dwindling food supplies, and of a small influx of refugees from other villages. These refugees, familiar with the land near the coast, helped villagers slip behind enemy lines under the cover of night to harvest crops and slaughter cows for meat. When the Haganah entered the half-deserted village, it blew up Shoufani's house as a signal of the fate of those who kept their guns. After the village priest had arranged for a formal surrender, villagers headed back to their homes: "It was a heartbreaking sight: a pile of stones and scattered suggestions of the house's former structure."[69]

Unlike residents of Miilya, many fellaheen, such as those in the nearby village of al-Ghabisiya, moved on to Lebanon or another country once the Israelis completed their capture of the Galilee at the end of October.[70] Others, such as Najib Asad of the neighboring village of al-Birwa, were driven by Israeli soldiers to the border of the Gaza Strip and told to run as fast as they could without looking back.[71]

Partly for security reasons, partly under pressure from Jewish communities that had already taken abandoned Arab property, and partly with an eye to space for incoming Jewish refugees, Israeli leaders moved towards a decision between April and August, 1948, to bar the return of the refugees. For those accustomed to a pattern of leaving trouble through a swinging door that would soon bring them home, the Israeli ban became a disaster. The Israeli government destroyed most of the approximately 350 abandoned Arab villages and towns,[72] and arguing that the concept of land ownership was meaningless in a total war, Ben-Gurion initiated the allocation of the refugees' land to Jews. Through the middle of 1949, Israeli leaders also established about 130 new Jewish settlements where Arab villages and towns had stood, most to be populated by European victims of the Holocaust and Jews fleeing Arab countries, pouring into Israel following its declaration of independence. Both groups also occupied abandoned Arab houses in the big cities, such as Haifa and Tel-Aviv/Jaffa.

A few Israeli cities, such as Nazareth and Acre, still retained a sizeable Arab population, and about 150,000 Arabs, mostly villagers, took on Israeli citizenship. Outside the Jewish state, hundreds of thousands of refugees crowded into camps in the Gaza Strip (administered by Egypt), in Syria, and in Lebanon (see map 5). The greatest number, almost 400,000, joined the suddenly beleaguered population of the old towns, led by Nablus in Palestine's hilly eastern portion, as well as the villages—that realm of peasant society least integrated into external markets. Absorbed in 1950—in a territory that would come to be known as the West Bank—into the newly dubbed Hashemite Kingdom of Jordan, these Palestinians found their political environment changed almost as drastically as did their compatriots left in Israel.

Now, with the coastal cities practically empty of Arabs and with Jerusalem truncated and divided, the mountainous area again took on the core role in Palestinian society. This encapsulated region, the one least subject to the influences of the West over the last century, would preserve the nucleus of a dispersed Palestinian nation and foster its social and cultural reconstruction. Precious few of the institutions necessary for this task had survived, and the ayan had all but disintegrated, no group standing ready to seize its mantle.

King Abdallah of Jordan had either implicitly supported the Zionists or actively colluded in preventing the emergence of another Arab state.[73] For the next 20 years, Jordan and Israel, though apparently enemies, would often adopt policies revealing a set of shared interests: to thwart Palestinism, to dissolve the emerging separate Palestinian collective identity, and to prevent the reemergence of Palestinian nationalism.

PART THREE

RECONSTITUTING THE PALESTINIAN NATION

The Odd Man Out: Arabs in Israel

During the nearly half century since al-Nakba, the struggle to refashion a Palestinian nation has necessarily had a double focus: Arabs in the West Bank and Gaza maintained the distinct character of camp society and the largest intact population in towns such as Nablus, representing a certain staying power. The newly formed satellite communities outside Palestine signified cosmopolitanism, mobility, and, in time, agitation against the existing international order. Between 1948 and the 1967 war, those who did not leave the Jewish state occupied a position as uncertain and ambiguous within Israel as in the eyes of other Arabs. Mostly fellaheen during the British mandate, Israeli Arabs heard distant echoes of the political vocabulary being forged in exile, which was recreating Palestinism. Transformed by their passports into the pariahs of the Arab world, they were also cut off from the huge waves of outward migration to more distant Arab countries—the West Bank alone had nearly 300,000 such emigrants before the 1967 war and another quarter of a million through 1975.[1] The war finally inaugurated a process of reintegration. Even then, while many began to think of themselves as Palestinians and to support the ideals of Palestinian nationalism, their experience as Israeli citizens psychologically and socially separated them from that of dispersal and longing.

In any event, from its inception, the state of Israel had developed two distinct personalities. For Jews, it was one of the few vibrant, participatory democracies in Asia, Africa, and Latin America. For Arabs, it represented a system of control and was the distributor of key resources—a state for which its Arab citizens had limited emotional attachment. As citizens of a country formed for them, Israeli Jews had, beyond simple feelings of civic responsibility, those of proprietorship towards the political institutions—the army, the flag, and the national anthem. Correspondingly, a predominant concern of government officials and academics was absorbing waves of Jewish immigrants into a new society and culture.

The state leadership certainly did not intend such absorption to involve the Arabs, especially as they came to compete with Jewish immigrants for land, water, welfare, and jobs. Their formal rights were initially counterbalanced by the harsh realities of military government, isolating them from the rest of the population, fostering dependence, preventing the creation of significant local institutions, and transforming them into a voting bloc that supported the ruling political party. Later, they would find their civic participation offset by continued national alienation. What sociologists have called the civil religion of Israeli national life—Independence Day, the Sabbath, school and work holidays on Jewish festivals, and so on—held little meaning for them.[2]

FROM MAJORITY TO MINORITY

Just after the 1949 armistice, the approximately 150,000 Israeli Arabs comprised slightly more than 10 percent of all Palestinians and about the same percentage of the Israeli population. Three-quarters of them lived in villages in the western Galilee and the Little Triangle—a part of the country adjacent to the coastal plain annexed to Israel in the armistice agreement with Jordan. These villages had not experienced mass exodus, nor the same sort of social decimation as Haifa, Jaffa, and other cities.

This apparent stability was deceiving: The 1948 war had left an Israeli Arab society as disoriented, in many ways, as those in the refugee camps ringing Israel. Although not officially exiles, between one-sixth and one-half of all the Palestinians in Israel were internal refugees.[3] Some would manage to return to their original villages, as would others who had fled the country.[4]

Nonetheless, Israeli authorities continued to expel concentrations of Arabs after the fighting subsided.[5] Citing their rights as citizens of the state, such uprooted Christian Maronites from Birim and Iqrit used the Israeli courts in an unsuccessful struggle to return that lasted several generations.[6] And many of the few thousand young men who were not exiles were war prisoners, leaving the Arabs without a significant part of their productive potential.[7]

Other Israeli Arabs faced a double bind, facilitating the confiscation of their land: The military barred them from their original homes, but since they were classified officially as "present absentees," the state could claim their "abandoned" land through the Absentee Property Act of 1950. One estimate is that as much as 40 percent of Arabs' land (half a million acres) was confiscated through the act.[8] After resettling Arabs (and compensating them for about a quarter of its worth), Israeli officials would use the land for people who were themselves uprooted, simultaneously thinning out a population that—reflecting a bitter legacy—they believed was threatening to the state:[9] a fifth column. In fact, broadcasts from neighboring Arab states continuously suggested just such a role to the Arabs in Israel. In this context, the land transfer was viewed as a means of disabling a major tool for undermining Israel's right to exist—the Arabs' claim to possession of the land.

Even where they held onto their plots, the Arabs found it difficult to stay in farming. The state severely limited their water and electricity quotas, particularly when compared to the more productive neighboring Jewish communal and cooperative farms (kibbutzim and moshavim).[10] And the Arabs found themselves excluded from the country's powerful marketing, credit, and purchasing cooperatives.[11] Arab-owned citrus groves all but disappeared; in the 1950s, the fellaheen fell back on subsistence production, with supplemental marketing of olive oil.

It is thus not surprising that many Israeli Arabs abandoned agriculture altogether. In this respect, at least, they resembled the Palestinians scattered in most other countries—in Zureik's terms, they underwent a process of depeasantification.[12] The land became the domain of those with the machinery to exploit it. By the 1960s and 1970s, Arab agriculture in Israel would undergo significant mechanization and cash cropping, Israeli research organizations speaking of a shift from fellah to farmer.[13]

In earlier decades, however, it would have been more apt to speak of a shift from fellah to wage earner. The shrinking Arab land base and the preference given to Jewish commercial agriculture simply continued the process that was well established, already, in the mandate period—the movement of fellaheen into nonagricultural, unskilled and semiskilled wage labor. Approximately three quarters of urban Arab workers, one study has found, had no training at all.[14] As Israel moved from labor surpluses to labor shortages, many Palestinian Arabs ended up integrated into the national economy, working in Jewish industries and construction companies as the lowest group on the social ladder.[15]

The transformation was rapid and thorough. By 1963, the fraction of Arabs in farming was slightly more than one-third (compared to just over 10 percent of the Jews); a decade later, it was one-fifth. Arabs entered what is often called a split- or a dual-labor market:[16] Jews filled the skilled and higher paying positions, while Arabs settled into those that were lower-paying and often seasonal, demanding little technical skill. As we have seen, even during the mandate, Palestinian Arabs found themselves at a disadvantage compared to the more skilled, technologically sophisticated Jews. The post-1948 power of the Jews in the society's central institutions only heightened the disparity.

Israel's rapid economic growth did not only produce disorientation, but also a rising standard of living for Palestinian Arabs and a gain in their rights as citizens: They now had access to the Histadrut and the benefit of a law opening state employment offices to them. But hovering behind such gains were the costs of being a weak minority. Even when state employment offices accepted applications from Arabs, they tended to give preference to Jewish applicants for jobs in Jewish areas.[17] All Arabs experienced related major and minor favoritism towards Jews. Being barred (aside from Druze and Bedouin) from army service, they found benefits, jobs, even housing, open only to those who had served in the military. And sellers and real estate agents often greeted Arabs seeking housing in predominantly Jewish areas with outright discrimination.

It is also important to note the trauma involved in any sudden transformation from national majority to small, fairly powerless minority. While now in the latter category, "it does not necessarily follow that [the Israeli Arabs] have developed a minority self-concept."[18] Compounding the trauma was the absence of any effective national leadership to deal with their Jewish counterparts. Those who remained, noted the first Israeli adviser on Arab affairs, "were like a headless body . . . the social, commercial, and religious elite had gone";[19] even among the Christians, making up a disproportionately high 21 percent of the Israeli Palestinian population, there were few remaining representatives of the mandate period's middle and upper classes.

Like the refugees, the Arabs in Israel thus looked to local leaders, many of whom were clan heads, gaining new prominence as they played key mediating roles between their relatives and Israeli state and party officials. In fact, the clan heads filled an even more central niche than local leaders in the refugee camps, and interclan rivalries took on far greater intensity than those of the mandate period.[20] In the camp society of Gaza, Jordan, and Lebanon, the old village chiefs gave way in the two decades after 1948 to a young, educated national leadership; in Israel, the Arabs found themselves cut off from it and barred from generating a broader leadership of their own. Even when increasing urbanization and education began to undermine the old local clan leaders, starting in the mid-1970s, the Arabs in Israel could not produce a countrywide leadership to represent them. A series of Israeli government policies, reflecting lingering Jewish fear that the Arabs would form a spearhead for Israel's avowed enemies, was aimed at forestalling its creation—and with it, a revitalized Palestinian identity.

No policy rankled more than the imposition and maintenance of military government for the Arabs. Drawing on mandate regulations dating back to 1936 and 1945 (to thwart Arab and then Jewish rebels), the government established military administration in the fall of 1948, while the fighting raged. In 1950, the government organized the administration into a military government, maintained until 1966. It resembled emergency powers in other countries, restricting freedom of speech, freedom of movement, and so forth. It provided an easy way to shove the Arab minority aside—in order to focus on the pressing problems of creating a new state administration, assimilating hundreds of thousands of immigrants, stimulating economic growth, and building military capabilities to face the next round, which neighboring Arab states repeatedly promised would soon come.

Perhaps for the Arabs the military government's most onerous aspect was its severe restriction on movement. Journalist and poet Fouzi El-Asmar recalls the situation in Lydda right after the 1948 war: "The Arabs were not allowed to leave their own ghetto [practically all Arab villages or clusters of villages were designated as closed areas[21]] without a permit from the authorities [i.e. the military governor], and the most infuriating thing for us was that our area and the other areas in Lydda which were inhabited by Arabs were under military command, while the rest of the city in which Jews lived, was not. We were not allowed out without special licences until the early fifties, while the Jews, of course, were free to walk anywhere except in our neighbourhood."[22]

The effect of the restrictions on free movement was to fragment the population even further (by limiting contacts among Arabs) and to make it more difficult to find employment in the larger labor market. Several years before its demise in the 1960s, the hand of the military government became much lighter. In part, the liberalization was due to the fact that Arabs in Israel did not prove to be disloyal or subversive. In part, it was due to the tragic events in the Little Triangle village of Kafr Qasim, in 1956, spawned by the harsh restrictions on movement.

For Arabs, Kafr Qasim became a symbol; for Jews, it was the catalyst removing one of the many veils shrouding the Arab issue. The events unfolded at the beginning of the Suez war—that second Arab-Israeli war, following fast upon the first one and (in light of Nasser's pan-Arab appeal) intensifying Jewish fear about the disposition of the country's Arabs. On October 29, at the outset of the fighting, military authorities clamped a curfew on Arab villages, starting at 5 P.M. In Kafr Qasim, workers had been toiling in the fields; not having heard about the curfew, they drifted home after five. The village chief, having learned of the curfew at 4:30, had cautioned the local military unit's NCO that the returning laborers would have no way of knowing about it. Similar situations occurred in other villages, but in Kafr Qasim the military unit lined up the returning workers and shot them. Forty-seven were killed.

For the Arabs, Kafr Qasim took on a symbolic importance almost rivalling that of Dayr Yasin. El-Asmar writes of:

a turning point in my political development. I spent so much time talking about the incident to my friends, who were also greatly affected to varying degrees. We asked ourselves: "What will happen next? When will our turn come? What had these poor workers done?" We dwelt on these and a thousand other questions. From these unanswerable questions, I arrived at the conclusion that in all truth this had happened simply because these people were Arabs, despite the fact that Arabs in Israel had kept the peace since the creation of the State.[23]

The response of the Israeli government offered little reassurance. At first, it tried to cover up the events. Once they became public, officials expressed outrage and brought the members of the military unit to trial, but Arabs openly questioned whether the punishments fit the severity of the crimes. Eight men received sentences ranging from eight to seventeen years in prison, but in the end none served more than three and a half years.

Along with Dayr Yasin, Hebron, Gush Etzion, and similar incidents, Kafr Qasim encouraged Arabs and Jews to demonize each other. The absence of routine contacts, exacerbated by the military restrictions, made the process easy: The two peoples resided in segregated neighborhoods, attended different schools, almost never intermarried; they met only in the workplace—and then, usually, as boss and worker.

For the Arabs, still reeling from their defeat in 1948, Kafr Qasim dramatized the weakness of their position as a national minority. Israeli policy was not simply aimed at subduing the Arabs through sheer force, but controlling them in ways that denied their connection to a larger Palestinian society and its nationalism, thus thwarting unity among them. One political scientist has identified this policy as segmentation,[24] resembling the system of divide and rule made much use of by the imperial powers earlier in the century and still used by many states to handle their populations. As with Jordanian policy during the same period (examined in the next chapter), the Israeli political leadership worked consciously to nullify the Arabs' Palestinian identity. But its approach differed from Jordan's in having no goal of integrating them into a larger state identity. As Israeli Arabs, they were designated as neither Israeli—in the ways that Jews could be Israeli—nor Palestinian.[25]

Israeli citizenship would bind Jews and Arabs in a civic sense, enabling Arabs to secure a relatively fair share of resources and assure their civic rights, but they would forego *any* national identification, any means of membership in a close-knit collectivity.[26] The Law of Return, conferring rights of immigration and instantaneous citizenship on any Jew, reflected the status of Jews as automatic members of such a collectivity, as did the continuing functioning of nonstate organizations such as the Jewish Agency, bestowing benefits on Jews only.[27] (Only the Law of Return and military service officially differentiated Jews from Arabs.)

The experiences of a group called *al-Ard* (The Land) reflected how the authorities moved against those aiming to speak for broad sectors of the Arab population. The al-Ard group of nationalist intellectuals, who published a magazine starting in 1959,[28] attempted to create an Arab party list in 1964 to run in the upcoming Israeli national elections. Lustick describes the events that followed:

> The Military Administration moved hard and fast. Permission for the Arab Socialist List to appear on the ballot was refused, el-Ard's leaders were separated and banished to remote Jewish towns, many members were put under administrative detention, and the organization itself was finally declared illegal. Subsequently several of its leaders were offered a choice of imprisonment or exile from the country.[29]

Al-Ard raised fears among Israeli officials that the Arabs were about to reopen the old, finally dormant political struggles of the mandate period. The Arab party, troublingly Nasserite and pan-Arab in its stance, did not recognize the right of a Jewish state to exist, certainly not within the enlarged boundaries of the 1949 armistice.[30] It also saw the Arabs of Israel as an integral part of the dispersed Palestinian people. Israel's High Court finally banned the group, finding that its core ideology contradicted the very existence of the state.

Working to fragment the Arab population into numerous different minorities, such as Druze, Circassians, Bedouin, and the like, Israeli officials turned to the clan as their institutional link.[31] In the 1950s and 1960s, clan leaders served as the village conduits for government investments in education, social services, and infrastructure. This status—depending on the continuing largesse from the Israeli government, the Histadrut, and the major political parties (especially the Labor party, or, as it was formerly known, Mapai)—thus gave them a newfound discretionary power. Their co-optation was demonstrated in 1963, when a move to abolish the military government failed by a single Knesset vote: Two of the negative ballots came from Arabs.

Not surprisingly, the older clan leaders began to lose their followers' confidence even as they continued to deliver important benefits. At the same time, Israeli officials put obstacles in the way of any other organizations taking over. They confiscated, froze, or took control of the Muslim religious endowments, the waqfs, which had played such an important political and economic role in earlier periods. And quite effectively, they drew activist students away from community leadership roles with well-paying positions in the Histadrut or state agencies. Between 1948 and the 1967 war, such policies were generally successful. But they also had an unintended effect, producing new social groups—including small numbers of elites—who sometimes subtly, sometimes openly, forged the elements of an Arab identity running counter to the official vision.

No policies had more impact in this regard than those involving education. Education for Arabs in Israel has sustained a built-in tension since the state's inception. On the one hand, the state has controlled all of it, Arab and Jewish alike, in a highly centralized manner, with the curriculum completely controlled by the Ministry of Education in Jerusalem. On the other hand, the Arab and Jewish educational systems have led almost totally separate lives at least up to the university level. With a few exceptions in several cities (Jaffa, Haifa, Nazareth), Jewish children have attended school with other Jewish children, Arab children with other Arab children—and Arab teachers. This has allowed, amidst Jerusalem-imposed uniformity, the emergence of an educational milieu with a distinctly Arab personality.

Both the Arabs and Jewish officials have seen the education of Arab children as a key resource for achieving important goals: for the Arabs, political and socioeconomic progress;[32] for the Jews, both overall Arab modernization and the creation of the "new Israeli-Arabs," with their various subdivisions of identity, their religious and ethnic fragments. Soon after the guns fell silent in 1948, the Knesset passed a compulsory education law, which overwhelmed Arab schools with droves of new students. Ministry of Education personnel promptly drafted Arab teachers, many poorly qualified, to staff the classrooms. Makeshift schoolhouses and two-a-day shifts became the norm in most villages.[33] Textbooks were almost nonexistent.[34] Setting a pattern for other government offices, the Ministry of Education established an Arab Department, led and in large part staffed by Jewish civil servants. Much as in the Bureau for Indian Affairs in the United States, a certain paternalism became its standard operating procedure.

In many respects the results of the crash program were impressive, dwarfing British educational efforts in earlier decades. The great majority of Arab children became not only literate but conversant in Hebrew as well as Arabic. By 1955, the Israelis had doubled Arab enrollment percentages from prestate levels. And even that figure is somewhat misleading, since it incorporates nomadic Bedouins, of whom only a negligible number attended state schools, and girls, still enrolled at less than one-third the rate of boys. But in one important respect the Israeli enterprise did evoke the mandate period: As the Arabs gained in the classroom, they nonetheless continued to fall farther behind the Jews. For example, while the compulsory education law led to truly universal education among Jews at the elementary level, in 1973 only four-fifths of Arab children attended school regularly.[35] In fact, their pre-1967 elementary school enrollment was closer to the levels of West Bank Palestinians than to those of Israeli Jews. In high schools and universities, the disparity was even greater.

The educational system, in an odd way, fed upon itself. For educated Arabs, many Israeli offices employing white collar workers, both in government and in the private sector, were off limits—Arabs were simply not hired. Furthermore, at the time Israeli investment policies discouraged the creation of autonomous economic sectors in Arab areas, severely limiting career possibilities for educated young Arabs. The result was that education and law became virtually the only careers open to the growing number of graduates. Soon, many of the best students returned to the schools as teachers, raising the level of education substantially. In 1962, for example, the Arab failure rate in the state high school matriculation exams was 90 percent; three years later it had dropped to 70 percent.

Even if the Israelis could point with some pride to such

achievements, their goal of reshaping Arab consciousness into a new Israeli-Arab identity had more mixed results; the development of Arab education within a dominant Jewish culture was bound to cause confusion. Note the ideals articulated in the 1953 educational laws: "To base education on the values of Jewish culture and the achievements of science, on love of the homeland and loyalty to the state and the Jewish people, on practice in agricultural work and handicraft, on pioneer training and on striving for a society built on freedom, equality, tolerance, mutual assistance, and love of mankind."[36] The actual curriculum adapted these statements for Arab schools and Arab students, but the Jewish cultural thrust continued to be very strong: Arab students around the country studied more hours of Jewish history than they did of Arab history.[37]

In some important ways, formal education was thus a disorienting experience for Israeli Arab children, represented a bilingual and bicultural experience, with both cultures being somewhat out of place. Anomalous in schools where all the students were Arab,[38] Jewish culture still established the norms for achievement—the matriculation exams, entrance into all the country's universities, facility in Hebrew. The limited professional career opportunities that did exist depended on mastering a curriculum including Hebrew literature, Jewish history, Zionism, and the like. The relationship to Arab culture was equally anomalous, since Israel's Arab minority was cut off from the centers of Arab culture and learning in Cairo, Beirut, and elsewhere. Its isolation came not only from Israeli policies but also from being shunned by other Arabs in the coffee houses of Europe, and by Arab governments. Inversely, in Israeli schools, the Arabic component of the curriculum included classical Arabic language and literature and Muslim history, without any reference to contemporary Arab or Palestinian developments. The implicit message to the students was that the Ottoman Empire represented the end of their history.[39]

Israeli officials had hoped that children's educational experiences in the state's highly centralized school system would create the new Israeli-Arab man and woman, an identity autonomous of those being forged in refugee camps and Palestinian satellite communities outside Israel. The values implicit in a modern education would break down the Arabs' old parochial perspectives, the appreciation of both Arab and Jewish history creating a minority that identified itself with classical Arab culture and, in a civic sense, with the Israeli state. The formation of new identities, however, is far more complicated and confusing than the officials imagined. The disorienting experience that Arab children faced within school, compounded by the contradictory pulls they faced in the larger society, resulted in the emergence of a rather different perspective.

It did not emerge immediately. In the 1950s and 1960s, the Arabs in Israel did not have the resources to recreate an autonomous cultural life, especially given the restrictions of the military government. Caught between the pull of local Arab culture and the efforts of Israeli educational officials, they remained largely quiescent, both on a political and cultural level. When asked by Israeli sociologists in the summer of 1966 to state their core identities, those in a sample gave the following rank order: Israeli, Israeli-Arab, Arab, and Palestinian.

A short time after, other factors led to a strikingly different order: Arab, Muslim/Christian, Israeli-Arab, and Israeli.[40] No doubt the intervening 1967 war had shaken up existing Arab understanding. But the war also made manifest the educational system's virtue of offering both Jewish and Arab students the tools to challenge the truths taught them. What may have mattered even more than such critical skills was the educational system's fostering of new groups in Arab society. Despite efforts to prevent Arab national integration, high schools and universities brought together students from far-flung villages and towns to explore their common experiences and construct their own view of the world.

In this manner, a fragile, narrow new Arab elite emerged out of the Israeli educational system. It would never manage to play a social and political role similar to that of the old notables before 1948 or of the exiled educated element in the Palestine Liberation Organization. Nonetheless, those who rose out of peasant society through school ranks in Israel provided the basics for an emerging, collective self-identity, as Israel's Arabs struggled to clarify their relationship with other Palestinians and other Israelis.

What sorts of people made up this elite? As Khalil Nakhleh suggests, foremost among them were "people of the pen."[41] A number of school teachers began to achieve recognition beyond their local communities by publishing poetry and short stories. In 1954, they established the League of Arabic Poets (including Jewish members writing in Arabic), which gave way in 1955 to the League of the Arab Pen. Through their verse, often recited in public forums, they expressed the pent up grievances of the Arab minority as a whole.

It is important to note that in the Palestinian Arab context both inside and outside Israel, politics and art were almost never differentiated. The *only* nonpolitical poet with stature in the 1950s was Mishel Hadad. The most important Arab writer in Israel was Emile Habibi, a Communist activist. (His best-known book is *The Opsimist*—a mixture of "optimist" and "pessimist"—an ironic description of the Jewish-Arab reality in Israel.) Likewise the most important literary periodical remains *al-Jadid*, also issued by the Communist party. It was a vehicle for poets and political activists such as Samih al-Qassim, Mahmoud Darwish, Zaki Darwish, Salim Jubran, and Tawfiq Zayad.[42]

In the period leading up to the 1967 war, "few Israeli Arabs defined themselves publicly as Palestinian Arabs or just as Palestinians," writes Aziz Haidar, but in the work of some of these writers one could discern signs of a renewed Palestinian identity.[43] A handful eventually left Israel and joined the armed resistance. Others stayed in their teaching positions, using symbolism and allegory to "write protest poetry and to communicate with the readership under the watchful eyes of the Israeli censor."[44] They also railed against the clan leaders for working hand-in-glove with the Israeli authorities.

Until the mid-1960s, the Zionist political parties did not accept Arab members in their ranks; instead, they created affiliated lists, or so-called Arab slates, populated largely by clan heads or their designated representatives, the only exception being the left-wing Zionist Mapam party. Allied with the writers, a small number of political leaders now managed to gain a foothold outside the framework of the clan heads.[45] Most rose to prominence within Israel's Communist party, but some joined Mapam. With the top leadership of both parties being Jewish,[46] the immunity of the parties themselves, along with the privileges of party activism—access to publications, participation in local seminars, travel to conventions in communist countries, interaction with Jewish intellectuals—enabled this small group to gain invaluable experience and contacts, as well as access to Eastern-bloc universities for their children.

The graduates of both Israeli universities and those in communist countries eventually joined the emerging elite, mostly as a small core of professionals, especially teachers, lawyers, physicians, and pharmacists. Although most of their education was financed by their clans, seemingly grounding them within village society, they became cultural oddities. Their Hebrew was often flawless, certainly superior to that of the Jewish man in the street; they read the same books and newspapers, attended the same plays, and hummed the same tunes as their Jewish middle-class counterparts. (In fact, after 1967, many Gazans and West Bankers commented on how "Jewish" these Arab men appeared.) Nevertheless, they played an important role for other Arabs, providing an important bridge to the dominant Jewish culture. Lawyers, in particular, became skilled at advancing Arab interests through the adept use of the courts and Israel's democratic institutions.[47]

Like the cultural and economic leaders who had emerged on the coast during the mandate period, these intellectuals, professionals, and party activists could not create a comprehensive leadership by building political parties or other institutions. One writer notes that the "Arab elites, on the whole, are few in number relative to the size of the community. They are also a bitter and frustrated lot. . . . Finally, they are economically and politically marginal, rarely occupying positions that enable them to influence or contribute to the development of their society"[48]—a judgment that seems overly harsh. The elite did fill an important function in defining possibilities and directions for the Arabs of Israel. They did so at a time when old social institutions had been eviscerated and new ones were threatening the foundations of Palestinian Arab life.

AFTER 1967: ECONOMIC AND POLITICAL TRANSFORMATION

In the years leading up to the June war, the old patriarchal system based on the clan was in disrepair. Much of its strength had come from its pivotal role in the distribution of land and of government benefits tied to agriculture during Israel's first two decades. But with a declining number of Arabs in farming, and as work lives expanded beyond the village's physical and social boundaries, its special position in Arab society had begun to vanish. After 1967, its economic strength ebbed quickly and it moved further towards the community's margins. The process accelerated when the Labor party weakened and then, in 1977, fell into opposition; much of the vitality of the early brand of politics had rested on the ties of the clan heads to the party.

Even the marriage system that had sustained the clan fell into disarray. The prevalence of wage labor meant that the family's arrangement of marriages and the old standards determining bride price, or dowry, disappeared. In the post-1967 period, young women from outside the village, or at least outside the clan, no longer were the most desirable brides. According to tradition, marriages were within the patrilineal clan, with villagers prizing outside brides because they could enhance its political alliances. Now, such carefully arranged unions gave way to personal choice.

In that respect, the old system did not entirely vanish after the June war. In the town of Shafa Amr, Majid al-Haj found more traditional marriages still prevalent—even if young Arabs reported that their selections were made through their personal choices, rather than family arrangement.[49] Nonetheless, as one anthropologist puts it, "The marriage system has become ineffectual. . . . At best, the system is accommodated to individual strategies promoting personal or (nuclear) household viability or need. . . . The 'end purpose' of a marriage strategy is personal well-being. . . ."[50] Once questions of bride price and the basis of selection of mates changed, so did other aspects of family life. Increasing individualism, for example, made it much more likely for young couples to set up separate households, rather than moving in with their extended families.[51]

Corresponding to these social changes, new organizations were appearing with political potential—for example, those consisting of internal refugees from various destroyed villages. Yet even as the clan heads' local stature suffered, the new, more individualistic Arab community faced an Israeli political system still working through them. And government policies continued to stifle the possibility that the educated elite would emerge as a comprehensive leadership, prepared to help the Arabs in Israel confront the changes setting in after 1967.

Some of these changes had already been evident in preceding decades, now simply intensifying dramatically. Others were real breaks with earlier patterns, partly growing out of the resumed relations with other Palestinians in the West Bank and Gaza. Two trends, in particular, were central to a reshaping of Arabs' social life in Israel: the end of agricultural society, with the Arabs adopting a different role in the Israeli economy, and the development of a new politics.

The economic surge in the years following the June War affected both the standard of living of the Arabs and what anthropologist Henry Rosenfeld has termed their "latitude and scope in the economy."[52] Many became self-employed, owning small workshops and—in several instances—large-scale industries. They went, Rosenfeld notes,

> from unskilled laborers and service workers, often at the most menial of tasks over the past decades, to an increasing hold in construction . . . ; from a readiness to undertake jobs in manual labor that many Jews were leaving, to the gaining of skills, experience and know-how in the labor market, and the ability to provide these, and workers, as sub-contractors for Jewish contractors in building, defense projects, road construction, public works, and in a huge variety of enterprises many of them, directly or indirectly, state development projects.[53]

Just as Jews from Arab countries escaped low-status, unskilled manual labor in the 1950s and 1960s by moving past the Israeli Arabs, who filled such positions, now these jobs were handed on to commuters from the West Bank and the Gaza Strip. Even those remaining in wage labor forfeited temporary work on construction sites and in the fields to their West Bank brothers.

By the 1980s, an Arab industrial sector was also forming, employing as much as 30 percent of the Arab industrial labor force and about 6 percent of the Arab work force.[54] Unlike an earlier period when authorities frowned upon investment in Arab villages and towns, small manufacturing enterprises were now opening there, often with clear Jewish approval—if not material support. Arabs started smaller businesses (e.g., garages) servicing mostly local Arab clients. A 1985 field survey of such businesses, and of industries and development projects, points to their strength.[55] Correspondingly, agriculture itself was becoming less a peasant society's linchpin than another in a series of businesses; the attractiveness of wage labor outside the village eliminated underemployment and forced farmers to raise wages and their own productivity.[56]

The autonomy of the Arab economy should not be overstated, industrialization in the Arab sector still being quite limited. Palestinian-owned businesses tended to be small, devoted to trade and commerce, subcontracting, crafts, and transportation.[57] Many of the enterprises continued to be wholly or partially dependent on Jewish industries, contractors, and employers. An Arab clothing industry, for example, emerged to supply a larger, Jewish-owned textile industry and its design houses.[58] Industries owned by Arabs tended to be in traditional sectors, such as textiles and food processing, while Jews owned the more sophisticated manufacturing concerns. State policies continued to encumber Arab economic activities much more than Jewish ones (although Jewish businessmen might have wondered how that was possible). State intervention assisted politically favored groups, which included Jews but not Arabs.[59] Nonetheless, lacking state investments or the advantages accruing to an area designated as an industrial zone, but finding informal, innovative ways to bypass state policies (the so-called black economy),[60] the Israeli Arab achievement by the 1980s was remarkable.

The economic vitality and the mobility in Israel after the June war helped make it possible. One researcher has pointed to approximately 300 Arab families becoming big investors, with another 2,000 moving up to the middle ranks.[61] Along with the intellectuals and professionals, whose numbers had risen to over 4,000, these entrepreneurs comprised the most influential force in Israel's Arab society.

Such prosperity had a marked impact on less privileged Palestinians—most notably, on village women. Increasing numbers entered the labor force, corresponding to the growing demand for workers. In the town of Shafa Amr, 11 percent of the working-age women did so by the 1980s.[62] But if there existed a dual labor market for Arabs and Jews, internally one emerged for Arab men and women: Because Arab economic growth was not accompanied by significant urbanization—the inhospitality of the larger society meant that Arabs continued to live in their villages—and cultural mores kept women much closer to home, they found

themselves limited to the opportunities in their immediate localities. Nearly three-quarters of industrial workers in Arab industries were women, filling the lowest status and lowest paid
positions. Now, they were part of a rhythm in society reflecting
wage labor rather than agriculture, but still cut off from the
mobility and autonomy that could change their status. The new
marriage system and labor opportunities may have translated
into a slight relaxation of the difficult conditions wives traditionally had endured, chipping away at the husband's dominance; at the community level, however, women's positions did
not noticeably improve.[63]

In general, the transformation of the Israeli Arab economy did
not come without important problems. Arabs still had to deal
with a wider society that frequently suspected their motives and
discriminated against them; they had to participate in a political
system continuing to prefer working through clan heads and
failing to address some of their most pressing needs. Perhaps no
problem better illustrates this reality than that of house construction. The Arab population in Israel rose from the 150,000
remnant after the 1948 war to over three-quarters of a million by
the end of the 1980s. At times the rate of natural increase soared
to over 4 percent per year, an almost unheard of figure among
demographers. For the decade of 1972–82, the figure was 3.7
percent, translating into a rate that would double the population
in less than 20 years. The pressure on housing grew correspondingly; nearly 2 out of 5 Arab households included 7 or more
people, and more than a fifth held more than 4 people to a room.
(The rates for Jews were 5 and 1 percent, respectively.)

Two other factors made the housing situation even more difficult: the lack of rapid urbanization to take pressure off the
villages, and the fact that the new prosperity brought both the
desire and ability to build more and larger homes (a source of
great prestige in the society). But such construction was no simple matter since Israeli law demanded that it conform to a local
municipality's master development plan, and Arab villages simply did not have the resources to undertake such projects. Construction on current agricultural lands, almost the only plots
available in Arab villages, also demanded special permission
from the Ministry of Agriculture. Village representatives frequently lacked the clout to gain the necessary waivers. And
Israeli officials systematically denied Arab communities the re-

sources—from building permits to official recognition as a city—to develop comprehensive town plans.

The result was an explosion of illegal construction in village after village, probably comprising 30 percent of all housing. Some of it came to be accepted de facto by Israeli authorities. The rest became the source of bitter controversy, leading to the bulldozing of new houses. At a protest against a housing demolition, reflecting a change from the political quiescence of previous decades, security forces killed one Arab and 12 others were injured.[64] A separate episode, the House Day general strike of 1988, also demonstrated that Arabs were increasingly seeing their grievances in national terms.

The housing crisis points to the development of a new politics among the Arabs in Israel. Within a decade after the 1967 war, a wave of political activism rolled over the community, rekindling some of the Jews' worst fears. The Arabs continued to find an effective independent political movement beyond their grasp, but their orientation within Israeli politics altered dramatically. The event making this clear came on March 30, 1976, in a violence-marred general strike. The National Committee for the Defense of Arab Lands—the first political organization claiming to represent the entire Israeli Palestinian population—called the strike and dubbed it Land Day. As in the past, the immediate issue was proposed expropriation of Arab-owned land by the state, announced by the government in February, 1976. In the Galilee, where the expropriations were slated to occur, villagers clashed with army units, leading to six Arab deaths plus many injuries and arrests. For many Arabs, the events echoed those in Kafr Qasim, twenty years earlier. But the Arab community now demonstrated a sense of assurance and political awareness totally absent in 1956.

In some ways, the strike represented the coming of age of Rakah, the Communist party, which had created the National Committee. Born in petty factional disputes leading to a Communist split in 1965, the party emerged in the mid-1970s as the voice of Arab grievances. More than a third of Arab votes in national elections were going to Rakah, and in the 1977 elections, when it was in coalition with a largely Jewish party (the Democratic Front for Peace and Equality), half the Arabs voted for its list. Before Land

Day, it had succeeded in breaking the Labor party's near stranglehold on elective offices in Arab municipalities by gaining the office of mayor of Nazareth, the sole Arab city at that time. Now the new mayor, Tawfiq Zayyad, led the general strike, albeit with qualified success in terms of mass involvement. Rakah did come with baggage limiting its appeal: Many Arabs rejected its atheism, and some younger nationalists reacted against its calls for Jewish-Arab worker solidarity. Nonetheless, the party was the closest the Arabs came to a broad-based organization expressing many of their nationalist aspirations.

Other groups besides Rakah, also began to express nationalist sentiments. Arab university students and graduates formed the Arab Academic Union in Israel in 1971, which affirmed that the country's Arabs were part of the Palestinian people and Arab nation.[65] A movement called *Ibna al-Balad* (Sons of the Village) picked up momentum in the late 1970s, partly because it presented itself as an alternative to Rakah. Starting in 1974, Arab mayors came together in the Committee of the Heads of Arab Local Councils. Later this organization evolved into the Supreme Follow-Up Committee, which in effect became the recognized representative of the Palestinian community in Israel. It included leading political figures and cultural leaders along with the heads of the municipalities.

Precisely the sorts of Arab community integration that Israeli policy had long sought to prevent were now occurring. The Supreme Follow-up Committee, in particular, managed to emerge as a forum for overcoming the debilitating factionalism that had plagued the Arabs. Attempts by the authorities to stress the solidarity of Arab subdivisions foundered on an emerging sense of community, cutting across the old lines.[66]

Land Day, declared a national Israeli Palestinian festival in 1992 and acknowledged by annual demonstrations and a general strike, led to newfound respect for its participants among Palestinians in the West Bank and the Gaza Strip. The immediate reaction of Israeli authorities was one of alarm. In September 1976 a highly controversial document, called the Koenig Report, was leaked to the press. In it, Israel Koenig, who had been a high placed official in the Interior Ministry, stated that the Arab majority in the western Galilee posed a threat to the state's security, and argued for settling Jews in the area, suppressing Arab political activity, and encouraging Arab emigration. But in the following years, the same disinterest that had existed earlier crept back into Israeli policy, punctuated periodically by a gesture of good will, an enticement to follow one party or another, or a clamping down on Arab political activity. With time, Israeli officials grew increasingly distracted by events on the West Bank and Gaza, especially after the outbreak of the Intifada in December, 1987. Two weeks later, a general strike by Israel's Arabs in solidarity with the revolt raised concerns that it might spread to Israel proper. But those concerns also seemed lost to distraction once the strike was over.

Israel's Arabs were becoming more responsive to outside Palestinian political currents, the two most important being Palestinian nationalism, as expressed by the PLO, and a revived Islamic consciousness. For its part, the PLO leadership treated the Arabs of Israel with a studied indifference—as if, along with the Israeli government, they looked through them rather than at them—for the first two decades after it reorganized in 1968. The PLO would only address them as a community in the 1988 Israeli elections, when it suggested which choices would best serve the Palestinian national cause. While many Arabs in Israel lined up with those wings of the PLO supporting the creation of a Palestinian state alongside Israel, their feelings about the PLO as the spokesman for all Palestinians remained more obscure. Partly, the obscurity derived from Israeli restrictions on any form of contact with the organization. But it also certainly stemmed from authentic, continuing ambivalence at their own position—the one fragment of the Palestinian community not facing dispersal, and not really fitting into a national culture being reconstructed in exile, ghurba.

Like other Arabs, those in Israel were not left untouched by the Iranian Revolution of 1978. By the mid-1980s, Islam was clearly ascendant in the Muslim population, vying for a central role in the definition of the community. This became most obvious in the municipal elections of 1988, when Islamic political forces won majorities on a number of councils, including that in Umm al-Fahm, a former village that had grown so large it was accorded the legal status of a city, after a protracted political battle of its residents with Israeli officials. The Islamic movement was now the most important political rival to Rakah.

The roots of Islamic activism in Israel lay in a group of students who were involved in the Islamic revival on campuses in Nablus and Hebron during the 1970s. A charismatic figure, Abdallah Nimr Darwish, led an underground group, Usrat al-Jihad (the Family of Holy War), discovered by Israeli officials in 1981. Darwish and others were jailed for secreting arms. Upon their release, they turned to ground-level community welfare projects as a means of political organizing, much as other Islamic groups in Gaza and the West Bank were doing. Their influence spread, as they created community centers around mosques and self-help circles to combat drugs, prostitution, and alcohol. Groups of youngsters undertook sanitation and clean-up campaigns in local villages. In some ways, their mundane activities made the activities of Rakah—fighting for national equality and civil rights— seem somehow misplaced, because the communists now appeared removed from the everyday problems of the people.[67]

The shift of Islamic political leaders from clandestine activities to the provision of routine services was reflected in their orientation to Israel and the Jews. At first, their magazine al-Sirat (banned since 1990) was very militant, preaching for jihad and complete Islamization of the country. In time, their radical political slogans gave way to advocacy of "two states for two nations," their entry into the fray of Israeli elections seeming to moderate their stance at the very moment that Islamic groups on the West Bank and in the Gaza Strip were demonstrating increased militancy. Once again, Israel's Arabs seemed out of step with the activities of other Palestinians.

The Arab public in Israel at the turn of the 1990s was neither the subdued, traumatized group it had been four decades earlier nor the revolutionary force that many Jews had feared it would become. Its self-definition as a distinct and cohesive group, crystallizing with Land Day in 1976, stemmed from the political events of 1967, from the vast social and economic changes that they underwent afterward, and from the experience of living in Israel for over forty years. Their identities were increasingly Palestinian (in surveys over two-thirds felt so) but in ways quite distinct from other segments of the people.[68]

The dissolution of the sealed frontiers to the West Bank and Gaza in June, 1967, had ended two decades of isolation from other Arabs, offering access to both the basis for a recreated Palestinian identity advocated by Israel's Arab writers for several years—the symbols and longings in the refugee camps—and the resistance that would soon coalesce in the PLO.

At the same time, it highlighted major differences with other Palestinians. In a survey comparing their position in 1968 to that of their counterparts under Jordanian rule, Israel's Arabs found themselves with better economic and cultural conditions, higher morale, and more political freedom. Their only real envy was for the intensity of both religious observance and patriotism in the West Bank. Few of them seemed ready to trade their positions in the Jewish state for the lot of their brothers.[69] Other surveys showed a willingness to have Jews as friends, a reluctance, by a vast majority, to leave Israel, even if a Palestinian state were to come into being, and a dwindling number (below 10 percent by 1980) denying Israel's right to exist as a state.[70] In general, they developed a sense of themselves as participating in a legitimate political entity.[71] And a substantially greater number reported feeling more at home in Israel than in Arab countries. Here is Smooha's summary of his survey:

> Israeli Arabs are a Palestinian national minority, destined to live permanently in the Jewish state. They avail themselves of Israeli democracy to wage a struggle for greater equality and integration. They are bilingual and bicultural, Israeli Palestinian in identity, and are in solidarity with the submerged Palestinian nation, but loyal to Israel. They support the PLO and a two-state solution to get their people settled and their own national aspirations fulfilled, but their fate and future are firmly linked to Israel.[72]

Once the uprising against Israeli rule broke out in the occupied territories, the ambivalence of Israel's Arabs became even more pronounced. To be sure, the Intifada unleashed strong feelings strengthening a sense of Palestinian identity and support for political Islamic movements.[73] A sense of sharing a common fate with Palestinians in the West Bank and Gaza became palpable.[74] At the same time, except for a slight increase in the number of individual hostile acts,[75] they did not join in the uprising directly. Even at the tensest moment in the midst of a clash with police during the general strike in December, 1987 (named Peace Day), they were careful to draw a firm boundary between support for the Intifada—consisting for the most part of raising money for its Arab victims—and their own participation in it, a caution that served to emphasize their separateness.[76]

In the difficult days of the Intifada, one prominent Arab summed up the tortured position of his community, a people relegated to marginality among both Palestinians and Israelis: "They will not manage to draw the Intifadeh into the Green Line [the armistice line after the 1948 war, which appeared on the maps in green]. There is a difference between players and fans. We are the fans. Our goal is to live in Israel with equal rights, while the aim of the residents in the West Bank is to form a separate state."[77]

The Arabs of Israel made considerable gains in the country's strong economy and democratic political atmosphere. From a remnant of mostly fellaheen, shorn of leaders and institutions in 1948, they managed to rebuild a complex, stratified society, with a stable working class, a growing middle class of professionals and entrepreneurs, and its own talented cadre of intellectuals. As nearly a fifth of Israeli society, the Arabs became more and more aware of themselves as a community and more articulate about their needs.

At the same time, they continued to suffer through personal and national humiliations. In 1990, the beatings of Arabs on the street after one terrorist attack or another sent shudders through their community. So, too, did the anti-Arab legislation proposed in the Knesset, although the laws were rarely passed. (An example was an amendment to the Prevention of Terror ordinance of 1948, which would have allowed confiscation, without due process, of money from organizations receiving funds—knowingly or otherwise—from terrorist sources. Without defining the term "terrorist," the amendment would have put many Arab social service agencies, which received financing from abroad, into serious jeopardy; one Jewish Knesset member argued that the amendment was "nothing but a tool for political persecution."[78])

Continued discrimination, both at the personal level and in official policy, contributed in the period after 1967 to what one Arab scholar has termed "an intensive process of re-Palestinization"[79]—a process led by the new Arab elite. Nevertheless, the central motifs and symbols that became the building blocks of the new Palestinism—longing for the homeland, the conception of the Lost Garden, even the glorification of a piece of land or an olive tree—could not evoke the same powerful feelings for the Arabs in Israel, living in their original villages, as for those in ghurba, including residents of the far-off refugee camps.

Even the poetry, now as much a part of Israeli as Palestinian life, could not be as evocative. When, for example, Fadwa Tuqan wrote

> How can I see my land, my rights usurped,
> And remain here, a wanderer, with my shame?
> Shall I live here and die in a foreign land?
> No! I will return to my beloved land.
> I will return, and there
>   will I close the book of my life.[80]

she could bring empathy but not visceral identification. Anton Shammas, the best known of Israel's Arab writers, wrote his best-selling novel *Arabesques* in eloquent Hebrew. In this autobiographical account recalling his childhood in the village of Fassuta, he indicates how closely the Arabs in Israel are wedded to the Jewish culture around them—how their Palestinism is laced with what we might call their Israelism:

> My Jew will be an educated Arab. But not an intellectual. He does not gallop on the back of a thoroughbred mare, as was the custom at the turn of the century, nor is he a prisoner of the IDF [the Israel Defense Forces], as was the custom at the turn of the state [of Israel]. . . . He speaks and writes excellent Hebrew, but within the bounds of the permissible. For there must be some areas that are out of bounds for him, so nobody will accuse me of producing the stereotype in reverse, the virtuous Arab. He might be permitted the *Kaddish* [the Jewish prayer of mourning], as it were, but not the *Kol Nidre* [the Yom Kippur prayer]. And so on and so forth. A real minefield.[81]

The pain of this ambivalence emerges as yet another echo of the myth of Scylla and Charybdis. Twenty years before Shammas, another Palestinian in Israel noted, "I sometimes think that we are neither real Arabs nor real Israelis, because in the Arab countries they call us traitors, and in Israel, spies."[82] More recently, this refrain has been articulated by a teacher: "When I educate my pupils toward loyalty to the State I am considered a traitor . . . and when I emphasize the national character of my pupils and try to nurture in them a sense of national pride, I am told I am a traitor."[83] Such a mutual ill fit has relegated the Arabs of Israel to the sidelines in the nearly half century after al-Nakba. The central task of national reconstruction has fallen to those remaining outside Israel—both in Arab Palestine and in the new Palestinian communities beyond the borders of the old British mandate.

Dispersal, 1948–1967

O Lost Paradise! You were never
too small for us
But now vast countries are indeed
too small
Torn asunder your people
Wandering under every star.

—Mahmud al-Hut

In the century leading to 1948, the Crimean War, the First and Second World Wars, even the American Civil War had altered economic and social patterns in Palestine, on occasion taking the lives of its young men. But the Palestinians were essentially peripheral to such conflicts, and the wars themselves had not often intruded into their fundamental routines. With the founding of Israel, the situation changed completely—the Arab-Israeli wars of 1948, 1967, 1973 (to a lesser extent), and 1982 revolved around the question of Palestine's future: They wove themselves into the fabric of Palestinian Arab life and shaped the fate of the community as a whole.

As we have seen, following an extensive process of unravelling that had already begun after the UN partition resolution, the Palestinian community dissolved under the impact of the 1948 war. Seeming at first to represent only further displacement and defeat, the 1967 war in fact inaugurated a period of national reintegration and institutional renewal, along with the daily burdens of Israeli occupation. The intervening years marked a certain limbo. The Palestinians were severed from the old foundations of society and politics, scarred by exile, and still stunned by the fate that had befallen them. The leaders and formal groups characterizing the post-1967 era had not yet appeared on the scene. It was the moment in Palestinian history most bereft of hope.

With 1948, in the words of Fawaz Turki, "The nation of Palestine ceased to be. Its original inhabitants, the Palestinian people, were dubbed Arab refugees, sent regular food rations by the UN, and forgotten by the world."[1] After Palestine's dust began to settle, a migration began from the hilly regions, out of the old villages and towns and out of the refugee camps, not to the coast, as in previous times, but to distant places outside Palestine. To the degree that there was any remaining Palestinian cultural center, it was Nablus, now the largest entirely Palestinian town. While Jerusalem retained its religious stature and some of its old administrative role, it was a diminished city under the Jordanians, who jealously guarded the prerogatives of their capital Amman. Never a significant economic center (apart from tourism and some commercial enterprises for the eastern part of the country), it had suffered through emigration, combat, and finally, partition between Jordan and Israel. Severed from its economic lifeline, the road to the Mediterranean coast, "it became an economic backwater."[2] With their traditional hinterlands and markets cut off, smaller towns such as Tulkarm, Jenin, and Qalqilya turned towards Nablus as the leading economic center of the West Bank.

Because of the steady erosion of peasant life, along, now, with the physical fragmentation of the Palestinian community, this preeminence was shaky at best. It contended with an increasing outward migration, motivated by economic survival and educational opportunity, to various countries, mainly in other parts of the Middle East, which became Palestinian satellite centers. (The American University in Beirut and the American University in Cairo became their most prominent institutions.) Taking on the role previously served by Jaffa, these centers reflected the influence of European, world-market values, challenging the cultural dominance of Palestine's eastern heartland, symbolized by Nablus.

As in the past, such values offered the basis of an alternative national leadership. The conditions prevailing between 1948 and 1967, even more than those during the mandate, undermined the claims of the old notable leaders. But this time, their demise was complete. In 1948, Amin al-Husseini established the All Palestine Government in Gaza. Those who stayed with him found it reduced within a few years by the Egyptians and the Arab League to window dressing. And those who threw in their lot with the Hashemites in Jordan, once it annexed the West Bank after the 1948 war, discovered that the attractive governmental positions they were offered only alienated them from the Palestinian population.[3] In ghurba, the ayan could not salvage their special status.

Ironically, when a new national leadership finally emerged in the 1960s, its experience would in some ways mirror the ayan's, as it found itself distant from those it sought to lead. After 1948, four out of every five Palestinians remained within the former mandate's territory, even if most could no longer return to their homes. But the leadership would grow disproportionately from those who had migrated, both to the Middle East and to the West.

In the period of the mandate, the idea of a Palestinian people distinct from other Arabs and Muslims had originated with members of the ayan, eventually moving down to other groups as well. After al-Nakba, this process was reversed: Former fellaheen and workers—and especially their children—many cramped in squalid refugee camps, defined a new Palestinian consciousness. To be sure, there were numerous important links between the old and new types of Palestinian nationalism, but the "bottom-up" nature of the new type had a distinctly different character.

The 20 percent of Palestinian Arabs who left Palestine went to Lebanon (over 100,000) and Syria (75,000–90,000), as well as to Iraq (4,000) and Egypt (7,000–10,000) (see map 4). In time, the steady emigration would result in exiled Palestinians outnumbering their brethren,[4] with formidable communities emerging in Kuwait (nearly 400,000 until the 1991 Gulf War), Saudi Arabia (150,000), other Gulf states (65,000), and the United States (100,000). But in the crucial, disorienting period following the 1948 war, the three communities within the old boundaries of British Palestine (the West Bank and the Gaza Strip, in particular, but also Palestinian Arabs in Israel) were instrumental in defining ghurba, not necessarily as exile from the country, but as displacement from original homes, villages, neighborhoods, and lands (see map 5). Long afterward, these refugees helped shape the national Palestinian aspiration as one for a homeland, rather than merely for a return to Palestine.[5]

FIRST STEPS TOWARDS A NEW IDENTITY:
JORDAN AND THE PALESTINIANS

The evictions and mass flight of the 1948 war had taken place in Palestine's coastal plain, the Galilee, and the south, while the eastern region—encompassing Al-Khalil (Hebron), Ramallah, Nablus, Tulkarm, Jenin, and the Arab part of Jerusalem—which would be grafted onto Transjordan, remained largely intact. More than half of the pre-war Palestinian population of over 1.3 million was in the area now called the West Bank, the elements of its previous society still in place at the end of the war. Nevertheless, life would not be what it had been; demography and politics were the grounds of the transformation.

Only in the Gaza Strip was the pressure caused by the influx of refugees more intense than in Jordan. The population of the West Bank had grown from 400,000 to more than 700,000. While it would stabilize after 1948, this influx of desperate refugees strained all existing resources.[6] Approximately a third of the newcomers ended up in refugee camps, another third in villages, and the remainder in towns.[7] If the eastward migrations during the Arab Revolt and at the start of World War II had strained village and town institutions, the 1948 migrations simply overwhelmed them.

Demographic pressure was particularly intense along the new armistice lines with Israel.[8] Deprived of their fertile fields to the west, old villages had to turn to poorer land in the rocky hills. They also had to contend with over 130 new villages appearing between 1948 and 1967. For decades, the Palestinians had steadily moved from being part of a largely peasant society to one centered in towns and cities. And that process—Zureik's "depeasantification"—accelerated after 1948.[9] Nevertheless, Palestinians in Jordan sustained and nurtured the idea of themselves as a people of the soil, fostering symbols of lost olive trees and vineyards.

Interconnected with the impact of this population rise on both the physical and social landscape, a new set of questions emerged concerning social structure and Palestinian self-definition. Since its implanting in what became Transjordan at the beginning of the 1920s, the Hashemite dynasty under King Abdallah had tried to bind diverse peoples and tribes into a cohesive whole. After 1948, the Jordanian regime began to treat the Palestinians as but one more group or tribe that would contribute to the process of the Jordanization of the country.

For Abdallah and his regime, this would have seemed a realistic enough goal: After all, the ties between Palestinians and Jordan were not remote. In 1920, Palestinian activists had stood with the Hashemites as Abdallah's brother, Faysal, made his bid to rule Syria. In fact, part of the British compensation to the Hashemites for their loss in Syria had been a carving out, from the territory envisioned by both Zionist and Palestinian Arab leaders as part of the new Palestine mandate, of the Emirate of Transjordan for Abdallah.

With Palestinians staffing key political institutions, Abdallah had seen the territory as a beachhead for eventual rule of a larger kingdom, including Palestine, Syria, and Lebanon—and possibly other parts of the Fertile Crescent.[10] With its Islamic sites and shrines, most notably those in Jerusalem, Palestine played a large role in these ambitions, the Emir welcoming Palestinians as a reservoir of skilled and educated manpower from the time he won a degree of limited autonomy for Transjordan in 1923 (Britain granted independence only in 1946). In 1924, when Sir John Philby, the British High Commissioner for the Emirate, was replaced with Colonel P. Cox, the latter reorganized the Emirate's civil service—expelling all the Istiqlal members, who had fled from Syria in 1920 and had formed the early backbone of Abdallah's administration—with British-trained Palestinians. Roughly 10,000 took up the welcome, serving as bureaucrats, educators, businessmen, and financiers, in Amman and elsewhere.

When Abdallah's Arab Legion moved over the border into Palestine in 1948, the new Transjordanian state took on the challenge of expanding more than its territorial boundaries.[11] Longstanding relations with key Palestinian families such as the Nashashibis—the leading opposition to the Husseinis—may have encouraged Abdallah to believe that smooth absorption and integration of the Palestinians was possible. It is difficult to know whether he hoped from the start to completely replace Palestinian and other parochial identities with a tight-knit Jordanian nation.[12] In any event, after al-Nakba, he declared Jordan the only legitimate inheritor of Arab Palestine (a policy that the state more or less maintained until 1988). Abdallah's regime banned the use of the word Palestine—substituting the term

West Bank in most cases. (There is thus an odd irony to the present Palestinian insistence on use of this term to confirm national identity, fighting off the Israeli effort to substitute the biblical "Judea and Samaria.") Even if Abdallah was not thinking in terms of complete assimilation—a loss of Palestinian self-definition—at the very least he believed that bringing the West Bank and its population under his control would not shake the foundations of his dynasty and his state, its social and political balance. (This offers a pronounced contrast to Lebanon, whose leaders deeply feared an upsetting by the refugees of the country's fragile equilibrium.)

In order to consolidate its control over the Palestinians, the Jordanian state executed policies on political and social levels. Following the 1948 war, it arranged two Palestinian national congresses, which provided the appearance of mastery by the Palestinians over their own political futures (although, in fact, these were largely staged events). The congresses rejected the Mufti's continuing bid for leadership through the All Palestine Government in Gaza and called upon His Majesty, King Abdallah to unify the West Bank with Jordan—"as a prelude to the unification of all the Arabs."

At both congresses, aides to Abdallah worked hard to stifle differences between the Palestinian perspective and that of the king. To a large extent, the disagreements revolved around the Palestinian insistence that the king publicly commit himself to reunifying all of Palestine and eliminating both the Jewish state and Zionist community that had settled the land—a position that ran counter to the spirit of his ongoing negotiations with the Zionist (now Israeli) leadership. Over the next two decades, first Abdallah's policies, then those of his successor King Hussein, toed a fine line between maintaining nonbelligerent relations with Israel and convincing Palestinians the regime was adequately representing them in their struggle for repatriation. In 1956, the director of UNRWA (the United Nations Relief and Works Agency) reported to the General Assembly that the Palestinian refugees "bitterly oppose anything which has even the semblance of permanent settlement elsewhere."[13] With Palestinians at the bottom of the social scale now thus defining the parameters of an emerging new Palestinism, the Jordanian government's one serious bid to resettle the refugees foundered on the rocks of their opposition.[14]

The regime also weighted representation in its own institutions to favor the minority of non-Palestinians, and it clamped down on any exclusively Palestinian political institutions. In this way, Abdallah eliminated any semblance of Palestinian political autonomy. During the 1948 war, the Arab Legion had already disbanded Palestinian political organizations and fighting groups in the areas it occupied; now it set the stage for absorption of Palestinians into Jordanian state political institutions, staffed by a combination of East Bankers and Palestinians—the ayan's remnants, along with other local Palestinian leaders, some eventually becoming prime ministers. And Jordan was the only state besides Syria that accorded the Palestinians citizenship en masse: Two-thirds of all Palestinians ended up as Jordanian citizens.

In the social sphere, the Jordanian state acted on a number of fronts. It established a comprehensive educational system for the East and West Banks to help promote a harmonious, Jordanian social whole. At the same time, it established a number of welfare and development agencies to assist refugees and others affected by the recent traumatic events. As in the period before 1948, it encouraged the gradual settlement of Palestinians on the East Bank. And, not least of all, the state used active suppression and repression to prevent any public voicing of a national Palestinian identity. Following Abdallah's 1951 assassination in Jerusalem at the hands of a Palestinian, and the abdication of Abdallah's son, Talal, because of failing mental health, his young grandson, Hussein, succeeded to the throne in 1953; his policies regarding the Palestinians did not significantly change direction.

These policies had in fact born some fruit, Abdallah succeeding for a time in building significant support among many Palestinians. For most, their loyalty rested on the hope that he could "liberate" Palestine and bring about their repatriation. They expressed a Jordanian identity passively, through simple acceptance of the new political order; had Jordanian rule continued beyond two decades, it perhaps would have eventually absorbed most West Bankers.

Some wealthier Palestinians—including those from the old notable families—feeling a stigma in being Palestinians, went further than offering such loyalty, taking on Jordanian identities.[15] While, as Brand indicates, the Jordanian effort to eliminate Palestinian nationalism played a part in the process, the effort also ran up against formidable obstacles: A tiny state, scarcely a society, was attempting to impose itself on a larger, more educated, and urbane community. From the day of annexation, Palestinians outnumbered the original Jordanians two to one. The West Bank remained exclusively Palestinian, a potential breeding ground for nationalist revival, while the East Bank was a heterogeneous mixture of Palestinians and others.[16]

Those others, the 350,000–400,000 people of the East Bank prior to the 1948 war, had much lower levels of literacy (Jordanian schools had enrolled about a quarter of school-age children; Palestinian schools, approximately half).[17] Nearly half the Transjordanians had been nomadic Bedouins; another third, small peasant farmers; most of the rest, residents of four towns whose population had ranged from 10,000 to 30,000. Amman, the capital and largest of the towns, has been described as "a hamlet with unpaved roads in the nineteen-thirties."[18] As a point of contrast, ten cities in Palestine had more than 10,000 Arabs before 1948, and three (Jaffa, Haifa, and Jerusalem), more than 60,000.[19] The more skilled Palestinians now overwhelmed the original Jordanian population in many domains—its Bedouin core only kept control of key political ministries and the army through skillful manipulation.[20]

The differences are even more striking if we take account of the distribution of Palestinians in the kingdom. The elite—the notables, merchants (particularly Christian businessmen), and professionals—settled in West and East Bank towns. Uneducated fellaheen disproportionately filled the refugee camps on both sides of the Jordan River.[21] In short, when Palestinian society began to recrystallize in Jordan, it followed the old patterns of stratification from the mandate: Palestinians living in cities were even more likely to be skilled and educated, competing for key economic and political posts.

Continuing migration to the East Bank only reinforced their dominance. The flow began during the 1948 debacle, and by 1952 over 100,000 Palestinians had crossed the river, many settling in the urban areas. Today, well over 1,000,000 of the more than 2,000,000 East Bankers are Palestinians.[22] Their absorption into Jordan was further complicated by the organization of refugee society, especially in the camps, and the discrimination against the West Bank (21 of the 24 camps were west of the

Jordan River).[23] The camps created a new Jordanian underclass, only marginally integrated into the national economy at the end of the 1940s. Opportunities for wage labor fell far short of available supply.[24] Agriculture was able to absorb some camp dwellers as laborers and sharecroppers, but this was limited by slow advances in farming technology and a severe shortage of cultivable land and water—only about a fifth of the refugees actually remained in farming, although many continued to think of themselves as fellaheen. The economic difficulties were reflected in abject conditions in the camps, where families lived in makeshift tents, replaced after five or six years by small shacks made from concrete blocks and covered with corrugated metal.

Rapid economic growth, beginning in the late 1950s and gaining momentum in the half-dozen years leading up to the 1967 war, did spur greater Palestinian integration. So did a project of irrigation and electrification: the East Ghor Canal Project, opening land in the eastern Jordan Valley (the state could not complete it, nor the land distribution that went along with it, before the war).[25] But that first decade of hardship after 1948 had helped set the Palestinians apart. Cut off from the national economy, the refugee camps tended to be societies unto themselves, and the rest of the West Bank also suffered from exceedingly low investment. This was partly because of the low savings rate there, and partly because of the state's preference for East Bank investment.[26]

A key factor in reinforcing the isolation of the refugees was UNRWA. Established by the U.N. in late 1949 as a response to the refugee crisis,[27] the agency gradually became a kind of overpowering paternal force. Most camp dwellers depended on it for their sustenance, especially in the early years after the exodus,[28] marked by severe economic depression in Jordan and known as "the years of famine." Besides the rations it provided, the agency promoted many Palestinians into staff positions; its teachers, in particular, would form the basis of a new Palestinian leadership. In general, some of UNRWA's most notable achievements have involved education, improving on the desultory efforts of the British, especially for girls.

Although the agency took on an odd sort of permanence for the refugees, it also represented the impermanence of their situation: a beneficent host insuring material necessities until they could return to their homes and land. Originating, again, at the bottom of society, that sense of impermanence became a mark of the emerging Palestinian consciousness. The camps thus served as its reinforcers and rebuilders, rather than as conduits into a Jordanian social whole. (Although the Jordanian regime did try to maintain a semblance of control by demanding its headquarters be in Amman, UNRWA was largely independent.) The refugees' isolation reinforced not only family and clan ties, but those of neighborhoods and villages. Unlike Palestinians outside the camps, those in the camps, forming approximately a quarter of Jordan's population, provided almost no representatives to national political institutions—not a single one to Parliament between 1950 and 1965.[29]

At times, the refugees even managed to establish public institutions and symbols to express the reformulation of their identity. Their al-Wahda soccer team, for instance, won the Jordanian championship, as well as the avid support of Palestinians throughout Jordan. Even Arabs in Israel became fans when it beat the Ramtha team, symbolizing the East Bank and loyalty to the kingdom. Having a good understanding of the team's significance, the Jordanians reorganized and renamed it, adding non-Palestinian players to its roster.

The camp and area committees, occasionally formed by elders, village mukhtars, and notables in the immediate aftermath of the 1948 war, were less successful than the soccer team.[30] Their purpose was to represent refugee interests to the Jordanian and international authorities (the UN and various relief agencies such as the Red Cross) on questions of aid, the status of property in Israel, and so on. But they were undercut by old rivalries of clan and region and by differing interests among camp dwellers, such as the divisions between those who had owned land and those who had not. About the only division that did not reappear in the camp was that between Christians and Muslims, since the camps were 99 percent Muslim. Active interference by Jordanian officials in the committees' nomination process also kept them weak and ineffective. The government disbanded a number after receiving complaints of favoritism, jealousy, and so forth. It also kept a close and suspicious eye on any groups seeking to represent general Palestinian interests.

The most serious challenge to Jordan's claim to representation came through the General Refugee Congress, organized in Ramallah in March, 1949. The Congress empowered delegates to negotiate with Israel at forthcoming armistice talks, but they were rebuffed by the Jordanians, by other Arab delegations (which had their own advisory refugee contingent), and by Israel (which sought to deal exclusively with Arab states). It lasted as an organization into 1950 but faced opposition from all sides, including poorer refugees who felt it represented rich landowners, and other Palestinians who looked for their salvation in Arab unity.[31]

In the first decade after al-Nakba, political impotence and the failure to construct meaningful public institutions fueled the disorientation and petty bickering rife among the Palestinians. But ground-level activities (charitable, professional, and cultural) quietly continued. While they did not carry explicit Palestinian messages or symbols, organizations such as the Jaffa Muslim Sports Club and the Haifa Cultural Association (in Nablus) had an exclusively Palestinian membership; they helped both to keep alive the memory of now inaccessible places and to create new bases of association among West Bankers in their changed circumstances—often, ironically, with the support of funds from the government in Amman.

In a broader manner, the intensity of their shared experience in refugee camps and their strong sense of having suffered a common injustice helped preserve and reshape a solidarity evident even in the context of feuding and resentment. This solidarity was strengthened all the more by the West Bank's local population, which had become irritated by the refugees—they "occupied public buildings (mosques, schools, etc.), encroached on farm land, picked local crops, used scarce local water, and so on."[32] Much of that population, particularly in the border areas, expressed dismay as refugees infiltrated into Israel in desperate attempts to regain property left behind or to harvest crops, thereby prompting severe Israeli retaliation. But such divisions did not prevent the gradual development of a sense of suffering a common fate.[33]

In face of such feelings—rather than any overt political organization—the minimal political stability Abdallah had counted on when he annexed the West Bank proved highly elusive. By the mid-1950s, the Hashemite regime was confronting new factors, pan-Arab and pan-Islamic, that both further impeded Palestinian assimilation and gnawed away at this stability.

Several years after Nasser's 1952 revolution, pan-Arabism penetrated the West Bank, along with the rest of the Middle East. Perhaps no Arabs had more to gain than the Palestinians from the denigration of specific loyalties (Iraqi, Egyptian—indeed Palestinian) in favor of devotion to broader Arab unity, and they became among pan-Arabism's most fervent exponents.[34] They were, as a Palestinian who had been a member of the Communist party put it, "more Nasserist than Nasser."[35] Pan-Arabism's emphasis on national liberation, both social and political, transformed the Palestinian dilemma from the particular to the general—it placed this dilemma in the broader historical context of the regeneration of the entire Arab people, their shedding of imperialism's shackles.

The lure of pan-Arabism was not a totally new phenomenon in Palestinian intellectual circles. Following World War I, the Palestinian alliance with Faysal, in his bid to wrest control of Syria from the French and establish a broad Hashemite kingdom, had strong pan-Arab overtones. Then too, the tension between pan-Arabism and the more exclusivist Palestinian nationalism derived from the special challenges of Zionism: Generalizing these challenges offered an attractive route towards broad mobilization against Jewish encroachment in the Middle East.

If Arab disunity was responsible for the fiasco of 1948, as Musa Alami and other Palestinian nationalists argued, then Arab unity could undo the writ of exile.[36] An Egyptian newspaper noted in 1963, "If there is any absolute and complete joy to Arabs in the establishment of a large, new and united state, it is the joy of the Palestinians. . . . The Palestinians see in the new state the beginning of their salvation from the suffering, humiliation, dispersion and despair with which they have been living for fifteen years. . . . Arab union is the only path by which they will regain their natural existence."[37] In Jordan, the combination of the voice of Arab unity emanating from Egypt and the active support of Palestinians and others from within appeared to threaten the kingdom's basis in 1956 (marked by particularly serious demonstrations and riots) and 1957: "To many Palestinians, complete Arab unity seemed just around the corner."[38]

Pan-Islam also served to generalize the Palestinian issue, tapping deep-seated loyalties among the Muslim majority, while of course once again excluding the sizeable Christian minority. It did not develop anywhere near the organization and momentum of pan-Arabism at the time, but it did evoke sentiments that many Palestinians considered far more important than those represented by fashionable contemporary ideologies. Like pan-Arabism, it rejected Western imperialism, understood as the vehicle for Zionism's success.

Many of the political parties then active in other Arab countries of the Middle East, offering their own social vision to the Palestinians, established legal and underground branches in Jordan. In the early 1950s, a number of younger Palestinians tried to create a new leadership through these parties, which—in the confusion and grinding poverty—failed to attract a significant following. (The largest had only 300–350 members, recruiting students and teachers while ignoring workers and peasants).[39] In any event, after an attempted coup—growing pan-Arabism in the Middle East and pressure by the United States to join a new anti-Communist security alliance, the Baghdad Pact, had created increasing unrest in Jordan—Hussein cracked down, banning all parties in April, 1957; although several continued to exist underground, they thus closed, as would other forms of public life, as avenues for Palestinian political expression.

Not least of the factors contributing to this dead end was the failure of unity talks among Egypt, Syria, and Iraq in 1963.[40] Arab unity held "an irresistible fascination for all political parties in the West Bank, even those parties whose self-proclaimed ideal was primarily a new social or religious, rather than national, order in the area."[41] The failure of the unity talks—like the French rout of Faysal in 1920—deepened a painful period of reassessment that began in the late 1950s, leading towards a renewed commitment to Palestinian self-reliance. But as previously, the tension between pan-Arabism and Palestinism would not entirely disappear in the 1960s; rather more recently, we have seen the former option loom large again in Palestinian support for Saddam Hussein.

A PALESTINIAN RESERVATION AND THE EMERGENCE OF CAMP SOCIETY

Nowhere did Palestinians find more brutal conditions than in the Gaza Strip, the single, tiny part of Palestine remaining in the hands of the Egyptian army after its humiliating defeat in the

1948 war. Approximately 28 miles in length and 5 miles in width, it became one of the most densely settled regions in the world. With three-quarters of Gaza's Palestinians living in eight refugee camps, even the small comforts that Jordan could provide were absent here. Jordan's population growth came disproportionately in the rural areas, as displaced fellaheen attempted to regain some foothold in agriculture. In Gaza, where most refugees were fellaheen and agriculture continued to employ approximately a third of those able to find work, overall opportunities were so limited that, by 1967, 80 percent of the Palestinians were urban—one of the highest rates in Asia. Border villages and towns on the West Bank had lost their agricultural zones and their accustomed markets in 1948, but in Gaza the losses were much more devastating: Of the 5,000 acres of citrus plantations, barely 1,000 remained; of the 250,000 acres of grain-growing land in the Negev, less than 10 percent was still accessible.[42] In fact, only 2.5 percent of the original Gaza District remained as part of the Strip.[43] Some Palestinians, especially those who made their way to the East Bank, assimilated into the upper echelons of Jordanian society; Gazan refugees (except for a very small number of Jaffa upper-class families) failed to accomplish a similar feat.[44]

For all the upheaval Jordan's Palestinians faced, their society still retained vestiges of the past and of normalcy: farms, villages, towns and cities, citizenship, even, for a time, a lively political arena. Those in Gaza had no such vestiges. Gaza became the quintessential representation of a new culture—what we might call camp society.

The Gaza Strip's moment of political glory came with the establishment in 1948 of the Mufti-inspired All Palestine Government, with Gaza City as its provisional capital.[45] With thriving citrus exports as its lone claim to some centrality, the Gaza region had long been a fairly peripheral corner of Palestine (the poorest in the country during the mandate period). Now, it rode the back of Arab League and Egyptian power to become the nucleus of a Palestinian state. But the effort was short-lived; even the government's chosen name contained a strong dose of irony: Without control of more than a symbolic remnant of Palestinian territory, it fell upon the same hard times as other governments-in-exile in the mid-twentieth century. A number of key officials "deserted" to Jordan. Others faced the reality of an authority derived exclusively from their benefactors, Egypt and the Arab League. In September, 1952, the League dissolved the All Palestine Government and empowered the Arab states to represent the Palestinian cause.

Grim poverty and social misery became the defining characteristics of the Gaza Strip. Personal income was among the lowest in the world (one source put the figure at $80 per capita per year).[46] The Egyptian government denied Gaza's Palestinians even the limited opportunities for institution building and political participation (including citizenship) that the Jordanians granted Palestinians. After the failure of the All Palestine Government, the only attempt under Egyptian rule to carve out some political autonomy came with the establishment of an elected Council of Representatives, nominated by local committees and not destined to enjoy great success. The Egyptians reserved a meaningful political role for the already-powerful Gazan families, the mass of camp refugees finding themselves, as in Jordan, almost entirely excluded from formal public life. To the extent that the Egyptian authorities dealt with them at all, they did so through pre-1948 institutions such as the village mukhtar.[47] In 1955, the Egyptian government also selected refugees for units of fedayeen to take part in operations against Israel. This offered some important military experience, and common lore has it that the veterans of such actions became the nucleus for resistance against Israeli military occupation after 1967. But the units were always under strict Egyptian control.

Like the people crammed in there, the political status of the Gaza Strip remained in limbo from 1948 on. Egypt did not annex it, as the Jordanians had the West Bank, which reinforced a sense of temporariness—now prevailing for almost half a century—on the part of the refugees. Egypt maintained its dominion for two decades (losing control briefly between October, 1956, and January, 1957, as a result of the Sinai war), and the Israelis have held it, also without annexation, since the 1967 war. Even more than in Jordan, the "permanence of temporariness" became an emblem of Gazan society.

Egyptian government policies and the sentiments of the refugees themselves transformed the Gaza Strip into a closed reservation in the 20 years following the 1948 war. Anxious about the effects of Palestinian influx on the stability of Egyptian politics and the level of competition in the workforce, first the monarchy and then its successor, the Nasser-led regime, restricted migration from the Strip into Egypt proper. One exception was the opening of Egyptian universities to Palestinians; another, the granting of jobs as village teachers to Palestinian graduates of UNRWA vocational schools. But the border was basically sealed, and emergency law was administered by the military there until 1962. After the Sinai war, the Egyptians began to incorporate some Palestinians into the Strip's administration, along with easing some of their restrictions.

For their part, the refugees, like their counterparts in Jordan, rejected several Egyptian resettlement schemes, including one that, with UNRWA support, would have diverted Nile waters into the nearly empty Sinai Desert.[48]

As was the case in Lebanon, under these circumstances, "the only strangers who ventured into the camps were cops, invariably drunken ones at that and in groups."[49] Despite the fact that it held the second largest concentration of Palestinians, Gaza would fail to become a center of new Palestinian institution building as a result of Egyptian repression. Its contribution lay rather in the realm of consciousness and identity. The character of the society that developed there was unique, weaving memories and culture from pre-war Palestine with the poverty-stricken, harrowing life in the camps.

Deprived of its traditional agricultural lands, the Strip became an economic cripple, even the original population losing most of its previous sources of income. The refugees' income was limited principally to UNRWA aid, Egyptian administrative and military expenditures, and the smuggling of goods through the port of Gaza into Egypt. Almost no industry developed, so entrepreneurial activity was channeled into commerce, the most important means for penetrating the wall that seemed to surround the Strip. Gaza became a kind of duty-free port, which prompted the smuggling, along with shopping sprees by Egyptians wishing to circumvent the high taxes in Egypt.

Gaza's commercial life picked up when Nasser moved towards closer relations with the Soviet Union in the latter half of the 1950s. Farmers, merchants, and smugglers took advantage of the markets opening in Eastern Europe, the Gazan citrus industry expanding more than tenfold to meet the increased demand. The East Europeans exchanged construction materials and machinery for the exports.[50] In turn, many of those goods went to Lebanon for consumer items—the ones that, along with locally made goods such as wool rugs, attracted the Egyptians to shop in Gaza. Some merchants managed to prosper in this manner, but for most, economic conditions remained extraordinarily difficult—even the money sent home by those who had migrated faced stiff Egyptian currency controls.

Such migration gained momentum in the second decade of Egyptian rule, bringing badly needed income to hard-pressed families. But Gaza also paid a price for the migration, those with education, training, and some resources being the first to leave. Following the trail of petrodollars, they went to Saudi Arabia, Kuwait, Qatar, Bahrain. The result was that Gaza was left virtually without an intellectual or professional class. More than any other territory, the section of Palestinian society it harbored was homogeneous. Even before the start of the professionals' emigration, 65 percent of the refugees were classified as unskilled laborers or agricultural workers, and an estimated 90 percent were illiterate.[51]

Camp society developed distinct features from country to country and camp to camp. Those surrounding Beirut, for example, were unusual for the high proportion of their work force in industry: the camp of Tal al-Zaatar had 60 percent of its total force employed in the nearby industrial area of Mukallas, the refugees working, as usual, without government papers and thus tending to receive lower pay and fewer rights than Lebanese workers.[52] The Rashidiyya camp near Tyre developed as a reservoir for agricultural labor on the plantations of local wealthy landholders.[53]

Important similarities also developed among the camps. The Palestinian sociologist Bassem Sirhan has argued that "in fact such differences as exist consist of a descending scale of general physical conditions—space, housing, basic amenities, etc. . . . those in Lebanon and the West Bank ranking highest, Syria and Jordan next and Gaza lowest."[54]

In all camps, UNRWA was an overpowering presence—what Turki has referred to as "our contemptuous stepmother."[55] Oth-

ers compared UNRWA services to "a shot of morphine," a pal-
liative that could not cure the refugee's basic alienation.[56] Its
educational and employment projects, and of course its direct
relief aid, were nevertheless of obvious value in helping Palestinians reconstitute their lives after 1948. The old institutions of
family, clan, and village also offered support in the face of a
strange and often hostile new environment. Life in the camps
thus mirrored normal Palestinian life before the war, tending to
reinforce—indeed, even reinvigorate—its social institutions.

This trend was highly evident in Gaza, where the centrality of
such institutions was kept alive not only by the actions of the
Palestinians themselves, but also by the policies of Egyptian
officials and relief workers: In the initial confusion of the refugee influx, Quaker relief workers struggled to reestablish village
groupings and administer programs through the old village leadership.[57] The very process focused attention on the life that had
been lost. "If a refugee in Gaza is asked where he comes from, he
will answer with the name of his original village whether or not
that village still stands; that is where his roots lie."[58] Fawaz
Turki has commented on the recreation of Palestinian identity
in exile:

> The social structure of the Palestinian family, whose atmosphere
> engendered a deep and constant hope for the return to Palestine,
> and the official discrimination against the refugee himself, cre-
> ated pressures that served to perpetuate the notion in the mind of
> the young Palestinian that he was the member of a minority, thus
> enhancing his Palestinian consciousness. In his home a Palestin-
> ian child, whether born in Beirut, Amman, or Damascus, would
> be instructed to identify himself as a Palestinian from Haifa or
> Lydda or any other town that had been his parents' birthplace,
> and his own experience would constantly remind him of this.[59]

Within the gap between remembered home and present circumstances lay deep wells of bitterness, directed at those considered the usurpers, the Israelis. Writing from the Middle East in
1951 and 1952, Stewart Alsop described the refugees as surrounding Israel "with an iron ring of hate," the refugee camps as "a reservoir of smoldering antagonism against the State of Israel and its
Western backers."[60] But the alienation was not only from the de-

spised Israelis. Perhaps no better indicator exists of the profound segregation between Egyptians, Lebanese, and Jordanians, on the one side, and the refugees they hosted, on the other, than the marriage barriers that developed. Even in the absence of religious differences, there was no common market of brides and grooms.

The social institutions of the camp created this invisible wall, drawing the refugees away from confrontation with larger Arab society,[61] into a world of memory—and, as memory itself dimmed, into their mythological Lost Garden of Palestine.[62] The Garden contrasted starkly with present conditions—poverty, humiliation, and the sense of loss of control over their personal and collective futures. At the same time, the isolation of the camps exacerbated a widespread disdain for the refugees. (Turki evokes this disdain in the form of a banal Lebanese epithet, "two-bit Palestinian."[63]) Both the isolation and disdain fed the slow formation of a new "diaspora consciousness," and an institutional infrastructure to support it.

It was not that Palestinians failed to venture outside the camps—which in Lebanon, especially, tended to be located on the edges of important cities. They did so frequently (adults and children alike, especially males), even if few city residents reciprocated. Many camps soon became strange suburbs for the cities they bordered. Surrounding land values were often quite high, and, as birth rates soared and the camps gained population, state officials took steps to make sure that the refugees' dwellings did not spread beyond the established boundaries. The result was a sort of involuted expansion, the camps becoming increasingly dense environments. Brick-built homes replaced the original tents and subsequent shacks, contrasting with the traditional Palestinian stone houses. Some poor Lebanese and Syrians, unable to find affordable housing in the cities, added to the burden by moving in.

Efforts to eke out a few square meters more for housing put intense pressure on any remaining space for mosques, schools, clinics, and the like. Sanitation and other public services, handled by UNRWA and the host municipalities, also suffered from severe neglect. Eventually water and sewage systems, indoor toilets, electricity, and even paved streets began to appear in the camps, but their escalating population kept public services at frighteningly inadequate levels. Like the hostility of nearby cities, the suffocating living conditions reinforced the distinctive-ness of camp life. Studying together in segregated schools (in Lebanon, no Palestinians attended public schools), playing to-gether in narrow alleys, sitting together in all-Palestinian cafes, the refugees developed a society—even with incessant, interne-cine conflict and a leadership that proved constantly inadequate.

The old village and town leadership continued to play a role in camp life until 1968—in Gaza, as we have seen, they were used as go-betweens by the Egyptians. But with the drastic decline in their power and authority before 1948, they now possessed very little real authority. In their place, economic entrepreneurs qui-etly began to vie for leadership, one variety being a new kind of go-between: the *rais* (boss, head). The rais would act as a con-tractor supplying agricultural and industrial laborers for nearby fields and companies, thus building important economic rela-tionships outside the camp. In time, he would offer an array of other services, including permission to move within those coun-tries where the Palestinians lacked official papers. Economically desperate refugees would pay him in both cash and loyalty.

With growing prosperity in Lebanon beginning in the 1950s and Jordan in the 1960s, many Arabs sank their savings into new homes, a traditional sign of prestige. A number of Palestinians became building contractors, accumulating significant wealth. Some of these contractors chose to escape camp life altogether, but many others became the new upper class of the camps, and another power center, surrounding themselves with entourages of relatives and friends.

Camps in the West Bank, Lebanon, and—to some degree—Syria thus began to take on a more complex social structure. Nevertheless, while exerting some influence and wielding some power, neither the old leadership nor the new entrepreneurs played a powerful role in the reshaping of a destroyed society, or managed, in fact, to rise above a purely local level. Many shied away from overt political participation altogether. They con-fronted a scattering of the Palestinian community, a distinct limit to the resources for developing leverage, and a grave risk in associating too closely with the host authorities. For the time being, the definition of what it meant to be a Palestinian seemed to grow spontaneously from the community's poorest, most hard-pressed members, the former fellaheen who made up the bulk of camp society.

FIRST STEPS TOWARDS REGENERATION:
EDUCATION AND MOBILITY

The ambivalent feelings that Palestinians harbored for UNRWA did not belie its importance. Although UNRWA adopted the school curricula of each host state (in Lebanon, Lebanese history; in Jordan, Jordanian history), it was solely responsible for elementary education, which became nearly universal. By the 1980s, 95 percent of all refugee children attended school at the elementary and preparatory levels,[64] one study noting that "never before in the Arab Middle East has there been as inclusive an educational system as that of the UNRWA, reaching as it does to all classes and both sexes."[65] This resulted in both the employment of many teachers and the creation of an educated generation of Palestinians, whose essential, marketable resource would be skills based on that very education. Offering the hope of "economic security in a situation where political security was virtually unachievable,"[66] and of escape from the misery of camp life, it was a strategy for survival.[67] For this reason, as one of the first teachers there has indicated, even before UNRWA established itself in the Gaza Strip, groups of Palestinians and relief workers

> began recruiting teachers for a rudimentary teaching programme. They only took people who had a secondary school education—I think there were about 80 such people in the whole Strip at that time—so I began working in 1949 as a volunteer teacher. We were all volunteers then and we used to get paid two sacks of flour per month. . . . When I think back over this period, the thing that sticks clearest in my mind is just how enthusiastic we all were—teachers and pupils. I suppose for the refugees who had lost all their possessions, there was nothing else but to learn. But I also think that there was a very strong sense that we were taking things into our own hands and building our own future. Believe me, I am not the only one who thinks that things were better then with the sacks of flour than they are now with all the UNRWA dollars.[68]

A Lebanese refugee has echoed these sentiments: "In spite of all this [the pitiful conditions of the camp], we had faith that there was no road but education."[69] Sayigh has raised doubts as to whether the sacrifices involved in sending children to school were worth the payoff: The education itself was often of poor quality, there was a general fall-off in enrollment after age 14, and the opportunities for most youngsters, even with this elementary education, were severely limited.[70] What is certain is that by the 1950s, "for all but the wealthy, UNRWA schools remained virtually the only avenue to higher education."[71] From the early 1950s, the small but growing stream of secondary-school graduates found places in universities in Egypt, Syria, Lebanon, Western Europe, and North America. The establishment of a Jordanian university in 1962 was, in large part, a Palestinian undertaking, and its faculty and students were both disproportionately Palestinian.

For the Palestinians as a whole, the new generation of university graduates had two important outcomes: physical mobility and leadership. The graduates entered skilled positions in the oil economies, civil services, and schools of Arab states across the Middle East. They spearheaded the transformation of the Palestinian people into a mobile, internationally oriented society; along with events such as the 1967 war, this emigration would finally leave fewer than half of all Palestinians in Palestine. It did not occur at equal rates for all Palestinian communities—so many people poured out of the West Bank to the East Bank and beyond that its population growth was negligible; the more limited exit from Gaza allowed a growth of nearly 3 percent a year.

In Kuwait, which until the Gulf War of 1991 would house the largest Palestinian concentrations outside the original homeland, the community seemed to develop in strata. Educated male Palestinians were the first to migrate there; they became the fodder for state agencies, staffing everything from post offices to schools. Male ex-fellaheen followed, filling a wide variety of open semiskilled and unskilled positions in the developing country. Finally, wives and children followed suit and the Palestinian population of Kuwait gained a complex, fairly autonomous set of social structures.[72] In the United States, by contrast, Palestinians tended to join the cultural, academic, and scientific communities, as well as the business class. Scattered across the American expanse and absorbed into the public school system, they lacked the autonomy of their Kuwaiti counterparts.[73]

Whether autonomous or relatively assimilated, these scattered Palestinian communities, lacking their own political institutions, succeeded in forming what Ghabra has called a cross-national entity.[74] The evolution of memories of the Lost Garden, the labelling of places and institutions with names from Palestine, the emphasis on the temporariness of present life (even when people seemed well settled-in), the importance put on education as the most crucial resource, the undying hostility towards Israel, and a general insistence on maintaining a Palestinian identity were cultural vehicles that transversed great distances from the camps. The process was facilitated by regular international travel, the mobility of capital (i.e. staking a family member's emigration and receiving the remittances he would later send back), and the concentration of parts of families in different countries.

Equally important for understanding this Palestinian self-awareness was the emergence of professionals and intellectuals lacking the political reticence of the old village chiefs and new entrepreneurs. Many became outright activists, turning to a variety of ideologies centered around pan-Arabism but always focused on the Palestinian problem.[75] In the late 1950s and early 1960s, the repression they faced and the failure of Arab unity muted their social role. But after the debacle of 1967, the investments they were making would result in a new national leadership.

In the meantime, other parties staked their claims to leadership, all failing to garner much enthusiasm: most notably the Jordanian monarchy, but also Amin al-Husseini, continuing to operate his claim through the nearly moribund Arab Higher Committee, existing (albeit with very little influence) through the 1967 war.

In 1959, the government of Nasser played its own hand, leading a campaign of vilification against Amin and the Committee and forcing the Mufti to move from Egypt to Lebanon. Nasser also pushed hard for the creation of some alternative national body—what he termed a Palestinian entity—to represent the Palestinians and support his own pan-Arab ambitions.[76] King Hussein of Jordan countered with continued, severe repression of supporters of pan-Arabism; he even briefly entered a strange-bedfellow alliance with the Mufti, bringing the latter back to Jerusalem for a last visit in 1967. Another Nasser rival, President Abd al-Karim Qasim of Iraq, proposed establishing the "immortal Palestinian Republic," starting with the territory of the West Bank and Gaza.[77]

Educated Palestinians were starting to look beyond the framework of such possibilities for a national leadership. Their focus turned to self-generated organizations in the West Bank, Gaza, Lebanon, and elsewhere. Between 1959 and 1963, as many as 40 secret organizations had been formed, with anywhere from 2 to 400 members, expressing frustration with the passivity of their parents—as well as with the Arab states' propensity to use the Palestinian issue for their own purposes. After 1964, taking advantage of the renewed interest in the Palestinian problem that accompanied the formation of the PLO under Nasser's auspices, several tried to create an umbrella organization that could avoid the powerful state manipulation the early PLO experienced—a manipulation they saw as rendering it, in the words of Rashid Khalidi, "far from being an expression of autonomous Palestinian national feeling."[78]

With Arab universities bringing together talented, highly motivated Palestinians in an atmosphere of relative freedom, a scattered Palestinian leadership thus emerged in the 1960s. Its power derived, not from its traditional place in a largely agricultural society (as was the case in Nablus), but from its manipulation of the tools and values of a modern education. To be sure, dispersal would present this leadership with grave difficulties as well as opportunities. But for the time, it served as a source of cultural cohesion.

These university graduates did not labor to regenerate Palestinian society alone. The Palestinian National Charter, embraced by the new leaders in 1968, expressed a credo much more a product of the camps in their poverty and disorientation than a slogan imposed from above: "The Palestinian personality is an innate, persistent characteristic that does not disappear, and it is transferred from fathers to sons." Unlike the three decades of British rule, when leaders defined the meaning of the word Palestinian for their followers, the two decades after 1948 saw the least privileged social groups provide the cultural content for what it meant to be Palestinian.

The Feday:
Rebirth and Resistance

I am against boys becoming
  heroes at ten
Against the tree flowering explosives
Against branches becoming scaffolds
Against the rose-beds turning to trenches
And yet
When fire cremates my friends
  my youth
  and country
How can I
Stop a poem from becoming a gun?

                    —Rashid Hussein, "Opposition"

Israel's lightning victory in the Six Day War followed a month of dejection and demoralization in face of Nasser's bellicose maneuvers. Immediately afterward, things of course looked very different: In addition to taking the Golan Heights from Syria and the Sinai from Egypt, Israel's forces had driven Jordan's Arab Legion from the West Bank and the Egyptian army from the Gaza Strip, uniting the territory of the old Palestine mandate and bringing the majority of Palestinians under Israeli control (see Map 6). Over 600,000 West Bankers could now resume contact with the more than 300,000 Palestinians in the Strip and with a similar number living in Israel's pre-1967 boundaries.[1] The war also precipitated another exodus of Palestinians from Palestine. Approximately 250,000 fled for the remnant of Jordan, the East Bank. The war is one of several events in the latter half of the twentieth century (others being the dissolution of the French and British empires and the Soviet Union, and the reuni-

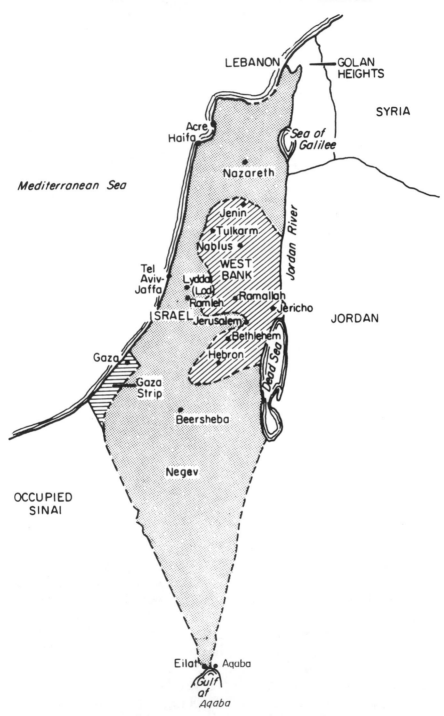

Map 6.   Israel and Occupied Territories of the West Bank and Gaza Strip

fication of Germany) that radically transformed the world map. Its results were correspondingly momentous for both Israeli Arab citizens and Palestinians in the newly occupied territories.

To everyone's surprise, the nature of the conflict in which Jews and Arabs were embroiled was now different. After 1948, the conflict had seemed largely international—the armistice agreements, continuing border tensions, the Suez war in 1956, all involved sovereign states. From this perspective, both to its own Jewish citizens and to a larger world public, Israel seemed small and beleaguered, surrounded by much larger, hostile states that refused to accept its right to exist.

Following the 1967 war, the focus gradually drifted back to the communal problem, as in the days of the mandate: two peoples—Jews and Palestinians—claiming the same piece of soil. Israel's image thus shifted, much to the frustration of its supporters, from beleaguered to all-powerful.

With the territory of historical Palestine reassembled under a single authority for the first time since 1948, the bulk of the Palestinians once more stood face to face with the Jews, their longstanding enemies, representing an alien culture and religion. The reality of what was an almost perfect reversal of the two communities' proportions in the last years of the mandate—three million Jews now ruling slightly more than one million Palestinians—has been shrewdly and succinctly captured by poet Samih al-Qasim:

> Ladies and Gentlemen.
> We are here
> On a crossroad.[2]

The Palestine Liberation Organization, led by Yasser Arafat and his Fatah faction, would now become the institutional vehicle for attracting and directing the charged emotions of the Palestinians. It would shape their self-understanding, although stumbling when it tried to mobilize their society under the single ideological umbrella of Palestinism—and under the noses of hostile governments. But despite its centrality, it was the resources of that society that would enable the organization to play such a prominent role.

Reflecting this interplay of leaders and followers, the Palestinians developed three heroic images in the face of the difficult post-1967 conditions: The *feday* (lit.: "one who sacrifices himself") was a modern metamorphosis of the holy warrior. Sacrificing himself in the battle against Zionism, he was portrayed with head wrapped in the distinctive checkered Palestinian kafiya, gripping a Kalishnokov. The image drew on memories of those who had manned the rebel groups from 1936 to 1939 and on idealized portraits of peasants as salt of the earth—even though the membership of the PLO, which heavily promoted the image, was primarily cosmopolitan and from the cities; its early popularity bolstered the PLO claim to be the sole legitimate Palestinian representative.

The image of the survivor also evoked the fast-disappearing fellah. But this was a more passive hero, demonstrating *sumud*, or steadfastness. Enduring the humiliations imposed by the conqueror, he confirmed his sumud by staying on the land at all costs—a bitter lesson learned from 1948. Eventually, even those not tilling the land but simply staying in the occupied territories came to epitomize sumud. Finally, the survivor's counterpart was "the child of the stone," often exemplified through portraits of the *shahid*, or martyr, offering his life for the national cause by fighting against all odds. Modelled partly on the role of the shabab in the 1936–39 revolt, this was the adolescent willing to confront the enemy through rock throwing, tire burning, manning shoulder-mounted antitank rockets, and so forth.

At the end of the 1960s and in the 1970s, the feday dominated the Palestinian symbolic universe, as Palestinians groped for a response to the new conditions wrought by the June war. In the 1980s, images of the survivor and the child of the stone became more prominent, challenging what had become basic tenets of Palestinian society.

FATAH

As two of his biographers put it recently, "The ordinary facts of Arafat's life—his place of birth, his parents, his childhood, his adolescence—lay buried in the soil of his distant homeland."[3] Later, this vagueness would fuel myths among the Palestinians, hungry for a larger-than-life leader. One common story is that Arafat was born in Jerusalem, although more reliable evidence indicates he was actually born in Gaza and grew up in Egypt;

another is that he was part of the Husseini clan—a connection that might have benefited him at one point, but became a liability as the ayan were discredited. He is also said to have been a member of the Muslim Brotherhood, and in fact, the Egyptians arrested him on such grounds in 1954, in connection with an attempt on Nasser's life. What is certain is that he ended up in Cairo in the early 1950s, studying to be a civil engineer and working hard as the head of the Palestinian Students' Union, which he founded with a small group of collaborators.[4]

In the 1950s, the political and cultural center of gravity in the Arab world, and an ideal site for the Union, was Cairo. Nasser swept to power, drastically altering the tenor of Egyptian and Arab politics. In the midst of Cairo's intellectual currents and crosscurrents, Arafat and his trusted colleague Salah Khalaf (who, under the name Abu Iyad, would remain Arafat's chief aide-de-camp until his assassination in 1991, probably at the hands of Iraqi agents) fashioned an agenda for the Palestinian people. Their thinking can be summed up as follows: First, the Palestinians had to take responsibility for their future—only an autonomous organization of their own could reverse their fortune. Second, their chief aim needed to be the liberation of Palestine, taking precedence over the goal of Arab unity (the key to the Nasserite revolution). Indeed, the liberation was a necessary precondition for that unity. Third, the key means to achieve liberation was armed struggle, undertaken by Palestinians themselves. And finally, Palestinians would work hand-in-hand with other Arabs and international forces on the basis of equality to help achieve the goal.[5]

Khalaf would later recall those early days at Cairo University. Approached by Arafat, who was attempting to recruit him for the Union, he found a welcome refrain in Arafat's approach: "[We] knew what was damaging to the Palestinian cause. We were convinced, for example, that the Palestinians could expect nothing from the Arab regimes. . . . We believed that the Palestinians could rely only on themselves."[6] When Arafat, in the growing fashion of educated Palestinians, moved from one exiled community to another, he transported this approach with him. But by the time of his forced move to Kuwait in 1957 to take up an engineering post, it had taken some hard knocks. Arrested earlier by Nasser, he was now harassed by him because of promises made to the Israelis to secure their withdrawal from the Gaza Strip following the 1956 Suez war. And Arafat found himself caught in the turmoil of Iraqi-Egyptian competition for Arab regional leadership.[7]

Despite the fact that the British kept their protectorate in Kuwait until 1961, Arafat and his colleagues found its Arab leaders offering them a relatively free hand to establish an organization based on the Cairo principles. They also found the growing oil wealth providing resources unimaginable in Egypt. Their underground cell, which in 1959 became *Fatah*—officially, the Palestine National Liberation Movement—began to take shape a few months after Arafat's arrival. Khalid al-Hassan, a Palestinian who had risen in Kuwaiti politics, joined the cell, giving it badly needed organizational skills. In time, Hassan became the leading ideologue of the right wing of the Palestinian movement.

The cell also began publishing a magazine, *Filastinuna* (Our Palestine: The Call to Life), which appeared every six weeks or so for the next five years.[8] Its primary purpose was to put forth Fatah's strategy of provoking the Arab states into a war that Arafat was certain would eventually end Israeli control of Palestine. In a less ambitious vein, editor Khalil al-Wazir (Abu Jihad)—Arafat's long-time aide and close companion—also saw the publication as a critical forum for diverse ideas about how to promote the Palestinian cause.[9] This worked well, and the magazine's success distinguished Arafat's small clandestine group from countless others forming in various Palestinian communities.

Both Fatah and the other groups drew their strength from the deep misery of the Palestinian situation, and from points of resistance elsewhere in the Arab world. Nasser's successful challenge to British control of the Suez Canal and the anti-French agitation of Algeria's FLN suggested it was possible to reverse the verdict of history. For all the clandestine groups, the FLN was a model of how to fashion a national liberation organization, and Arafat's own position was in fact greatly strengthened by the Algerian decision, immediately after independence in 1962, to recognize and support Fatah alone.

With Nasser beginning to use the term Palestinian entity, and Iraq's new revolutionary leader, Qasim, talking of the creation of a Palestinian republic, Palestinian militants gained confidence, despite limited resources and opportunities. In the late 1950s and early 1960s a sentiment seemed to emerge among the Arab republics to give the Palestinians an active role in the struggle against Israel—at least that is what the rhetoric suggested; actually, leaders such as Nasser and Qasim displayed extreme ambivalence towards Palestinian activists, regarding with the deepest suspicion any attempt to take the initiative or set the tone.

Along with the other groups, Fatah set out to sink roots in Palestinian society. But the task was difficult, partly because of its insistence that the sole realization of Nasser's wildly popular call for Arab unity was through Palestinian repatriation. This position did not find favor among Nasser or his avid followers—many of whom were young Palestinians. Nasser felt the Fatah militants were putting the cart before the horse. At the time, even George Habash, who subsequently became the leading Palestinian ideologue of the left, advocated working for unity of the Arab masses through revolutionary regimes as a prelude to the liberation of Palestine.

Arafat found himself moving against the current of popular feeling in the Arab world—Nasserism was pushing the entire Palestinian issue to the margins. His circumstances would eventually change, partly due to larger events—such as the failure of Egyptian-Syrian unity in 1961, and the Arab catastrophe in the 1967 war—and partly due to his own tenacity. Hassan notes how his unswerving dedication to the Palestine problem, before all else, paid off: "We reversed the slogan [of Arab unity first], and this is how we reversed the whole tide of thinking. And we managed to do that. Because when you want to talk about unity, then you have to work against the [present Arab] regimes. When we want to talk about liberation, we have to work on liberation."[10]

The 1960s catapulted Fatah and Arafat from obscurity to overall leadership of the Palestinian people. The evolution from a clandestine political cell, tucked away in a remote corner of the Arab world, to an international organization, involved several important steps. In 1963, Fatah moved towards some permanence by creating a central committee, consisting of Palestinians who eschewed the party and factional conflicts wracking the Arab world. With Arafat as chief and Wazir as second in command, the committee consolidated power and directed the organization and its membership. At the same time, in the face of objections by Khalid al-Hassan and others on the committee, Arafat pushed Fatah into a strategy calling for immediate military action against Israel.

Probably nothing but armed violence could have established the organization so quickly among the various Palestinian communities, after almost two decades of inaction and growing despair. Still, the nature of the dispersal and the disdain of Fatah's leaders for traditional party organization—cells, local committees, and the like—made it difficult for the group to educate, recruit, or consistently mobilize the larger population. The committee succeeded in coordinating the organization's own actions, less so in infusing Fatah into the everyday lives of the Palestinians. When Fatah did create some rudimentary regional subgroups, it found itself hemmed in by the governing Arab regimes.

For all these organizational liabilities, the group did capture the Palestinians' imagination, but not in ways that could have been the basis for systems of control and mass mobilization. This remained true after the 1967 war, when it built a complex central apparatus, covering areas from financial control to relations with Arab parties. Over the years, Arafat tried to make Fatah (and later the PLO, which Fatah came to dominate) into what the Jewish Agency had been for the Jews during the Palestine mandate—a state-in-the-making—but without the equivalent of the political parties and the Histadrut, which had given the Jewish Agency a firm foundation in the Jewish population.

Fatah's turn to violence came after the first Arab summit meeting, held in Cairo in January, 1964, voted to establish the Palestine Liberation Organization, the culmination of almost five years of ground-laying work by Nasser. The new PLO held its first convention in East Jerusalem's Palace Hall movie theater that spring. The motivation was Israel's completion of its National Water Carrier, diverting water from the Jordan River. Support for a Palestinian organization was a way for the Arabs to give the appearance of counteracting Israel without precipitating a direct confrontation. Nasser certainly did not intend the PLO to gain much autonomy—he wanted its semblance, while insuring that no underground groups dragged Egypt into war before it was ready.

Nasser selected a figure who had worked closely with individual Arab states and with the Arab League, Ahmad Shukayri, to build the new organization. Shukayri came from impeccable Palestinian lineage. His father had been a supporter of the Young Turks in 1908 and after being exiled by the sultan, had returned to Acre where he became a learned Muslim dignitary and an activist in the emerging Palestinian movement. Shukayri took the same route as spokesman for the Arab Higher Committee, the Arab League, and the Syrian and Saudi delegations to the United Nations. In his memoirs, he also claims a connection to al-Qassam, the Palestinian hero of the 1930s, noting that he offered his services as a lawyer to defend the surviving members of the Sheikh's group in 1935.

Shukayri had been advocating an organization to "liberate" Palestine for more than a year, but due to his bluster and self-promotion, few took him seriously. Alan Hart, Arafat's sympathetic biographer, vilifies Shukayri as the Puppet-in-Chief—a political mercenary selling himself to the highest bidder, and a demagogue who was a cross between Adolf Hitler and Ian Paisley.[11] The claim of Shukayri's opponents was that he was simply doing Nasser's bidding in creating an illusion of Palestinian autonomy while keeping the organization under tight wraps. But to the surprise of many, Shukayri was far more effective than his enemies (or their biographers) let on. To establish the PLO, he overcame the opposition of feisty old Haj Amin al-Husseini, despite the fact that his father had been an outspoken opponent of the Mufti, as well as the deep suspicions of the Jordanians and several other key regimes. His other efforts were undermined by unceasing hyperbole and demagogic statements: A "bombastic orator,"[12] perhaps best remembered for his purported threat before the 1967 war to drive the Jews into the sea, he had the temerity while in Amman to proclaim that all of Jordan, including the East Bank, was an integral part of Palestine.

The spring convention disgusted many of the Fatah activists, although several attended—Arafat, whose name was on the list of invitees, did not. They saw what they considered quiescent, hand-picked delegates ratify every proposal that Shukayri put before them. Some of those proposals, however, had long-term ramifications: the Palestinian National Covenant (revised in 1968 as the Palestine National Charter) was ratified, with its strong condemnation of Zionism and Israel—a bone in the throat of Israelis to this very day. "Zionism," the Covenant declared, "is a colonialist movement in its inception, aggressive and ex-

pansionist in its goals, racist and segregationist in its configura-
tions and fascist in its means and aims. Israel in its capacity as
the spearhead of this destructive movement and the pillar for
colonialism is a permanent source of tension and turmoil. . . ."[13]
The convention also emphasized the need for Palestinians to
amass forces, mobilize their efforts and capabilities, and engage
in holy war until complete and final victory has been attained.
Toward those ends, the PLO created the Palestine Liberation
Army (PLA) two years later.

For Fatah, the PLO proved a formidable competitor. A real
army of their own seemed highly attractive to destitute refugees
and political exiles. Droves of Fatah members abandoned ship,
hoping to join the projected new PLA.[14] With almost no levers of
influence and control among its own members, let alone in the
wider Palestinian population, the PLO needed some audacious
acts as a means of restoring its most important asset—its image.
Khalid al-Hassan put it this way:

> You can say, because it is the truth,that we were pushed down a
> road we did not want to take by the coming into being of the
> P.L.O. Because of its existence, and the fact that it was not the
> genuine article that so many Palestinians were assuming it to be,
> we decided that the only way to keep the idea of real struggle
> alive was to struggle.[15]

The road that Hassan had not wanted to take was, of course,
that of direct violence against Israel. Notions of armed struggle
and popular liberation were in the air in the 1960s, leading some
in Fatah to believe that they were part of a larger, inexorable
world force. The success of Algeria's FLN in expelling the deeply
rooted *pieds noirs* was but one of several important models.
Jomo Kenyatta's triumph against British colonialism in Kenya
and the efforts of the National Organization of [Greek] Cypriot
Struggle (EOKA) were others. Farther away, but still extremely
important in the minds of Fatah members, were the Cuban and
Vietnamese revolutions. The writings of General Giap in Viet-
nam, Che Guevara in Cuba, and Mao Zedong, were all appearing
in Palestinian refugee camps, newly translated into Arabic. Perhaps most influential of all was Franz Fanon's *The Wretched of
the Earth*, which, in the Algerian context, talked of the cathartic
benefits of violence against the occupier; Fanon himself was a
psychiatrist who had joined the FLN.[16]

The new strategy of armed violence had roots in Palestinian society as well. Some of the key figures involved in the early raids in 1965 had had direct experience in the 1936–39 revolt. Ahmad Musah, who led Fatah's first raid, had been part of Arab fighting groups carrying out action against Jewish settlements during that revolt.[17] Another key figure in these years was Subhi Yasin, who had been a member of the Black Hand group during the mandate period, as well as a direct disciple of al-Qassam. Yasin alternately competed and cooperated with Fatah, finally merging his own group, the Organization of the Vanguard of Self-Sacrifice for the Liberation of Palestine, with Arafat's in 1968.[10]

Fatah's decision was not the first time that the Palestinians had resorted to violence since 1948. Individuals such as Ahmad Musa had periodically slipped across the border to undertake personal acts of vengeance. Also, the Suez war of 1956 stemmed in no small part from the cycle of organized guerrilla raids from the Gaza Strip on Jewish settlements and Israel's strong retaliatory actions. In fact, in later years Arafat claimed some responsibility for those Gaza-based raids through his role as student leader at the time.

But Arafat's real military role began when a Fatah team operating under the name *Assifa* (The Storm) slipped into Israel and placed an explosive charge in the Beit Netopha canal. In some ways, the action was more a comedy of errors than a serious military expedition. The Lebanese arrested the group slated to carry out the attack on the last day of 1964, but, unaware of what had occurred, Arafat and his colleagues sped through Beirut distributing a military communique reporting the purported action. Later, laden with explosives, he was arrested and held for a short time by the Syrians, even though a high-ranking Syrian officer had pledged unfailing cooperation. When a group finally did plant the explosive charge on January 3, 1965, it set the timer so late that Israelis discovered and dismantled the bomb before it went off. And on its return from the action, the Palestinian unit ran into a Jordanian patrol that killed its leader, Ahmad Musa, and arrested the others.

What made the action more than merely a series of mistakes was the reaction to it. Fatah may have learned here that it is not how much actual damage they inflict on Israel that counts as how it perceives their actions. The Israelis publicized the attack and several others that Assifa undertook in early 1965, both in their Arabic radio broadcasts and in a speech by Prime Minister Levi Eshkol. Nothing could have better demonstrated the underground group's readiness to confront the enemy directly. After a second unit infiltrated into Israel, Fatah took public responsibility. Arab regimes also helped by branding Assifa the venal creation of Western intelligence agencies seeking to push the Arabs into war before they were fully prepared (Egypt) or as "communists bent on subversion" (Jordan). Egypt's army even declared itself at war with Assifa.

Wide publicity about the execution of real acts of violence and the furor they precipitated captured the attention and respect of the frustrated Palestinians around the Arab world. From an initial act of sabotage, Palestinians thus gained a new understanding of themselves as *jil al-thawra*, the revolutionary generation. At the same time, Fatah leaders learned the difficulty of making their way through minefields—not only those laid by the Israelis but also the political minefields set out by Arab regimes. Egypt, Syria, Jordan, Lebanon—all the states bordering Israel—either hunted down the underground group's members or, when professing cooperation, constrained their every move. Nonetheless, by the outbreak of the 1967 war, Assifa, which was by now the official military arm of Fatah, had undertaken nearly 100 acts of sabotage in Israel, killing eleven Israelis and wounding sixty-two.[19] Indeed, Israeli spokesmen cited these provocations as an important catalyst of the cycle of violence leading to the war.

RECREATING THE PLO

As humiliating as the 1967 war had been for the Arabs, it gave Fatah new opportunities in two important areas. First, the humiliation quieted the gales of Nasserite pan-Arabism. Fatah's opposition to Nasser's philosophy—i.e., Arab unification as a prelude to the liberation of Palestine—had previously seemed a form of spitting into the wind. Now the opportunity existed for alternatives to Nasser's discredited vision, to his handpicked PLO leadership, to his insistence on control.

Second, by reuniting the Palestinian majority—this time under Israeli occupation—the war made it much easier for Fatah to penetrate Palestinian society. The combination of its universal antipathy towards the Israelis with this shift from a logistically difficult fragmentation seemed to open the way for tactics reminiscent of Mao Zedong's or Ho Chi Minh's: Fatah could provide key social services and organizations to the people and, in turn, finally develop its means of mobilization and control. And such control would be a significant innovation in Palestinian society. While before 1948, the Husseinis had insinuated themselves into people's daily lives through landholding, the Supreme Muslim Council, and clan ties, neither they nor any other claimants to Palestinian leadership had created networks of influence that were truly national in scope.

In fact, Fatah was only able to capitalize on one of the opportunities, control of the PLO turning out to be its most far-reaching political achievement. Even with Nasser's firm backing, Shukayri had never managed to establish his own control over the organization, despite his claims that the PLO he led represented the general will of the Palestinians: He ended up precipitating and dealing with one factional split after another. His crowning accomplishment was the creation of the Palestine Liberation Army—in 1959, the Arab League had resolved to put such an army in the field, but little came of the effort or of several subsequent ones.[20] Eventually, Shukayri deployed several units in Gaza. But this did not save the PLO from overall ineffectiveness, and Shukayri from political demise. The army, which did not amount to more than four or five thousand men, came under the command of each host country, rather than the PLO's appointed commander-in-chief. Shukayri simply could not achieve even the most rudimentary form of autonomy, for either the army or the PLO as a whole. Jordan, in particular, fought to erode even the slightest gains by the PLO. This problem would later plague Arafat, as well.

The 1967 war recast relations among the Arabs as no other event would until Iraq's invasion of Kuwait. Pan-Arabism, which had electrified the Arab world from North Africa to the Fertile Crescent, slowly gave way to state relations reminiscent of those in other regions, based on standard diplomacy and international negotiation. Nasser's calls for unity, directed to the peoples of neighboring Arab countries above their rulers' heads, were replaced by conciliatory steps among kings and presidents. Even the dinosaur-like monarchs became legitimate nationalist leaders in this new diplomacy.

The result was a flagging interest by Arab heads of state in the PLO. At the Khartoum summit conference in the summer of 1968—the famous meeting in which the Arab League issued its notorious three no's to Israel: no negotiations, no recognition, no peace—the final communique did not even mention the PLO. Shukayri, who had enjoyed Nasser's support before the war, now felt his bone-chilling disinterest.

With the 1967 defeat, Palestinians felt the pan-Arab foundations of their hopes disintegrated. In the war's wake, many turned to the feday—especially as represented by Fatah and its record of direct, violent action against Israel—as their only chance for salvation. Fatah in turn, nourished by the new Palestinian support, used the growing disinterest of the Arab states to create some space for itself. Sending representatives to Arab capitals, it won both financial and rhetorical support. With Fatah thus catapulting into Arab consciousness, the PLO faded. By Christmas eve, 1967, Shukayri had resigned.

Arafat moved deliberately to replace Shukayri and revive the PLO. Probably no act furthered his aims more than the battle of Karamah (a refugee camp on the East Bank) on March 21, 1968. Nettled by Fatah guerrilla attacks, the Israeli government dispatched a large military force into Jordan, in order to destroy its local headquarters. In what turned out to be the first open battle between Jews and Palestinian irregulars since 1948, the Palestinians (aided by Jordanian artillery) ambushed the Israelis, killing as many as 25 soldiers in the course of a day-long firefight.[21] The Israelis retreated without achieving their objective.[22] While the Palestinians lost five times as many fighters as the Israelis, the psychological effect of the battle was overwhelming: Almost immediately assuming mythic proportions (Karamah means honor in Arabic), it confirmed the primacy of the feday, propelling thousands of teenagers into Assifa and Arafat to the top of the Palestinian national movement.

Within a year of the battle, he had assumed the chairmanship of the PLO, with Fatah the dominant group in the reconstituted organization. The PLO became an umbrella organization, enveloping a number of smaller ones dedicated to armed struggle and Palestinian autonomy, of which Fatah was by far the most important. It now controlled half the seats of the Palestine National Council (PNC), the PLO's emerging parliament-in-exile. Arafat and his associates controlled the 15-member Executive

Committee, while keeping rival organizations fragmented and in sight as part of the Committee and the larger Council.

For substantial periods, Arafat insisted on standing clear of Arab political in-fighting, his single-minded preoccupation with Palestine making it possible for Fatah to maintain the political, moral, and financial support of a wide variety of Arab regimes. (He paid a price for deviating from this policy—the most dramatic recent example being his support for Iraq's Saddam Hussein.) In general, Fatah also spurned questions regarding the future makeup of Palestinian society or arcane ideological debates over the need for social revolution, thus enabling it to gain a broad base of support. Such choices clearly differentiated it from other Palestinian groups now committed to striking against Israel, none of which managed to establish extensive Palestinian and Arab support.

Nonetheless, such groups did have a significant impact on the movement, setting much of the tone and tenor of the PLO, indeed of the entire Palestinian national movement. In July, 1968, Palestinians hijacked an El Al Israeli airliner to Algeria, the first of a spate of hijackings and other acts aimed at the vulnerable international air transportation system. Terrorism now became a key element of the struggle against Israel. Until 1988, Palestinian groups never admitted to it, using the term "external operations" for all armed action outside Israel and the occupied territories. In 1988, the possibility of a direct dialogue with the United States hanging in the balance, Arafat denounced—and seemed to renounce—it.[23]

Behind many such acts stood the Popular Front for the Liberation of Palestine (PFLP). Like those of Fatah, its leaders came from the student movement—but in this case from the American University in Beirut. There George Habash—its preeminent figure—and colleagues had established the clandestine Arab Nationalists' Movement; shortly after the 1967 war it merged with other groups to become the PFLP, finally joining the PLO in 1970. The Arab Nationalists' Movement's activists had originally advocated Nasserism. In the mid-1960s, it moved towards a Marxist perspective, demanding social revolution as a precondition for true Arab unity. After 1967, the Front took on a Palestine-first orientation.

Direct violent action was always at the center of its concerns. By 1964, even before Fatah, members of the Arab Nationalists'

Movement's guerrilla unit had attacked Israel. But even while furnishing enough notoriety to challenge Fatah among the Palestinian population, the themes of violence and ideology divided and redivided the organization.

The first acrimonious split came when Naif Hawatma demanded a more radical approach: to break the Popular Front's relations with the inherently conservative Arab regimes and to align itself instead with popular revolutionary forces throughout the Arab world. Out of the ensuing, sometimes bloody battle came a splinter group, the Popular Democratic Front for the Liberation of Palestine, headed by Hawatma. The split with the Popular Front in 1969 was finally brokered by Fatah, which in turn got the Popular Democratic Front to join the PLO. Interestingly, the new group took the lead, after long polemical debates, in distinguishing between Israel proper (as defined by the armistice agreements following the 1948 war) and the territories it captured in 1967. By the early 1970s, these debates moved many within the PLO away from the Charter's insistence on expulsion from Palestine of post-1917 Jews and their descendants to advocacy of a secular, democratic state including Jews and a majority of Arabs. Under Hawatma's prodding, this position evolved even further; by the 1980s, the Popular Democratic Front had persuaded most of the national movement to accept the principles of (a) more flexibility regarding what had formerly been considered the absolute right of Palestinian repatriation in their original homes and (b) an Arab Palestinian state in the West Bank and Gaza, rather—at least at first—than the democratic secular state in all of Palestine.[24]

The idea of creating a Palestinian state in the occupied territories had developed slowly, one of the first to raise the possibility being Mustaffa Akhmais, imprisoned by the Israelis shortly after the 1967 war.[25] The PLO has consistently emphasized three demands—the right of return, the right to self-determination, and the right to be an independent state. The 1947 partition was seen by PLO leaders as abrogating the right to self-determination.[26] The decision to found a Palestinian state in any "liberated" part of the country (i.e., the West Bank and Gaza) was finally taken at the eleventh PNC meeting (Cairo, June 9, 1974), and marked a major tactical turning point. Many Palestinians saw it as a withdrawal in principle from the idea of liberating the entire country and a movement towards the op-

tion of a "mini-state"—the backdrop to George Habash's resignation from the PLO Executive Committee on October 26 and
the establishment of a "Rejection Front."

Ahmad Jibril provoked another split. He had been a member of
Fatah's Central Committee before joining the Popular Front but
was dissatisfied in both cases with the insufficient commitment
to direct violent action. He, too, founded a new organization, the
Popular Front for the Liberation of Palestine—General Command. With an emphasis more narrowly focused on guerrilla
tactics, especially across Israel's northern border, it has been
implicated in scurrilous acts of violence, including the blowing
up of Pan Am flight 103 over Lockerbie, Scotland, in December,
1988. Even after Jibril withdrew his group from the PLO in the
early 1980s, he retained considerable influence over the worldwide image of the Palestinian national movement.

Drawing on theories of urban guerrilla warfare and cooperat-
ing with a terrorist network including Japan's Red Army, the
IRA, and the Baader-Meinhof group, the Popular Front and its
splinter organizations initiated a series of "external operations."[27] The most spectacular by far were the airplane hijackings. These and other acts—the mass murder of passengers by
the Red Army in Israel's principal airports; the murder of Israeli
athletes in the 1972 Olympics—made the Palestinian issue a
media event, pushing it to the top of the world political agenda.
Within Palestinian society, they offered new heroes and a sense
of power.[28] In the popular imagination, the feday was someone
who, like Joshua, could stop the sun in the sky. Among Palestinians everywhere, there was a renewed sense of pride and
autonomy, helping to rekindle a Palestinian national consciousness, battered in the decades since the Arab Revolt.

The emphasis on terror had its costs, as well, fostering a blood-
thirsty stereotype, both internationally and among those Israelis
who might have sought accommodation. Israeli leaders pointed
to the terrorism as proof that the Palestinian Covenant involved
not only the elimination of Israel but of Jews generally. And the
world's revulsion enabled these leaders to delegitimize Palestinian national claims. As indicated, Arafat and Fatah over time
distanced themselves from terrorist tactics, even while apparently creating their own deadly terrorist branches, Force 17 and
Black September, for a while the world's most formidable terror
organization.[29] The latter was responsible for many operations,

including the assassination of Jordanian Prime Minister Wasfi al-Tal in Cairo (November 28, 1971) and the attack on the Munich Olympics (September 5, 1972; death toll: eleven Israeli athletes, a German policeman, five guerrillas). It is clear, then, that while Fatah now headed the PLO, it could not control many of the organization's parts; also, the reputation and image of the PLO derived as much from acts of the smaller groups as from Arafat's and Fatah's leadership.

Arafat's new stature, and that of the reorganized PLO, were recognized implicitly at the Arab League's Rabat conference in December, 1969. To the surprise of many, the PLO—now the umbrella for a slew of guerrilla groups and much more consistent on freedom of action than Shukayri ever had been—won Nasser's enthusiastic support for engaging in direct resistance to Israeli rule. He even gave Fatah some military aid and a special broadcasting station annexed to Cairo Radio.[30]

Other states such as Syria and Iraq fell into line as well. Strains between them and the PLO did not disappear altogether: They appeared, for example, when Nasser agreed to the so-called Rogers initiative in 1970 (i.e., a cease-fire in Egypt's War of Attrition against Israeli forces dug in along the Suez Canal) or when Syria set up its own guerrilla group, Saiqa (along with Jibril's Popular Front for the Liberation of Palestine–General Command, it would quit the PLO altogether for most of the 1980s). But the overall situation was quite clear: Arafat and his Fatah colleagues had ridden the wave of Israeli success in the 1967 war, using the humiliation of the Arab states and the failure of their grand designs for Arab unity to seize leadership of the Palestinian national movement.

THE PLO'S SEARCH FOR ROOTS

Modelling his effort on those of the Chinese, Vietnamese, and Cuban revolutionaries, Arafat began a push immediately after the June war to establish a permanent, popular base for resistance and revolt in the occupied territories. His dramatic failure—the Israelis forced his and his entourage's ouster at the end of the summer of 1967—was a crucial development for the guerrillas and for Palestinian society in general (see chapter 9).

Ironically, Fatah's success in the battle of Karamah a year later was a result of this failure: Once driven from the occupied territories, it established its headquarters there. Nevertheless, the forced physical distance from the centers of Palestinian settlement would prove to be a persistent liability. Fatah did try to compensate for that liability with a Department of Popular Organizations, governing affiliated groups of students, doctors, peasants, and so forth, meant to mobilize the Palestinian population.[31] Compared with Shukayri's feeble efforts, Arafat's seemed quite robust.

Khalid al-Hassan has argued that the new PLO might have been all too robust: "After Karamah we were forced to make our mobilisation and ideological education [of] . . . the people in the camps by masses, by lectures, not by cells: and there is a big difference in both ways. There we deal with an individual; here we deal with the masses, with 100 at one time."[32] Within a year of Karamah, Fatah had members in eighty countries, but the cost of this growth was loss of organizational cohesion. Embraced as the symbolic representation of the national movement, the PLO found itself in a symbiotic relationship with the Palestinian people: On the one hand, it promoted—despite extreme dependence upon various host countries—a sense of their distinctiveness, autonomy, and empowerment. On the other hand, Palestinian refugees and others gave the PLO a foundation for action and a coherent audience by developing a shared culture, drawing on their memories of Palestine and the myths of the Lost Garden that they had created. But such emotional closeness notwithstanding, the Palestinians found the PLO rather distant from their practical needs and way of life.

Fatah's inattention to organization at the level of village, neighborhood, or camp made it difficult to mobilize people on a sustained basis, as well as to project a unified national will. To be sure, the proliferation of guerrilla groups complicated the task. It is impossible to account for all the organizations of "armed struggle" appearing and disappearing during this period. Some were cover names, or one-action groups, or mere paper organizations. Often, several groups would claim responsibility for a suspected or clear-cut guerrilla action. Free of the limits imposed on constituencies with everyday problems, their rivalries led each to work for preservation and dominance, often against the greater national good. The result was an odd mixture of ideological purity and political irresponsibility.

Arafat thus spent much of his time trying to preside over unruly groups and overcome frictions among them. Filling the seats of the Palestine National Council, which was seen as both a functioning parliament and a state-in-the-making, came only after intense and prolonged bargaining about precisely how much representation each group would have. Another formidable diversion involved the ever-more complicated world of Arab interstate relations, ensnaring the PLO in devastating, direct confrontations with the Jordanian and Syrian armies, as well as with numerous Lebanese militias.

Two factors led to such confrontations. First, the Palestinian communities located in Arab states often turned into points of contention between these states and the PLO. Local Palestinians frequently lacked basic rights and faced discrimination in their daily dealings. Attempts by the PLO to shield them from abuses meant a collision course with Arab regimes. Second, the PLO worked under a nigh-impossible dilemma. Among its most basic goals was autonomy in pursuing Palestinian interests—its own foreign policy, the right to initiate military action and develop unmediated relations with local Palestinians, and so forth. From the Palestinians' perspective, such autonomy was important, helping to define them in the Arab world as something other than refugees and victims. More concretely, if the PLO were to succeed in building viable institutions among them, autonomy could mean acquiring services that local governments would not or could not provide.

But that potential independence rankled Arab governments, none, in the postcolonial period, being ready to give even a hint of relinquishing any part of sovereignty within its assigned borders. This sentiment notwithstanding, Arafat had some success carving out areas of autonomy in particular states, but such cases were limited. One example was in Kuwait between 1967 and 1976, when the government, after greatly restricting the admission of non-Kuwaitis into the educational system, allowed the PLO to run schools for Palestinian children. Despite difficulties in keeping the schools afloat financially and in maintaining academic standards,

The PLO school experience contributed immeasurably to the development of national consciousness among Palestinian students. Children saluted the Palestinian flag each day, participated regularly in Palestinian cultural and social activities, and joined scouting troops as well as the Zahrat and Ashbal (associations that provided children with paramilitary and political training).[33]

This sort of success was rare. As we shall see below, the PLO managed to create broad zones of autonomy and independence for itself only in Lebanon. But there as elsewhere, its efforts led to disastrous conflict—perhaps none more so than the war with Jordan in 1970: what Palestinians came to call Black September.

After Fatah's failure to establish cells in the West Bank, Jordan became the center of its activities. Starting in the summer of 1967, first Fatah, then the PLO more generally, achieved a freedom of action calling King Hussein's control of his own territory into question. After the June war, Palestinian guerrilla suspects were released from Jordanian jails, and many fighters entered Jordan from across the Syrian border. Palestinian military units, which had been stationed in Egypt, also relocated in the Hashemite kingdom, coming under the PLO's direct command. For the first time, the feday appeared in refugee camps wearing his uniform and proudly bearing his arms.

A short honeymoon with the regime took place after the heady battle of Karamah, King Hussein proclaiming, "We shall all be fedayeen." But soon, rifle-toting guerrillas, unauthorized roadblocks they were manning, and related gestures prompted Jordanian officials to question whether the price for allowing the PLO free reign was worth it. Heavy Israeli artillery retaliation against Jordan's richest agricultural region, the Jordan Valley, only complicated the problem.

The smaller guerrilla groups heightened the tensions, some openly calling for the establishment of a "progressive regime" in Amman; the Popular Democratic Front for the Liberation of Palestine even tried to build local soviets of workers and peasants among concentrations of Palestinians in the north of the country. Fatah activists spoke of converting Amman into the Palestinian Hanoi, to be used as the headquarters for an assault on the Israeli Saigon, Tel-Aviv. King Hussein and his army became increasingly anxious about all of this.

Anxiety turned into humiliation on September 6, 1970. George Habash's Popular Front for the Liberation of Palestine hijacked three international airliners and forced them to land at the stark Jordanian desert airport in Zarqa. After the Popular Front blew up the aircraft, Jordan's army, the descendant of the British-trained Arab Legion, left its barracks to disarm the guerrillas. Several of the Palestinian organizations countered by declaring the northern part of the country a "liberated Palestinian area." Full warfare ensued; using heavy armor, artillery, and air attacks, the Jordanians inflicted a shattering defeat, around three thousand Palestinians dying in the fighting. Some units preferred crossing the Jordan River and surrendering to the Israelis rather than falling into Jordanian hands. When Syrian tanks threatened to intervene, Israeli forces, acting in coordination with the United States, redeployed to deter a southern thrust into Jordan.

In the aftermath of this episode, the Hashemites closed all PLO institutions and arrested those leaders who had not managed to flee.[34] The organization's prospects seemed bleak. In the course of three years, it had failed, first, in its efforts to gain direct access to the large Palestinian population in the occupied territories, and now to that in Jordan.

In subsequent decades, relations between the PLO and Jordan fluctuated.[35] For fifteen years they were very poor; the Amman Agreement of 1985 then envisioned a confederation between Jordan and a future Palestinian state, but a year later the agreement dissolved into bitter mutual recriminations. Alternating cooperation and disputes followed regarding whether Palestinian representatives could be incorporated into a Jordanian delegation for possible talks with Israel. Relations warmed again in 1990 and 1991, when both parties supported Saddam Hussein in the Gulf War. The new Jordanian government approved by the King in June, 1991, included seven Palestinian ministers, a clear signal of readiness to return to the confederation plan. The renewed cooperation laid the basis for the joint Jordanian-Palestinian delegation to the U.S.-sponsored peace talks that began in Madrid in the fall of 1991.

Hovering behind all the vicissitudes in the relationship between Palestinians and Jordanians after 1970 was a continued presumption of complete Jordanian sovereignty within its borders—including sovereignty over Jordan's Palestinian population. When in 1988 Jordan severed the tie forged with the West Bank forty years earlier, declaring the PLO the sole representative of the Palestinian people, the move's primary purpose was to underscore this presumption by excluding Palestinians in the East Bank.[36] (The move was, in any event, hedged somewhat—West Bank civil servants, for example, continued to receive Jordanian salaries.)

In any event, the PLO's grim circumstances in September, 1970, were to undergo a remarkable metamorphosis over the following five years—the greatest period of PLO success. With the uprooting from Jordan came the development of a state-within-a-state in Lebanon, that patched-together country with a large number of Palestinians (235,000). Arafat set up his headquarters in Beirut, but the real feday presence was in the southern part of the country, close to Israel's border, where much of this population lived without the political and civic rights of refugees in Jordan, or even Syria and Egypt: "Lacking work permits and generally employed in small enterprises, most Palestinians thus labored for low wages under poor working conditions with no fringe benefits, devoid of protection under Lebanese law."[37]

For the chronically weak Lebanese regime, carved up as it was among various religious sects, the presence of the PLO brought new risks. The Israelis had already made it clear in 1968 that Lebanon was running such risks, responding to the Popular Front's El Al hijacking, with an attack on Lebanon's main airport that destroyed thirteen civilian airplanes. The I.D.F. also initiated retaliatory attacks in southern Lebanon in response to Palestinian hostilities, leading droves of Shi'ite Muslims from the south to flee north to Beirut.

Battered from all directions—Israel, the PLO, Lebanese Muslim students sympathetic to the Palestinians, camp-dwelling Palestinians who undertook their own spontaneous uprising—the Lebanese government tried to contain the guerrillas, but with only marginal success. In 1969, Nasser brokered the apparently paradoxical Cairo Agreement, offering the PLO ample autonomy and latitude in southern Lebanon while somehow promising Lebanon "sovereignty and security." For the first time, Arafat had an opportunity to carve out institutional autonomy, seemingly free of interference by jealous Arab states.

Once they entered the camps, the guerrilla groups established courts, imposed taxes, conscripted young men. They revised the curriculum in the schools, which were funded and run by

UNRWA, so as to offer paramilitary training and change the tenor of social relationships in the camps. The entire spirit in them changed: The first appearance of the feday was received in mythological terms, as that of "giants [who] rose from the sea."[38] One man in the Tal al-Zaatar camp exclaimed,

> The first moment I got down from the car I saw the Palestinian flag instead of the Lebanese flag, and a group of Palestinians in fedayeen clothes instead of the Lebanese police. As I moved through the camp I saw happiness on people's faces. . . . The *sheikh* in the mosque now spoke clearly about the homeland. . . . In the homes, mothers spoke clearly with their children about Palestine—before this was only done in whisper. There were many new projects which weren't there before: social activities, sports, meetings where people could say what they thought clearly, without censorship.[39]

Service and administrative organizations quickly followed. By the early 1980s, the Palestinian Red Crescent Society had built 10 hospitals and 30 clinics, another 47 of the latter being run by the non-Fatah guerrilla groups. Two organizations with tens of thousands of members, the General Union of Palestine Workers and the General Union of Palestinian Women, gained most of their strength in Lebanon.[40] The PLO and its allies also set up the Voice of Palestine radio network, several newspapers, a news agency (WAFA), and a research institute. The organization "had grown from a loosely organized collection of *fida'iyyin* to a vast bureaucratic network, centered in Lebanon, employing perhaps 8,000 civil servants and a budget (including that of constituent organizations) in the hundreds of millions of dollars, three-quarters of which went to support the PLO's social and administrative programs."[41] In addition, it had gained diplomatic recognition from over 50 states, established more than 100 foreign missions of its own, and won observer status in the United Nations (the platform for Arafat's well-known 1974 speech toting a partially visible, holstered pistol). Rashid Khalidi describes the turn of fortune:

> PLO Chairman Yasser Arafat was now a head of a state in all but name, more powerful than many Arab rulers. His was no longer a humble revolutionary movement, but rather a vigorous para-state, with a growing bureaucracy administering the affairs of

Palestinians everywhere and with a budget bigger than that of many small sovereign states.[42]

Over time, the financial resources to sustain such a complex structure also developed, largely through aid from the Gulf states. Adam Zagorin estimates that the main financial body of the PLO, the Palestine National Fund, had yearly expenditures of approximately $233 million by the late 1980s, including over a third of that to support a standing army.[43]

While at the beginning, competition among the guerrilla organizations to control camp life was intense, by 1978 Fatah had achieved dominance. It appointed popular committees that looked after the most mundane human problems—road maintenance, the building of bomb shelters (for protection from both Israeli bombing and Arab militias) and providing proper hygiene. Fatah was especially successful in forming the youth groups mentioned above by Brand—the Zahrat (flowers) for girls and Ashbal (lion cubs) for boys—that stressed military training and the building of a revolutionary culture. This new culture emphasized the difference between the jil al-thawra—the assertive revolutionary generation—and the desolate, humiliating identities of the children's parents, the jil al-Nakba.

Some residents complained that these activities eroded the Palestinians' normally high academic motivation as well as the standing of the regular schools,[44] but there was no doubting the electrifying effect that the feday had on the Lebanese camps:

> On dark alley walls
> our comrades' deaths are announced
> posters show their smiling faces[45]

Such posters plastered the walls of the camps, and graffiti, folk songs, poetry, and stories all grew around the quasi-mystical icon of the feday, recognized as one who would gladly offer his (or in some versions, her) life to liberate Palestine.[46] These idolized recruits earned relatively high salaries, and their families gained preferred access to PLO services and jobs. Families of martyrs received special pensions.

The PLO's control went far beyond the Palestinian camps. The guerrillas had nearly free reign in a wide swathe of Lebanese territory, including the coastal cities of Tyre and Sidon. Over

time, the Lebanese police all but disappeared from the streets
(they simply removed their uniforms, while continuing to receive their salaries from the central government); Lebanese
courts and administrative services gave way to "revolutionary"
courts and to private arrangements with the guerrilla groups,
especially Fatah.[47] Naturally, this power and success came with
a variety of dangers, fears, and resentments, hidden and not-so-
hidden. Within the camps, the old leadership felt particularly
vulnerable. Sayigh quotes a camp school director:

> Most of the *wujaha* [traditional notables or leaders] collaborated
> with the authorities and informers, not because they were unna-
> tionalistic, but because they feared the new generation which was
> threatening their influence. These were the people on whom the
> Mufti depended—they worked together against the new current.[48]

A number of ordinary Palestinians also came to bridle under
the rule of the feday. A few had established close relations with
their Lebanese neighbors, even intermarrying, and opposed the
wedge now dividing the two peoples. Others saw the guerrillas,
many of whose families had come from the Hebron mountains
and Gaza, as socially and intellectually inferior to the Haifa and
Galilee Palestinians in southern Lebanon. For their part, guerrillas spoke of the Lebanese Palestinians as uncommitted to the
revolution, as they called their new order, and as "embour-
geoised." And to complicate matters even more, the various
factions of the PLO often squabbled among themselves for control. The popular committees that they appointed were frequently underskilled, disorganized, and ineffective.

The greatest dangers, however, did not come from resentful
Palestinians—most of whom gladly put up with inefficiences or
even occasional indignities in return for a true Palestinian leadership—but from the Lebanese, who, like the Jordanians, feared
that the guerrillas' autonomy would bring disaster. From the
signing of the Cairo Agreement on, powerful elements in Lebanon were convinced that the Palestinian state-within-a-state
could not coexist with Lebanese sovereignty—a conviction
sharpened by Israeli retaliation for any Palestinian armed incur-
sions, based on a faith that Lebanese pain would translate into
restrictions on the PLO. The Phalangist party of the dominant
Maronite sect—the religious group most closely identified with

the modern Lebanese state[49]—led the outcry. It watched Palestinian control expand from what the Israeli media called Fatahland in the south to territorial enclaves in the north and the Biqa valley, as well as to the PLO's "capital" in the Kakakhani district of West Beirut.

In March, 1970 (that is, before the expulsion of the PLO from Jordan) armed clashes broke out between units of the Lebanese army and guerrilla groups. A few years later (spring 1973), an Israeli raid in Beirut's rue Verdun, killing three leading PLO figures, provoked wide-scale fighting between Lebanese and Palestinian forces. The Milkart Protocols, signed in May, 1973, temporarily put an end to the warfare by precisely spelling out the boundaries for guerrilla forays and enjoining them to self-restraint. But in the end those agreements may have made the situation worse by prompting certain Lebanese factions, particularly among the Christian sects, to create their own militias. In the context of deteriorating relations among Lebanese confessional groups, the tensions helped generate one of the bloodiest communal conflicts of the twentieth century: the Lebanese civil war, lasting from 1975 until 1990 and resulting in well over 100,000 fatalities and endless human tragedy.

For the PLO and the Palestinians, this war would bring previously unimagined brutality and disasters, some of which would make Black September seem relatively benign. They would end up facing two Israeli invasions—a limited incursion in 1978 (the Litani Operation) and a full-scale attack in 1982—besides battles with numerous Lebanese militias. Encountering periodic hostility from the Syrian army, they would suffer a devastating defeat at its hands in 1976.

In the most ignominious blow of all, the PLO found its own factions mauling each other at several points during the war. In 1983, several guerrilla groups, including the Syrian-sponsored Saiqa and Jibril's Popular Front for the Liberation of Palestine—General Command, withdrew from the PLO. And a Fatah colonel, Abu Musa (Said Musa Muragha), led a mutiny against Arafat, involving pitched battles with Fatah forces. The opposition was based on a wide variety of grievances. But the key element was, as the critics saw it, the PLO's treasonous appeasement of its enemies—and its gradual abandonment of the claim to total repatriation, its acceptance in theory of an independent state limited to the West Bank and Gaza. Both Syria and Libya supported Abu Musa, and Syria went so far as to deport Arafat from Damascus (he ended up in Tunis). About 400 men were killed, and another 1,900 wounded, in this brief civil war within a civil war.[50]

Confronting such ordeals, Arafat and the PLO tottered badly. The 1982 Israeli invasion routed the 15,000-strong PLO fighting force and put its entire infrastructure under siege for nearly the entire summer. At the end of August, Palestinian military, administrative, and political forces were evacuated from Lebanon under U.S. supervision—their only shred of honor being the ability to hoist their weapons as they boarded ship in Beirut port. Arafat's personal exit on August 30 marked an end to *ayam Beirut*, the era of PLO political and military presence in Lebanon. Sixteen months later, after Israel had withdrawn from most of Lebanon and PLO fighters had infiltrated back, Abu Musa's rebellion again forced Arafat and his forces to leave.

Reestablished in Tunis, the organization moved some of its branches and training centers to Saddam Hussein's Iraq—paving the way for Arafat's support of that country in the 1991 Gulf War—after an Israeli bombing attack. By the late 1980s, the PLO was again engaging in international initiatives. Arafat engineered a short-lived dialogue with the United States, denouncing the use of terrorism and publicly recognizing the right of Israel to exist—both major concessions on his part. He also managed to reestablish his own tattered image among Palestinians and to have the Palestine National Council finally declare a state that would eventually rule in the West Bank and the Gaza Strip. Without defining its borders or establishing a government, the extraordinary 19th session of the Council, convened near Algiers from November 12 to 15, 1988, authorized a declaration of independence bearing a striking resemblance to that of Israel in 1948. Arafat proclaimed the state, with its capital in Jerusalem, on November 15, 1988.

But despite the international dazzle, the PLO had not altered the dilemma that had become evident in September, 1970: Its most basic aim, to create enough autonomy to shape Palestinian society and confront Israel, lay hostage to the whims of embattled Arab states—or of their unofficial militias or threatening or opportunistic neighbors. In 1991, for example, when the Lebanese state was taking its first steps towards reestablishing a semblance of effective rule, it turned, with the support of its powerful patron Syria, on the PLO in the south, ending its rule after several violent clashes. Arafat's desire to avoid the entanglements of Arab politics could not protect him from such fury. Indeed, writes Rashid Khalidi, "the fact that Palestinian nationalism has been in nearly constant conflict over the past few decades with both Israel and various Arab regimes is perceived as inevitable by most Palestinians."[51]

Even worse, at such times Arafat and his organization could not protect the Palestinian population. By the last half of the 1980s, this fundamental inadequacy changed the relationship of the PLO to Palestinian society in subtle but substantial ways. One of its first indications came shortly after Syria's intervention, aimed in part directly against the PLO, in the Lebanese civil war in 1976. The intervention offered the PLO's Lebanese opponents an opportunity to launch an attack on the two remaining Palestinian refugee camps in mostly Christian East Beirut. One fell quickly, but the other, Tal al-Zaatar, was besieged for almost two months, with the PLO nearly helpless to relieve the suffering and anguish. Despite substantial concessions to the Syrians, the Christian forces finally razed the camp, killing 3,000 Palestinians and evicting the others.

Another such indication was the notorious sequence of events on September 16, 1982, in the suburban Beirut camps of Sabra and Shatilla: Using Israel's protective presence around Beirut, the Phalangists entered the camps and in less than two days slaughtered anywhere between 460 and 3,000 Palestinians, including women and children—as well as Lebanese, Syrians, Algerians, Pakistanis, and Iranians who happened to be in the camps.[52] The camps thus were added to the list of places marking Palestinian martyrdom, alongside Dayr Yasin, Kafr Qasim, and Tel al-Zaatar.

The PLO's impotence did not seem to affect its popularity, or that of Arafat, among the Palestinians. Polls in 1988, for example, gave the PLO a 90 percent and Arafat a 75 percent approval rating.[53] But there were nonetheless indications of a changed relationship. On the one hand, while remaining popular through its long ordeal in Lebanon, the heroic image of the feday appeared increasingly distant from the immediate needs of the Palestinian population, and another cultural hero was beginning to challenge its dominance—the "RPG kid," named after the anti-tank shoulder rockets he toted to slow the Israeli advance.

The stiff price the Israelis paid for the invasion of Lebanon (over 650 dead; 3,500 wounded) catapulted the image of the young martyr, the shahid, into the limelight. The professionally paid feday now had to share the cultural stage with the spontaneous, untrained RPG kids. Later, in the West Bank and Gaza Strip, similar adolescents throwing rocks and taunting Israeli troops would mark the rise of the children of the stones.

On the other hand, many Palestinians were now falling back on their own tenacity for self-protection, a situation reflected in the increasing evocation of the image of the survivor, whose heroism is based on sumud. Perhaps somewhat grandiloquently, Ahmad Dahbur has reflected on such poles of vulnerability and tenacity in Palestinian life:

> You hear the news about the Palestinian?
> Wherever he is they knife him
> famine strikes him and flees
> rumor hacks off an arm here, a leg there,
> the media joyfully spread the news
> the Palestinian rejects
> he accepts his days as a sword
> a hand that scatters the illusions of others
> I testify "endurance is his strength."[54]

Regardless of Lebanese fears, the PLO's power in southern Lebanon remained over an isolated enclave. Once the civil war had ended, the Lebanese state wasted little time in targeting remaining PLO control. Arafat had succeeded in creating a popular leadership among the Palestinians for the first time in their history, and in Lebanon he had even built the semblance of a state. But his attempts to transform that leadership into one that could penetrate and shape Palestinian society beyond the Lebanese arena continued to meet impossible barriers.

PLO leaders had always understood that capturing the imagination of the Palestinians or appealing to them through an attractive ideology would in itself have been insufficient to gain the control they wanted and needed. Moreover, as the dominant faction, Fatah was often at a disadvantage compared to other groups in elaborating an effective ideology. Certainly, none of the others came close to Fatah in garnering outside material support or in sheer size (it probably had 10,000–15,000 men under arms at the end of the 1960s). But, often, their narrower bases allowed them to project more effective ideologies: Fatah seemed a catchall, sending loosely defined, often contradictory messages. It believed in "not engaging in ideological debates about the character of the regime of the liberated state at the present stage as it might split the Palestinians and divert their attention from the struggle against Israel."[55] Sometimes its voice had deep Islamic resonances; at other times, it spoke a language of secularism.[56] Sometimes it seemed to appeal to the downtrodden with the language of social revolution, at others it courted the growing Palestinian middle class. Alain Gresh has rather understated the case in noting that "Fatah is a movement with a variety of tendencies and sensitivities."[57]

Given all its difficulties, the PLO, under the control of Fatah, had managed to establish itself as the recognized leadership of the Palestinians. It had nurtured a national mythology of heroism and sacrifice, the portrait of the downtrodden refugee giving way to that of the feday—which, in turn became the catalyst for the reconstruction of the national movement. In time, armed struggle would give way to more nonviolent activity, both for the sake of international legitimacy and because of the Israeli abilities to deal with armed threats. But even if violence had failed to reverse al-Nakba, it had succeeded in projecting the Palestinian issue into the center of international concern. The PLO's continuing frustration was that its longstanding enemy, Israel, had also consolidated its power; as it did so, its readiness to make concessions to the Palestinians decreased. Facing this formidable opponent, the PLO, at the end of the 1980s and the beginning of the 1990s, was unable to show tangible gains, despite its political evolution. Along with its other difficulties, the organization's want of definition left its leadership vulnerable to challenges from within and to the rising tide of Islamic movements.

Steering a Path Under Occupation

Yasser Arafat and George Habash first met in a cafe in Damascus shortly after the end of the 1967 war. Habash was utterly despondent; turning to Arafat he cried, "Everything is lost." Arafat's answer seemed little more than whistling in the dark. "George, you are wrong," he said. "This is not the end. It's the beginning."[1]

Arafat's brave words met not only with Habash's doubt but with the skepticism of Arafat's lieutenants. Abu Jihad recalled, "I myself was crying. Because of the way in which the Arab armies had been broken, some of our colleagues were saying that everything was finished. Some were talking about giving up the struggle and making new lives outside the Arab world."[2] But in a heated debate during the Fatah Central Committee meeting, Arafat prevailed over such skepticism, and over the opposition of his aides, gaining support for an armed popular uprising in the occupied territories.

The effort began the month after the war, when Arafat and several of his associates infiltrated into the Israeli-controlled West Bank. Hoping to establish cells there and, eventually, in the Gaza Strip, he set up his headquarters in Nablus—the city that had played such a critical role in the earlier Palestinian uprisings of the 1830s and 1930s. Several months before the Israeli occupation of the city, Arabs witnessed a revolt against the Hashemite regime. Mass demonstrations were organized and about twenty inhabitants were killed by the Jordan security forces; law and order were reestablished only after two weeks of curfew. Nablus seemed to be the ideal base for the guerrillas, with the winding alleys of its densely populated core, the Kasba, and its hinterland of remote, mountain villages. Arafat's aides established other cells in East Jerusalem and Ramallah. But for all of the optimism and the hopes promoted by these initiatives, by early fall there were practically no remnants of Fatah's presence in the West Bank. The organization had picked up stakes and relocated to Karamah, Jordan.

After the fall of the West Bank underground, few organized guerrilla activities originated there except for sporadic hit-and-run attacks. Using Palestinians previously trained by the Egyptian army, Gaza managed to sustain some limited operations, but Ariel Sharon ruthlessly crushed them, resettling about 160,000 refugees—including 70,000 in the West Bank—killing over 100 guerrillas and arresting almost 750 others in the half year beginning July, 1971.[3] Individual Palestinians or small groups maintained violent and nonviolent protest in subsequent decades, but PLO-directed attacks were almost entirely absent. The organization had become another Middle Eastern refugee.

For the nearly 1,000,000 Arabs in the West Bank and Gaza Strip, Fatah's failure had long-term consequences. After slowly emerging from the disorientation of al-Nakba, the 1967 defeat, with the annexation of East Jerusalem, had been almost as great a shock.[4] Now the Palestinians seemed all the more incapable of formulating an answer to the occupation. Anticipating what would take place in Gaza, the Israeli military had made short order of Arafat's dreams of infiltrating into the heart of Palestinian society—assisted, in part, by Fatah's own loose organizational methods. Israel's policies were summed up in the title of a book written by the first Israeli military governor of the occupied territories: *The Stick and the Carrot.*[5] The stick, in the mode of nearly all modern occupying forces, was a series of harsh, repressive measures in response to almost any demonstration of resistance; it included arrests (almost a thousand prisoners were in Israeli jails by the end of 1967), deportations, blowing up houses, and detention without trial or formal charges. Israeli military authorities also meted out collective punishments—closing schools, shops, and markets, as well as imposing strict curfews on the Arab population, in response to nearly any provocation.

The innovative aspect of Israel's occupying policies involved the carrot. Almost from the very beginning of its rule, the military rulers granted a relatively large degree of self-government to the municipalities, later allowing nearly 20 percent of the 1967 refugees to return through a family reunion program. They orchestrated two municipal elections in the 1970s, the second of which greatly expanded the roll of eligible voters and resulted in pro-PLO officials holding office. Moshe Dayan, the defense minister through 1973 and the primary architect of these policies, insisted on open bridges for the movement of people and goods between the West Bank and Jordan, as well as a permeable border between the territories and Israel. He also kept Jordan firmly at the center of all considerations of the West Bank's future. In Dayan's notion of a functional division of rule between Israel and Jordan, the area's inhabitants would continue to be subjects of the Hashemite Kingdom, while the land would be under Israel's control. Although there were qualifiers for many of his measures, the Israelis did try to foster the image of an enlightened, liberal—perhaps, even friendly—occupier. It even oversaw the establishment of the first Palestinian universities—Bir Zeit (1972), Al-Najah (1977), and Gaza Islamic (1978).

As long as both Israelis and Palestinians regarded the occupation, excluding East Jerusalem, as a temporary state of affairs, there was little motivation on either side to exacerbate tensions unduly—little cause for the Palestinians to risk their precarious situations by abetting the cells Arafat tried to establish in 1967. Still, the Israeli policies and the prowess of Israeli intelligence services were only superficial causes for Fatah's failure, interacting with a set of developments in Palestinian society that are the subjects of this chapter.

FROM RESISTANCE TO INSTITUTION BUILDING

In June, 1967, the West Bank's character was shaped primarily by farming, as in the period of the mandate.[6] But what had then been a backwater now contained refugees who were more educated, less likely to have been peasants, than the rest of the West Bank population. Many had lived in the towns and cities of the coastal plain before their descent into refugee status in 1948. While the East Bank had probably changed more due to Palestinian migration than the West Bank had due to initiatives from Amman, efforts at "Jordanizing" the West Bank had made some limited headway before the June war. Nonetheless, few West Bankers considered themselves primarily Jordanians.[7] Nor did they think of themselves as "Palestinians"; indeed, use of the phrase to indicate nationality was just beginning to gain currency. Perhaps the best description of who they were in 1967—more so for the original inhabitants than for the refugees—was simply West Bankers. This did not exclude other dimensions of their identity, whether local, pan-Arab, or Islamic. Nor did it totally mask the deep rifts in the society, especially between the refugees and other residents. This said, it remains the case that the forces acting on the West Bank population had created a unique people, doggedly attached to the Palestine they now inhabited as well as the Palestine of their memories.

Gazans, also using the memory of Palestine as the basis for a new refugee identity during the nineteen years of Egyptian rule, but more cut off from the influences of other national cultures, had also developed their own distinctive subculture. The West Bank and Gazan strands of Palestinian culture only began to reconnect after the 1967 war, in the unexpected environment of a Jewish state.

Even as PLO leaders in Lebanon established their organization as an international force in the early 1970s, many seemed to realize the futility of a policy in the occupied territories resting solely on a general armed uprising. Key Palestinians on the West Bank and in Gaza were putting their energies, not into fomenting such an uprising, but into limited, local political initiatives and the creation of a variety of social organizations. An alternative strategy began to evolve at the tenth and eleventh sessions of the Palestine National Council in 1972 and 1973: aid to grassroots efforts in the West Bank and Gaza Strip—to labor unions and other sorts of organizations and institutions.

This strategy did not come easily. When Rashad al-Shawwa agreed to the Israeli entreaty to become mayor of Gaza and form a municipal council in the fall of 1971, local nationalists objected loudly. At first, the PLO refused to endorse the council. But al-Shawwa persisted, devoting himself to such issues as reviving Gaza's citrus industry. Sara Roy has observed that "with the reinstatement of a locally based municipal structure and the defeat of the resistance movement, political struggle began to challenge armed struggle as a tactical approach for dealing with the realities of the occupation."[8]

As in the early nineteenth century, Nablus was at the center of these changes. But, unlike that period, when Nablus was the heart of an agricultural hinterland, and unlike the early twentieth century, when it played the parochial foil to Jaffa's cosmopolitanism, the new Nablus was a locus of innovation: the generation of indigenous organizations that could create new social parameters.

It was imperative for the PLO, if it hoped to stay relevant, to be in the forefront of this process. Its very charisma insured that it would have an ongoing, forceful say in almost all forms of organizational life—the policies of municipal councils, the setting up and running of the new universities, the editorial policies of the Jerusalem newspapers, even the programs of the Boy Scouts.[9] But its control was limited by two important factors: its physical distance from events in the territories, and the tendency of local organizations to develop and assume autonomous capabilities as their activities expanded.

The PLO's complex relationship with the Palestine National Front, which emerged in the early 1970s to coordinate organizational activities in the territories, demonstrates the PLO's struggle to come to terms with this dilemma.[10] The shift in policy reflected in these activities raised difficult questions about precisely who was in charge. Officially, the creation of the Palestine National Front was the result of a secret decision, divulged later, by the Palestine National Council at its eleventh session, in January, 1973.[11]

In fact, the Front was the creation of a number of young Communist leaders in the West Bank. One of its initiators, the mayor of the small town of al-Birah, has noted that "following the [1973] war, we felt that we needed a collective leadership, so that our political stands and resistance to the military occupation would not be individualistic."[12] Much of this leadership was identified with the Palestine Communist party; the rest included various guerrilla groups, the Baath party, labor unions, professional associations, student groups, and women's organizations.

It gradually became apparent that the Front more closely reflected the shape of events on the West Bank and in the Gaza Strip than it did the desires of the PNC or the PLO leadership.

All of its local leaders publicly accepted the authority of the PLO, while both quietly positioning themselves to influence its decision making and taking on increasing autonomy.[13] Their chief concern was reducing the West Bank's utter dependence on the Israeli economy.

As the Front's popularity grew in the West Bank and Gaza Strip, so did the suspicions within the PLO. The Palestine Communist party represented an organized force with strong roots that PLO leaders feared they could not control. In 1975 and 1976, they demanded that it refrain from propagating any messages in the territories other than those issued by the PLO. They also demanded prior review, and censorship, of any Front publications, accusing it of trying to out-maneuver the PLO.[14] Israel's own harsh response to the Front, like many related policies, ironically played into the hands of PLO members who felt excluded as a result of its activities. Through a curious coalition of the PLO, Israeli authorities (who deported numerous Front activists), and pro-Jordanian figures in the West Bank, the Front declined, finally disappearing in 1977. (It was not until 1987 that the local Communists gained a seat on the Palestine National Council.)

Rather than being exceptional, the PLO's experience with the Front was symptomatic of events to come. The Jordanians were continuing to promote the dominant leadership from the post-1948 period, naturally much more inclined to support its positions than the PLO's. Israel was scanning the horizon for leaders who would cooperate with its administration, looking either to existing local leaders or, later, to new ones through an abortive Israeli invention called the Village Leagues. With the distance from the West Bank, and in the context both of Jordan's open competition and what appeared to be Israel's policy of creeping annexation, it is not surprising that the PLO felt pressed to cement alliances with viable figures in the territories. But its sense of urgency continued to be offset by the fear of finding its authority challenged. To deal with the dilemma, it ended up granting significant latitude on local issues to its allies in the territories, while retaining for itself all "state" issues.

But the solution may have been more rhetorical than practical. Local leaders intent on creating a Western-style, democratic state, such as lawyer Aziz Shehadah of Ramallah, were as aware of the larger importance of their institution building as were the leaders of the PLO.[15] During the Jordanian period, Shehadah had already come under surveillance by the King's security forces for his views on Palestinian autonomy; by 1968, he had earned the wrath of both Fatah and Jordan. Bypassing the PLO in expressing his views to Cyrus Vance (then the U.S. secretary of state), Shehadah was subsequently assassinated.

After the demise of the Palestine National Front, other groups arose that tried to accommodate the PLO's needs and demands with those of Israel and the local population. In response to the Camp David accord, a twenty-one-member National Guidance Committee formed in 1976, serving as a meeting point for heads of the municipalities—elected in 1976—as well as for those of other nascent institutions. Both local and PLO leaders felt that the accord and subsequent Israeli-Egyptian peace treaty validated permanent Israeli control over the territories under the fig-leaf of a theoretical Palestinian autonomy. With the rush of events brought on by Sadat's visit to Jerusalem, the Committee played a key role in mobilizing local Palestinian opposition to what was occurring.

Even that consensus could not hide the conflict between those inside the territories and those outside. Despite more institutional tinkering—this time, the reconstitution of the Palestine National Front to guide the Guidance Committee—the latter organization now fell victim to the complicity of Israel, the PLO, and Jordan. First crippled, it was finally outlawed by Israel in 1984.

Fatah's leaders had somewhat more success in direct attempts at mobilizing youth than in the coordination of ongoing activities. In the early 1980s, they built "The Youth Committee for Social Work," popularly known as Shabiba (The Youth).[16] With projects designed to ingratiate itself into Palestinian society, the organization offered little challenge to the social order—it sanctified the family, separated boys and girls, encouraged the traditional village value of mutual aid, and glorified village life. Its first project was to clean and rehabilitate cemeteries, thus stressing the ties of today's youth with their ancestors.[17] And it followed by cleaning mosques, schools, and other public areas. Soon, it took on a more explicitly political role, working against land expropriations; it also aided families whose houses had been demolished by the Israeli military as a form of collective punishment, or whose members had been detained or deported.

Shabiba's success became particularly evident in the early stages of the Intifada, when it was outlawed by the Israeli authorities.

But even in the case of such volunteer organizations, a tension emerged with Fatah. As we shall see below, university students rallied behind leftist political groups—the Communist party in conjunction with the Popular Front for the Liberation of Palestine and the Democratic Front—to establish a network of cells gaining far more independence than Fatah was willing to grant. Local labor unions similarly threatened Fatah's position, and were thus wrested from their democratically elected leadership, inducing a split in the General Federation of Palestinian Union Workers.

Such differences were probably inevitable. PLO leaders saw themselves as building the foundations for a Palestinian state. Local organizers, although talking of their role in this state, were in fact engaged in a very different project—erecting a civil society out of the diverse Palestinian population. In any case, the PLO faced other formidable barriers to the entrenchment in the territories its leaders sought. First, the Fatah leadership faced competition from other elements in the PLO—a rivalry not limited to youth groups—which fragmented the organization's efforts.[18] Second, the Israelis engaged in an ongoing process of deporting individuals with connections to the PLO from the territories. Their absence, coupled with difficulties the organization had with those allies who were available, reflected difficulties running much deeper than the population's unresponsiveness to the initial call to arms in the summer of 1967.

Perhaps the provisional character of the occupation made popular armed resistance seem superfluous: In the case of the 1956 Sinai war, Israel had been compelled to return the land it conquered—the Gaza Strip and most of the Sinai Peninsula—in less than half a year, without any serious public protests from the Gazan population. The image of Israeli invincibility coming out of the 1967 war may also have made such resistance seem somewhat futile. For both these reasons, the warrior was fading as a rallying point in the popular imagination—replaced, as we have suggested, with more indigenous, less remote archetypes, especially that of the survivor possessing infinite steadfastness, sumud.

Like almost any cultural concept that takes on increasing

power and meaning, sumud became a subject of controversy.[19] Palestinians in the territories differed over the correct form of steadfastness in the face of an occupation turning out, in fact, to be prolonged. The more passive school argued for preserving the status quo: minimal interaction or cooperation with the enemy, and opposition, whenever possible, to any territorial or demographic change. The emphasis was on endurance and, as time went on, avoiding any pretexts for deportation.[20] Others argued for active institution building, seeing local politics as part of the process of state making.

Understood either actively or passively, the image of the steadfast survivor was endowed with an aura of glamour by West Bankers and Gazans eager to avoid the stigma attached to those who had stayed in Israel in 1948 and, many assumed, collaborated with Israel. It gave their daily lives a larger meaning and purpose—ironically, in the context of wide cooperation with the occupier: paying taxes, seeking the many permits needed for various routines, and working for Israelis, even as builders of Jewish settlements or as aides to Israeli military and police officials. Only selling land to Jews, serving Israeli intelligence, and negotiating on wider political issues without PLO permission could jeopardize that standing.

The PLO leaders understood the importance of steadfastness, of preventing a mass exodus of Palestinians from the West Bank and Gaza Strip, and subsequent land sales to Israelis. It supported a project by the Arab states—valued by them as a lever of control—to establish *Sunduq al-Sumud*, the Steadfastness Fund, to discourage migration.

But the theme of the survivor represented a threatening self-sufficiency. A newfound respect for the West Bank's indigenous forces was manifest in the incorporation of the Palestine Communist party into the Palestine National Council in 1987. While Arafat—the archetypal feday—remained the personification of Palestinian nationalism in the occupied territories, it was becoming crystal clear that the vast majority of Palestinians were not prepared to take up arms.

THE CHANGING STRUCTURE OF SOCIETY

In 1987, patterns of West Bank life ranging from marriage to migration looked very different from twenty years before—a change starting in the wake of an overheated Israeli economy in the period following the war.[21] Pent-up demand generated an extraordinarily high need for workers—especially low-skill, low-wage labor that Palestinians could readily provide—and they were gradually integrated into the Israeli labor market.[22] By the 1973 war, as much as one-third of the total work force in the occupied territories was employed in Israeli agriculture, industry, building construction, and services. This drew labor from indigenous economic activities in the West Bank and Gaza, mostly agriculture but some local industry as well.

As in the period before 1948, Palestinians now found their economy uncompetitive with, and overwhelmed by, the adjoining Jewish economy: In agriculture, Israeli gross produce per worker was four times as high as that in the West Bank.[23] Under these circumstances, the possibilities for self-sufficiency there vanished—it became a reservoir of cheap labor for Israel and its second biggest export market, after the United States.

An initial drop in production for farm produce from the occupied territories was followed by a recovery. Continued access to Jordanian markets as a result of the open-bridges policy, coupled with Israeli purchases—despite their official ban—of specialized goods, precipitated a period of recovery from a postwar slump for larger West Bank farmers. Faced with rising agricultural wages due to the lure of jobs in Israel, they began to mechanize and become more productive through use of plastic coverings for vegetables, drip irrigation, and so forth.[24] They also drew more women and children into the labor market, largely as low-paid day workers, filling the gap in the agricultural sector caused by the draw of jobs in Israel.

Overall, however, agriculture—the economic mainstay during Jordanian and Egyptian rule—played a diminishing role in the territories,[25] made even more salient by the overall rapid growth of their economy.[26] Along with the magnetic effect of the Israeli labor market, the decline was caused by a closing of large tracts of land on the West Bank as military security zones and for Jewish settlements and a severe limitation put by Israeli authorities on water use. It is ironic that even as the guerrilla groups resuscitated and glorified the cultural portrait of the heroic peasant, economic changes were making such traditional farmers historical anachronisms—a situation reminiscent of the period of the Arab Revolt in the 1930s.[27]

Throughout the West Bank and Gaza, employers were now Jewish, not Arab; banks were Israeli branches, not Arab ones. Israel had forced banks in the West Bank to break their ties to Jordanian parent companies, causing the shutdown of the local branches (it allowed the branches of the Cairo-Amman Bank to reopen in the mid-1980s). The largest local industry was still olive oil. It was followed by textiles, quarrying, and food processing.[28] Industries were increasingly coming to be subcontractors for larger Israeli manufacturers. While investment in local industry and infrastructure remained pitifully low—continuing a trend of inadequate investment begun under Jordanian and Egyptian rule[29]—consumption grew, as reflected in a remarkable boom in family-home construction. Salim Tamari observes that "the average peasant, after saving some money, tends to put it into a separate housing unit for his own nuclear household, and converts the rest into gold jewelery."[30]

The new prosperity rested on the multiple sources of income possessed by many families, as husbands and sons worked in Israel proper. In 1987, shortly before the outbreak of the Intifada, the numbers of workers officially crossing daily into Israel peaked at 107,000—61,000 from the West Bank and 46,000 from the Gaza Strip—and the actual number was probably greater, perhaps as high as 120,000.[31] The official figure alone translated into a full 40 percent of the work force in the territories.

Indications exist that poorer families with many children were able to narrow the economic gap by sending as many as three or four workers to Israel to engage in construction, agriculture, industry, and services for Jewish employers. While their wages were low by Israel standards, in the context of the West Bank and Gaza Strip they were considerable and, when added together, allowed a rise in status and standard of living.

In the 1970s, with the migration of Palestinians to high paying jobs generated by the oil boom in the Persian Gulf, remittances from abroad—an important source of income in the West Bank and Gaza Strip since the 1950s—further supplemented wages earned in Israel. At times, the absolute number of people in the labor force on the West Bank actually decreased due to the continuing exodus. Higher skilled laborers served as engineers and teachers in the Gulf and in Jordan, which had its own economic boom in the years after 1967. The influx of capital back to the territories from all these workers probably totalled $100–200 million each year.

Other sources of capital also fueled the economic changes. Trade with Israel for industrial and agricultural goods increased considerably,[32] and there were continuing payments of salaries by the Jordanian government to civil servants on the West Bank. About $150 million came from the Steadfastness Fund, supported by the Arab states,[33] with additional aid from continuing UNRWA expenditures on education and salaries, as well as from the U.S. (about $5 million per year from 1975 to 1985) and private voluntary organizations in the West (about $20 million per year).[34] Finally, the Israelis—mainly after 1977—invested in public works, such as road building and electrification, although these were directed largely towards security and the needs of the expanding Jewish settlements.

One author has observed that "the economy of the Gaza Strip is an excellent example of how certain levels of economic prosperity can be achieved with little, if any, economic development."[35] Much the same could be said for the West Bank. For Fatah and the PLO, this combination held portentous implications, almost all the sources of vitality—the Israeli economy, the oil boom, outside capital flows, even the continuing salaries paid by the Jordanian government to civil servants—lay beyond their control. At the same time, the basis for the growth of Palestinian resentment was widening—the territories becoming mere markets for Israeli produce and suppliers of cheap labor[36]— and this generated sympathy for the PLO and feday. PLO leaders were not oblivious to this paradox. At the tenth session of the Palestine National Council in 1972, they passed resolutions calling for new trade union and welfare organizations that could mobilize the public in the territories under their auspices.

THE FOUNDATIONS FOR UPRISING

The remarkable thing for both Palestinians and Israelis was that, despite all the difficulties the PLO encountered in establishing control and a capacity to mobilize, an uprising finally did materialize in the West Bank and Gaza Strip. It was not the armed rebellion Fatah advocated, but it was a massive act of resistance.

It erupted in December, 1987, two decades after Arafat's call to arms, without the direction of the resistance cells he had tried to establish then. In fact, it may have surprised him as much as anyone.

The hopes that the Israeli occupation would be short-lived had proved ever-more fleeting. In October, 1967, a small group of Israelis had formed the Land of Israel movement, asserting the right of the Jewish people and the Israeli state to rule all of what had been the earlier mandated territory of Palestine. The assertion was made more and more stridently, rendering any departure from what had now become the status quo increasingly costly. The terms of the high-decibel political debate centered on the disposition of the territories—questions of defensible borders, the historical (including biblical) rights over the land, the possibilities of trading land for peace, and the settlement of Jews on the newly captured lands—while little was said about the people in them.

Almost precisely a year after the war, the Labor party–led Israeli government tabled the Allon Plan. Named after Yigal Allon, former army general and a minister with several different portfolios in the Labor government, the plan proposed a return of about two-thirds of the West Bank to Jordan, while holding onto a Jewish-settled security strip along the Jordan River. It also would have retained other areas near the old Israeli borders that would attract Jewish settlers. In the first version of the plan, the Gaza Strip was to remain a part of Israel—a preference echoed by Prime Minister Levi Eshkol and Defense Minister Moshe Dayan —although in a later one Allon conceived of Gaza as part of a Jordanian-Palestinian state.[37]

The government never adopted Allon's design, and the plan did not lead to Israel's ceding the Gaza Strip or parts of the West Bank. It did, however, legitimate the settling of Jews within the lines it advocated, adding yet another complicating factor to the difficult relations with the Palestinian Arabs. Behind the settlement, and much of the refusal to return captured territory, was a new social movement—Gush Emunim, or the Bloc of the Faithful, founded after the 1973 war.[38] By 1977, about 11,000 Jews had put down stakes in 84 mostly tiny new communities in the occupied territories, among the most important being Elon

Moreh (Sebastia), Ofra, and Maale Adumim. That was the year the Israelis voted the Labor government out of office, in favor of the Likud party's nationalistic coalition, led by Menachem Begin. Under the new government and its successors, about 100,000 Jewish settlers took up residence in the occupied territories by the end of the 1980s. Most of these were concentrated in 15 settlements, largely metropolitan satellites of Tel-Aviv and Jerusalem.

The Palestinians in the West Bank and the Gaza Strip found themselves facing a two-sided process of change. While their own society was undergoing major transformations, in good part because of a growing symbiotic relationship with the tumultuous Israeli economy, a powerful ethnic group was settling in their midst. The settlers posed an immediate problem through their exclusive and preferential rights: The Israeli government granted them a set of laws different from those of their neighbors—and, in some respects, from those of Jews inside Israel, preferred access to water and land, special security arrangements.[39] The glaring reality of second-class status now confronted the Palestinians not only during sojourns into Israel.

The settlers were also causing longer-term complications. They lobbied with considerable success for the Israeli government to include the West Bank and Gaza Strip, but not their Arab inhabitants, within the state borders, and to redefine Israeli identity to legitimate this inclusion.[40] This implied granting the Palestinians far fewer rights than the Jews or, at best, a separate set of rights altogether, within some context of local Palestinian autonomy. By the 1980s, it interacted, at times, with the ominous notion of "transferring" the Arabs—through economic inducements or deportation, depending on who was proposing the "transfer"—from the territories. While this new threat emanated from marginal political parties, once the Intifada was under way, as much as half the Jewish public subscribed to one or another of its forms.[41]

The political menace to Palestinians, then, was dynamic in nature. It did not stem from military occupation alone, but from the powerful economic forces and incrementally changing legal code that came with it, from the growing Jewish presence (increasingly after 1977 in the most heavily populated parts of the West Bank), from shifting Israeli opinions about the ultimate disposition of the territories and their inhabitants, and from the reordering of Israeli society and its politics.[42] By the early 1980s, occupation-with-a-smile had turned into hardened military rule—a stick far more than a carrot. A clear shift came as early as 1978, with the Likud's appointment of Menahem Milson to the position of administrator of the West Bank. Milson, a Hebrew University professor of Arabic literature, felt Palestinian nationalism had been allowed to grow unhindered long enough. By 1985, the term "iron fist" had entered the Israeli lexicon, introduced by the former prime minister and now defense minister of a national unity government, Labor's Yitzhak Rabin. For both Palestinians and Israelis, the occupation was having a wearing effect, exacerbating the existing proclivity to demonize one another. With pallid international initiatives failing to bring an end to Israeli rule, some Palestinians—including those born under occupation—began to advocate a move beyond steadfastness.

Along with the nature of the occupation, the character of the Palestinians was changing. West Bankers and Gazans had begun to demonstrate their solidarity with Israeli Arabs by marking Land Day. Palestinians adopted a common hymn, "Biladi, Biladi" ("My Country, My Country") from an Egyptian patriotic tune, along with composing or adopting many other songs to articulate a growing sense of common identity and protest their circumstances. A literature of resistance appeared and quickly expanded. In 1982, the military government banned the distribution of approximately one thousand books, including fiction, nonfiction, and poetry[43]—a doubtful gesture, since the items can be bought in East Jerusalem, where the military has no authority. East Jerusalem also became the base of the Palestinian press—a major tool in creating national consciousness—with newspapers distributed semi-illegally in the West Bank and Gaza, Israel, and abroad.[44] The authorities outlawed the display of the black, white, red, and green Palestinian flag, as well, but without noticeable success. In very important ways, the meetings, discussion, and political activity of the 1970s had had a cumulative effect, resulting by the 1980s in a much more tightly woven society.[45]

Probably no structures played a more important role in this regard than the new universities. Fearful of the emergence of an independent center of West Bank life, the Jordanian authorities had stood in the way of the creation of a Palestinian national university in Ramallah in 1970–71. (One of the key figures behind the effort had been Aziz Shehadah, who ran afoul of the PLO as much as he did the Jordanians; another was Sheikh Ali al-Jaabri, the traditional, pro-Jordanian leader of Hebron.) Despite this failure, local colleges did emerge on the West Bank, mostly out of well-established high schools. Besides the three major universities authorized by Dayan, there was the Islamic College of Hebron, Jerusalem University (which included three separate colleges), and Bethlehem University. The motivation for building these colleges was not so much nationalism as necessity, given the difficulty of attending outside universities and the higher incomes of Palestinian Arab families.

Once built, the colleges became centers for interpreting the occupation's common meaning. They also became the cornerstone of a quiet demand for autonomy in other spheres. With almost fourteen thousand students by 1985, their weight was considerable.[46]

In Bir Zeit, the student council put great effort into nationalistic cultural activities, including festivals, exhibits, and "Palestinian weeks." A typical one involved poetry readings, presentations of plays, and song recitals, all with strong nationalistic themes. Shinar reports that "Palestinian flags and posters with the national colors, both banned by the authorities, are usually raised and decorated with slogans such as 'Palestine, fight till the end,' 'Blessed art thou, Palestine, the ancestors' land,' 'With Allah's help we shall come back,' 'We shall return in battle with the most courageous soldiers,' and 'Death to the Jews.' "[47]

University and college students were determined to carry their activities beyond the campus. Those at Bir Zeit sought to provide economic and social services to fellaheen and to the villages. Behind their participation in plowing, harvesting, road-building, and village cleaning lay the cultural theme of sumud. Its new vitality owed much to the Palestine Communist party and its strong indigenous roots. Backed by the party, the students worked to bridge the divide between rural and urban Palestinians and head off Israeli efforts to purchase land from farmers. In 1980, in the face of opposition from Fatah, Jordan, and various elements who feared activities mixing men and women, they established the Supreme Committee for Voluntary Work.[48] The committee included about 40 branches and more than 1,000 volunteers. Its credo was as follows:

> We do not only build a wall or pave a road. We are building a new human being. . . . Our purpose is to turn voluntary work into a workshop and a school, both able to provide our Palestinian people with pioneering individuals, bound by national ethics, firmly anchored into the land and highly dedicated to the national cause. . . .[49]

As we have seen in chapter 4, the mandate period had already witnessed the beginning of a trade union movement among Palestinian Arabs, with Communists, Zionists, and others scrambling to organize the emerging working class. Some activity had continued in the Jordanian period, especially by the Jordanian Communist party, but harsh repression had choked these grassroots efforts—in1961, there were 16 active local trade unions in various economic sectors, compared to approximately 40 four years earlier.

After the 1967 war, union activity increased dramatically, more as a vehicle towards national unity than of class struggle. Growth was most rapid after 1975, especially in the West Bank, although the unions did not incorporate that half of the work force commuting daily to Israel, where they were not recognized. With the larger union rolls, internal battles abounded, particularly between the Communists and Fatah.[50] At stake was not only who would have his hand on the levers of power in society but also the distribution of funds provided by Arab states as a result of the 1979 Baghdad conference.

Like the student-led groups, the unions were part of an intense effort by leftist organizations to mobilize the population. Nationalism was never far from the top of their agenda. In several strikes of the important Jerusalem Union of Hotel, Restaurant, and Coffee Shop Workers—which had over one thousand dues-paying members and probably almost as many nonpaying sympathizers—demands over wages and working conditions comingled with those to expel Israeli union organizers.[51] The trade unions, with their highly democratic settings and generally fair elections—at least until Fatah's effort to control their activities[52]—were models for a common effort transcending family and other ties. They also served as excellent schools for local and regional leadership, most union leaders eventually being detained or deported by the Israelis.

There is some evidence of Palestinian women's activism as far back as 1884, protesting the establishment of the first Jewish settlements.[53] During the mandate, small groups of women, mainly from the ayan and prosperous Christian merchant families, took advantage of their relative freedom to participate in the national struggle: About 200 women participated in the Palestine Congress of October, 1929, then marching through the streets of Jerusalem chanting anti-British slogans.[54] But these efforts were very limited. It was only from the mid-1960s that broad-based women's associations became critical components in the building of a new civil society. In the West Bank—as in Israeli Palestinian society—they provided a wide array of social services for community centers, orphanages, homes for the elderly, and families facing the imprisonment of sons and husbands. The most important of these associations, Inash al-Usra (which roughly translates as "family support network"), was actually created in 1965, before Israeli occupation began. Its founder, Samiha Khalil (popularly known as Umm, mother of, Khalil), came from a middle class refugee family. She and her colleagues built branches all through the West Bank, offering women diverse training projects and employed them in a variety of ways, mainly producing traditional wares and textiles.[55] More explicitly political organizations, such as the Palestinian Women's Association and the General Union of Palestinian Women, also began to take hold on the West Bank.

Student groups, labor unions, and women's associations constituted only a small portion of the institutional network that existed at the outbreak of the Intifada in 1987. Sports clubs, a sophisticated and politicized central theater, other amateur acting groups, charities, branches of the Red Crescent Society, the Palestinian Physicians', Pharmacists' and Lawyers' Association, other professional organizations, all thrived—especially when compared to the period of Jordanian rule—helping make life under prolonged occupation viable.[56]

Occupation had also made it more likely that such voices would be heard, and that enough cohesion existed for a collective response to be effective. The occupation had substantially weakened what ordinarily would have been the most prominent and influential social class—that of the landowners and mer-

chants.[57] While certainly not eclipsing all the differences between rich and poor, the new institutional activities, led by the
university and high school graduates and aided by the general
antipathy to Israeli occupation, served as meeting grounds for
diverse groups of Palestinians. The occupation thus resulted in
the first steps toward a political levelling of the society and in
bases for association across formerly unbroachable sexual and
class lines[58]—key elements in the spontaneous outbreak of the
Intifada. Equally important was the deteriorating standard of
economic life in the territories during the 1980s, a major factor
in the semblance of normality during the occupation's first fifteen years having been the burgeoning economy. As in the first
half of the 1940s, fast-paced economic growth had served as a
damper on collective resistance.

Three sources of prosperity had fueled this economy—Israel
itself, with its developed, labor-intensive market; Jordan, with
its strong agricultural build-up; and the Persian Gulf states, with
their seemingly endless supply of petro-dollars. By the early
1980s, each had entered a prolonged crisis, in turn choking the
West Bank and Gaza. A sense of economic hopelessness now
combined with flagging hopes that international diplomacy, the
PLO, or outside Arab armies would bring an end to the occupation. (Internationally, the period had witnessed the dissolution
of the alliance between Hussein and Arafat, the disappointing
Arab summit in Amman, and the Reagan-Gorbachev meeting,
all of which indicated lack of momentum towards a diplomatic
solution.) A much more educated, mobile, and nonagricultural
population found a world of shrinking economic opportunities.

The contrast between the pre- and post-1980 economy in the
West Bank and the Gaza Strip is dramatic. With overall economic growth in the period from 1967 to 1980 averaging over 5
percent annually, the territories had witnessed an easing of the
harsh material conditions the Palestinians had endured under
Jordanian and Egyptian rule. Gazans, in particular, had entered
the era of occupation with annual per capita incomes averaging
$80.[59] By the beginning of the Intifada, that figure had reached
$1,700. Even in the West Bank, which had been part of Jordan's
rapidly growing economy—over 8 percent annual economic
growth between 1954 and 1967—personal consumption was far
greater than at the beginning of Israeli rule, the gross domestic
product more than tripling between 1968 and 1980: an extraor-

dinarily high rate of growth by world standards.[60] Even if those economies demonstrated little self-generating potential, they at least had made life materially palatable for most of the population.

During the late 1970s, worrisome economic signs were on the horizon. The Israeli economy, which had been a textbook case of rapid growth until the 1973 war, slipped into a long period of slow growth and stagnation.[61] Inflation, always something of a problem, became hyperinflation, with annual rates reaching 1,000 percent. In many areas of the world, inflation has been a precipitant for social unrest; its corrosive effects on wages and savings combined with the uncertainty that it fosters has often served as a mobilizing force among workers. For Palestinians, now deeply integrated into the Israeli economy, stagflation had dire consequences. By 1980, it was evident that real wages for those working in Israel were eroding, and by 1985 the slippage was quite pronounced. Workers from one West Bank village reported that their real wages were cut in half by inflation in the five-year period before 1985.[62] The resulting economic discontent, combined with the occupation, formed the basis for easy nationalist fervor.

Unemployment, first evident in Israel in the late 1970s, began to hit the territories seriously in the early 1980s. Rates of unemployment in the West Bank more than quadrupled between 1980 and 1985 to over 5 percent, hitting the young and the educated particularly hard. In the latter part of the decade, the influx of Soviet Jews exacerbated the problem of unemployment, reaching double-digit figures in Israel. The immigration had both an indirect effect on Palestinians by straining the already fragile economy they depended upon and, later, a direct impact as Soviets filled the menial jobs Arabs had formerly held. In the early 1990s, overqualified Palestinians—the products of the expanding educational system—and overqualified Soviet Jews eyed the same low-level jobs.

Just as immigration levels were rising, Israel found itself with a rapidly declining rate of new job creation, to less than 1.5 percent by 1980. The country had moved from a labor-hungry economy at the start of the occupation to one in which the work force could not be absorbed. As the politically and economically weakest part of that work force, Palestinians found the change particularly ominous.

Complicating the situation in Israel was that in outside economies. Through the 1970s, Palestinians had left the West Bank and Gaza in large numbers for opportunities elsewhere. The net outflow was as high as twenty thousand people a year—even with all the emphasis on the survivor's sumud.[63] For both migrants and family members depending on their remittances, the performance of other Middle Eastern economies was crucial.

Jordan had served both as a transit point and end point for those leaving the West Bank. For the overall period 1965–86, its economy had rapidly expanded. But high average rates of economic growth can mask sharp vacillations.[64] In the few years after the 1967 war and the loss of the West Bank, Jordan's national product had declined by one-third to two-fifths. By the time Israel assumed control of the West Bank in 1967, as many as 400,000 Palestinians had migrated in search of a better life. In the 1970s, Jordan rebounded, achieving the stupendous growth rate of 10 percent in the five years following 1977. It benefited from the good fortune of the oil states—whose petrodollars meant aid, financial investments, and remittances—and from the ill fortune of Lebanon, which lost its key financial role among the Arab states to Amman during its long civil war.

But during the 1980s, the country's absorptive capacity dried up in the wake of the larger Middle Eastern economic crisis. Remittances slipped steadily through the decade, leading to large declines in per capita income.[65] The Gulf War of 1991 simply capped an already eroding position, aid from the oil states ending and the economy contracting severely, due to Jordan's support of Saddam Hussein. Clearly, Jordan was no longer an attractive stop for West Bank workers.

The oil-producing states were also facing severe contraction. World fears of an international oil shortage at the outbreak of the Iran-Iraq war in 1980 had driven prices to unprecedented heights: A standard barrel had reached $40, compared to a figure less than one-third of that after the first series of oil price hikes following the Arab-Israeli war of 1973. But this boom was not to last long—overpumping in the face of such attractive rates and slackening demand due to both high cost and world recession led to a precipitous decline in prices. By the late 1980s, with a barrel selling for around $15, the real price had fallen to less than half of what it had been at the end of 1973, and less than one-third what it had been in 1980. The slump cut deeply into Palestinian economic life. Jobs disappeared, making emigration much less attractive. Remittances from workers in the Gulf countries diminished drastically.

Palestinian Arabs in the West Bank and Gaza were thrown back on the local economy and that of Israel at precisely the wrong time. Perhaps a third of those working in Israel still cultivated land and could gain some income from farming: Happily, the failure of capitalist, mechanized farming in the mountainous villages of the West Bank meant that those who could hold onto postage-stamp–sized plots had a fallback when all else failed, also serving as a source of income to share tenants who worked the land.[66] But many workers were rural dwellers without access to land; still others lived in the towns or refugee camps. The Israeli policy of carrots and economic opportunities—something for Palestinians to contemplate losing when the thought of resistance crossed their minds—meant little to a generation raised and educated under stiffening occupation, many of whose members were now unemployed and with little economic hope for the future.[67]

The bleakness of national prospects thus combined with despair over individual and family prospects. Added to this dismal brew were the personal experiences of routine harassment, occasional beatings, arrests without formal charges, and humiliating searches by security forces at roadblocks and checkpoints. Young Palestinians increasingly felt there was little to lose if they broke the rules of the game.

INTIFADA

On December 8, 1987, an Israeli truck hit two vans carrying Gaza laborers in Jabalya, a refugee camp packed with sixty thousand residents. The crash instantly killed four of them. Rumor—an essential ingredient in the prelude to any ethnic violence—spread quickly that the wreck was no accident, but an act of vengeance on the part of the relative of an Israeli stabbed to death several days earlier in the Gaza market. A denunciatory Palestinian leaflet—one of the uprising's major motifs—appeared in the evening.

At the funeral that same evening, thousands of mourners turned on the nearby Israeli army post, assaulting it with a barrage of stones. By the morning, the streets and alleys of the camp were filled with quickly fashioned barricades, and full-scale violence broke out, inaugurating the uprising.

Acts of violence against the occupying forces were certainly not unheard of in the territories: Between 1968 and 1975, the Israeli military counted an average of about 350 incidents a year; from 1976 to 1982, the number doubled. After that, it jumped precipitously to 3,000, which itself dramatically paled next to the outbreaks starting in December. Over the next six months, there were 42,355 recorded incidents.[68] For the first time since the occupation began, the Israeli forces lost control of the population in the occupied territories. On the uprising's first day, rioting spread to other camps in the Gaza Strip, and the next day it fanned across those in the West Bank as well. During the rest of December, the confrontations occurred largely in the camps—the sites of the most extreme misery as well as the centers of nationalism over the previous decades. Between mid-January and mid-February, villages and towns also became actively involved in the resistance.[69]

Just as important as the spontaneous extension of the rioting was the Palestinian perception of its meaning: not as expressing individual grievances, but those of all the individuals and localities together. The events soon acquired a name, Intifada ("shaking off"), which was consciously compared to the 1936–39 revolt.[70] The mythic qualities of the survivor now stood alongside a new cultural form—direct and sometimes violent resistance. For the third time in the last two centuries, the Arabs of Palestine had risen up in revolt.

Its fighters were not professional guerrillas, but children of the stone, faces shrouded by kafiyas or masks, standing ready to confront Israeli soldiers openly and head-on. In the popular image, they stood without feelings of inferiority—the soldier with his modern weapons, the shabab armed only with stones. Here is one among countless poems glorifying the new hero—and making the important jump from the child to the shahid, or martyr:

> Have you seen his mark in the streets
> In my bloodstream rave winds
> Flames spurt from my fingers . . .
>
> He dawned
> On people's horizon

He woke us
He joined us
He bonded us all . . .

Lo the moon has now risen
He lived and was roaring
He died and was roaring:
Hail the stone!
Hail the stone!
Hail the stone![71]

Martyrdom became the means to make legendary the acts of children of the stone. The family of a martyr was accorded special honor, and posters of him were carried at demonstrations and appeared on walls. The omnipresent leaflets and folk songs acclaimed his heroic acts. Penny Johnson notes that "in the intifada, the rebellious young men, the shabab, have become the sons of all the people and their exploits legendary."[72]

The PLO financially supported the martyr's family, although canonization as a shahid occasionally led to a process of bargaining about the precise amount of support. While the popular imagination was fixed on individual, youthful heroism—indeed, often the stone throwing consisted of such spontaneous acts, and often by groups of shabab—existing organizations, such as Shabiba, and numerous new youth groups, stood behind the uprising's more institutionalized "strike forces." Within a short time, the image of the child of the stone became so powerful that Israeli soldiers were instructed to direct their fire at the "chief instigators"—those with the shrouded faces.

If the shock troops of the Intifada were represented by a young masked face, the new local leadership was represented by the anonymous leaflet, itself a way "to shroud [its] true face."[73] Territory-wide leaflets appeared by the end of December, and by January they carried the signature of the Unified National Leadership of the Uprising in the Occupied Territories, later accompanied by the signature of the PLO.[74] The Leadership consisted, at least in the first half year or so, of the second-rank representatives of the various outside guerrilla organizations—Fatah, the Popular Front for the Liberation of Palestine, and the Democratic Front for the Liberation of Palestine plus the Palestine Communist party. This mirrored the heavier influence of leftist groups inside the territories compared to outside, where Fatah's dominance was much more pronounced. (In fact, leftists claimed that the outside should be organized along the same lines.) Not naming top figures made it more difficult for the Israelis, but also for the uprising's leaders, to develop the autonomy that the Fatah-dominated PLO feared. The Leadership drew up the leaflets in the territories, based on local circumstances, and then sent them outside for modification and approval by the PLO, which broadcast them over Baghdad Radio.[75] Local shabab then distributed them in the West Bank and the Strip.

Besides containing eulogies of the shahid, the leaflets set out specific directives for the strike forces, the popular committees that had formed to implement the plans, and the general population. A primary goal articulated in the leaflets was to break the dependency of the territories on Israel, as a prelude to the establishment of a Palestinian state.[76] They called for a shunning of the Israeli civil administration, a boycott of Israeli products, a mass resignation of Palestinian police officers and tax collectors, a refusal to pay taxes, a search for alternatives to work in Israel (especially in agricultural enterprises), attacks on Jewish settlers and an end to work in the settlements, a closing of shops for part of each day, and an attempt to create alternative Palestinian institutions in industry, agriculture, education, and the like.

The results were decidedly mixed. Police officers and tax collectors did indeed resign, much to the consternation of the Israelis, who futilely used a variety of means to try to reverse the mass walkout. At great economic cost, shopkeepers heeded the call for a partial commercial strike, shuttering their stores each afternoon. But the boycott of Israeli products only partially succeeded (it did provide a boom for local workshops, benefiting from an increased demand for their own products[77]). And except for announced general strikes, which were quite effective, a substantial proportion of laborers continued to cross into Israel to work, albeit in reduced numbers; many others continued to work for the settlements.

This mirrored the mixed success of the Intifada as a whole. Its triumph in a number of areas was unprecedented. Images of the shahid electrified the population, leading to new, sustained levels of mobilization and revolutionary fervor. The poet Mahmoud Darwish captured the mood in words addressed to Israelis:

We have that which does not please you: we have the future
And we have things to do in our land.

Another partisan declared that "An air of popular democracy has
pervaded the atmosphere."[78]

Self-reliance grew, as well. When the Israelis closed schools
for prolonged periods, many Palestinians set up their own clandestine classrooms. Economically, they became increasingly
self-sufficient in a number of fields, such as dairy farming—by
buying cows from Israelis, they managed to satisfy 80 percent of
their dairy needs—and animal husbandry. At the same time, the
uprising bloodied the already faltering Israeli economy. The
Bank of Israel reported that after two years of rebellion the direct
cost to Israel had been 1.4 percent of its national wealth, or over
$1 billion, and the indirect costs even higher.[79]

But after four years of sometimes bloody battles, the Palestinians had not managed to bring an end to the occupation or create
national independence. This failure, notes one researcher, led to
the redefinition of their goals, now "generally defined as the
reestablishment of the Palestinian political agenda internationally, and the reaffirmation of Palestinian identity."[80] It is not
surprising that after the first six months the uprising lost some
of its spontaneity and autonomy. The original Unified Leadership was decimated: 69 leaders sent into exile by mid-1991, well
over 600 shooting deaths,[81] and 40,000 arrests through May
1990. And the Arafat-led PLO exercised firmer control over those
who replaced them.

Local leaders also found that they had to temper some of their
demands on the population. Later leaflets modulated the stigma
on working in Israel, imposing a ban, instead, on certain days or
on specific sectors that competed with the Palestinian economy.
The boycott on Israeli products was modified so that it applied
to products for which a local substitute was available.[82]

Large-scale violence by a nearly permanently mobilized population gave way to small groups of resisters or even individuals
who used hit-and-run tactics and sabotage—including arson in
Israeli forests, torching of cars, and knifing and kidnapping of
Israelis, especially soldiers and settlers in the occupied territories. By the 1990s, the Israelis were content to station their
military forces safely outside most refugee camps and other com-

munities, allowing an unanticipated degree of community autonomy. The new deployment also reduced the opportunities for head-on confrontations between mobilized groups of Palestinians and Israeli soldiers.

A sense of hopelessness had pervaded the territories in November, 1987—a feeling that all the diplomatic jet-setting by PLO Executive members and Arab statesmen would not bring an end to occupation. The Arab summit meeting that month had placed the Iran-Iraq war, not the Palestinians, at the top of the Arab agenda. That message, in fact, helped spark the uprising, as a self-reliant way of emerging from a political cul-de-sac.[83]

After more than two years of frenzied rioting and backbreaking hardship, renewed despair about the uprising's limited potential now led the Palestinians to look outside again for some way to end the occupation. By spring of 1988, the Unified Leadership's leaflets were openly calling for outside diplomatic support. Later, Palestinian support of Saddam Hussein in the Gulf War reflected a desperate hope of thus achieving what the Intifada clearly could not. After Iraq's ignominious defeat, Roy wrote of those in the Gaza Strip, "Palestinians feel totally abandoned, increasingly helpless, and very fearful. They are harassed by the army on a daily basis and have no institutional recourse or form of appeal. Daily life is impossibly oppressive and people genuinely despair of protection."[84] And in fact, in a widely quoted statement, Defense Minister Rabin defined the measures needed to maintain security as "might, force, and beatings" and "breaking their bones." In the third year, some easing occurred, as the Israeli forces gave up on efforts to impose order on every square meter of the territories, focusing instead on central strategic areas.

Outside economic opportunities for the Palestinian Arabs had almost entirely disappeared, the support for Saddam Hussein by both the PLO and the rank-and-file having made them unwelcome in many parts of the Middle East. The once prosperous community of nearly four-hundred thousand Palestinians in Kuwait was shattered upon the Iraqi defeat—and the return of the Kuwaiti government. In late 1991, less than half of the community remained. In Jordan, the economy had suffered a dramatic slide, affecting both Palestinians there and those on the West Bank whose salaries were in Jordanian dinars: The value of the dinar in January, 1989, was less than half of what it had been only six months before. Once the Gulf crisis began in August, 1990, the decline intensified.

In the occupied territories themselves, the dismal economic performance in the period leading up to the uprising turned drastically worse: Communities were reporting unemployment rates of 30 to 40 percent. Conditions deteriorated further with the UN coalition's bombing of Iraq and the Iraqi Scud missile attacks on Israel starting in January, 1991. The standstill of the Israeli economy and the Palestinians' exclusion from it once the war ended were combined with the cut-off of Arab aid to the PLO, some of which had been funnelled to the territories. With a drastic cut in their cash flow, retailers in the territories complained of a falloff in business of almost 80 percent.

Although accurate figures are hard to come by, some collected for Gaza indicate, at the very least, the magnitude of the problem. In the first three years of the Intifada, Palestinians in Gaza saw a 30 percent decline in their gross national product; a drop in per capita income from $1,700 to $1,200, with some families losing as much as three-quarters of their income; a 75 percent decline in remittances from outside; and a sharp drop in income from work in Israel. Once the Gulf War began, work in Israel stopped altogether and after the war did not even come close to the depressed prewar level. Soviet immigrants, who themselves were desperate over the lack of economic opportunities, now stepped into the open jobs. In the month after the end of the war, ten thousand West Bank and Gazan Palestinians worked in Israel—less than 10 percent of the pre-Intifada numbers. Large increases in child labor, requests for UNRWA supplementary feeding programs (up 200 percent), and sharp rises in the numbers requiring emergency food aid are a few indicators of the desperate economic straits in Gaza.[85]

Some early, sketchy figures for the West Bank indicate similarly dire conditions. Four months after the start of the Intifada, West Bank gross domestic product had declined by 29 percent, individual consumption by 28 percent, and employment by 36 percent.[86] The $200 million share of both Gazan and West Bank subcontractors in Israel's construction industry evaporated. Exports to Israel dropped by 50 percent in the first year of the uprising, and then continued to decline.

Despite all these difficulties, the Intifada still stands as the preeminent event in the Palestinians' recent history, galvanizing a sense of community and nationhood; it has fostered what Laurie Brand has termed their reempowerment.[87] But, like its predecessor, the Arab Revolt of 1936–39, it has exposed rifts corresponding to this greatly heightened sense of unified purpose.[88] Any communal uprising brings conflicts over what the new society will be into much starker relief—who will lead it, what the relationship of leaders to followers will be, which beliefs and symbols will prevail. This occurs despite efforts to paper over tensions and project an air of unity.

With hindsight, we can see how the 1936 revolt allowed a surfacing of important questions about the Palestinians' future. Conflicts between merchants and shabab, coastal city dwellers and inland villagers, Christians and Muslims, all revolved around that future. The closeness of the Intifada makes us somewhat myopic on this score, but we can still form an idea of the important questions regarding Palestinian leadership and the role of religion in the definition of their society. The fact that nearly half as many Palestinians in the occupied territories have been charged and killed as collaborators by other Palestinians as have died at the hands of the Israeli military hints at some very strong clashing currents beneath a unified oppositional front.

The 1987 outbreak of sustained revolt by a mobilized population took the established national leadership by surprise just as had that of the Mufti and his colleagues at the general strikes rocking Palestine in April, 1936. Like Amin al-Husseini, Yasser Arafat was quick to associate himself with the new revolt, speaking on the second day of "the children of the stones in our beloved, holy country" as the contemporary achievements of the Fatah–PLO revolution—a connection that proved very important for the PLO's effort to reestablish its international position after the Lebanese fiasco.

Even with the association between the PLO and the Intifada, some strain between the organization's top echelons and the Unified Leadership seems to have emerged during the first half year or so. There is considerable disagreement about the level of overt conflict afterward. Some argue there was complete harmony between the outside and inside leadership—that the Unified Leadership simply "sees itself as the local political and activist arm of the PLO."[89] Others see a continuation of the battle for local autonomy at work between them.[90]

But open conflict is less the issue than the more subtle tensions determining the place of the local leadership in the overall national movement. In the period leading up to the uprising, Gazan and West Bank leaders had been afforded short shrift by the PLO leadership. The Intifada now enabled residents in the territories to influence the PLO's political positions more strongly and directly, to play a major role in determining the national political agenda, and to transform the accepted national tactics. In particular, the local leadership pushed the PLO towards acceptance of Israel, a two-state solution to the conflict, and participation in U.S.-sponsored peace talks with Israel despite the formal exclusion of the PLO.[91] In fact, according to a Helena Cobban interview with Arafat, it pushed the PLO Executive to abandon armed struggle within the context of the Intifada.[92] Communications from West Bank and Gaza leaders, notes Cobban, "could no longer be downgraded by the PLO leaders as had sometimes been the case before December 1987."[93] Teitelbaum and Kostiner echo this point: "Not only had the Palestinian movement become a mass movement, but its political center of gravity had shifted."[94]

The relatively smooth process by which the PLO incorporated the Unified Leadership into a more prominent national role was attributable, in part, to a single individual. He was Arafat's aide Abu Jihad, the editor of *Filastinuna*, who also served as the PLO's overall coordinator in the occupied territories, and who worked endlessly to avoid open rifts with the young leaders there. It is simply too soon, at the time of this writing, to assess whether his assassination in April, 1988, in Tunis—almost certainly by the Israelis—may have led to a long-term erosion of that link.

For Arafat's PLO, the ability to gain the public deference of the Unified Leadership and to have other Arabs identify the organization with the dramatic and popular Intifada was critical. It enhanced the PLO's own position in face of others still trying to shape the future of the Palestinians—King Hussein of Jordan and President Hafiz al-Asad of Syria, in particular. Abandoning his long struggle with the PLO for influence on the West Bank, the Jordanian king formally disclaimed his sovereignty on July 31, 1988. (This was something of a shock. Even after the 1976 municipal elections in the West Bank resulted in the rise of pro-PLO officials, the Jordanians had continued to press their influence.[95]) This step allowed the final triumph of an educated, internal leadership with few attachments to the Hashemites. (It should be added that King Hussein did not shut the door altogether—West Bankers, for instance, still held Jordanian citizenship and passports.)

At the same time, the dogged Syrian opposition to Arafat began to lessen, although no reconciliation took place until 1991. With such pressure behind it, the PLO recognized Israel's right to exist, renounced terrorism, initiated diplomatic contacts with the United States, and had the Palestine National Council declare the creation of a Palestinian state at its November, 1988, meeting in Algiers. Unfortunately for the PLO, it could not sustain its new international position. After its refusal to condemn a terrorist attack, the U.S. broke off the contacts; later, its ties to Saddam Hussein eroded much of the goodwill it had accumulated. But it still served notice that, by deftly incorporating the Unified Leadership, it had gained power in the struggle to control Palestinian society. The remaining question was whether Palestinians from the West Bank and Gaza Strip—the so-called inside leadership—could wrest meaningful influence and control from the Tunis-based, outside leadership. Once again Nablus, now termed "the city of martyrs" in the Arab press for its sacrifices during the Intifada, faced off against a contending center of power—but in this instance the contender lay far from the shores of Palestine.

No struggle for the future of Palestinian society became more clear in the course of the Intifada than that over the future role of Islam. Even the most secular and national figures appropriated cultural symbols that had strong Islamic resonances. But the conflict went deeper than such appropriation. Just as in the 1936–39 revolt, the uncertainty associated with rebellion thrust the question of religion back into popular concerns. In the 1930s, the Mufti had used his religious office and the institution of the Supreme Muslim Council as a springboard for national leadership. Sheikh Qassam had employed his position as a Haifa preacher to touch off the general strike and the peasant uprising. And the Arab Revolt itself had revealed intense anti-Christian sentiments by some of those agitating against the British and Jews.

The last two decades of the twentieth century have been a

period in which Islam has played a much more overt role in Middle East politics, from Algeria to Iran. While to some of the educated, urban population of the 1930s it may have appeared a living anachronism, by the time of the Intifada it had emerged as a self-assured and active alternative to European-style nationalism. In the Gaza Strip, especially, Islamic organizations challenged the entire worldview of the various elements comprising the PLO and the Unified Leadership.

The major Islamic group, Hamas (or the Islamic Resistance Movement, which was the Palestinian branch of the Muslim Brethren), and a smaller faction, Islamic Jihad, aimed to establish an Islamic state in Palestine and, perhaps later, throughout the Arab Middle East. They rejected the nationalists' aim of a secular, religiously pluralistic state.[96] Their target was not so much individual Christians or Druze, as in the 1930s, but the very foundation of the inclusive nationalist conception of who the Palestinians are. The sorts of bridges between nationalist and religious activism that had dominated the 1930s, including the view of the Mufti himself, were now much less in evidence. Hamas thus posed not just an ideological challenge but—like the Communist party and other indigenous groups—an internal social challenge to the movement based in Tunis and Baghdad.

As in the rest of the Middle East, the prime mover of the Islamic revival in the occupied territories was the Iranian Revolution of 1978. But even that event came in the midst of a dramatic rise in prayer attendance and the building of mosques, especially in the Gaza Strip. By the 1980s, there was clear evidence of Islamic entry into the Palestinian political realm. In 1979, student elections at Bir Zeit University—the most important and the most secular of the Palestinian universities—had led to important victories for avowedly Islamic candidates. They came away with 43 percent of the vote, and in subsequent years regularly garnered 30–35 percent in universities throughout the West Bank. This success was the result of determined, grassroots organizing, stressing the importance of individual and moral change.

Standing behind Hamas was the imposing figure of Sheikh Ahmad Ismail Yasin of Gaza. The military court had sentenced him to thirteen years in prison in 1984, after Israeli authorities had discovered sixty rifles in his home, but he won early release as part of a larger prisoner exchange. His influence was evident in Islam's growing activism in the Gaza Strip—in his success at gaining control of the Islamic University and ridding it of pro-PLO forces. Once the uprising began, Sheikh Yasin moved to forestall a complete PLO appropriation of the Intifada. He broadened his base in the West Bank and, breaking with his long-time practice, began to allow his movement's use of some nationalist symbols and language.

The desire of both Yasin and Arafat to keep the fires of the uprising burning, and to direct Palestinian fury against the Israelis, not each other, helped minimize the number of open clashes between their followers. Both the Islamic and nationalist forces encouraged resistance to the Israelis, with the Muslims usually calling for more violent action and the Unified Leadership shunning arms and direct violence. But sniping between them still occurred. Differences had already been evident after the founding of the precursor to Hamas in the Gaza Strip in the mid-1980s. Yasin's group—deeply influenced by the Egyptian Muslim Brethren—undertook both verbal and physical assaults on the PLO and its allies, particularly on the pro-PLO Red Crescent Society.

During the course of the Intifada, Hamas began to disregard directives set out in the Unified Leadership's leaflets, issuing its own instructions to the population. The two sets of leaflets called for different strike days, offered different instructions, and used different language. Nearly a year into the Intifada, Hamas issued a convenant that implicitly challenged the near-sacrosanct National Covenant adopted by the PLO in 1968. It emphasized that the land of Palestine is an Islamic trust (or waqf), to be guarded by Muslims until Judgment Day.[97]

Like their Jewish fundamentalist counterparts, Hamas activists stressed the holiness of the land itself and the consequent impossibility of considering any trades of land for peace. It was this notion that made Hamas so critical of the PLO's diplomacy in 1988, and its sanctioning in 1991 of the peace talks starting in Madrid: "Such conferences are nothing but a form of judgement passed by infidels on the land of the Muslims."[98]

Given the twin tragedies of 1948 and 1967, both the PLO and the Unified Leadership saw this sort of rhetoric as threatening the reconstruction of the nation, and they began to respond in kind. In one leaflet they demanded that fundamentalist elements cease playing on factional interests, "displaying negative stands and manifestations. For, they are serving the enemy, whether they wish it or not."[99] Hamas insisted on continuing unity, dismissing the leaflet as an Israeli forgery. Whether it was one, the growing divergence was becoming a worrisome factor for the national forces—as was the deepening Islamic orientation of lower-level PLO members themselves.[100] The Israelis, who at first thought they might employ the Islamic groups as a tool to weaken the PLO and undermine the uprising, had also begun to grasp the implications of their success. They moved against the Islamic leadership in 1989, eventually arresting Sheikh Yasin.

The conflicts among Palestinians about the shape and character of their society are far from over. As indicated, in the context of the ongoing struggle with Israel, there were strong pressures to downplay them.[101] But when tactics and strategy are matters of life and death, it is difficult to keep differences under wraps. It is thus not surprising that the Intifada sparked both debate about and changes in the role of women in society. Women seemed pulled in two directions: Especially in the West Bank, many participated publicly in the rebellion,[102] some believing it would be the road to their own liberation.[103] At the same time, within a year of its outbreak, all but a few determinedly leftist women had donned the hijab (headscarf) in the Gaza Strip, at least in part because of pressure from the militant Islamic organizations. Early in that campaign, the male leadership of the nationalist groups offered little support for those not wanting to do so.[104]

Given previous experience of Palestinian Arab women activists in Lebanon, the disregard for women was not so surprising. While taking a stand for more equality, in the end, the organization had "declined to be an arena for a radical restructuring of the gender order"; its first priority was in building national unity, not in dealing with the specifics of women's circumstances.[105]

In leaflet 43, the Unified Leadership finally took a firm stand against harassment of women, and the split in this respect at least was now open. A few years before the Intifada, Rosemary Sayigh addressed a predicament that became acute in its course: "With Palestinians increasingly polarized between progressive [nationalist] and reactionary [religious] currents, women are likely to pay a heavy price for over-visibility."[106] Novelist Sahar Khalifa would echo this theme. Because she wrote on the plight of women, her critics were "astounded and shocked. They feel that I exaggerate, that I focus on peripheral matters and not on what is germinal. In their opinion what is most important is to write about our conflict with Israel, with imperialism, with the Arab world." Her goal was to show "how our society stifles women, puts them in cages, blocks up their vast reserves of energy." But critics claimed that she "was imitating American feminist views by ignoring the real solution for women which is to be found within the framework of the national struggle. . . ."[107]

Social upheaval can catalyze and confirm changes incipient for years or decades. The Intifada validated the replacement of the old landed elite with a new leadership bred in the schools and universities of the West Bank and Gaza. When the rioting broke out, Israeli civil administrators turned to the village mukhtars and the old notable leadership,[108] who, to the astonishment of the Israelis—and perhaps the old leaders themselves—could do little to stem the tide of resistance. It had become uncertain precisely where authority within Palestinian society lay.

The question had been complicated over the years by the Israeli, Jordanian, and PLO discouragement of any visible, independent new leadership. Those personalities who did emerge in the occupied territories to offer political or social initiatives, including the elected mayors, faced arrest, deportation, detention, assassination. Nonetheless, university teachers, journalists, and other professionals gained enough respectability and political support to be seen as "inside" representatives of the West Bank and Gaza. In the early 1990s, their claim was reinforced by the international discrediting of the "outside" PLO leadership for siding with Saddam Hussein, by the insiders' active role at the Palestine National Council meeting in Algiers in 1991, and—most importantly—by their role as the Palestinian delegation to the new peace talks. Among the most prominent of these figures is Faysal al-Husseini, the son of the canonized shahid, Abd al-Qadir al-Husseini, who led Palestinian fighting forces in the Arab Revolt and the 1948 war. (He is also the grandson of Musa, the first leader of the national movement in the 1920s and early 1930s, and nephew of Jamal.) Probably the most public figure has been Hanan Ashrawi, a Christian Palestinian and professor of English literature at Bir Zeit University, who has articulated the Palestinian case in an international arena better than ever before. Another Bir Zeit professor, Sari Nusayba, also comes from a prominent Palestinian family—his father was Jordan's minister of defense and director of the most prestigious "national" Palestinian economic institution, the Eastern Jerusalem Electric Company.

The ultimate influence of these and other insiders[109] or of younger less visible members of the Unified Leadership is still unclear; what is quite apparent is that social changes would no longer be dictated by a Palestinian leadership from on high—and certainly not by a leadership based in Amman or Damascus. Nor should the conflicts among Palestinian groups be understood as simple leadership struggles, although they certainly constitute an important element of the larger conflicts. The symbols and practices evolving among the entire population of the West Bank and Gaza Strip from 1948 to 1967, and then again after the onset of Israeli rule, created the possibility of Palestinian action. Whether they now offer the hope for an end to occupation, for national independence, and for reconciliation with Jews and Israel, is too soon to tell.

Afterword

In some important ways, the history of the Palestinians over the last two centuries has echoed that of other people in Asia and Africa. The social rift between Jaffa's metropolis and the eastern hills around Nablus is one of a number of such divisions in the countries skirting the Mediterranean coast. Throughout the region, the impact of the European market and closer administrative and political control widened the gap between coast and hinterland.

As elsewhere, the Palestinian fault line underscored two very different responses to the challenges that made village life and old beliefs unviable. The first was to embrace the new ways—Western education, values, dress, technology—as the basis for molding the nation. The second highlighted the emptiness and alienation accompanying the penetration of Palestine by Europe. This response called for reaffirmation of the old pillars of society—religion, village, kinship—now within the context of a heightened sense of peoplehood. Here, the cultural artifacts of the West were not seen as weapons to secure a rightful place on the world stage but as elements confirming Palestine's relegation to the wings.

The struggle across this divide did not develop smoothly, but rather was shaped in social eruptions suddenly mobilizing the society and pitting the contending worldviews against one another. Those eruptions—the Revolt of 1834, the Arab Revolt of

1936–39, and the Intifada—functioned as points of exclamation in a meandering narrative of change, marking the response of society as a whole to other forces (Egyptian, British, and Zionist) imposing themselves on Palestine. They also brought into stark relief the contending forces in Palestinian society itself: a struggle over how to proceed in the minefield of tightened administration, an aggressive market economy, and a contending claim for the national right to the soil on which they lived.

In all three rebellions, the Palestinians fielded a political leadership strong enough much of the time to prevent the struggle from obscuring the overall message to outsiders, but incapable of imposing its will on the society as to how to proceed towards the future. Both the Arab Revolt and the Intifada were initiated by groups outside the official Palestinian leadership, and both proceeded while the leadership remained far from the battle scene—in Lebanon and Syria in the case of the 1936 revolt and in Tunisia in the case of the Intifada. In the periods between the revolts and during the uprisings themselves, what it meant to be Palestinian was defined and redefined, not so much by these leaders, as by a changing array of social groups: migrating fellaheen, wealthy merchants, village heads and landowners, cadres of students and professionals, the shabab—and, finally, the refugees.

In the period after al-Nakba, refugees first emphasized individual and collective rights of return. The culture they subsequently generated in the camps, however, laid the basis for a major change: from the right of return to the development of a true Palestinian nationalism. The Palestinian movement went from the promotion of the rights of an aggrieved group to a national movement asserting the broad collective will of an entire people.

All these groups contributed to the painful process of drawing boundaries that would socially and culturally define the Palestinians. The press of outsiders on these boundaries forced Palestinians, at various points during the century, to reevaluate the adequacy of their institutions. At times, they leaned towards more closely identifying with other Arabs in various pan-Arabist schemes or with other Muslims through Islam; at other times, towards a more particularistic self-definition as Palestinians. But the alternatives were never mutually exclusive; one or the other became prominent depending on the internal balance of power and the nature of external forces pressuring the society.

Despite the fractures among the Palestinians, threatening to undermine the meaning of Palestinism, one element united them and distinguished them from the other Arabs—indeed from all other peoples in Asia and Africa contending with modern economic and political forces. That special element was of course Zionism, and later Israel. The prominent Palestinian place on the agenda of international politics and world opinion resulted from a territorial struggle with the Jews. The ancient conflict between two great civilizations, the Arab and Israelite, and two great religions, Islamic and Jewish, only amplified the political conflict of the last hundred years.

Jewish–Arab antagonism simmered in the last decades of Ottoman rule and then erupted into full-scale conflict in the years of the British mandate. The importance of these 30 years of British government cannot be overestimated. Not only did the British define the physical boundaries of the state, which by the logic of colonial rule would eventually be given to the country's majority—the Arabs—but they also carved out what would be the social boundaries of the Palestinian Arab people. Yet the formation of such a people in this case did not ensure that the logic of colonialism would be played out, as the mandate also fostered the formation of a Jewish society in Palestine, a society able to establish its own state-in-the-making that frustrated the Arabs' aspirations. When the colonial state collapsed, the Palestinian Arabs lacked the organization to challenge Jewish society effectively, in good part because the British had decimated Palestinian institutions during the Arab Revolt.

As our own account may have suggested, it is impossible to tell the story of Zionism or Palestinism without understanding the impact they had on one another. For the Palestinians, the story centers on al-Nakba, a catastrophe that produced, ironically, a strong collective consciousness transcending all the fractures. In the misery of the camps—in the permanence of temporariness—refugees developed a powerful new nationalism. Its fuel was longing and injustice, humiliation and degradation—bitterness and hatred towards Jews, the West, other Arabs, and the cosmic order itself. At its heart was a vision of returning to a Lost Garden. The right to do so was perceived as self-evident and a condition for rebuilding the cosmic order destroyed in al-Nakba.

While the communities of exiles, scattered through the countries of the Middle East, formed the foundation of the new Pal-estinism, the 1967 war returned the focus to the reunited territory of the old Palestine mandate. Israel's overwhelming victory produced not only another wave of refugees, but also the rise of a new outside leadership, and the creation of a civil so-ciety within the occupied territories. The PLO outsiders and insiders in the West Bank and Gaza Strip cooperated and con-tended, struggling over the image of the Palestinians' future, all within the context of the Palestinian consciousness created in the refugee camps in the decades following al-Nakba. They pushed and pulled at the edges of the meaning of Palestinism, so that now the images of the Lost Garden and the inalienable right of return to their original homes contend with the pragmatic possibility of independence in only part of Palestine.

At this point, the struggles taking place within Palestinian society have no more clear an outcome than those between Jews and Arabs. What is unmistakable is that both Israelis and Jews worldwide will have a significant role in determining the Pales-tinian future, as will Palestinians in determining that of the Israelis, and thus the Jews. History has linked the two peoples and national movements. Neither can make the other disappear, and neither can achieve peace without fulfilling some of the most deeply held aspirations of the other.

It was this sense of being locked in an embrace in which neither side could make the other disappear that finally drove Israel and the PLO to the bargaining table in the 1990s. After several years of false starts, the two sides finally approved a joint Declaration of Principles on September 13, 1993, laying out a blueprint for their intertwined future. At this writing, it is im-possible to say whether that agreement will lead to the peace that both sides covet. What can be said is that the single act of signing that document changed Israel's and the PLO's relation-ship to each other. Until that time, the primary tactic of each side had been to make the other fail. After that historic moment, each understood that its own success depends, in great part, on the success of the other.

CHRONOLOGICAL LIST OF MAJOR EVENTS

Date	Palestinian History	Events Related to Palestinian History
635–37	The Arab tribes capture Jerusalem from the Byzantines and make the province of Palestina Prima into a jund (military district) of Filastin; Arabization and Islamization of the region	
641		Arab conquest of Byzantine Egypt
661		Muawiya, the founder of Umayyad dynasty, proclaims himself caliph in Jerusalem, having Damascus as his capital
685–705	Caliph Abd al-Malik builds the Dome of the Rock mosque to emphasize the holiness of the city, in opposition to his rival who controls Mecca and Medina	
705–715	His son Walid builds al-Aqsa mosque in Jerusalem	
715–717	Suleiman, the seventh Umayyad caliph, builds Ramleh as his residence	

Date	Palestinian History	Events Related to Palestinian History
1095		The famous scholar Abu Hamid al-Ghazali from Nizamiyya Academy of Baghdad resides in Jerusalem, where he begins work on his volume *The Revivification of the Science of Religion*, one of the major efforts of Islamic theology
1099–1187	The Crusader invasion of Palestine, and the establishment of the Latin Kingdom of Jerusalem; major massacre of Arab and Jewish population of the territory	
1187	Salah al-Din (Saladin) reconquers Jerusalem and creates a new Islamic dynasty; the Ayubidis rule over a part of the region	
1260		In the battle of Ayn Jalut (Nazareth) the Egyptian-based Mamluks defeat the Mongol hordes of Hulagu (grandson of Genghis Khan) and overcome the remaining Crusader fortifications
1260–1515		The region is under the rule of the Mamluk military caste and their sultans, after they

Date	Palestinian History	Events Related to Palestinian History
1260–1515		depose the Ayubid dynasty
1515–1917	During the rule of Suleiman the Magnificent (1520–66), the old city of Jerusalem is walled	With some interruptions, the country is incorporated into Turkish Ottoman rule
1798		Napoleonic campaign in Egypt; battle of the Nile
1799	Ahmad al-Jazzar, the governor of Acre, turns back the French army, gaining control over most of Palestine	
1808	Muslim revolt in Jerusalem against Ottoman governor; more power for local families	
1826	Second rebellion of the Jerusalem Muslims; Christians and Jews attacked	
1830	Ibrahim Pasha, the Ottoman governor, gains considerable control and autonomy over the country	
1831–40	Egyptian conquest of the region, including Palestine, and its incorporation into the Egyptian state	
1834	Major revolt of the region against the Egyptians, focused mainly in Palestine	

Date	Palestinian History	Events Related to Palestinian History
1839		Proclamation of a program of reorganization in the Ottoman Empire
1854–56		Crimean War
1856		Reform in the Ottoman Empire with a more detailed statement than in 1839, followed by land tenure changes
1860–61		Intercommunal rifts in Lebanon and Syria
1861–65		Civil War in the U.S.
1863	Creation of the municipality of Jerusalem under Ottoman law, first nucleus of modern local government	
1868–75		Ottoman civil code
1876		Ottoman Constitution
1881–82		Pogroms in Eastern Europe against the Jews; Arab revolt in Egypt; British occupation of Egypt
1882–1904		First wave of Jewish settlers immigrate to Palestine (First Aliyah)
1878	Establishment of Petah Tikvah, the first Jewish colony in Palestine	
1891		Ahad Ha'am (Asher Ginzberg) publishes his article "Truth from

Date	Palestinian History	Events Related to Palestinian History
1891		Eretz Israel [Palestine]" warning his fellow Jews of the danger of ignoring Arabs' feelings in Palestine
1892	Establishment of Palestinian branches of Crédit Lyonnais in Jaffa and Jerusalem	
1897		First Zionist Congress launches the Basel Program with the aim of resettling the Jewish people in Palestine and establishing the World Zionist Organization
1899– 1902	Arab-Jewish tension following large Jewish land purchases in the Tiberias region	
1904–14	Second wave of Jewish immigration; demand by Jews for exclusive use of Jewish labor in Jewish colonies and in Zionist-funded enterprises	
1905		Nagib Azouri publishes his *Le reveil de la nation arabe*, envisioning the conflict between major national movements in the Middle East—those of the Arabs and Jews
1907		Yitzhak Epstein, a Hebrew teacher from Galilee, publishes in

Date	Palestinian History	Events Related to Palestinian History
1907		*Shiloach* an essay warning the Zionist settlers that uprooting Arab tenants from the land will cause hatred against the colonization and the crystallization of a common Arab consciousness that will turn against the Jewish settlement
1908	Appearance of the first Palestinian newspaper in Haifa, *al-Karmil,* with the major aim of fighting against land transfers from Arab to Jewish ownership	Young Turks revolution in Istanbul
	Palestinian delegates, elected to the Ottoman parliament, warn against "Judification" of the country; frequent tension between Arabs and Jews	
1911	*Filastin,* a large Palestinian newspaper, is launched in Jaffa	
1914		World War I breaks out
1915–16		Correspondence between the British high commissioner in Egypt (Henry McMahon) and Sharif Hussein of Mecca leads to agreement between British and Arabs on

Date	Palestinian History	Events Related to Palestinian History
1915–16		establishment of an Arab kingdom in the Middle East in exchange for an Arab military revolt against the Ottomans; Arabs believe Arab kingdom includes Palestine
1916		Secret Anglo-French agreement to divide Ottoman Middle East provinces (Sykes-Picot agreement)
June 1916		Hussein proclaims Arab independence and revolts against the Ottomans
1917	Ottoman forces in Jerusalem surrender to British forces	The Balfour Declaration: British support for establishment of a Jewish national home in Palestine
1918	All of Palestine occupied by British forces	End of World War I; Treaty of Versailles and League of Nations Covenant approved; General Arab (Syrian) Congress, including prominent Palestinians, held in Damascus rejects Balfour Declaration and considers Palestine part of southern Syria
1919	Arab Literary Club and Arab Club founded to propagate Arab nationalism; Kamil	

Date	Palestinian History	Events Related to Palestinian History
1919	al-Husseini appointed by the British as grand mufti of Jerusalem; emergence of a new Muslim hierarchy in place of the center in Istanbul	
1919–20	Muslim-Christian Associations formed countrywide, protesting against Balfour Declaration and claiming Palestine as part of Syria	
1920	As part of Arab unrest in Syria against the French, Arab rebels attack two Jewish settlements in the north of Palestine	
	Faysal's proclamation excites the Arab population of Palestine; riots in Jerusalem and Jaffa (following the Nabi Musa festival); some notables arrested by the British; Amin al-Husseini's flight; Musa Kazim al-Husseini, the mayor of Jerusalem, replaced by Raghib al-Nashashibi	Faysal proclaims the independence of Syria and himself as king; the revolt is suppressed by French troops
	First Palestinian National ("Third Syrian Arab") Congress meets in Haifa, constituted	San Remo Peace Conference assigns Britain the mandate over Palestine

Date	Palestinian History	Events Related to Palestinian History
1920	from delegates from Muslim-Christian Associations and other notables; the Congress nominates the Arab Executive Committee, which is perceived (and recognized de facto) by the British as the political leadership and representative of the Arab community in Palestine (until 1935); the Congress demands British recognition as representatives of the Arab Palestinian population, as well as independence, an immediate halt to Jewish immigration and land acquisitions	
1921	Kamil al-Husseini dies	
	Riots in Jaffa; Arabs kill 46 Jews; a British commission of inquiry attributes the disturbances to Arabs' anxiety about increasing Jewish immigration; Amin al-Husseini is appointed Mufti of Jerusalem, and pardoned by High Commissioner Herbert Samuel	
1922	Creation of the Supreme Muslim Council to fill the vacuum left by the removal of	

Date	Palestinian History	Events Related to Palestinian History
1922	Islamic Ottoman rule; Amin al-Husseini elected president of the Council	
	Britain issues a "White Paper" emphasizing that only a part of Palestine is considered the Jewish national home and excluding East Palestine (Transjordan) from the mandate	
1925	Establishment of Palestinian Workers' Society (PAWS) as a moderate trade union movement led by Sami Taha	
1927	Municipal elections end in a resounding Nashashibi-led opposition victory	
1929	Countrywide riots against Jews, including the massacre of many members of the old non-Zionist community of Hebron, following fears and rumors of Jewish intentions to gain control over the Wailing Wall; Arab Women's Congress in Jerusalem adopts strong nationalist positions	
1930	The Arab Bank established by the Abd	

Date	Palestinian History	Events Related to Palestinian History
1930	al-Hamid Shuman family, competing with Barclays	
1931	Pan-Islamic Congress held in Jerusalem, attended by 145 delegates from the Muslim world, reinforces Amin al-Husseini's position as an Islamic leader	
1932	National Congress of Arab Youth convened in Jaffa	
	Formation of the first modern Palestinian political party, the Istiqlal ("Independence"); strong pan-Islamic ideology and revival of the idea of Palestine as a natural part of southern Syria; creation of additional quasi-parties: Palestine Arab party (Husseinis), National Defense party (the opposition, or the Nashashibis), and Reform party (Khalidis)	
1933	Establishment of the Arab Agricultural Bank to grant loans to fellaheen (from the 1940s, it is called the Bank of the Arab Nation)	
	Meetings of some Palestinian leaders (Musa	

Date	Palestinian History	Events Related to Palestinian History
1933	Alami, Awni Abd al-Hadi, and George Antonius) with the just-appointed chair of the Jewish Agency, David Ben-Gurion, in attempt to find some accommodation between the contrasting demands of the two national movements; no understanding achieved	
	Arab Executive Committee declares a general strike and mass demonstrations are held in the major cities; the protest is directed solely against British rule, demanding independence, immediate halt of Jewish immigration and land acquisition, and establishment of a local government based on proportional representation; British police and troops suppress the protest movement	
1935	Sheikh Izz al-Din al-Qassam, leader of a small guerrilla group, killed by British forces	
1936	Following minor clashes with Jews, National Committees are established in all towns and some	A 45-day general strike in Syria against French rule; French promise to consider granting independence

Date	Palestinian History	*Events Related to* Palestinian History
1936	villages; the Jerusalem committee adopts the slogan "No taxation without representation." Some local leaders call for a general strike, forcefully implemented by the shabab. All Arab political parties and organizations merged into the Arab Higher Committee, led by Amin al-Husseini; waves of violence; the British lose control over the country despite reinforcements; the Great Arab Revolt breaks out	
	A Syrian officer, Fawzi al-Qa'uqji, enters Palestine, leading volunteers from Arab countries to conduct guerrilla warfare against the British	
	The Arab Higher Committee accepts the call of the Arab states to end the 175-day general strike that exhausts the Arab economy	
1937	The Peel Commission publishes its report recommending partition of Palestine into a Jewish state, an Arab state incorporated into Transjordan, and British enclaves; both parties	

Date	Palestinian History	Events Related to Palestinian History
1937	reject the proposal; the Arab revolt is renewed	
	Nazareth district commissioner assassinated by Palestinians; the British outlaw the Arab Higher Committee and other Arab political organizations; five leaders deported to the Seychelles; two hundred arrested; Amin al-Husseini escapes to Lebanon	
1938	Insurgence and counterinsurgence escalate; thousands of fellaheen join guerrilla rebel forces; Amin al-Husseini establishes the Central Committee of the National Jihad and the Council of Rebellion in Damascus	Close cooperation between mainstream Jewish para-military organization (Haganah) and British forces; Col. Charles Wingate trains and leads joint counterinsurgence units
	Rural rebels control most of the inland towns, such as Nablus, Hebron, Ramallah, Tiberias, Beersheba, and even parts of Jaffa and the walled portion of Jerusalem; well-to-do families leave Palestine; Palestinian counterinsurgence groups fight the rebels; civil war among the Arabs	

Date	Palestinian History	Events Related to Palestinian History
1938	British military rule over the country; reinforcements from Britain; military pressure on the hilly regions; recapture of the Arab Old City of Jerusalem by British troops; guerrilla groups disbanded and leadership killed or captured	
	Opposition leaders organize and fund "peace bands," fighting against rebel groups and defending villages and neighborhoods	
	Partition (Woodhead) Commission declares Peel Commission partition proposal "impractical"; proposes an Arab-Jewish-British conference for solving the problem of Palestine; deported Palestinian leaders released	
1939	London Conference convened; talks end without agreement; Malcolm MacDonald, colonial secretary of state, launches a new British policy for Palestine (1939 White Paper): after ten years of a transitional period, an independent, unitary (i.e., Arab-ruled)	George Antonius publishes *The Arab Awakening*, the first comprehensive history of the Arab nationalist movement

Date	Palestinian History	Events Related to Palestinian History
1939	Palestinian state, annual Jewish immigration of 15,000 and heavy restrictions on Jewish land purchases; de facto withdrawal from Balfour Declaration; House of Commons approves the new policy	World War II breaks out
1940	Publication of Land Transfer Regulations, restricting official Jewish purchases; de facto sales continue	
1941	Economic prosperity; establishment of the Congress of Workers and Union of Section of Arab Workers, both unions under communist influence	Formation of Jewish shock units (Palmach)
		German invasion of Soviet Union; British troops sent to overthrow pro-German regime in Iraq, with assistance of Jewish units
		The U.S. enters World War II
1942	Following a Nablus conference, PAWS splits; formation of communist-led Federation of Arab Trade Unions	Ben-Gurion declares the policy of prompt creation of a "Jewish Commonwealth" in Palestine; awareness of the scope of the Holocaust

Date	Palestinian History	Events Related to Palestinian History
1944	Revival of Arab National Fund; new board of directors, replacing Amin al-Husseini's supporters	Etzel (the Irgun) declares an anticolonial revolt against Britain
1945		End of World War II; millions of uprooted people, among them hundreds of thousands of Jewish survivors of the Nazi Holocaust; formation of Arab League; the Jewish leadership begins a policy of sending ships to Palestine with unauthorized immigrants
	Najjada, a para-military organization, founded by Nimr al-Hawari in Jaffa	Declaration of the "Jewish Revolt" against British by the mainstream paramilitary Haganah; negotiations with other Jewish underground organizations on coordination among them
	New statement of policy (White Paper of 1945) launched by British Foreign Secretary E. Bevin; more restrictions on Jewish immigration; proposal to set up Anglo-American Committee of Inquiry	
	Reconstitution of the Arab Higher Committee	

Date	Palestinian History	Events Related to Palestinian History
1946	Jamal al-Husseini allowed to return to Palestine; takes control of a reorganized Arab Higher Committee	
	The Anglo-American Committee of Inquiry recommends the immediate entry of 150,000 Jewish immigrants and abolition of the 1940 Land Transfer Regulations	
	Amin al-Husseini arrives in Egypt trying to regain control over Palestinians; new attempt of unity by creation of an Arab Higher Executive; full-scale Jewish underground operations, mainly against British targets and infrastructure (railroads and bridges); Etzel blows up the British administration headquarters (a wing of Jerusalem King David Hotel)	Transjordan gains independence from Britain
1946-47		Another London Conference; Britain submits an autonomy plan based on division of the country into provinces; first round attended only by Arab states; second round includes participation of Palestinian and Jew-

Date	Palestinian History	*Events Related to* Palestinian History
		ish delegations; Arabs demand a unitary state; conference ends without results
1947	Bevin submits the problem of Palestine to the UN; UN special commission (UNSCOP) appointed and sent to Palestine; organization of a second para-military organization, the Futuwwa, under the control of Jamal al-Husseini	
	Publication of UNSCOP report: majority recommend partition, minority a federative solution	Arab League meeting in Aley (Lebanon) reaffirms Bludan resolution to use oil as a weapon in the struggle over Palestine
November 29, 1947	The Palestinians and the Arab states reject partition; the Zionists accept	UN General Assembly adopts Resolution 181, recommending the establishment of Jewish and Arab states in Palestine and the internationalization of the Jerusalem area
1948	Arab Higher Committee declares a general strike; full-scale inter-communal war breaks out in Palestine;	
	Abd al-Qadir al-Husseini returns to the country and proclaims himself the chief commander of Palestinian forces	

Date	Palestinian History	Events Related to Palestinian History
1948	Arab League calls for volunteers for an Arab Liberation Army (ALA) under the command of Fawzi al-Qa'uqji	
	Brigades of ALA irregulars arrive in North Palestine in January; selective abandonment of middle and upper class members from the big cities, and flight from the villages captured by Jewish forces in the coastal plain	Political Committee of Arab League rejects all demands of Amin al-Husseini and declares that the Arab Higher Committee does not represent the Palestinian people; all funds allocated to the League's Palestinian Council
	Fawzi al-Qa'uqji establishes his headquarters in central Palestine; ALA irregulars arrive in Jaffa; significant successes for the Arab irregulars; the main roads of the country are blocked; Yehiam, Gush Etzion, Hulda, and Neve Daniel convoys destroyed; Jewish Jerusalem under siege	
	Successes for Jewish forces facing ALA in the north; in March, they capture and demolish Arab villages on the coastal plain, including Abu Kabir and Jabalya; Plan D adopted, allowing for	

Date	Palestinian History	Events Related to Palestinian History
1948	securing Jewish settlements and the roads to them even beyond the territories allocated for the Jewish state and for destroying Arab localities and expelling their inhabitants if necessary for security reasons	
	In April, Abd al-Qadir al-Husseini is killed in a counterattack by Jewish forces on the strategic village of Castel, dominating the way to Jerusalem; major demoralization among Palestinian irregulars; massacre in the village of Dayr Yasin, about 120 villagers killed; Palestinian leadership tries to halt the flight; Arab Higher Committee calls on Palestinian Arabs not to leave	Mass demonstrations in Damascus, Baghdad, Cairo, and Tripoli calling to "save the Palestinian brethren"; pogroms in local Jewish communities; Arab League committee meets to discuss the ALA failures and the Dayr Yasin events
	Qa'uqji withdraws from Mishmar Haemek; Jewish forces take over Tiberias, Haifa, and additional villages; Arab population flees or is expelled; Jaffa under siege; a Jewish convoy to the Mt. Scopus campus of Hebrew University massacred	Lebanon and Syria announce the intention of sending troops to Palestine in April; Iraq concentrates troops in Transjordan

Date	Palestinian History	Events Related to Palestinian History
1948	In April, battle over Jaffa continues; an ALA unit reinforces its defenders; all Arab neighborhoods of West Jerusalem are captured by Jewish forces and their inhabitants driven out	
	In May, Jewish forces capture Safed and its rural hinterland; Jaffa surrenders and the majority of its Muslim population leaves; the remaining Jewish settlements of Etzion bloc (in the mountain region) surrender to the Arab Legion	
	The end of the British mandate in May; the State of Israel is proclaimed; Egyptian regular forces cross the border into Palestine; Arab Legion (Transjordanian) forces cross the Jordan River westward; Syrian troops move to cross the border; the 1948 war breaks out on May 15	The Soviet Union and the United States recognize Israel; creation of the Israel Defense Forces (IDF)
	Major battles between advancing Arab armed forces and Israeli forces; most Arab villages are evacuated following the force	

Date	Palestinian History	Events Related to Palestinian History
1948	movements; Israeli decision prevents Arabs from returning to evacuated villages; formation of refugee camps in May and June in Gaza, territories controlled by the Arab Legion, and Lebanon	
	The All Palestine Government, with a temporary site in Gaza, is established by Amin al-Husseini	
	End of first truce in July; major Israeli offensive on three fronts, mainly to clear the Tel Aviv–Jerusalem road including the Lydda–Ramleh region; this action leads to a new wave of about 100,000 Palestinians fleeing to territories held by Arab Legion, ALA, and Egypt; a portion of the Palestinians evacuated by force	
		Lausanne peace talks fail in September, mainly due to Israel's refusal to "repatriate" the Palestinian refugees
	The Jericho Conference in November calls on Abdallah to annex the West Bank to Transjordan	

Date	Palestinian History	Events Related to Palestinian History
1948	Continuing battles and expulsion of Arabs from the conquered territories by Israeli armed forces; remaining Arab population is moved from one place to another according to perceived security requirements	
	In December, the UN General Assembly Resolution 194 (III) recognizes the right of the Palestinian refugees to return "and live at peace with their neighbors"	
1949		Armistice agreements between Israel and Lebanon, Transjordan, and Syria are signed; Israel holds about 80% of the total territories of Western Palestine; the eastern mountain area ("West Bank") is under Transjordanian rule; the "Gaza Strip" is under Egyptian occupation
1949–56	Constant infiltration of Palestinians across the armistice lines causes casualties and unrest in Israel, which adopts a policy of retaliation against the Arab states and the "sources of	

Date	Palestinian History	Events Related to Palestinian History
1945–56	infiltration"; military clashes along the armistice lines	
1950	Military government imposed on most Israeli Arabs; in April, the West Bank is formally annexed to Jordan; the United Nations Relief and Works Agency (UNRWA) begins operations	
1951	Yasser Arafat reorganizes the Palestinian Students' Union in Cairo	Nationalization of oil in Iran
	George Habash organizes the Arab Nationalists' Movement, with a leftist pan-Arabist ideology; its Palestinian branch will develop into the Popular Front for the Liberation of Palestine (PFLP); it initiates some sabotage activities against Arab and "imperialist" targets	King Abdallah of Jordan killed at prayer in al-Aqsa mosque
1952	The Arab League dissolves the All Palestine Government and empowers the Arab states to represent the Palestinian cause	Free Officers coup in Cairo; the end of the monarchy
1955		Alliance among Iraq, Pakistan, and Turkey

Date	Palestinian History	Events Related to Palestinian History
		("Baghdad Pact") links them to Britain and the Western bloc
1956	47 Israeli Arabs killed in Kafr Qasim village after violation of curfew	Nationalization of Suez Canal; Israel conquers Gaza Strip and most of Sinai Desert; Anglo-French intervention
1957	Most of the Arab members of the Israeli Communist party (MAKI) split away, forming the almost purely Arab Communist list (RAKAH)	Israeli withdrawal from the Sinai Desert and Gaza Strip
1958		Formation of Egyptian-Syrian federation, creating the United Arab Republic, arouses pan-Arab sentiment
1959	Fatah is created by Arafat and associates; al-Ard group starts to publish an Arab nationalist periodical in Israel; Khalil al-Wazir (Abu Jihad) issues in Lebanon the clandestine Fatah magazine *Filastinuna*; the Arab Higher Committee and Amin al-Husseini forced to move from Egypt to Lebanon	Muamar Qaddafi overthrows the monarchy in Libya
1962		Civil war in Yemen, removing the monarchy; Egypt backs the republicans, sending a military expedition

Date	Palestinian History	Events Related to Palestinian History
1964	Al-Ard outlawed by Israeli authorities after an attempt to establish it as an Arab nationalist party in Israel	In January, the first Arab summit in Cairo concludes with a statement about the need to "organize the Palestinian people enabling them to play their role in the liberation of their country and to achieve self-determination"
	In May, the First Palestinian National Council (PNC) convenes in Jerusalem, chaired by Ahmad Shukayri; it adopts the Palestine National Charter as the Basic Constitution of the Palestine Liberation Organization; a Palestine Liberation Army is also planned	
1965	Fatah launches its armed struggle for the liberation of Palestine; Communique No. 1 of al-Assifa, its military branch, is issued	
1966	Abolition of the Military Government that had ruled Israeli Arabs	Syrian Baath party conference decides to establish a Palestinian para-military organization, Saiqa
1967	Following Israel's victory in the June war, the entire territory of the former Palestine mandate comes under	In August, an Arab leaders' summit in Khartoum rejects any negotiations with Israel

Date	Palestinian History	Events Related to Palestinian History
1967	Israeli control, including about 650,000 Palestinians of the West Bank and East Jerusalem and 356,000 in the Gaza Strip; East Jerusalem is annexed to Israel and the rest of the captured territories, including the Golan Heights and the Sinai Desert, are put under military administration	
	Arafat attempts to establish his headquarters inside the occupied territories, trying to provoke and lead a popular uprising; by the end of December, all of his network is destroyed by Israeli intelligence and Arafat has left the territories	
	In September (through November), teachers and students strike against Israeli occupation in the West Bank; first general strike in Nablus	
	George Habash's group joins other small guerrilla organizations to form the Popular Front for the Liberation of Palestine (PFLP)	
1968	In March, Fatah fighters, aided by Jordanian	

Date	Palestinian History	Events Related to Palestinian History
1968	artillery, repel an Israeli attack on Fatah's headquarters at Karamah (in the Jordan Valley). At the 4th session of PNC in July, the guerrilla groups led by Fatah take over the PLO, which becomes an umbrella organization of different streams, with Fatah predominance; the National Convenant is revised, an Israeli civilian airliner is hijacked by the PFLP and lands in Algiers	
	A Syrian-backed guerrilla group headed by Ahmad Jibril splits from the PFLP and forms its own PFLP—General Command	
1969	Naif Hawatma splits from the PFLP and founds the pro-Maoist Democratic Front for the Liberation of Palestine (DFLP). At the 5th session of the PNC in February, Arafat nominated as chair of the ruling Executive Committee (EC). The "Cairo Agreement" between Arafat and the Lebanese Army commander, Emile Bustani,	

Date	Palestinian History	Events Related to Palestinian History
1969	permits "regulated guerrilla activities" in Lebanon; this agreement will be the basis of the state-in-a-state infrastructure built by the PLO in Lebanon	
1969–71	Demonstrations against Israeli rule in all major cities of the West Bank; sporadic Palestinian uprisings and guerrilla activities in the Gaza Strip	
1970	A multiple hijacking is initiated by the PFLP; planes land in the desert area of Zarqa in Jordan and are blown up	
	Jordan armed forces begin to destroy the infrastructure of the guerrilla forces around Amman and the refugee camps; civil war between Palestinians and Jordanian troops; the guerrilla forces are defeated in what comes to be known as "Black September," and their headquarters are moved to Lebanon	
1971	Israeli security forces "pacify" the Gaza Strip	Assassination of Wasfi Tal, Jordanian premier and minister of defense, the first operation of "Black September," a Fatah-led
	Foundation in Israel of the Arab Academic Union	

Date	Palestinian History	Events Related to Palestinian History
1971		organization under the command of Ali Hasan Salamah and Salah Khalaf (Abu Iyad)
1972	PLO's Executive Committee establishes a central council as an intermediate level between the EC and the PNC, making the decision-making process more flexible.	
	The Japanese "Red Army" guerrilla group, in coordination with Wadi Haddad, PFLP's chief of operations, hits Ben-Gurion Airport ("Operation Dayr Yasin"); Black September takes Israeli Olympic team as hostages in Munich; most of the hostages and guerrillas are killed during an abortive German police attempt to rescue the athletes	
1973	In April, Israelis launch a commando action against Fatah headquarters in Beirut, killing several Fatah commanders	The October War begins with a surprise Egyptian–Syrian attack on Israel; Henry Kissinger brokers separation of forces agreements in preparation for a Geneva peace conference
	Formation in the West Bank of the Palestine	

Date	Palestinian History	Events Related to Palestinian History
1973	National Front (controlled by the Communist party) challenging the "outside" PLO leadership	
1974	Arab Summit recognizes the PLO as the sole legitimate representative of the Palestinian people; Arafat speaks to the UN General Assembly in New York	
	In July, the 12th PNC adopts the idea of establishing "a Palestinian national authority in any area liberated from Israeli control," the so-called "mini-state option"; George Habash (PFLP) resigns from the PLO Executive Committee, establishing with the pro-Syrian guerrilla organization the "Rejectionist Front"; faced with the possibility of Palestinian participation in the Geneva Peace Conference, the Rejectionist Front is enlarged to include the PFLP-GC, the Arab Liberation Front (Iraqi backed), another small guerrilla groups	

Date	Palestinian History	*Events Related to* *Palestinian History*
1974	Creation of the Committee of the Heads of Arab Local Councils, which becomes the Supreme Follow-Up Committee and acts as the leadership and representatives of the Israeli Arabs	
1975–91		Civil war in Lebanon with PLO participation; Syrian intervention in the civil war leads to gradual Syrian control over Lebanon, except for a small "security zone" in southern Lebanon which is dominated by Israel
1976	Municipal elections in the West Bank lead to PLO supporters being swept into office (Bassam al-Shaka in Nablus, Fahd Qawasma in Hebron, Karim Khalaf in Ramallah, Ibrahim Tawil in al-Bira); the elected mayors and other prominent figures form a nucleus of an internal leadership, the National Guidance Committee	
	The first Land Day (March 30) includes a general strike and protests of Israeli Arabs	

Date	Palestinian History	Events Related to Palestinian History
1976	against land expropriations; six Arabs are killed; in 1992 it is declared a national holiday	
	Christian right-wing militias in Lebanon, supported by Syria, enforce a siege on Tal al-Zaatar, a Palestinian refugee camp; the siege ends with a massacre of the camp inhabitants	
1977	Abu Abbas splits from PFLP-GC and forms Palestine Liberation Front (PLF)	The nationalist right-wing party Likud comes to power in Israel; the settlement of the occupied territories by Jews accelerates
	Appearance of the radical nationalist group "Sons of the Village" among Israeli Arabs	President Sadat of Egypt visits Jerusalem and speaks at the Knesset
1978	Seaborne Fatah guerrillas hijack a bus on the main coastal highway of Israel; 37 people are killed including six guerrillas	Israel undertakes a limited invasion of Lebanon (Operation Litani) and occupies a strip in southern Lebanon, constructing a buffer zone held by a local Israeli-supported militia
	Israeli-Fatah ("Habib") agreement on a cease-fire along the Lebanon-Israel border	Camp David accords signed; Israel recognizes the "legitimate rights of the Palestinians" and commits to granting them "full

Date	Palestinian History	Events Related to Palestinian History
1978		autonomy" after a transitional period of five years; Israel also commits to withdrawal from the Sinai Desert in exchange for peace with Egypt
	Menahem Milson appointed as civilian administrator of the West Bank; tries to establish a local counterbalance to the PLO by forming the Village Leagues, armed groups headed by Mustafa Doudeen	Revolution in Iran; a radical Muslim regime is established promoting a militant Islam throughout the Arab world
1982	The National Guidance Committee is outlawed; general strike and mass demonstrations in the West Bank and Gaza Strip	
	In June, Israeli troops invade Lebanon in collaboration with the Maronite-Christian forces; Israel's major aim is to destroy the PLO's quasi-state infrastructure; the first large-scale Israeli–Palestinian war since 1948; heavy battles and casualties on all sides; West Beirut comes under siege and bombardment	

Date	Palestinian History	Events Related to Palestinian History
1982	In August, the PLO evacuates its forces and headquarters from Beirut to Tripoli, with its fighters carrying only their personal arms; a new headquarters is established in Tunis In September, Christian-Maronite militias, under Israeli protection, massacre Palestinians in the Sabra and Shatilla refugee camps	Bashir Gemayel elected president of Lebanon in August; 22 days later, he is killed by an explosive probably planted by Syrian agents
1984		Jewish settlements in the West Bank and Gaza Strip increase and now have about 80,000 settlers
1985	The Amman Agreement on a confederation between a future Palestinian state in the West Bank and Gaza Strip and Jordan is signed by King Hussein and Arafat; after a year the agreement is voided by King Hussein	
1987	On December 9, a general popular uprising, the Intifada, breaks out in the Gaza Strip and spreads to the West Bank; popular committees are formed; a unified leadership of the	

Date	Palestinian History	Events Related to Palestinian History
1987	revolt is formed inside the territories; its directives are ratified by the "outside" PLO and are spread mainly by leaflets; power shifts towards "inside" leadership	
1988	In March, the Unified Leadership calls for Palestinian policemen to quit	
	In April, Khalil al-Wazir (Abu Jihad) is assassinated, most probably by Israeli agents	
	In November, the 19th session of the PNC convenes in Algiers and declares an independent Palestinian state; following heavy pressure by the U.S. which holds out recognition of and a dialogue with the PLO, Arafat declares in Geneva that the PLO recognizes the rights of all parties concerned in the Middle East conflict to exist in peace and security, including the State of Palestine, Israel, and other neighbors; Arafat denounces terrorism, and U.S. opens dialogue	

Date	Palestinian History	Events Related to Palestinian History
1988	The Islamic Movement wins the municipal election in the Israeli Arab town of Umm al-Fahm	
1989	When Arafat refuses to condemn a terrorist attack by a PLO constituent organization, the U.S. suspends the dialogue with the PLO	
1990	In December, 17 Palestinians are killed and nearly 200 wounded after jittery Israeli security forces open fire near al-Aqsa mosque	Iraq invades Kuwait; a multi-national force is created by the U.S.
1991	In January, Salah Khalaf (Abu Iyad) is assassinated, probably by the Abu Nidal organization, perhaps at the behest of Iraq	Massive Jewish immigration from the Soviet Union to Israel
	The Intifada turns inward as collaborators and other "suspects" are killed by Palestinian "shock troops" or individuals; vigilante activities on the part of Jewish settlers	The U.S.-led force defeats Iraq in the Gulf War; the PLO is hurt diplomatically by its support of Iraq; the Palestinian community in Kuwait of over 350,000 is reduced to several thousand and is badly persecuted

Date	Palestinian History	Events Related to Palestinian History
1991	In November, peace talks begin in Madrid (continue later in Washington) between Israel and Arab delegations (including Palestinians from the occupied territories as part of a joint Jordanian–Palestinian delegation); the peace talks are the product of U.S. diplomatic efforts and are held under the auspices of the U.S. and USSR	
1992		The Labor party returns to power in Israel, promising to implement Palestinian autonomy within a year
	In December Islamic organizations intensify terror attacks inside Israel; Israeli government decides on a temporary deportation to Lebanon of 415 Hamas and Islamic Jihad members; Madrid talks in Washington grind to a halt	
	Deportations lead to a rise in Palestinian support for the Islamic groups in the occupied territories, with a corresponding drop in support for the PLO	

Date	Palestinian History	Events Related to Palestinian History
1993	Secret negotiations between Palestinian and Israeli officials in Norway; a Declaration of Principles (DOP) is drafted; the DOP includes Israel's recognition of the PLO as the legitimate representative of the Palestinian people and the agreement to grant full autonomy to the Palestinians under PLO leadership for 5 years, starting in the Gaza Strip and Jericho; the final status of the autonomous entity will be negotiated later; Palestinians interpret the agreement as an interim stage towards the establishment of an independent state	
	On September 13, the Declaration of Principles is signed in Washington by Yasser Arafat and Yitzhak Rabin, including an understanding that by December 13 an agreement will be reached on the withdrawal of Israeli troops from the Gaza Strip and Jericho, and that by April 13, 1994, Israeli troop redeployment will be completed; the PLO will assume civil authority in those regions and deploy its own police forces	

Date	Palestinian History	Events Related to Palestinian History
		Jordan and Israel conclude a framework for a peace agreement
		Intensification of terror acts by Jewish settlers against Palestinians as part of their political protest movement against the PLO-Israel agreement; with similar motives, Hamas members and other figures step up the murder of Jews in Israel and the Occupied Territories
	Most of the non-Fatah elements within the PLO and the Islamic movements reject the DOP; some Fatah leaders express objections to Arafat's concessions to Israel	
		Some progress in the Israeli-Arab multinational negotiations in Washington and other locations; Syria takes a hard line by supporting the groups rejecting the PLO-Israeli agreement

Date	Palestinian History	Events Related to Palestinian History
	In December, difficulties occur in PLO-Israeli talks; the December 13 deadline for the "Gaza-Jericho plan" is missed and high-level negotiations continue; most of the members of the Islamic movements who were expelled are returned to the occupied territories	
1994		Presidents Bill Clinton of the U.S. and Hafez al-Assad of Syria meet in Geneva; Syria indicates its readiness to negotiate a full peace with Israel in exchange for full Israeli withdrawal from the Golan Heights
	Several months after missing the December 13, 1993 deadline, Israel and the PLO sign an agreement opening the way for Israeli troop withdrawal from the Gaza Strip and Jericho and the beginning of limited PLO self-rule there	
	In May, the first Palestinian self-government begins with PLO self-rule in Jericho and the Gaza Strip	

Notes

INTRODUCTION

1. The term *al-Nakba* (catastrophe, disaster) was coined by Syrian scholar Constantine Zurayk in the event's immediate aftermath: "The defeat of the Arabs in Palestine is no simple setback or light, passing evil. It is a disaster in every sense of the word and one of the harshest trials and tribulations with which the Arabs have been afflicted throughout their long history—a history marked by numerous trials and tribulations." See *The Meaning of Disaster* (Beirut: Khayat's College Book Cooperative, 1956), p. 2. The Arabic title of the book is *Ma'na al-Nakbah*.

2. Frank C. Sakran, *Palestine, Still a Dilemma* (Washington, D.C.: American Council on the Middle East, 1976), pp. 104–5. There are numerous other works making similar points. See, for example, Samir S. Saleeby, *The Palestine Problem* (London: The Institute of International Studies, 1970), ch. 2.

3. Cited in *The Sunday Times*, London, June 15, 1969.

4. *From Time Immemorial: The Origins of the Arab-Jewish Conflict over Palestine* (New York: Harper & Row, 1984), pp. 402–3.

5. Her numbers were characterized by Norman Finkelstein (*In These Times*, September, 1984) as "the most spectacular fraud ever published on the Arab-Israeli conflict . . . a field littered with crass propaganda, forgeries and fakes. . . ." Similar evaluations were expressed by notable historians: Albert Hourani, *The Observer*, March 5, 1985; Yehoshua Porath, "Mrs. Peters' Palestine," *The New York Review of Books*, January 16, 1986. In *Trends in the Demographic Development of Palestinians, 1870–1987* (Tel-Aviv: Shiloach Institute, Tel-Aviv University, 1989) [Hebrew, mimeo], Gad Gilbar shows that, contrary to what Peters contends, the migration factor was far less significant than natural increase. See also Justin McCarthy, *The Population of Palestine: Population History and Statistics of the Late Ottoman Period and the Mandate* (New York: Columbia University Press, 1990), who writes "These and myriad other methodological and factual errors make Peters' work demographically worthless" (p. 41). Besides the manipulative use of facts, the book suffers from a failure to take account of Palestinian social structure and its inner dynamics and development. (More interesting, perhaps, is the acceptance the book gained in intellectual circles.) In any case, our position is in line with this statement from Porath's review: "But even if we put together all the cases [Peters] cites, one cannot escape the conclusion that most of the growth of the Palestinian Arab community resulted from a process of natural increase" (p. 37).

6. Turki, a refugee who grew up in Lebanon, has written some of the most poignant and biting material about the condition of exile, most notably in his book, *The*

Disinherited: Journal of a Palestinian Exile (New York: Monthly Review Press, 1972).

7. See Muhammad Y. Muslih, *The Origins of Palestinian Nationalism* (New York: Columbia University Press, 1988), passim. For the best overall account of the history of Palestinian nationalism, see the three-volume history by Y. Porath, *The Emergence of the Palestinian-Arab National Movement: 1918–1929* (London: Frank Cass, 1974); *The Palestinian Arab National Movement: 1929–1939* (London: Frank Cass, 1977); and *In Search of Arab Unity* (London: Frank Cass, 1986).

1. THE REVOLT OF 1834 AND THE MAKING OF MODERN PALESTINE

1. The image—cultivated, among others, by Lawrence of Arabia, the British soldier, intelligence agent, and diplomat who assisted the Hashemite revolt against the Ottoman Empire during World War I—was a relatively late one in Western culture. It was preceded by a depiction of Arabs, Bedouins, and the Orient in general as evil. See Maxime Rodinson, *Europe and the Mystique of Islam* (Seattle: Near Eastern Studies Dept., University of Washington, 1987), p. 66. The move towards a more favorable view began with the Renaissance and Enlightenment. The image was created by poets, novelists, playwrights, and painters, as well as by travelers and diplomats: Delacroix, Chateaubriand, Mark Twain. As Albert Hourani describes it, some of its elements were "The Arab horseman as savage hero, the seductiveness of beauties in the *harim*, the charm of the bazaar, the pathos of life continuing among the ruins of ancient grandeur" (*A History of the Arab Peoples*, Cambridge, Mass: Harvard University Press, 1991, p. 300). Among the important works conveying the image were Antoine Galland's translation of *The Arabian Nights*, Walter Scott's *The Talisman*, Disraeli's *Tancred*, and Goethe's *Westöstlicher Diwan*. This process has been well described in Edward Said, *Orientalism* (New York: Vintage Books, 1978), esp. ch. 1.

Even earlier Jewish proto-Zionist and Zionist writers and painters depicted the original "healthy" Jews of the area, back to biblical times, as typical Bedouin. The message was that Jews had to return to that sort of virtuous life. The first Jewish paramilitary organization in Palestine, Hashomer (the Guard) dressed its men as Bedouins and explicitly socialized them to behave as noble Bedouins. Along with Lawrence's *Seven Pillars of Wisdom: A Triumph* (London: Jonathan Cape, 1935), pp. 2–11, see Tovia Ashkenazi, *Tribus semi-nomades de la Palestine du Nord* (Paris: Libraire orientaliste Paul Geuthner, 1938), pp. 7–19.

2. On Egyptian occupation and rule and the revolt against the Egyptians, see Assad Jibrail Rustum, *The Royal Archives of Egypt and the Disturbances in Palestine, 1834* (Beirut: American University of Beirut, Oriental Series, No. 11, 1938). For engrossing descriptions of this affair, see Rustum, *A Corpus of Arabic Documents Relating to the History of Syria under Mehemet Ali Rasha*, vols. 1–5 (Beirut: American University of Beirut, 1929–34); idem, *The Royal Archives of Egypt and the Causes of Egyptian Expeditions to Syria, 1831–1841* (Beirut: American University of Beirut, 1936). See also Moshe Ma'oz, *Ottoman Reform in Syria and Palestine, 1840–1861: The Impact of the Tanzimat on Politics and Society* (Oxford: The Clarendon Press, 1969), pp. 12–16; and Shimon Shamir, "Egyptian Rule (1832–1840) and the Beginning of the Modern Period in the History of Palestine" in Amnon Cohen and Gabriel Baer, eds., *Egypt and Palestine—A Millennium of Association (868–1948)* (New York: St. Martin's Press, 1984), pp. 214–31.

3. Ma'oz, *Ottoman Reform in Syria and Palestine*, 16.

4. Faruk Tabak, "Local Merchants in Peripheral Areas of the Empire: The Fertile Crescent during the Long Nineteenth Century," *Review* 11 (1988): 179–214.

5. For pioneering discussion of this episode see Mordechai Abir, "The Revolt of the Year 1834 against Egyptian Rule and Its Background" (unpublished M.A. thesis, Hebrew University, 1961) [Hebrew]. The account that follows is mostly taken from Abir's excellent study. See also Rustum, *The Royal Archives of Egypt*, p. 411; Neophytos of Cyprus, *Extracts from Annals of Palestine, 1821–1841*, trans. S. N. Spyridon. (Jerusalem: Ariel, 1979), pp. 78–80, 106–8.

6. Gabriel Baer, "Fellah Rebellion in Egypt and the Fertile Crescent" in Baer, *Fellah and Townsmen in the Middle East* (London: Frank Cass, 1982), pp. 253–323.

7. The division between Qays and Yaman goes back to rivalries between the two main tribes in the Arabian peninsula during the initial period of Muslim conquest of the Middle East and the establishment of the Ummayad dynasty (661–750). See Hourani, *A History of the Arab Peoples*, 30. This division continues to have some meaning for Syrian, Lebanese, and Palestinian Muslim society, as an organizational principle of local factionalism. See Miriam Hoexter, "The Role of the Qays and Yaman Factions in Local Political Divisions: Jabal Nablus Compared with the Judean Hills in the First Half of the Nineteenth Century," *Asian and African Studies* 9 (1973): 249–311. However, the continuing factionalism did not necessarily reflect the original lineages that divided the two leagues, but was used in contemporary times as a principle of legitimacy for any coalition formation—what Salim Tamari calls fictive alignments. See "Factionalism and Class Formation in Recent Palestinian History," in Roger Owen, ed., *Studies in the Economic and Social History of Palestine in the Nineteenth and Twentieth Centuries* (Carbondale: Southern Illinois University Press, 1982), pp. 181–86. See also R. A. Stewart MacAlister and E. W. G. Masterman, "A History of the Doings of the Fellahin during the First Half of the Nineteenth Century, from Native Sources: Part III," *Palestine Exploration Fund Quarterly* (January, 1906): 33–50.

8. More than three-quarters of the Arab population still farmed for a living in the 1920s. See Eric Mills, *Census of Palestine—1931* (Jerusalem: Government Printer, 1933), pp. 17, 23. The 1931 November census updated and corrected the first British census of October 1922.

9. See Alexander Scholch, "European Penetration and Economic Development of Palestine, 1856–82" in Owen, ed., *Studies in the Economic and Social History of Palestine*, 10–87; Haim Gerber, *The Social Origins of the Modern Middle East* (Boulder: Lynne Rienner Publishers, 1987); Charles Issawi, *An Economic History of the Middle East and North Africa* (New York: Columbia University Press, 1982), pp. 62–76. Iris Agmon argues that the impact of foreign capital on the building of the Palestinian economy was highly fragmentary and unbalanced: The roads and ports were developed, the land tracks enlarged, new crops and types of cultivation introduced, and banking, postal, and transportation services were founded, but basically cultivation techniques remained very primitive. See "Foreign Trade as a Catalyst of Change in the Arab Economy in Palestine, 1879–1914," *Cathedra* (October 1986): 107–32 [Hebrew]. See also Sa'id B. Himadeh, ed., *Economic Organization of Palestine* (Beirut: American University Press, 1938); Joel S. Migdal, *Palestinian Society and Politics* (Princeton: Princeton University Press, 1980), pp. 19–32 (on socio-political aspects of the problem); I. M. Smilianskaya, "The Disintegration of the Feudal Relations in Syria and Lebanon in the Middle of the Nineteenth Century" in Charles Issawi, ed., *The Economic History of the Middle East* (Chicago: University of Chicago Press, 1966), pp. 227–47. For the attempts to intensify Ottoman rule over Palestine, see Ma'oz, *Ottoman Reform in Syria and Palestine*, part II; Carter V. Findley, "The Evolution of the System of Provincial Administration as Viewed from the Center" in David Kushner, ed., *Palestine in the Late Ottoman Period: Political, Social and Economic Transformation* (Jerusalem: Yad Ben Zvi, and Leiden, Netherlands: E. J. Brill, 1986), pp. 3–29.

10. Neville Mandel, *The Arabs and Zionism Before World War One* (Berkeley: University of California Press, 1976), pp. 13–25 and 76–79; Baruch Kimmerling, *Zionism and Territory: The Socioterritorial Dimensions of Zionist Politics* (Berkeley: Institute of International Studies, University of California, 1983), pp. 8–21; Kenneth Stein, *The Land Question in Palestine, 1917–1937* (Chapel Hill: University of North Carolina Press, 1984), pp. 4–7 and 36–39; Abd al-Wahab Kayyali, *The Modern History of Palestine* (London: Croom Helm, n.d.), pp. 13–21 and 171–74.

11. John Pinkerton, *Modern Geography* (1802), p. 27. While Europeans viewed Palestine as poor and marginal, many Arabs saw it as the heart of the Arab world. See Muhammed al-Nahhal, *Palestine: Land and History* (Amman: Dar al-Galeel, 1984), pp. 7–24 [Arabic].

12. Ruth Kark, *Jaffa—A City in Evolution, 1799–1917* (Jerusalem: Yad Ben Zvi, 1984), pp. 116–79, 204–13 [Hebrew]; Resat Kasaba, Caglar Keyder, and Faruk Tabak, "Eastern Mediterranean Port Cities and Their Bourgeoisies: Merchants, Political Projects, and Nation States," *Review* 1 (1986): 121–35; Ruth Kark, "The Rise and Decline of Coastal Towns in Palestine" in Gad G. Gilbar, *Ottoman Palestine, 1800–1914: Studies in Economic and Social History* (Leiden: E. J. Brill, 1990), pp. 69–89.

13. Other parts of the country responded to the new opportunities. By 1872, for example, 90 percent of the fertile Marj Beni Amer, or Esdaelon plain, in the north, was under cultivation, half with wheat and barley. See C. R. Conder, *Tent Work in Palestine* (London: Palestine Exploration Society, 1878), pp. 112–13.

14. The intense labor the orchards required meant that wealthier farmers, who could afford the substantial investment in irrigation and young seedlings, had to recruit numerous share tenants or wage laborers from the hills. From 1880 until the outbreak of World War I, the acreage for citrus orchards more than quadrupled. The number of cases of fruit shipped through Jaffa's port increased more than thirtyfold in the half century before the war, partially due to the increased acreage and partly as a result of new, more efficient agricultural techniques. See for example, A. Aaronsohn und S. Soskin, "Die Orangengarten von Jaffa," *Trupenpflanzer: Organ des kolonial wirtschaftlichen Komitees* 6 (1902): 341–61. Usually the most reliable sources for trade data are the Great Powers Consuls' reports. For a general survey see Roger Owen, *The Middle East in the World Economy 1800–1914* (London: Methuen, 1981).

15. It is estimated at 350,000 for 1870, at 600,000 for 1914, and at 1,290,000 for 1947. This followed a long period of stagnation and even population losses (in part due to the cholera epidemic of 1865–66). The portion of immigrants (mostly from Egypt, Syria, and Lebanon) was about 10 percent, and the annual natural growth seems to have been one of the highest in the Middle East, above 20:1,000. Our demographic proximations on the Ottoman period are mainly based on Gad Gilbar, "Trends in Demographic Developments of the Palestinian Arabs, 1870–1948," *Cathedra* 45 (1987): 42–56 [Hebrew] and Alexander Scholch, "The Demographic Development of Palestine, 1850–1882," *International Journal of Middle East Studies* 17 (1985): 485–505.

16. Scholch, "European Penetration"; Issa Mustafa Alami, "Some Aspects of the Development of Palestinian Peasant Economy and Society, 1920–1939" (unpublished Ph.D. dissertation, University of Edinburgh, 1984), pp. 117–247.

17. The source of capital was not always that market. Since Muslim religious law prohibits moneylending for interest, the need for capital created a new socioeconomic arrangement, the *sharika* contract, considered valid by the Sharia courts. This was a small-scale but well-established form of economic entrepreneurship: a contract of partnership between a worker or peasant and a person of resources (land and/or money) to share in the profit from growing any cash crop (mainly

grains), olive trees, cattle husbandry, and camel or motor transportation. See Ya'a-
kov Firestone, "Production and Trade in an Islamic Context: Sharika Contracts in
the Transitional Economy of Northern Samaria," *International Journal of Middle
East Studies* 1 (1975): 185–209; 2 (1975): 308–25; Gabriel Baer, "The Impact of
Economic Change on Traditional Society in Nineteenth-Century Palestine" in
Moshe Ma'oz, ed., *Studies on Palestine During the Ottoman Period* (Jerusalem:
The Magnes Press, 1975), pp. 495–98.

18. This argument is confirmed by later developments in the economic, social, and
political spheres around Nablus. See Sarah Graham-Brown, "The Political Economy of the Jabel Nablus" in Owen, ed., *Studies in the Economic and Social
History*, pp. 88–177.

19. Ma'oz, *Ottoman Reform in Syria and Palestine*, 78.

20. Ibid., 77.

21. Ibid., 85.

22. The *Nizam-i Cedid*—the remodeled Ottoman army—helped impose the rule of
the Abd al-Hadi clan and the Tuqans in the area surrounding Nablus, the Abd
al-Rahem Amir family (rooted around the large village of Durah) in the Hebron
region, and two rival peasant-based clans, Abu-Ghush and Samhan, in the mountainous countryside around Jerusalem.

23. Ma'oz, *Ottoman Reform in Syria and Palestine*, 196; Yehosua Porath, "The Social
Aspects of the Emergence of the Palestinian Arab National Movement" in
M. Milson, ed., *Society and Political Structure in the Arab World* (New York:
Humanities Press, 1973), pp. 93–144.

24. Kemal Karpat, "The Land Regime, Social Structure and Modernization in the
Ottoman Empire" in W. Polk and R. Chambers, eds., *Beginnings of Modernization
in the East* (Chicago: University of Chicago Press, 1968), pp. 68–89.

25. Stein, *The Land Question in Palestine*, 3–28. The legislation's original purpose
was to grant the peasants land directly in exchange for the payment of an entry fee,
Tapu (pronounced "Tabu" in Arabic), and a tithe. But the state was unable to
collect the farm taxes (determined mostly by the *Mejlis*, the local councils) on its
own, and needed the service of local notables. They "became patrons of villages
and this was one of the ways in which they came to establish their claims to
ownership over them" (Albert Hourani, "Ottoman Reforms and the Politics of
Notables" in Polk and Chambers, *Beginnings of Modernization*, 49). See also S. J.
Shaw, "The 19th Century Ottoman Tax Reforms and Revenue System," *International Journal of Middle East Studies* 6 (1975); Doreen Warriner, "The Real Meaning of the Land Code" in Charles Issawi, ed., *The Economic History of the Middle
East*, 72–78; Frederic M. Goadby and Moses Doukhan, *The Land Law of Palestine*
(Tel-Aviv, 1935); Samuel Bergheim, "Land Tenure in Palestine," *Palestine Explo-
ration Fund Quarterly Statement* 26 (1894): 191–99.

26. David Grosman, "Rural Settlement in the Southern Coastal Plain and the
Shefelah, 1833–1945," *Cathedra* 45 (1987):57–86 [Hebrew]. Much has been written on share tenancy from the mandate period on, but little has focused on the
formative period at the end of the nineteenth century. See Ya'akov Firestone,
"Crop-sharing Economics in Mandatory Palestine," *Middle East Studies* 11
(1975): 3–23, 175–94; Salim Tamari, "From the Fruits of their Labour: the Per-
sistence of Sharetenancy in the Palestinian Agrarian Economy" in Kathy and
Pandeli Glavanis, eds., *The Rural Middle East: Peasant Lives and Modes of Production* (New Jersey: Zed Books, 1990), pp. 70–94.

27. *Palestinians: From Peasants to Revolutionaries* (London: Zed Books, 1979), pp.
15–16.

28. See Ya'akov Firestone, "The Land-equalizing Musha Village: A Reassessment" in
Gilbar, ed., *Ottoman Palestine*, 91–129; Stein, *The Land Question in Palestine*,

10–15; Alami, *Some Aspects of the Development of Palestinian Peasant Economy*, ch. 2.

29. Hilma Granquist, *Marriage Conditions in a Palestinian Village* (Helsingfors: Societas Scientrarium Fennica, 1935). Some of these patterns are vividly described in Yusuf Haddad, *Society and Folklore in Palestine: A Case Study of al-Bassa Village* (Nicosia: Research Center, Palestine Liberation Organization, 1985), pp. 67–110 [Arabic]. For an excellent analysis of the changes that occurred in the Palestinian family before and after the mandatory period, see Majid Al-Haj, *Social Change and Family Processes: Arab Communities in Shefar-A'm* (Boulder: Westview Press, 1987).

30. See E. A. Finn, "The Fellaheen of Palestine—Notes on Their Clans, Warfare, Religion and Law," *Palestine Exploration Fund Quarterly Statement* (1897): 31–45. (Finn, whose sharp observations are an important record of the period, was the spouse of the British Consul in Jerusalem between 1845 and 1863); P. J. Baldensperger, "Morals of the Fellahin," ibid, 123–34. For a comparison with similar patterns, see Richard Antoun, *Arab Village: A Social Structural Study of Trans-Jordanian Peasant Community* (Bloomington: Indiana University Press, 1972), pp. 88–91. Also see C. T. Wilson, *Peasant Life in the Holy Land* (London: J. Murray, 1906); Sayigh, *Palestinians*, 10–24. Compare with the contemporary structure of Palestinian village and fellaheen subculture as described by Shukri Araaf, *The Palestinian Arab Village: Structure and Land Usage* (Jerusalem: Arab Studies Society, 1986) [2nd ed., Arabic]. *Fidya* was later used as a mobilizing mechanism against the Zionists and the British.

31. The woman's inferior status was reinforced by jokes, folktales, and the tradition of machismo in village life. See Haddad, *Society and Folklore in Palestine*, 189–230, for a detailed account of this subculture. Much later, the rise of Palestinian nationalism and the resistance movement considerably changed the social position of Palestinian women. See Matiel Mogannam, *The Arab Woman and the Palestinian Problem* (London: Herbert Joseph, 1937), pp. 57–84; Yvonne Haddad, "Palestinian Women: Patterns of Legitimation and Domination" in K. Nakhleh and E. Zureik, eds., *The Sociology of the Palestinians* (London: Croom Helm, 1980), pp. 147–99; Mariam Mar'i, "The One Good Thing That Has Resulted From the Intifada," *Israeli Democracy* (Summer 1989): 15–17.

32. For a vivid recollection of this aspect of village life, see Sayigh, *Palestinians*, 18.

33. See, for example, Eliezer Volcani, *The Fellah's Farm* (Tel-Aviv: Agricultural Experimental Station, The Jewish Agency for Palestine, Bulletin No. 10, 1930); John Hope Simpson, *Report on Immigration, Land Settlement and Development* (London: HMSO, 1930, Cmd. 3686); Government of Palestine, *Report by Mr. C.F. Strickland of the Indian Civil Service on the Possibility of Introducing a System of Agricultural Cooperation in Palestine* (Jerusalem: Government Printer, 1930), p. 11; Stein, *The Land Question in Palestine*, 14–15.

34. Kimmerling, *Zionism and Territory*, 32–33; Abraham Granott, *The Land System in Palestine: History and Structure* (London: Eyre and Spottiswood, 1952), p. 218.

35. There is debate among historians about how entrenched the institution was in the late Ottoman period. Some claim that virtually all the land in the central mountain region was co-owned prior to the Ottoman land law of 1858. According to this view, the steady erosion of musha that continued into the second quarter of the twentieth century resulted from increased government intervention: first the Ottoman reforms and later British policies. Others read the fragmentary evidence to say that it was already in decline by 1858, the Ottoman legislation simply nudging the process along. Whatever the precise situation, the element of musha that became a casualty of the 1858 (and subsequent) reforms was its freezing of land ownership. See, for example, Granott, *The Land System in Palestine*, 218.

36. The authorities also reassessed taxes on the gross value of the harvest rather than the net value and finally tried to collect their revenue in hard cash, which was extremely difficult for smallholders to lay their hands on, rather than as a portion of the harvest. See Migdal, *Palestinian Society and Politics*, 14–17.

37. Salim Tamari describes this patronage system as follows: "A single peasant or a whole village crushed relentlessly under despotic taxes and debts placed themselves, together with their lands, under the protection of the town notable, who then interposed himself between his dependents and the tax collectors or creditors, and he looked after their taxes and court cases." For the entire process see Tamari, "Fractionalism and Class Formation in Recent Palestinian History" in Owen, ed., *Studies in the Economic and Social History*, 188–200. Another pattern was sharetenancy, by which the tiller was remunerated for his labor by a share of his yield; see Tamari, "From the Fruits of their Labour" in Glavanis and Glavanis, eds., *The Rural Middle East*, 53–94.

38. For the role of the mukhtar, see Gabriel Baer, "The Office and Functions of the Village Mukhtar" in Migdal, *Palestinian Society and Politics*, 103–23.

39. In fact, the office of the mukhtar was established by the Ottoman Law of 1864 as a *multazam*, or tax farmer, but the office's authority was actually much larger: Mukhtars possessed police power in all spheres of life. See Gabriel Baer, "The Economic and Social Position of the Village Mukhtar in Palestine" in Gabriel Ben-Dor, ed., *The Palestinians and the Middle East Conflict: Studies in Their History, Sociology and Politics* (Ramat Gan: Turtledove, 1978), pp. 101–18.

40. Sharif Kana'ni and Bassam Al-Kaabi, *Ein Houd*—Monographs on Palestinian Destroyed Villages Series, No. 1 (Bir Zeit: University of Bir Zeit, Center of Documentation and Research, 1987), pp. 22–29 [Arabic]; for a later variation of this phenomenon, see Dov Shinar, *Palestinian Voices: Communication and Nation Building in the West Bank* (Boulder: Lynn Rienner, 1987), pp. 86–87.

41. Kana'ni and Al-Kaabi, *Ein Houd*, p. 44. The University of Bir Zeit in the West Bank developed a project of documentation and oral history of Palestinian villages destroyed in 1948 and immediately after (see chapter 5). A number of our descriptions in the following pages are based on this documentation program.

42. Neville Mandel, "Turks, Arabs and Jewish Immigration into Palestine: 1882–1914," St. Anthony's College Papers Series, No. 17 (Middle Eastern Affairs Department, Oxford, 1965), pp. 77–108. The majority of the Jewish immigrants were subjects of foreign great powers and under the protection of consuls (of Russia, Austro-Hungary, Germany, France, and the U.S.) in the framework of the capitulations system.

43. For an excellent account of this period, see David Vital, *The Origins of Zionism* (Oxford: Oxford University Press, 1975). For the Jewish settlement process, see Alex Bein, *The Return to the Soil* (Jerusalem: Am Oved, 1952).

44. Walter Laqueur, *A History of Zionism* (New York: Schocken, 1972), pp. 75–83; Mandel, *The Arabs and Zionism Before World War One*.

45. Laqueur, *A History of Zionism*, 75. The immigrants generally did not see themselves as a part of the European colonization movement of the "non-white territories," but as a national movement. See Shlomo Avineri, *The Making of Modern Zionism* (New York: Basic Books, 1981).

46. On the Templars, who founded their first colonies in 1875–76, see Alex Carmel, "The German Settlers in Palestine and their Relations with the Local Arab Population and the Jewish Community, 1868–1918" in Ma'oz, ed., *Studies on Palestine*, 443–65. On September 22, 1866, American Christian colonists from "The Church of the Messiah," moved by similar religious feelings, tried to settle in Palestine but gave up after one year in face of the harsh conditions of the country.

47. Kimmerling, *Zionism and Territory*, 15.
48. Mandel, *The Arabs and Zionism*, 77–79, 102–7, 166–69.
49. The Abd al-Hadi clan, for example, used land to practice horticulture following the examples of the Templars. Scholch, "European Penetration," 23; D. Giladi, "The Agronomic Development of Old Colonies in Palestine, 1882–1914" in Ma'oz, ed., *Studies on Palestine*, 175–89; Shmuel Avitsur, "The Influence of Western Technology on the Economy of Palestine During the Nineteenth Century" in Ma'oz, ed., *Studies on Palestine*, 485–94. Later the interactions between Jews and Arabs became more complex. See Baruch Kimmerling, "A Model for Analysis of Reciprocal Relations between the Jewish and Arab Communities in Mandatory Palestine," *Plural Societies* (Autumn, 1983): 45–68.
50. It must be noted that not all the crops and agricultural technologies imported by Europeans fit local conditions, and the Templars as well as the Jewish settlers adopted many of the fellaheen technologies after the failure of the imported techniques. See Shaul Katz, "Ideology, Settlement and Agriculture during the First Decade of Petach-Tikvah," *Cathedra* 22 (1982): 74–81 [Hebrew].
51. Graham-Brown, "The Political Economy of Jabel Nablus," 90–92.
52. Stein, *The Land Question in Palestine*, 39.
53. *Land, Labor, and the Origins of the Israeli-Palestinian Conflict—1882–1914* (New York: Cambridge University Press, 1989), pp. 91–122; Baruch Kimmerling, *Zionism and Economy* (Cambridge, Mass: Schenckman, 1983), pp. 19–39.
54. Ahad Ha'am (pseud. for Asher Ginzberg), the famous Zionist writer and analyst, warned in 1893 that Jewish land purchases and employment policies would turn the local Arab population into an eternal enemy. A similar statement was made by the Galilean teacher Yitzhak Epstein in the seventh Zionist Congress (1905), reproduced under the title "The Hidden [Arab] Question" in the Hebrew Zionist organ *Ha'Shiloach* 17 (1908). Both figures forecasted the creation of a *local* Arab national movement as a reaction to Zionism. See also Yosef Gorny, *Zionism and the Arabs, 1882–1948* (Oxford: Clarendon Press, 1987), pp. 57–65. Later the policy toward tenants was changed, and in addition to the money paid for land, the Zionists also paid compensation to the displaced tenants, or preferred to buy lands already free of tenants. See Stein, *The Land Question in Palestine*, 38–48; also, Leah Doukham-Landau, *The Zionist Companies for Land Purchase in Palestine, 1897–1914* (Jerusalem: Yad Ben-Zvi, 1979) [Hebrew].
55. Mandel, *The Arabs and Zionism*, 38.
56. See Gilbar, "Trends in Demographic Developments," 47–49.
57. See Samir M. Seikaly, "Unequal Fortunes: The Arabs of Palestine and the Jews during World War I" in Wadad al-Qadi, ed., *Studia Arabica et Islamica: Festschrift for Ihsan ᶜAbbas on his Sixtieth Birthday* (Beirut: American University of Beirut, 1981), pp. 399–406.
58. I. al-Nimr, *Tarikh jabal Nablus wa-l-Balqa* (Nablus, n.d.), vol. 3, p. 132. The isolation of the territory from the outside world primarily hurt the Jewish settlement, but the war hurt the Arab community, too: Thousands of Jews and Arabs died from epidemics and famine; 11,000 Jews (up to 35 percent of their prewar population) emigrated or were expelled. The export of oranges and other items halted completely, and the abrupt devaluation of the Turkish currency made it completely non-negotiable. See Stein, *The Land Question in Palestine*, 3, 4, 16, 19, 24, and 41.
59. The Declaration was a statement of intent, issued in the form of a private letter from the British foreign secretary Arthur Balfour to Lord Rothschild. Arab historiography has argued that the Balfour Declaration has no value in light of the commitments of Sir Henry McMahon, the British ambassador in Cairo, to Sharif Hussein of Mecca, promising "freedom of the Arab peoples." See George Anto-

nius, *The Arab Awakening: The Story of the Arab National Movement* (New York: Capricorn Books, 1946), pp. 413–427. Even though Palestine was not mentioned in McMahon's letter, the Arab claims were that the western boundary of the Arab independent area, as proposed to Sharif Hussein, was the Mediterranean Sea. For the text of the declaration, see Chapter 3, p. 73.

60. Shalom Reichman, *The Development of Transportation in Palestine, 1920–1947* (Jerusalem: Ministry of Transportation, 1969) [Hebrew].

61. The three-year average yield of vegetables, for example, soared from 11,000 tons to 205,000 tons in just 20 years.

62. From roughly 5,000 to 35,000 acres. Most of the data and analysis on the economy of the Mandatory Palestinian state is based on Himadeh, *Economic Organization of Palestine*; David Horowitz, *The Development of the Palestinian Economy* (Tel-Aviv: Bialik Institute and Dvir, 1948) [Hebrew, second and enlarged edition], pp. 169–79; Jacob Metzer, *Technology, Labor and Growth in a Dual Economy's Traditional Sector: Mandatory Palestine, 1921–1936* (Jerusalem: Falk Institute, 1982); idem, "Growth and Structure of the Arab Economy in Mandatory Palestine—A Historical Overview," *Economic Quarterly* 137 (1988): 129–45 [Hebrew]; idem, *Growth and the Structure of the Palestinian Arab Economy* (Jerusalem: Falk Institute for Economic Research, Research Paper no. 200, 1988) [Hebrew]; Raja Khalidi, *The Arab Economy in Israel: The Dynamics of a Region's Development* (New York: Croom Helm, 1988), pp. 7–34; Jacob Metzer and Oded Kaplan, "Jointly but Severally: Arab-Jewish Dualism and Economic Growth in Mandatory Palestine," *Journal of Economic History* 45 (1985): 327–45; Z. Abramowitz and Y. Gelfat, *The Arab Economy in Palestine and Middle Eastern Countries* (Tel-Aviv: HaKibbutz HaMeuchad Press, 1944) [Hebrew]. For an analysis of the Palestinian state economic policy, see Nachum T. Gross, *The Economic Policy of the Mandatory Government in Palestine* (Jerusalem: Falk Institute, 1982) [Hebrew].

63. Oranges, lemons, and grapefruits—mostly shipped to the British Isles—accounted for 80 percent of the country's export revenue and over 90 percent of its agricultural exports. Abramowitz and Gelfat, *The Arab Economy in Palestine*, 44.

64. Vegetable fields and citrus groves expanded rapidly in the country as a whole, while the production of cereals was much flatter. Large tracts owned by town notables and Jews produced oranges; the small fragmented plots of the fellaheen, for the most part, produced the cereals. In the two decades following the war, Jewish investment in citriculture reached $75 million. See Hurewitz, *The Struggle for Palestine* (New York: Schocken Books, 1976), p. 30. Intensively cultivated field crops also gained, with up to a quarter of them sold to the growing Jewish market by 1935. The same pattern could be seen in raising animals: the number of fowl (more and more the commercial product of Jewish communal settlements) increased fourfold from 1930 to 1943, while sheepherding (still mostly the domain of poorer Arabs) inched up only slightly.

65. See Metzer and Kaplan, "Jointly But Severally," 339–41.

66. A British report noted that in one village in the hilly region 30 percent of the land titles passed from smallholders to largeholders in the 1920s. The report was popularly known as the French Report, after its author, Lewis French. Government of Palestine, *Report on Agricultural Development and Land Settlement in Palestine* (Jerusalem: Government Printer, 1931), pp. 23–25.

67. Government of Palestine, *Report on the Economic Conditions of Agriculturalists in Palestine and Fiscal Measures of Government in Relation Thereto* (Jerusalem: Government Printer, 1930). Popularly known as the Johnson-Crosbie Report, this survey was one of nine undertaken during the mandate, eight by the British and one Anglo-American. The commission that wrote it surveyed 104 villages.

68. Gross, *The Economic Policy of the Mandatory Government*, 4, pinpoints the

following major goals of the British mandatory state economic policy: to avoid any burden on the British taxpayer as a consequence of holding Palestine, to promote British exports and help British firms to operate in the country, to maintain a stable and efficient government accepted by a satisfied population, to support the country's economic and cultural development in the frame of reference of European capitalism, and all this with minimal interference in local traditions and the existing social fabric.

69. Ylana N. Miller, *Government and Society in Rural Palestine, 1920–1948* (Austin: University of Texas Press, 1985), pp. 49–54.

70. Migdal, *Palestinian Society and Politics*, 24–31.

71. Miller, *Government and Policy in Rural Palestine*, 84.

72. See Nabil Ayyub Badran, *Education and Modernization in the Palestinian Arab Society, 1: The Mandatory Period* (Beirut: Palestine Liberation Organization Research Center, 1968) [Arabic].

73. Even after the revolt was broken by the British in 1939, earlier events "left villagers with little reason to see the law as protective rather than intrusive or, at best, irrelevant." Miller, *Government and Policy in Rural Palestine*, 128. See also Muhammed al-Nahhal, *The British Policy toward the Arab Palestinian Land Question* (Beirut: Filastin al-Muhtallah, 1981), pp. 53–68 [Arabic].

74. Nachum Gross and Jacob Metzer, *Palestine in World War Two: Some Economic Aspects* (Jerusalem: Falk Institute, Discussion Paper No. 87, 1987 [mimeo]), p. 6; Metzer, "Growth and Structure of the Arab Economy in Mandatory Palestine," pp. 129–45.

75. David Ben Gurion, *My Talks with Arab Leaders* (New York: The Third Press, 1972).

76. Ben Gurion stated in 1928 that "according to my beliefs, we do not have the right to deprive even a single Arab child, even if by means of that deprivation we will achieve our [national] goals." David Ben-Gurion, *We and Our Neighbors* (Tel-Aviv: Davar, 1931), p. 150, and Ben-Gurion, *My Talks*, 23–24.

77. See Volcani, *The Fellah's Farm*, 74–77.

78. Stein, *The Land Question in Palestine*, passim; Kimmerling, *Zionism and Territory*, passim.

79. See Gilbar, "Trends in Demographic Developments," 45.

80. See Kark, *Jaffa*; Mahmud Yazbak, "Arab Migration to Haifa: A Quantitative Analysis Following Arab Sources, 1933–1948," *Cathedra* 45 (1987): 131–46 [Hebrew]; Yosef Washitz, "Villagers' Migration to Haifa in the Mandatory Period: Was It an Urbanization Process?" *Cathedra* 45 (1987): 113–29 [Hebrew].

81. Pamela Ann Smith, *Palestine and the Palestinians, 1876–1983* (New York: St. Martin's Press, 1984), pp. 52–53.

82. Between 1931 and 1939, the mandatory government's definition of an alienated *fellah* was narrowed. The landless were defined as "such Arabs as can be shown to have been displaced from the lands which they occupied in consequence of the land passing into Jewish hands, and who have not obtained other holdings on which they can establish themselves, or other equally satisfactory occupation" (Stein, *The Land Question in Palestine*, 128–29). Perhaps the major land transfers, which left many fellaheen families without lands, were the purchase of Marj Beni Amer (Jezreel Valley) and Wadi Hawarith (Hefer Valley). Following an inquiry in 1931–32, 2,663 claims were submitted by landowners and tenants who claimed to have been hurt by the Jewish land purchases; only 899 of these claims were accepted.

83. Kimmerling, *Zionism and Territory*, pp. 111–112.

2. THE CITY: BETWEEN NABLUS AND JAFFA

1. Ihsan al-Nimr, *Tarikh Jabal Nablus wa al Balq'a*, vol. 1 (2nd ed.) (Nablus: Matba⁣ᶜat ᶜummal al-Matabiᶜ al-Taᶜawiniyya, 1975), pp. 223n and 205–7 [Arabic].

2. See the colorful description of Amnon Cohen, *Palestine in the 18th Century: Patterns of Government and Administration* (Jerusalem: Magnes Press, 1973), pp. 27–29.

3. Ibid., pp. 69, 313. Ottoman rule tried to unify southern Palestine, combining the Jerusalem, Jaffa, and Gaza districts under the leadership of Muhammad Abu-Maraq, as a counterbalance to Acre's governor. However, in 1802 Jazzar forced Abu-Maraq to surrender. The second time the *sanjaq* (district) of Jerusalem was separated from the center and unified with the sanjaq of Nablus was during the preparation for the Egyptian Muhammad Ali's invasion of Palestine in 1830. See Adel Manna, "The Sanjaq of Jerusalem: Between Two Invasions (1798–1831)—Administration and Society" (unpublished Ph.D. dissertation, Hebrew University, 1986), p. ii [Hebrew].

4. Cohen, *Palestine in the 18th Century*, passim.

5. Bernard Lewis, *The Emergence of Modern Turkey* (New York: Oxford University Press, 1976), pp. 34–37. The "Sublime Porte" refers to the center of the Ottoman authorities, the palace from which the Sultan ruled. The term comes from the manifold gates, or doors, leading up to the palace, which in Turkish are referred to as "the big gate."

6. Based on figures of Ruth Kark, "The Contribution of the Ottoman Regime to the Development of Jerusalem and Jaffa, 1840–1917" in David Kushner, ed., *Palestine in the Late Ottoman Period*, 46.

7. Among the visitors writing on Jaffa and the rest of Palestine were Laurence Oliphant, *The Land of Gilead* (Edinburgh: W. Blackwood, 1880) and (as noted above) Mark Twain, in *The Innocents Abroad, or The New Pilgrim's Progress: Being Some Account of the Steamship "Quaker City's" Pleasure Excursion to Europe and the Holy Land* (New York: Harper, 1905). For an anthology of other travelers' descriptions, see Thomas Wright, ed., *Early Travels in Palestine* (London: H. G. Bohn, 1848).

8. They also exported to Jericho, Nablus—and even to the Galilee and Gaza. See Amnon Cohen, *Economic Life in Ottoman Jerusalem* (Cambridge: Cambridge University Press, 1989), pp. 86–87.

9. As the eminent Palestinian historian A. L. Tibawi put it, the great powers' rivalry in Palestine "was often manifested during the nineteenth century in one power upholding the claims of one Christian sect against those of another Christian sect, upheld in turn by another power, or against the Turkish authorities." *Arab Education in Mandatory Palestine: A Study of Three Decades of British Administration* (London: Luzac, 1956), p. 6.

10. According to an Egyptian census, of 466 villages in central and southern Palestine in 1833 (including the districts of Gaza, Jaffa, Lydda, Ramallah, and Hebron), the Nablus and Jerusalem districts claimed 323 or nearly 70 percent. In fact, the Nablus district accounted for over 200 villages. See Mordechai Abir, "Local Leadership and Early Reforms in Palestine, 1800–1834" in Ma'oz (ed.), *Studies on Palestine*, 285.

11. Like much else in these towns, for years the olive industry resisted changes that, by the turn of the twentieth century, entrepreneurs along the coast openly welcomed. As late as 1928, mechanical engines had been introduced into a mere 6 percent of the approximately 500 oil presses in the country. In the 1930s, change began to overtake the industry: By 1941, one-quarter of the presses were engine-driven.

The data for this section were compiled from Yaacov Shimoni, *The Arabs of Palestine* (Tel-Aviv: Am Oved, 1947), pp. 186–89 [Hebrew]; Abramowitz and Gelfat, *The Arab Economy in Palestine*, 212–23 [Hebrew]; Yosef Waschitz, *The Arabs in Palestine* (Merhavia: HaKibbutz HaArtzi, 1947) [Hebrew] pp. 87–94; Baruch Kimmerling, *The Economic Interrelationships between the Arab and Jewish Communities in Mandatory Palestine* (Cambridge: Center for International Studies, Massachusetts Institute of Technology, 1979), pp. 47–58; Nachum Gross, *The Economic Policy of the Mandatory Government in Palestine* (Jerusalem: Falk Institute, Discussion Paper No. 816, 1982 [mimeo]), pp. 1–66.

12. Another common specialty was woven fabrics. The largely Christian town of Bethlehem, exploiting the increasing numbers of European pilgrims from the 1830s on, manufactured holy items and souvenirs sculpted from local olive wood.

13. al-Nimr, *Tarikh Jabal Nablus*, 152.

14. Abir, "Local Leadership and Early Reforms in Palestine," 286–89.

15. Abir argues that by the time of the Egyptian invasion, the autonomy of the Nablus chiefs was about to be undone by the Ottoman authorities, in any case: that the possibilities for maneuvering between Sidon and Damascus were largely gone, and the drive for centralization in the Empire was very strong. Ibid., pp. 301–2.

16. Shimon Shamir, "Egyptian Rule (1832–1840) and the Beginning of the Modern Period in the History of Palestine," in Cohen and Baer, eds., *Egypt and Palestine*, 220–21.

17. al-Nimr, *Tarikh Jabal Nablus*, 319–34.

18. The inland families sent them to Ottoman or Muslim academies, while those on the coast were more likely to provide a Western education.

19. Owen, *The Middle East in the World Economy*, 174.

20. Ma'oz, *Ottoman Reform in Syria and Palestine*, 93.

21. al-Nimr, *Tarikh Jabal Nablus*, 325–28.

22. Charles Issawi, "The Trade of Jaffa, 1825–1914" in Hisham Nashabe, ed., *Studia Palaestina: Studies in Honour of Constantine K. Zurayk* (Beirut: Institute for Palestine Studies, 1988), pp. 42; 50–51. The rise of Jaffa and Haifa coincided with the incorporation into a world trade network of towns such as Beirut, Alexandria, and Port Said. See Kark, "The Rise and Decline of Coastal Towns in Palestine" in Gilbar, ed., *Ottoman Palestine*, 69–89. See also Kark, "Transportation in Nineteenth Century Palestine: Reintroduction of the Wheel" in *The Land that Became Israel: Studies in Historical Geography* (New Haven: Yale University Press, 1989), pp. 67–70.

23. Through the eighteenth century, Beirut "remained a curiously small and insignificant agglomeration." In the nineteenth, it assumed cultural, social, and economic dominance in Lebanon. See Samir Khalaf, *Lebanon's Predicament* (New York: Columbia University Press, 1987), p. 219. Also, see Yasar Eyup Ozveren, "The Making and Unmaking of an Ottoman Port-City: Nineteenth-Century Beirut, Its Hinterland, and the World-Economy" (unpublished Ph.D. dissertation, State University of New York at Binghamton, 1990). For the classic analysis of the distinction between Mediterranean coast and hinterland, see Fernand Braudel, *The Mediterranean and the Mediterranean World in the Age of Phillip II*, vol. 1 (New York: Harper & Row, 1972).

24. This trend was diametrically reversed during the years of the Arab Revolt. See Rachelle Leah Taqqu, "Arab Labor in Mandatory Palestine, 1920–1948" (unpublished Ph.D. dissertation, Columbia University, 1977), p. 64.

25. See, for example, Alexander Schölch, "The Economic Development of Palestine, 1856–1882," *Journal of Palestine Studies* 10 (1981): 48.

26. Alex Carmel, *The History of Haifa Under Turkish Rule* (Jerusalem: Yad Ben-Zvi, 1977), p. 161 [Hebrew].

27. Kark, "The Contribution of the Ottoman Regime" in Kushner, ed. *Palestine in the Late Ottoman Period*, 46–47. Construction continued as a major activity after the First World War. Not surprisingly, building along with work in quarries and cement factories constituted the largest sector absorbing migrants to the coastal cities between the wars.

28. Issawi, "The Trade of Jaffa, 1825–1914," in Nashabe, ed. *Studia Palaestina*, 43–45.

29. Jaffa became the orange capital of Palestine, and citrus the country's major export: by 1910, it accounted for about one-third of the total income from exports shipped through the city, with the number exported quintupling in the three decades leading up to the Great War. Gad G. Gilbar, "The Growing Economic Involvement of Palestine with the West, 1865–1914" in Kushner, ed., *Palestine in the Late Ottoman Period*, 191; Owen, *The Middle East in the World Economy*, 265.

30. To this day, movies are prohibited in the town of Hebron.

31. Neil Caplan, *Palestine Jewry and the Arab Question, 1917–1925* (London: Frank Cass, 1978), p. 133.

32. In 1966 the Histadrut officially removed the word "Jewish" from that title.

33. David Ben-Gurion, quoted in Neil Caplan, "Arab-Jewish Contacts in Palestine After the First World War," *Journal of Contemporary History* 12 (1977): 647.

34. See Gershon Shafir, *Land, Labor and the Origins of the Israeli-Palestinian Conflict* (New York: Cambridge University Press, 1989), pp. 55–60 and 69–78; Michael Shalev, *Labour and the Political Economy of Israel* (Oxford: Oxford University Press, 1991), pp. 1–18.

35. Rachelle Taqqu, "Peasants into Workmen: Internal Labor Migration and the Arab Village Community under the Mandate" in Migdal, *Palestinian Society and Politics*, 271.

36. On the Communist effort, see Musa K. Budeiri, *The Palestinian Communist Party, 1919–1948: Arabs and Jews in Struggle* (London: Ithaca Press, 1979). The author himself was a leading figure in the mandate period Communist party.

37. Maher al-Charif, "Le premier congrès ouvrier arabe: l'émergence du mouvement ouvrier arabe en Palestine" in René Gallissot, ed., *Mouvement ouvrier, communisme et nationalismes dans le monde arabe*, Cahiers du Mouvement Social 3 (Paris: Les Éditions Ouvrières, 1978), pp. 147–56.

38. For an idea of how World War II affected labor patterns, note the statistics for Haifa: Out of a total of 15,000 workers in 1943, almost 10,000 worked for the government and the British army (7,000 just for the army). Another 2,000 worked for international oil companies. See Itzhak Klein, "The Arabs in Haifa under the British Mandate: A Political Economic and Social Survey," Occasional Papers on the Middle East (New Series), No. 5 (University of Haifa, The Jewish-Arab Center, Institute of Middle Eastern Studies, 1987), p. 59 [Hebrew].

39. This is discussed in chapter 5.

40. Taqqu, "Peasants into Workmen," 271.

41. Shulamit Carmi and Henry Rosenfeld, "The Origins of the Process of Proletarianization and Urbanization of Arab Peasants in Palestine," *Annals of the New York Academy of Sciences* 220 (1974): 470–85.

42. This distinction was so meaningful in Palestinian society that it continued to be used in the refugee camps even 30 years after it had lost any practical meaning. See Sayigh, *Palestinians: From Peasants to Revolutionaries*, 25–40; and Danny Rubinstein, *The Fig Tree Embrace—The Palestinian "Right of Return"* (Jerusalem: Keter, 1990), pp. 23–32 [Hebrew].

43. Muslih, *The Origins of Palestinian Nationalism*, 162.

44. This is discussed in chapter 4.

45. Adnan abu-Ghazaleh, "Arab Cultural Nationalism in Palestine during the British

Mandate," *Journal of Palestine Studies* 1 (1972): 39. In the cities, these figures reached 85 percent, while in the villages they remained around 20 percent. More boys were in schools than girls: in the villages, more than 10 times as many; in the towns, more than 50 percent. From 1914 under the Turks to 1944 under the British, the number of public schools for Arabs went from 98 to 480 and the number of pupils from 8,248 to 71,662. See Tibawi, *Arab Education in Mandatory Palestine*, 20, 49. Still, chronic underfunding and the lack of sufficient places for children prompted Arab protest in the 1930s and a subsequent British inquiry by the Department of Education. Public schools began to accommodate Christians as well as Muslims, although disproportionately large numbers of Christians continued attending private foreign schools.

46. One estimate placed the number of Palestinians studying at the American University of Beirut in 1945 at approximately five hundred, with an additional three hundred at Egypt's universities and colleges. See Shimoni, *The Arabs of Palestine*, p. 387.

47. In the 1940s, the Arab College evolved into a university-level college, qualifying its graduates for a London University certificate.

48. Tarif Khalidi, "Palestinian Historiography: 1900–1948," *Journal of Palestine Studies* 10 (1981): 59.

49. *Awdat al-Safina* (Returning of the Ship), pp. 37–39 [Arabic].

50. Khalidi, "Palestinian Historiography," 60.

51. Abd al-Karim al Karmi (Abu Salma), cited in A.M. Elmessiri, ed., *The Palestinian Wedding: A Bilingual Anthology of Contemporary Palestinian Resistance Poetry* (Washington, D.C.: Three Continents Press, 1982), p. 26.

52. Cited in *Poetry of Resistance in Occupied Palestine*, translated by Sulafa Hijjawi (Baghdad: Al-Jumhuriya, 1968), p. 12.

53. Muhammad Siddiq, *Man Is a Cause: Political Consciousness and the Fiction of Ghassan Kanafani* (Seattle: University of Washington Press, 1984), p. xi.

54. Cited in Richard J. Ward, Don Pertez and Evan M. Willson, *The Palestinian State: A Rational Approach* (Port Washington, NY: Kennikat Press, 1977), pp. 6–7.

55. In 1928, 1939, and 1942, the mandate government surveyed the industry, and additional data are available from the general population survey of 1931 and other sources. Unfortunately, the figures are not comparable as definitions of industry and handicrafts varied. In 1942–43, the survey reported a total of 1,558 small plants and workshops for all of Palestine. See Government of Palestine, *A Survey of Palestine*, 3 vols. (Jerusalem: Government Printer, 1946); Supplement (Jerusalem, 1947); see also P. J. Loftus, *National Income of Palestine* (Jerusalem: Government Printer, 1946); E. Mills, *Census of Palestine* (Jerusalem: Government Printer, 1933).

56. Shimoni, *The Arabs of Palestine*, 189.

57. The largest share was food processing (43 percent). The other figures: shoe production—16 percent; tobacco products including cigarettes—9 percent; metallurgy and textiles—5 percent each. The increasing availability of hydroelectric power from the Jordan River and power plants in Tel-Aviv and Haifa made this expansion and diversification feasible. From 1921 to 1939, the number of Arab enterprises using mechanical power went from 7 to 541.

58. Government of Palestine, *Report of Committee on the Economic Condition of Agriculturists and the Fiscal Measures of Government in Relation Thereto* [Johnson-Crosbie report] (Jerusalem: Government Printer, 1943), pp. 60–61. One report in the 1930s estimated that the fellaheen bought £P700,000 to £P800,000 worth of goods from the towns, including clothing, matches, oil, rice, and sugar. "Under the Ottoman Empire, Palestine, like other parts of the Empire, used the Turkish pound as the legal money in circulation. This continued until the occu-

pation of Palestine by the Allies, when the Egyptian pound was made legal tender along with the British gold sovereign in 1917. In 1926 the Palestine Currency Board was established and the Palestinian currency was legally defined in 1927. The Egyptian pound and the British gold sovereign were withdrawn from circulation as the Palestinian pound [£P] took their place. The monetary standard for Palestinian currency was the sterling exchange standard." Ahmad K. Katanani, "Economic performance of Palestine before 1948," *Dirasat* 13 (1986): 52.

59. In 1927, the government listed 259 Arab importers and 133 exporters; those numbers expanded to 317 and 160 respectively in 1933.

60. The total volume of Arab foreign trade in this period appears impressive. Imports expanded by more than 50 and exports by 67 percent in the 15 years after 1922. On a per capita basis, however, the results are less striking, less than 4 percent growth for imports and 22 percent for exports.

61. Katanani, "Economic Performance of Palestine," 35.

62. In fact, Jews purchased approximately a quarter of the net Arab national product in 1935, Arabs in turn consuming about 8 percent of that of the Jews. In that year, the Arabs shipped about £P2 million worth of products abroad and sold another £P1 million to the Jews, and about 12,000 Arabs worked for Jewish enterprises. See Metzer and Kaplan, "Jointly but Severally," 328; Abramowitz and Gelfat, *The Arab Economy in Palestine*, 104; Zvi Sussman, *Wage Differentials and Equality within the Histadrut* (Ramat Gan: Massada, 1974), p. 40 [Hebrew].

63. One survey found a cumulative peasant debt of about £P1 million in 1930, on which the fellaheen paid an average annual interest of 30 percent. (In the 1940s, peasants retired much of that debt as a result of the good economic conditions brought on by the war.)

64. From £P55,000 in 1931 to £P376,000 two years later, £P775,000 by 1942, and £P7 million at the end of the Second World War.

65. A similar attempt to found the Arab Industrial Bank failed. Shimoni, *The Arabs of Palestine*, 232.

66. Khalil al-Sakanini, *Palestine after the Great War* (Jerusalem: Beit al-Maqdas Printer, 1925), ch. 3 [Arabic]. Sakanini, an Arab patriot, was an educator who wrote scores of textbooks for the modern Palestinian Arabic schools. While his general views were humanist and liberal, he took a hard line against Jewish settlement. His selected diaries were published in Hebrew under the title *Such Am I, O World* (Jerusalem: Keter, 1990) and provide the Hebrew reader a unique window into the world of a Palestinian intellectual between 1914 and 1950.

67. Shai Lachman, "Arab Rebellion and Terrorism in Palestine 1929–39: The Case of Sheikh Izz al-Din al-Qassam and his Movement" in Elie Kedourie and Sylvia G. Haim, eds., *Zionism and Arabism in Palestine and Israel* (London: Frank Cass, 1982), p. 61. For more on Qassam's influence, see chapter 4. See also S. Abdullah Schleifer, "The Life and Thought of Izz-id-Din al-Qassam," *Islamic Quarterly* 23 (1979): 78.

68. This was not the first time that the name Black Hand was used by Arab nationalists. An attack in 1920 by more than 2,000 Bedouin fighters on a British military installation was suspected of being the signal for a general uprising against the British, which never materialized. The aim was unification with Syria under Faysal. One of the key forces in planning the uprising and stockpiling weapons was the Black Hand, an underground organization that spread from Jaffa to other towns, possibly under the direction of the Arab Literary Club. It existed from about 1919–23.

69. Ted Swedenburg, "Al-Qāssam Remembered," *Alif: Journal of Comparative Poetics* 7 (1987): 17.

70. Members of the Nashashibi and Khalidi families dissociated themselves from the violence of Qassam's group. Only after Qassam's death did most of the leadership

identify itself with him. See Yuval Arnon-Ohanna, *The Internal Struggle within the Palestinian Movement—1929–1939* (Tel-Aviv: Hadar, 1981), pp. 270–71 [Hebrew]. Also see Ghassan Kanafani, *The 1936–39 Revolt in Palestine* (Beirut: Committee for Democratic Palestine, Popular Front from the Liberation of Palestine, n.d.). Even the eventual leader of the Palestinian nationalist movement, Amin al-Husseini, seemed to oppose the violence of November 1935 at a time when he was involved in intensive diplomatic discussions with Britain and hoped to achieve an agreement for autonomy in stages. See Yehoshua Porath, *The Palestinian National Movement: From Riots to Rebellion, 1929–1939* (London: Frank Cass, 1977), p. 139. Subhi Yassin argues that Amin was always hostile to Qassam, but this seems to be a distortion of Amin's attitudes. See *The Great Arab Revolution in Palestine, 1936–1939* (Cairo, 1959), p. 22 [Arabic].

3. JERUSALEM: NOTABLES AND NATIONALISM

1. Aliza Auerbach quoted in Cornell Capa, ed., *Jerusalem: City of Mankind* (New York: Grossman, 1974), p. 118.
2. *Jerusalem: The Holy City in the Eyes of Chroniclers, Visitors, Pilgrims, and Prophets from the Days of Abraham to the Beginnings of Modern Times* (Princeton: Princeton University Press, 1985), p. ix.
3. Cited in Peters, *Jerusalem*, p. 562.
4. *The Innocents Abroad* 2: 326.
5. An excellent account of conditions can be found in Yehoshua Ben-Arieh, *Jerusalem in the Nineteenth Century: The Old City* (New York: St. Martin's Press, 1984), pp. 2–4 and 82–83.
6. Cited in Ruth Kark and Shimon Landman, "The Establishment of Muslim Neighborhoods in Jerusalem, Outside the Old City, During the Late Ottoman Period," *Palestine Exploration Quarterly* 112 (1980), 113–114. Kark and Landman show that in the early part of the century there were scattered Muslim buildings (religious structures, seasonal residences) outside the walls, but that serious Muslim construction there did not begin until the 1860s. It mostly involved the upper classes, and was limited compared to that of the Christians—the first to undertake large-scale construction—and that of the Jews.
7. See Amnon Cohen, *Economic Life in Ottoman Jerusalem* (New York: Cambridge University Press, 1989), pp. 6–10.
8. Edward Robinson, *Biblical Researches in Palestine, Mount Sinai and Arabia Petra. A Journal of Travels in the Year 1838*, vol. 2 (Boston: Crocker & Brewster, 1841), p. 81.
9. Twain, *The Innocents Abroad*, p. 329.
10. Kark, "The Contribution of the Ottoman Regime" in Kushner, ed., *Palestine in the Late Ottoman Period*, 46–49.
11. Gilbar, *Trends in the Demographic Development of the Palestinians*, 12; Butrus Abu-Manneh, "The Population of Palestine in the 1870s According to Ottoman Censuses," paper delivered for a conference on "Palestine 1840–1948: Population and Migration," Haifa University, June, 1986.
12. Manna, *The Sanjaq of Jerusalem*, vi–vii. The position of deputy to the Mullah in Jerusalem was for generations the monopoly of the al-Khalidi family, and, by virtue of this position, this family managed to accumulate great influence over public affairs in Jerusalem and beyond. Khalidis were appointed as deputies in Nablus, Jaffa, Gaza, and other cities.
13. In judicial and military matters there was some subordination to governors in Beirut and Damascus, but in most matters, the chief administrator of the Jerusalem sanjak was equivalent to a provincial governor. See Haim Gerber, "The Otto-

man Administration of the Sanjaq of Jerusalem, 1890–1908," *Asian and African Studies* 12 (1978): 37.

14. Butrus Abu-Manneh, "The Rise of the Sanjak of Jerusalem in the Late 19th Century," in Ben-Dor, ed., *The Palestinians and the Middle East Conflict*, 25.

15. See Kushner, ed., *Palestine in the Late Ottoman Period*, 247–330.

16. Gabriel Baer, "Jerusalem's Families of Notables and the Wakf in the Early 19th Century," in Kushner, ed., *Palestine in the Late Ottoman Period*, 109–22.

17. "The Ottoman Administration of the Sanjaq of Jerusalem," 44.

18. In most instances, the Ottomans simply appointed the members of the council, but in 1908 an election for the council took place. The voters consisted of 700 Muslims, 300 Christians, and 200 Jews. See Ruth Kark, "The Jerusalem Municipality at the End of Ottoman Rule," *Asian and African Studies* 14 (1980): 124.

19. See Daniel Rubinstein, "The Jerusalem Municipality under the Ottomans, British, and Jordanians" in Joel L. Kramer, ed., *Jerusalem: Problems and Prospects* (New York: Praeger, 1980), pp. 62, 74.

20. Abu-Manneh, "The Rise of the Sanjak of Jerusalem," 26–28.

21. "Factionalism and Class Formation" in Owen, ed., *Studies in the Economic and Social History of Palestine*, 181.

22. See Yehoshua Porath, *The Emergence of the Palestinian-Arab National Movement, 1918–1929* (London: Frank Cass, 1974), pp. 160–62.

23. For a full account of all drafts of the text—including this, the final one—and for a full history of it, see Ronald Sanders, *The High Walls of Jerusalem: A History of the Balfour Declaration and the Birth of the British Mandate in Palestine* (New York: Holt, Rinehart, Winston, 1983).

24. *Bitter Harvest: Palestine between 1914–1979* (Delmar, NY: Caravan Books, 1979), pp. 299–300.

25. Mandel, *The Arabs and Zionism*, 39–40.

26. Ibid., 174.

27. *Le Réveil de la nation arabe dans l'Asie Turque* (Paris, 1905), p. v.

28. See Porath, *The Emergence of the Palestinian-Arab National Movement*, 39–69, 307–9.

29. For a brief account of it and other post-war arrangements, see Charles D. Smith, *Palestine and the Arab-Israeli Conflict* (New York: St. Martin's Press, 1988), pp. 55–66.

30. Porath, *The Emergence of the Palestinian-Arab National Movement*, 89. See also Porath, *The Palestinian National Movement*, 7–10; 14–24. The movement is also analyzed in Ann Mosley Lesch, *Arab Politics in Palestine, 1917–1939: The Frustration of a Nationalist Movement* (Ithaca: Cornell University Press, 1979), and Ann Mosely Lesch, "The Palestinian Arab Nationalist Movement Under the Mandate" in William B. Quandt, Fuad Jabber, and Ann M. Lesch, eds., *The Politics of Palestinian Nationalism* (Berkeley: University of California Press, 1973), pp. 7–42.

31. See Aaron S. Klieman, *Foundations of British Policy in the Arab World: The Cairo Conference of 1921* (Baltimore: Johns Hopkins University Press, 1970), pp. 117–22 and 129–31.

32. For details, see Porath, *The Emergence of the Palestinian-Arab National Movement*, 69–105.

33. Ibid., 84. Porath writes of the divisions at the congress: "It is hardly coincidental that it was the heads of two important families of Jerusalem, ᶜArif Pasha al-Dajani and Ismaiᶜil al-Husayni, who led the movement for 'Palestine for the Palestinians,' just as it was no coincidence that they were supported by the class of notables and community elders, in contrast to the opposition of the youth. The establishment of a separate government for Palestine would turn the notables of Jerusalem and the heads of the influential families into office-holders, ministers,

and future heads of state. On the other hand, the youthful partisans of unity could only gain from unity with Damascus. Around Faysal converged their contemporaries and ideological comrades from Syria and Iraq, who had been the decisive element in his regime, pre-empting the veteran Damascene élite." On the contribution of the Emir Faysal to Palestinian nationalism, see Muslih, *The Origins of Palestinian Nationalism,* 115–30.

34. Porath, *The Emergence of the Palestinian-Arab National Movement,* 86–87. See also Abu-Manneh, "The Rise of Jerusalem in the Late 19th Century," 28: "Even after the establishment of mandatory Palestine through the joining of the sanjaks of Jerusalem, Nablus and Acre, Jerusalem held its primacy; yet, for a long time, there existed another two centers, Nablus and Acre (Haifa), the notables of which were not always ready to take the lead of those in Jerusalem."

35. Kayyali, *Palestine, A Modern History* (London: Croom Helm, n.d.), pp. 70ff.

36. *The Arab Awakening,* 312.

37. Cited in Porath, *The Emergence of the Palestinian-Arab National Movement,* 107.

38. Ibid., 117–18; 175–81.

39. The only demand that the British completely—and promptly—accepted was giving the Arab Executive the same official status as the Jewish Agency. In exchange, they demanded official Arab recognition of the mandate, which the Palestinian politicians never gave. The idea of establishing an elected representative body of the entire population met with strong Zionist resistance; they proposed parity—a body half of Arab representatives and half of Jews, with veto power for the British. The Palestinians boycotted an election held in February–March, 1923 for secondary electors to an advisory council. In the late 1920s the Arabs accepted the establishment of such a council, but now the Zionists opposed it. See Porath, *The Palestinian National Movement,* chs. 1 and 3; Kayyali, *Palestine,* 84–129.

40. "The Bases of Arab and Jewish Leadership During the Mandate Period," *Journal of Palestine Studies* 6 (1977):113.

41. For a detailed description and analysis of the British motives and the developments leading to the rise of the new religious establishment, see Porath, *The Emergence of the Palestinian-Arab National Movement,* chs. 2–3. For a general discussion, see Uri Kupferschmidt, "Islam on the Defensive: The Supreme Muslim Council's Role in Mandatory Palestine," *Asian and African Studies* 17 (1983): 204–5.

42. For more on al-Husseini, see Philip Mattar, *The Mufti of Jerusalem: Al-Hajj Amin al-Husayni and the Palestinian National Movement* (New York: Columbia University Press, 1988); Zvi Elpeleg, *Grand Mufti* (Tel-Aviv: Ministry of Defence Publishing House, 1989) [Hebrew]; Taysir Jbara, *Palestinian Leader Hajj Amin al-Husayni: Mufti of Jerusalem* (Princeton: The Kingston Press, 1985). See also Muhammed Amin al-Husseini, *Truths Regarding the Palestinian Problem,* 2nd ed. (Cairo: Dar al-Kitab al-Arabi bi-Masr, 1957) [Arabic].

43. Mattar, *The Mufti of Jerusalem,* 25.

44. Uri Kupferschmidt, "Attempts to Reform the Supreme Muslim Council" in Ben-Dor, ed., *The Palestinians and the Middle East Conflict,* 35.

45. See Porath, *The Emergence of the Palestinian-Arab National Movement,* ch. 4.

46. For an excellent description of Palestinian notable politics between 1929 and 1936, see Porath, *The Palestinian National Movement,* 234–40; 184–206.

47. On the use of religious symbols in cases where Muslims faced Western powers, see Rudolph Peters, *Islam and Colonialism: The Doctrine of Jihad in Modern History* (New York: Mouton, 1979), pp. 3–5. For special reference to the Palestinian case, see pp. 94–104.

48. What role Amin played in these events, especially in their early stages, remains controversial. Arab writers have stressed his moderation—a view shared by many British officials of the time—Jewish writers the incendiary nature of his speeches.

It is a fact that he and other Jerusalem-led notables signed a proclamation dissociating themselves from Arab mob action, once it was well under way.

49. See Daphne Tsimhoni, "The Arab Christians and the Palestinian Arab National Movement During the Formative Stage," in Ben-Dor, ed., *The Palestinians and the Middle East Conflict*, 73–98.

50. Cited in ibid, 76.

51. See Nels Johnson, *Islam and the Politics of Meaning in Palestinian Nationalism* (London: Kegan Paul International, 1982), pp. 9–30; Donna Robinson Divine, "Islamic Culture and Political Practice in British Mandate Palestine," *Review of Politics* 45 (1983): 71–93.

52. Porath, *The Emergence of the Palestinian-Arab National Movement*, 276.

53. *The Mufti of Jerusalem*, 33.

54. "Factionalism and Class Formation," in Owen, ed., *Studies in the Economic and Social History of Palestine*, 192.

55. Kayyali, *Palestine*, 150.

56. *Palestine. Statement of Policy by His Majesty's Government in the United Kingdom* (London: HMSO, 1930, Cmd. 3692).

57. For the text of MacDonald's letter see Walter Laqueur, ed., *Israel Arab Reader: A Documentary History of the Middle East Conflict* (Middlesex: Penguin Books, 1970), pp. 50–55. For a good analysis of British-Zionist relations at that time, see Norman Rose, *The Gentile Zionists: A Study in Anglo-Zionist Diplomacy, 1929–1939* (London: Frank Cass, 1973), esp. pp. 1–40.

58. Cited in Kayyali, *Palestine*, 172.

59. See Joseph Nevo, "The Palestine Arab Party, 1944–1946," *Asian and African Studies* 14 (1980): 99–115.

60. See for example, Jaber Shibli, *Conflict and Cooperation in Palestine* (Jerusalem [Jordan]: al-Umma Press, 1950) [Arabic]; Naji Allush, *The Arab Resistance in Palestine: 1917–1948* (Beirut: Dar al-Talia, 1970) [Arabic]; Isa al-Sifri, *Arab Palestine Under the Mandate and Zionism* (Jaffa: New Palestinian Bookstore, 1973) [Arabic].

61. See Nabil Ali Shaath and Hasna Reda Mekdashi, *Palestine Stamps (1865–1981)* (Beirut: Dar al-Fata al-Arabi, 1981), pp. 7–8.

4. THE ARAB REVOLT, 1936–1939

1. *Al-Thawrah al-Arabiyyah al-Kubra fi Filastin*. For detailed descriptions and analysis of the revolt, see John Marlowe, *Rebellion in Palestine* (London: Crescent Press, 1946) esp. chs. 10 and 12; Porath, *The Palestinian National Movement*, chs. 6–9, esp. pp. 233–73; Abd al-Wahab Kayyali, *Palestine: A Modern History* (London: Croom Helm, n.d.), pp. 155–227; Tom Bowden, "The Politics of Arab Rebellion in Palestine, 1936–1939," *Middle Eastern Studies* 11 (1975): 147–74.

2. The strongest argument to this effect is made by Shai Lachman, "Arab Rebellion and Terrorism in Palestine 1929–39: The Case of Sheikh Izz al-Din al-Qassam and his Movement" in Kedourie and Haim, eds., *Zionism and Arabism in Palestine and Israel*, 78. In *Arab Politics in Palestine*, 217, Lesch notes that the attack on the Jews was carried out by a group led by Sheikh Farhan al-Saadi, who had been a follower of Sheikh Qassam.

3. See Uri Ben-Eliezer, "Militarism, Status and Politics: The First Israeli Generation and Political Leadership during the Forties" (unpublished Ph.D. dissertation, Tel-Aviv University, 1988), pp. 1–31 [Hebrew].

4. "The Road to Rebellion: Arab Palestine in the 1930's," *Journal of Palestine Studies* 6 (1977): 46.

5. Emile al-Ghawri, *Palestine Through Sixty Years* 2 (Beirut: Dar al-Taliya, 1973), pp. 132–34 [Arabic].

6. Kayyali, *Palestine*, 169–71.
7. Yehuda Slutsky, *The History of the Haganah: From Defense to Struggle* 2 (Tel-Aviv: Am Oved, 1964), p. 459 [Hebrew].
8. See Manuel S. Hassassian, *Palestine: Factionalism in the National Movement* (Jerusalem: Palestinian Academic Society for the Study of International Affairs, 1990), pp. 107–32.
9. September 17, 1931, edition of *al-Jami'ah al-Arabiyah*, quoted in Porath, *The Palestinian National Movement*, p. 111.
10. Ted Swedenburg, "The Role of the Palestinian Peasantry in the Great Revolt (1936–1939)" in Edmund Burke III and Ira M. Lapidus, eds., *Islam, Politics, and Social Movements* (Berkeley: University of California Press, 1988), p. 186.
11. Porath, *The Palestinian National Movement*, 123.
12. Cited in Yehuda Taggar, "The Arab Revolt of 1936 in the Perspective of the Jewish-Arab Conflict" in Shmuel Almog, ed., *Zionism and the Arabs* (Jerusalem: The Historical Society of Israel and the Zalman Shazar Center, 1983), p. 169. For more on the colorful figure of Alami as a British civil servant, Palestinian nationalist, and educator, see Geofrey Furlonge, *Palestine Is My Country: The Story of Musa Alami* (London: John Murray, 1969).
13. A group in the 1980s claiming credit for placing a bomb on a TWA flight even named itself after Qassam. In the summer of 1992, Israeli forces uncovered a clandestine group in Ramallah which was part of the Islamic Hamas faction (see Chapter 9), also named after Qassam. In fact, one Palestinian intellectual who himself became a revered martyr, Ghassan Kanafani, likens Izz al-Din to Che Guevara, Cuba's legendary revolutionary leader. See *The 1936–39 Revolt in Palestine* (Beirut: Committee for Democratic Palestine, Popular Front for the Liberation of Palestine, n.d.), pp. 3–5, 11–14. Perhaps a more apt analogy would be to Franz Fanon, the noted writer who in the Algerian context extolled the cathartic effect of violence by the colonized against the colonizer. Kanafani (1936–72) was not only a writer but a member of the Popular Front for the Liberation of Palestine. He was killed by a car bomb, probably by Israeli agents, in Beirut, on July 8, 1972. Among his most important literary works, which expressed the traumatic experiences of being uprooted and of refugee life, are the collections *Death of Bed No. 12* (1961), *Land of Sand Oranges* (1963), and *A World Not Our Own* (1965). See his *Men in the Sun and Other Palestinian Stories*, translated by Hilary Kilpatrick (Washington, DC: Three Continents Press, 1978). On his literary works and ideology see Stepan Wild, *Gassan Kanafani: The Life of a Palestinian* (Wiesbaden: Otto Harrasowitz, 1975), and Muhammad Siddiq, *Man Is a Cause: Political Consciousness and the Fiction of Gassan Kanafani* (Seattle: University of Washington Press, 1984).
14. Bowden, "The Politics of the Arab Rebellion."
15. Ghassan Kanafani accuses what he calls "the feudal clerical leadership" of being reactionary elements, colluding with the imperialists. See *The 1936–39 Revolt in Palestine*, 3–7.
16. Bowden, "The Politics of Arab Rebellion," 152.
17. Porath, *The Palestinian National Movement*, 173–74.
18. Baruch Kimmerling, *Zionism and Territory*, ch. 7. Over 35,000 acres of citrus and fruit trees were destroyed.
19. *Palestine Royal Commission Report* (London: HMSO, 1937, Cmd. 5479, Peel Commission).
20. Kupferschmidt, "Islam on the Defensive," 206; Porath, *The Palestinian National Movement*, 133–37.
21. See, Bayan Nuweihid al-Hout, "The Palestinian Elite during the Mandate Period," *Journal of Palestine Studies* 9 (1979): 109.

22. James P. Jankowski, "The Palestinian Arab Revolt of 1936–1939," *The Muslim World* 63 (1973): 227.

23. Yuval Arnon-Ohanna, "The Bands in the Palestinian Arab Revolt, 1936–1939: Structure and Organization," *Asian and African Studies* 15 (1981): 229–47. Among the most prominent band leaders were Abd al-Qadir al-Husseini (see below) and Abd al-Rahem al-Haj Muhammad, both self-styled commanders in chief; Arif Abd al-Razzaq, a loyal follower of the Mufti with a history of criminal activity in a rural gang; and Yusuf Abu Durra, who coordinated with Muhammad. Some bands and their leaders are discussed in Tom Bowden, *The Breakdown of Public Security: The Case of Ireland 1916–1921 and Palestine 1936–1939* (Beverly Hills: Sage, 1977), pp. 208–10. Also, see Bowden, "The Politics of Arab Rebellion," 156.

24. Arnon-Ohanna, "The Bands in the Palestinian Arab Revolt," 251.

25. See, for example, Jbara, *Palestinian Leader Hajj Amin al-Husayni*, 151. Haj Amin's relationship to Qa'uqji wavered through the years. As we shall see, in a later stage of the revolt, the Mufti's Damascus group asked Qa'uqji to lead the rural rebellion once again. In 1947, the Arab League appointed him leader of the newly formed Arab Liberation Army over Husseini's objections.

26. Ibid., 235.

27. Porath, *The Palestinian National Movement*, 190.

28. On the rebels' control see Smith, *Palestine and the Palestinians*, 64; on the actions of the British troops see Porath, *The Palestinian National Movement*, 299ff.

29. Bowden, "The Politics of Arab Rebellion," 153.

30. Swedenburg, "The Role of the Palestinian Peasantry in the Great Revolt," in Burke and Lapidus, eds., *Islam, Politics and Social Movements*, 192.

31. Dr. Khalil Totah, cited in Theodore Romain Swedenburg, "Memories of Revolt: The 1936–39 Rebellion and the Struggle for a Palestinian National Past" (unpublished Ph.D. dissertation, University of Texas at Austin, 1988), p. 25.

32. Kupferschmidt, "Islam on the Defensive," 204–5.

33. Smith, *Palestine and the Palestinians*, 64.

34. "The Story of a Palestinian under Occupation," *Journal of Palestine Studies* 11 (1981): 5.

35. Swedenburg, "Memories of Revolt," 213.

36. Antonius, *The Arab Awakening*, 405–6.

37. Cited in Miller, *Government and Society in Rural Palestine*, 124.

38. Swedenburg, "Memories of Revolt," 157–65.

39. Ibid., 153–54.

40. Miller, *Government and Society in Rural Palestine*, 138.

41. This is evident in the archive of one Palestinian group, captured by the Haganah, the Jewish underground paramilitary organization. The material includes reports from the field, correspondence between different local and district leaders, and decisions of military courts. See Ezra Danin and Ya'acov Shimoni, *Documents and Portraits from the Arab Gangs Archives in the Arab Revolt in Palestine, 1936–1939* (Jerusalem: Magnes Press, 1981) [Hebrew].

42. Dajani had broken with the Nashashibis, and some figures associated with the Husseinis have suggested it was the British, not the Mufti's men, who murdered him. See Swedenburg, "Memories of Revolt," 201.

43. Arnon-Ohanna, "The Bands in the Palestinian Arab Revolt," 284–85.

44. Abboushi, "The Road to Rebellion," 27.

45. Bowden tends to romanticize the rural nature of the bands, but correctly points to the organizational difficulties of basing a rebellion on rural groups with only attenuated connections to the major urban changes affecting the society: "It was in this remnant feudal society that the coterie of landed aristocrats, their class symbolized by the Mufti, attempted to politicize a rebellion which was for most

of its combatants an affair of the heart, the seasons, and above all the soil." *The Breakdown of Public Security*, 189.

46. Cited in Miller, *Government and Society in Rural Palestine*, 127.
47. See Abboushi, "The Road to Rebellion," 42.
48. Porath, *The Palestinian-Arab National Movement*, 251–54.
49. A division of the population into Husseini and Nashashibi camps is possible for some districts but not others. The northern portion of the country, for example, was largely removed from that conflict.
50. Elyakim Rubinstein, "Zionist Attitudes on the Jewish-Arab Conflict Until 1936," in Almog, ed., *Zionism and the Arabs*, 35–72, argues that the pre-1929 Zionist orientation to the Arab question was not one of complacency and reflected no comprehensive policy, consisting rather of ad hoc responses.
51. Cited in Shabtai Teveth, *Ben-Gurion and the Palestinian Arabs: From Peace to War* (New York: Oxford University Press, 1985), p. 166.
52. Cited in Yehoyada Haim, *Abandonment of Illusions: Zionist Political Attitudes Toward Palestinian Arab Nationalism, 1936–1939* (Boulder: Westview Press, 1983), p. 36. In *Collusion across the Jordan: King Abdullah, the Zionist Movement, and the Partition of Palestine* (Oxford: Clarendon Press, 1988), p. 14, Avi Shlaim states that "A wide gulf separated Ben-Gurion's public utterances on the Arab question from his real convictions."
53. Haganah forces, in the framework of the "Special Night Squads," were highly trained by the British Officer Charles Wingate. See Yehuda Bauer, *From Diplomacy to Resistance: A History of Jewish Palestine, 1939–1945* (Philadelphia: The Jewish Publication Society of America, 1970), pp. 12–13.
54. Bowden, *The Breakdown of Public Security*, 227, writes: "Palestine had in effect by 1936 become something of a haven for brigands, revolutionaries and escaped criminals seeking to avoid the comparative severity of justice in the neighbouring French territories."
55. Bowden, "The Politics of Arab Rebellion," 166–69.
56. See Aaron S. Klieman, "The Divisiveness of Palestine: Foreign Office Versus Colonial Office on the Issue of Partition, 1937," *The Historical Journal* 22 (1979): 423–41.
57. See Walid Khalidi, ed., *From Haven to Conquest: The Origins and the Development of the Palestine Problem* (Beirut: Institute for Palestine Studies, 1971), appendix 4, pp. 848–49.
58. Mattar, *The Mufti of Jerusalem*, 84.
59. Schleifer, "The Life and Thought of 'Izz-id-Din al-Qassam," 78, suggests that Qassam was "particularly vulnerable to the same process of political appropriation that to a lesser degree threatens all heroes."
60. Swedenburg, "Memories of Revolt," 175–77.

5. THE MEANING OF DISASTER

1. See Kimmerling, *Zionism and Territory*, 123.
2. Translated by Rivka Yadlin from an anthology edited by Abd al-Kahman al-Kayyali, *Palestinian Poetry and the Nakbah* (Beirut: Institute for Arab Studies, 1975), p. 235 [Arabic].
3. Turki, *The Disinherited*, 11.
4. Cited in Donna Robinson Divine, "Palestinian Arab Women and Their Reveries of Emancipation" in Susan C. Bourque and Divine, eds., *Women Living Change* (Philadelphia: Temple University Press, 1985), p. 57.
5. In the 1920s and the first half of the 1930s, the Arab sector grew 7.5 percent a year, the Jewish average being 22.5 percent. The Jewish economy had about one-fifth of

its workers in agriculture and an equal fraction in industry; in 1922 two-thirds of the Arab population were in agriculture, the figure still being over 50 percent in 1935. Manufacturing absorbed less than 10 percent of Arab workers throughout the period.

6. Al-Hout, "The Palestinian Political Elite during the Mandate Period," 89.

7. The rural economy also deteriorated: Weather was bad throughout the revolt, cutting into overall production, and with a frequent lack of urban markets, crops simply rotted.

8. A drop from almost three-quarters to only 2.5 percent of total exports. Government of Palestine, *Statistical Abstract* (Jerusalem: Government Printer, 1941, 1943, 1944–45). An excellent source of data on the wartime economy is found in Z. Abramowitz, "Wartime Development of Arab Economy in Palestine" in Sophie A. Udin, ed., *The Palestine Year Book*, vol. 1 (Washington, D.C.: Zionist Organization of America, 1945), pp. 130–44. See also Robert R. Nathan, Oscar Gass, and Daniel Creamer, *Palestine: Problem and Promise—An Economic Study* (Washington, D.C.: Public Affairs Press, 1946), pp. 155–62, and Nachum T. Gross and Jacob Metzer, "Palestine in World War II: Some Economic Aspects" (Jerusalem: Falk Institute, Discussion Paper No. 87, 1987 [mimeo]).

9. The effect on the Jewish economy was even more severe, since on the eve of the war citriculture composed 63 percent of its total agricultural product, compared to 21 percent for the Arabs. David Horowitz, *The Development of the Palestinian Economy*, 215.

10. Gross and Metzer, "Palestine in World War II," 4.

11. See G. H. Sealous, *Economic Conditions in Egypt* (London: Department of Overseas Trade, HMSO, 1936); A. Konikoff, *Transjordan: An Economic Survey* (Jerusalem: Economic Research Institute, The Jewish Agency, 1946). Konikoff described Transjordan as a poor, exclusively agricultural country, with all its economic survival based on the linkage with the Palestinian economy and British aid and support. In Syria and Lebanon, traditional industry was almost completely destroyed following the First World War; a new more developed and modern industry began to arise but not at the same rate as in Palestine. See George Hakim, "Industry," in Sa'id B. Himadeh, ed., *Economic Organization of Palestine* (Beirut: American University Press, 1938), pp. 119–76.

12. Taqqu, "Arab Labor in Mandatory Palestine," pp. 165–66. Taqqu notes that "the extensive recruitment of Arab villagers into wage labor had been the hasty by-product of war, accomplished over a brief span. It was a necessarily incomplete and inconsistent process, whose immediate effect was to fragment rural Arab society" (p. 187).

13. Miller, *Government and Society in Rural Palestine*, 141.

14. Abramowitz, "Wartime Development of Arab Economy in Palestine," pp. 130–35.

15. On the creation of the working class, see Haydar Rashid, "The Formation of the Arab Labor Movement in Palestine," *Shu'un Filistiniyya* (April 1981): 134 [Arabic].

16. Taqqu's comment: "The Arab labor movement suffered from an inherent structural weakness: its justification lay in the separate consciousness and claims of workers, while its attachments to a corporate image of Arab society continued on many levels. The movement thus reflected the growing disparity in the Arab community between the dominance of old elites on one hand and the emerging recognition of a new social reality which was no longer well served by those elites on the other." See "Arab Labor in Mandatory Palestine," 212.

17. Ibid., 287.

18. Ibid., 322.

19. Divine, "Palestinian Arab Women and Their Reveries of Emancipation" in Bourque and Divine, eds., *Women Living Change*, 76. Since 1948, the role of

women seems to have changed much more dramatically. See Ghazi al-Khalili, "Palestinian Women and Revolution, 1948–1967," *Shu'un Filistiniyya* (December, 1967), pp. 12–19; and Jamil Hilal, "Preliminary Notes on the Contribution of Palestinian Women in Production," *Shu'un Filistiniyya* (June, 1981), pp. 145–51 [both in Arabic].

20. All such intensive diplomatic efforts made by various factions of the British government during the war were to achieve an agreement that would satisfy the Palestinian Arabs. See Y. Porath, *In Search of Arab Unity* (London: Frank Cass, 1986), pp. 78ff.

21. Slutsky, *The History of the Haganah* 3: 112 [Hebrew].

22. Francis R. Nicosia, *The Third Reich and the Palestine Question* (Austin: University of Texas Press, 1985), p. 177.

23. Among the Axis forces, Amin al-Husseini's group was not the only one: An Iraqi group headed by Rashid Ali al-Kailani vied with it to represent the Arabs in Berlin and Rome. Al-Husseini never succeeded in receiving a public commitment from Hitler supporting independence for Palestine and the other Arab countries. Instead, in April, 1942, Count Ciano, the Italian foreign minister, declared that Italy would be ready to grant "every possible aid to the Arab countries in their fight for liberation, to recognize their sovereignty and independence, to agree to their federation if this is desired by the interested parties, as well as to the abolition of the national Jewish Homeland in Palestine." See Jbara, *Palestinian Leader Hajj Amin Al-Husayni*, 184–85. See also Elpeleg, *Grand Mufti*, 68. Postwar Zionist propaganda used the activities of al-Husseini as a powerful argument in favor of Jewish claims, depicting the entire Arab community as collaborators. In his own writings after the war, al-Husseini admitted his alliance with Germany and Italy against the common Jewish-British enemy, but emphasized his complete rejection of racist Nazi ideology. See *Truths Regarding the Palestinian Problem*, 115–17.

24. Shimoni, *The Arabs of Palestine*, 355–57.

25. Joseph Nevo, "The Renewal of Palestinian Political Activity 1943–1945," in Ben-Dor, ed., *The Palestinians and the Middle East Conflict*, 59–72; and Nevo, "The Palestinian Arab Party, 1944–1946," 99–101. See also Jamal Qadurah, "The Emergence of Political Parties in Palestine: The National Defense Party," *Shu'un Filistiniyya* (January–February, 1985).

26. The three main Jewish underground groups began their revolt against the British at different times and at some points worked against each other. The Lehi, or Stern Gang, fought the British in the early years of World War II. Members of the right-wing Irgun Zvai Leumi (commonly known as Etzel or just the Irgun) and the mainline Haganah worked with the British to eliminate Lehi's activities and jail its members. After the Irgun began to fight in February, 1944, the Haganah moved (at times, with the mandate authorities) to extinguish the revolt. Finally, for a short time starting in October, 1945, the Haganah joined the United Hebrew Rebellion. See Slutsky, *History of the Haganah* 3: 205–8; and David Niv, *Battle for Freedom: The Irgun Zvai Leumi* (Tel-Aviv: Klausner Institute, 1967, 1970), vols. 2–4 [Hebrew]. For the difficulties of the British authorities in dealing with the Jewish revolt, see David A. Charters, *The British Army and Jewish Insurgency in Palestine, 1945–1947* (London: Macmillan, 1989), p. 80. In the end, it was not Jewish revolt that drove the British from Palestine but fear of a renewal of the 1936–39 Arab Revolt. See Michael J. Cohen, *Palestine and the Great Powers, 1945–1948* (Princeton: Princeton University Press, 1982), pp. 223–27.

27. With Britain facing increasing pressure from Germany and stubborn resistance from the Arabs in their revolt, Malcolm MacDonald, the new colonial secretary, assembled a conference (known variously as the London Conference or St. James's Conference on Palestine or Round Table Conference) of Palestinian Arabs, Zion-

ists, and representatives of Arab governments, opening on February 7. The conference's wider Arab framework was intended to pressure the Palestinians into accommodating a solution to the problem of Palestine on British terms. See Porath, *In Search of Arab Unity*, chs. 1–2; Nicholas Bethell, *The Palestinian Triangle: The Struggle between the British, the Jews, and the Arabs, 1935–48* (London: Steimatzky, 1979), pp. 47–66.

28. Arif al-Arif, *The Disaster* (Sidon: Al-Maktaba al-Arabiyya, 1956), pp. 42–45 [Arabic]. The League, founded on March 23, 1945, was a political union of the independent Arab states meant to affirm their common historical, linguistic, and cultural heritage. When in March, 1943, the Egyptian prime minister called for a conference to establish the union, the composition of a Palestinian delegation immediately became an issue. See Robert W. Macdonald, *The League of Arab States* (Princeton: Princeton University Press, 1965), pp. 35–37. One of Alami's tasks for the League was to establish Arab information offices abroad. Following the emergence of the United States as a decisive influence on the future of Palestine and its growing involvement in the region, Alami established the Arab Office in Washington, D.C., in 1947. The Office was closed in May, 1948, at the start of the Arab states' military intervention in Palestine. See *Middle East Journal* 2(1948): 321.

29. Meir Pa'il, "The Problem of Arab Sovereignty in Palestine, 1947–1949: Arab Governments versus the Arabs of Palestine" in D. Carpi, ed., *Zionism*, vol. 3 (Tel-Aviv: Hakibutz Hameuchad for Tel-Aviv University, 1973), pp. 439–89 (Hebrew).

30. Benny Morris, *The Birth of the Palestinian Refugee Problem, 1947–1949* (New York: Cambridge University Press, 1987), p. 14.

31. *The Truth about the Palestinian Affair* (Cairo: Salafiya Press, 1954) pp. 43–47 [Arabic].

32. "The Arab Perspective" in Wm. Roger Louis and Robert W. Stookey, eds., *The End of the Palestine Mandate* (Austin: University of Texas Press, 1986), pp. 112–13.

33. Taqqu, "Arab Labor in Mandatory Palestine," 323.

34. Morris, *The Birth of the Palestinian Refugee Problem*, 17.

35. The phrase is used by J. C. Hurewitz, "Historical Overview" in Louis and Stookey, eds., *The End of the Palestine Mandate*, 145.

36. See Michael J. Cohen, *Palestine to Israel: From Mandate to Independence* (London: Frank Cass, 1988), ch. 12.

37. The formal decision was taken on September 20, 1947.

38. Three of UNSCOP's 11 members (India, Iran, and Yugoslavia) proposed an independent federal state following a three-year preparatory stage under a UN designated authority. There is some evidence that the Mufti would have accepted partition had he been the chief authority in the Arab sector (ironically, King Abdallah of Transjordan made the same stipulation). See Michael J. Cohen, *Palestine and the Great Powers, 1945–1948* (Princeton: Princeton University Press, 1982), pp. 267–68.

39. Robert Schaeffer, *Warpaths: The Politics of Partition* (New York: Hill and Wang, 1990), pp. 153–65.

40. The Jewish state was meant to include about 600,000 Jews and 500,000 Arabs, and the Arab state 20 Jewish settlements. See Baruch Kimmerling, *Zionism and Territory*, 121. For another view, see Walid Khalidi, "Plan Dalet: The Zionist Master Plan for Conquest of Palestine," *Middle East Forum* (November 1961): 22–28.

41. United Nations Palestine Commission, First Special Report to the Security Council, S/676, February, 1948, p. 6.

42. Again with deep reservations, they had also supported a British partition plan put forth in the Peel Commission report in 1937. The British and American Morrison-Grady Plan of 1946 contained a similiar idea—that for provincial or cantonal autonomy.

43. Government of Palestine, *A Survey of Palestine*, pp. 59–61. See also Cohen, *Palestine and the Great Powers*, 307.

44. Cohen, *Palestine and the Great Powers*, 304.

45. Cited in Morris, *The Birth of the Palestinian Refugee Problem*, 45–46.

46. Ibid., 41.

47. One source's estimate of 40,000 emigrants during the Arab Revolt, while a mere 5 percent of the same author's figure for refugees created in 1948–49, is formidable enough to suggest that psychological barriers were long gone. See Rony E. Gabbay, *A Political Study of the Arab-Jewish Conflict: The Arab Refugee Problem* (Geneva: Droz, 1959), p. 66.

48. Shlaim, *Collusion Across the Jordan*, 89ff.

49. Cohen, *Palestine and the Great Powers*, p. 306.

50. Sayigh, *Palestinians: From Peasants to Revolutionaries*, 77; al-Arif, *The Disaster*, 42.

51. Fauzi al-Qawuqji, "Memoirs, 1948: Part I," *Journal of Palestine Studies* 1(1972): 48.

52. Cited in Cohen, *Palestine and the Great Powers*, 311.

53. Ibid., 344.

54. See Morris, *The Birth of the Palestinian Refugee Problem*, 297–98; Gabbay, *A Political Study of the Arab-Jewish Conflict*, 167, 175; Janet L. Abu-Lughod, "Demographic Transformation of Palestine" in Ibrahim Abu-Lughod, ed. *The Transformation of Palestine* (Evanston: Northwestern University Press, 1971), pp. 139–64; Gilbar, *Trends in the Demographic Development of the Palestinians*, 3–12.

55. The lower figure is for the period through mid-March and was culled from the sources by Steven Glazer, "The Palestinian Exodus in 1948," *Journal of Palestine Studies* 9 (Summer 1980): 104. The higher figure comes from Morris, *The Birth of the Palestinian Refugee Problem*, 30. Morris, for all his oversimplifications of Palestinian life prior to the war, has done a masterful job of collecting the scattered evidence about the exodus. Unless otherwise noted, the numbers and composition of refugees presented here will come from his book.

56. Nur-eldeen Masalha, "On Recent Hebrew and Israeli Sources for the Palestinian Exodus, 1947–49," *Journal of Palestine Studies* 18(1988): 124, argues that "the objective [of the Jewish forces] was to shock, frighten, and throw the [Arab] communities off balance, forcing Arab neighborhoods and villages to evacuate."

57. Morris, *The Birth of the Palestinian Refugee Problem*, 62.

58. Ibid., 64. See also *The Conquest of the Arab and the Mixed Cities During the War of Independence* (Ramat Efal: Israel Galilee Center for the Study of the Jewish Defence Power—the Hagana, 1989 [mimeo]), pp. 9–12 [Hebrew].

59. Ibid., 63.

60. Many members of the Liberation Army were drawn from the margins of their own societies and included not only soldiers of fortune, but criminals and other deviant elements. See Muhammad Nimr al-Khatib, *As a Result of the Catastrophe* (Damascus, 1949) [Arabic].

61. Morris, *The Birth of the Palestinian Refugee Problem*, 73–95.

62. Sharif Kanani and Nihad Zitawi, *Dayr Yasin*, Monograph No. 4, Palestinian Destroyed Villages series, second edition (Bir Zeit: Center of Documentation and Research, Bir Zeit University, 1987), p. 6 [Arabic].

63. Israel's official Israel Defense Forces *History of the Independence War* (Tel-Aviv: Maarachot, IDF Publishing House, 1959), p. 117 [Hebrew], with a preface by David Ben-Gurion, makes this point.

64. Menachem Begin, *The Revolt* (New York: Henry Schuman, 1951), p. 155, argues that "what was invented about Deir Yassin helped in fact carve the way of Jewish victories on the battlefield."

65. Yehoshafat Harkabi, *Arab Attitudes Toward Israel* (New York: Hart, 1972), pp. 113–70, for an account of hostility and the concept of the enemy.
66. Khalidi, "Plan Dalet: Master Plan for the Conquest of Palestine," 6.
67. See Masalha, "On Recent Hebrew and Israeli Sources for the Palestinian Exodus," 129. Morris, *The Birth of the Palestinian Refugee Problem*, 113, here offers a somewhat different perspective:

> If at the start of the war the Yishuv had been reluctantly willing to countenance a Jewish State with a large, peaceful Arab minority, by April the military commanders' thinking had radically changed: the toll on Jewish life and security in the battle of the roads and the dire prospect of the invasion of Palestine by Arab armies had left the Haganah with very narrow margins of safety. The Yishuv could not leave pockets of actively or potentially hostile Arabs or ready made bases for them behind its geographically unnatural front lines.

68. "The Fall of a Village," *Journal of Palestine Studies* 1 (1972): 108 21.
69. Ibid., 113.
70. Nafez Abdallah Nazzal, "The Zionist Occupation of Western Galilee, 1948," *Journal of Palestine Studies* 3 (1974): 72.
71. Ibid., 76.
72. Morris, *The Birth of the Palestinian Refugee Problem*, 155.
73. The leading proponent of the thesis that Israel and Jordan actively conspired is Shlaim, *Collusion across the Jordan.* See also Dan Schueftan, *A Jordanian Option: The "Yishuv" and the State of Israel vis-a-vis the Hashemite Regime and the Palestinian National Movement* (Tel-Aviv: Yad Tabenkin and Hakibbutz Hameuchad, 1986) [Hebrew], pp. 75–99, which argues that there was de facto cooperation. For a Palestinian critique of the Jordanian role, see Anis Sayigh, *The Hashemites and the Palestinian Question* (Beirut: al-Muharir adn Asriya Library, 1966) [Arabic].

6. THE ODD MAN OUT: ARABS IN ISRAEL

1. George Kossaifi, "Demographic Characteristics of the Arab Palestinian People," in Nakhleh and Zureik, eds., *The Sociology of the Palestinians,* 25. On refugee numbers see United Nations, *Report of the Economic Survey Mission of the Middle East* (New York: United Nations, 1949), p. 22. Laurie A. Brand, *Palestinians in the Arab World: Institution Building and the Search for State* (New York: Columbia University Press, 1988), p. 150, estimates 900,000 Palestinians in Jordan in 1949, including 70,000 who already were settled on the East Bank. Gilbar, *Trends in the Demographic Development of the Palestinians,* 189, puts the number on the West Bank at 670,000. An estimate based on the 1950 Jordanian census was 742,000 on the West Bank and 184,700 Palestinians on the East Bank, demonstrating an already apparent tendency of Palestinians to migrate from the West Bank to the East.
2. Charles Liebman and Eliezer Don-Yehiyeh, *Civil Religion in Israel* (Berkeley: University of California Press, 1983), pp. 161–65.
3. The lower estimate is given by C. Kamen, "After the Disaster: The Arabs in the State of Israel, 1948–1950," *Collections on Research and Critique* 10 (December 1984): 18–20. The higher estimate is based on UNRWA data and is adopted by Ian Lustick, *Arabs in the Jewish State: Israel's Control of a National Minority* (Austin: University of Texas Press, 1980), p. 51. The same ratio is given by Sammy Smooha, *The Orientation and the Politicization of the Arab Minority in Israel* (The Jewish-Arab Center, Institute of Middle Eastern Studies, Haifa University, 1984), p. 79.

4. Moshe Dayan has suggested that as many as 1,000 refugees a month infiltrated back into Israel, either for brief periods or some to stay permanently. See "Israel's Border Problems," *Foreign Affairs* 23 (1955): 261.

5. Documentation is cited in Charles S. Kamen, "After the Catastrophe I: The Arabs in Israel, 1948–51," *Middle Eastern Studies* 23(1987): 453–95.

6. Baruch Kimmerling, "Sovereignty, Ownership and 'Presence' in the Jewish-Arab Territorial Conflict—The Case of Bir'm and Ikrit," *Comparative Political Studies* 10 (1977): 155–76.

7. Kamen, "After the Catastrophe," 476, estimates that 14 percent of the male population of military age (15–60) was in prison.

8. Don Peretz, *Israel and the Palestine Arabs* (Washington, D.C.: The Middle East Institute, 1958), p. 142. See also Sabri Jiryis, *The Arabs in Israel* (New York: Monthly Review Press, 1976), pp. 77–90.

9. Kimmerling, *Zionism and Territory*, 133–46.

10. The state gave a high priority to these farms, which were part of a nation-building process: They were heavily subsidized and protected from the competition of the Arabs' cheap agricultural labor economy. See Kimmerling, *Zionism and Economy*, 56–57. For the structure of Arab labor and its development in the first decade of Israel's existence, see Yoram Ben-Porath, *The Arab Labor Force in Israel* (Jerusalem: Falk Institute for Economic Research, 1966), pp. 7–18 [Hebrew].

11. See Raja Khalidi, "The Economy of the Palestinian Arabs in Israel" in George T. Abed, ed., *The Palestinian Economy: Studies in Development under Prolonged Occupation* (New York: Routledge and Kegan Paul, 1989), pp. 42–49. For an analysis of small villagers' entrepreneurship, see Aziz Haidar, *Types and Patterns of Economic Entrepreneurship in Arab Villages in Israel—1950–1980*, (unpublished Ph.D. dissertation, Jerusalem: Hebrew University, 1985) [Hebrew].

12. Elia T. Zureik, *The Palestinians in Israel: A Study in Internal Colonialism* (Boston: Routledge and Kegan Paul, 1979), pp. 131–41. Zureik analyzes the Arab situation in the Jewish nation-state in terms of "settler" or "internal colonialism" (viz. "colonies of exploitation" supported by an external power). Also see Herbert Adam, *Modernizing Racial Domination* (Berkeley, University of California Press, 1972), p. 31; and Najwa Makhoul, "Changes in the Employment Structure of Arabs in Israel, *Journal of Palestine Studies* 3 (1982): 77–102.

13. I. Arnon and M. Raviv, *From Fellah to Farmer: A Study on Change in Arab Villages* (Rehovot, Israel: The Volcani Center, Bet-Dagan, 1980 [Publications on Problems of Regional Development, no. 31]).

14. Sami F. Geraisy, *Arab Village Youth in Jewish Urban Centers* (unpublished Ph.D. dissertation, Brandeis University, 1970), p. 82.

15. By 1963, more Arabs worked in construction-related jobs than in agriculture. See State of Israel, *Labor Power Survey, 1963* (Jerusalem: Central Bureau of Statistics, 1964), pp. 52–53.

16. See Edna Bonacich, "The Past, Present, and Future of Split Labor Market Theory," *Research in Race and Ethnic Relations* 1 (1979): 17–64. See also Shlomo Swirski and Deborah Bernstein, "The Rapid Economic Development of Israel and the Emergence of the Ethnic Division of Labor," *British Journal of Sociology* 33 (1982): 64–85.

17. Michael Shalev, "Jewish Organized Labor and the Palestinians: A Study of State/ Society Relations in Israel" in Kimmerling, ed., *The Israeli State and Society*, 93–134.

18. Sami Khalil Mar'i, *Arab Education in Israel* (Syracuse: Syracuse University Press, 1978), p. xii.

19. Yehoshua Palmon (the first Israeli adviser to the prime minister on Arab affairs), cited in Lustick, *Arabs in the Jewish State*, 48.

20. Abner Cohen, *Arab-Border Villages: A Study of Continuity and Change in Social Organization* (Manchester: Manchester University Press, 1965), p. 118; and Subhi Abu Ghosh, "The Politics of an Arab Village in Israel" (unpublished Ph.D. dissertation, Princeton University, 1965), p. 33.

21. Jiryis, *The Arabs in Israel*, 9–71. (This book was first published in Israel in 1966, the Israeli authorities later trying to prevent its publication in France and keeping the author in administrative custody.)

22. Fouzi El-Asmar, *To Be an Arab in Israel* (London: Frances Pinter, 1975), p. 23.

23. Ibid., 52.

24. Lustick, *Arabs in the Jewish State*, passim.

25. Sammy Smooha, *Arabs and Jews in Israel 1: Conflicting and Shared Attitudes in a Divided Society* (Boulder: Westview, 1989), esp. pp. 130–39.

26. Kimmerling has found a built-in tension in the Israeli collective identity between its religious/primordial ingredients and the civil/modern ones. See "Between the Primordial and the Civil Definitions of the Collective Identity: Eretz Israel or the State of Israel," in E. Cohen, M. Lissak and U. Almagor, eds., *Comparative Social Dynamics* (Boulder: Westview, 1985), pp. 262–83.

27. Nadim Rouhana, "The Civic and National Subidentities of the Arabs in Israel: A Psycho-Political Approach," in John E. Hofman, ed., *Arab-Jewish Relations in Israel: A Quest in Human Understanding* (Bristol, Indiana: Wyndham Hall Press, 1988), pp. 123–53.

28. It appeared 13 times beginning in October 1959, using different names, since the authorities refused to grant permission for a regular journal. However, the suffix of each title was, "al-Ard" (the land). Circulated in runs of about 2,000 copies, it was finally banned in March, 1960, following the publisher's use of the same title twice.

29. *Arabs in the Jewish State*, 128.

30. See Yaacov Landau, *The Arabs in Israel* (London: Oxford University Press, 1969), ch. 4, and Jiryis, *The Arabs in Israel*, ch. 4. Jiryis himself was a young lawyer, a graduate of the Hebrew University, and one of the founders and leaders of this group. His book was the first on the Arab situation in Israel after 1948. Later, he left the country and become one of the most prominent intellectuals in the Palestinian resistance movement. He is considered an expert on the internal policy of Israel.

31. This policy was rooted in tradition: "In the agrarian, peasant society of eighteenth-, nineteenth- and early twentieth-century Palestine, strong village patrilineages gained recognition from the government and/or representatives of power (military governors, tax officials, administrators) in the form of derived local authority and titles (muhktar, shaikh) for its dominant personages/leaders and/or enjoyed minor economic advantages." See Henry Rosenfeld, "Men and Women in Arab Peasant to Proletariat Transformation," in Stanley Diamond, ed., *Theory and Practice: Essays Presented to Gene Weltfish* (New York: Mouton, 1989), p. 196.

32. On this faith being maintained by a minority of an Arab minority, see Gabriel Ben-Dor, "Intellectuals in Israeli Druze Society," in Elie Kedourie and Sylvia G. Haim, eds., *Palestine and Israel in the 19th and 20th Centuries* (London: Frank Cass, 1982), p. 232.

33. Although many of the problems have eased, overcrowding of classrooms, lack of qualified teachers, a shortage of vocational education, and other problems have continued to plague the Arab educational sector. See Mar'i, *Arab Education in Israel*, ch. 1.

34. All the textbooks of the mandatory period were outlawed, not only because they included expressions of hostility towards the Jewish community and Zionism, but also because most of them included expressions of Palestinian Arab political identity.

35. Mar'i, *Arab Education in Israel*, 19–20.

36. Ibid., 50.
37. Yochanan Peres, Avishai Ehrlich, and Nira Yuval-Davis, "National Education for Arab Youth in Israel: A Comparative Analysis of Curricula," *Jewish Journal of Sociology* 12 (1970): 156.
38. See Zureik, *The Palestinians in Israel*, 157–58.
39. For a content analysis of teaching materials in different classes, see Muhammad Miyari, *Contents of Teaching in Arab Schools* (Jerusalem: Ministry of Education, Educational Planning Project, 1975) [Hebrew], and Peres, Ehrlich, and Yuval-Davis, "National Education for Arab Youth in Israel," pp. 147–63. See also Mar'i, *Arab Education in Israel*, 70–89.
40. Ibid., 229. The categories on religious self-identification were added to the 1967 survey.
41. "Palestinian Intellectuals and Revolutionary Transformation" in Nakhleh and Zureik, eds., *The Sociology of the Palestinians*, 188–89.
42. Anton Shammas describes the poetry of Arabs in Israel as "bad," because thematically it never left the village to try to meet the real and much more complex "new Arab experience" in Israel. See *The Arab Literature in Israel* (Tel-Aviv: Shiloach Institute, Tel-Aviv University, 1976), pp. 5–6.
43. Aziz Haidar, "The Different Levels of Palestinian Ethnicity," in M. S. Esman and I. Rabinovich, eds., *Ethnicity, Pluralism and the State in the Middle East* (Ithaca: Cornell University Press, 1988), p. 108.
44. Zureik, *The Palestinians in Israel*, 183.
45. See Landau, *The Arabs in Israel*, 195–98.
46. Called Maki until 1965, the Communist party ended up entirely Jewish, as it denied the legitimacy of both Zionism and Arab nationalism—and thereafter Rakah, which drew both its rank-and-file and its voters largely from the Arab community. See Elie Rekhess, "Jews and Arabs in the Israeli Communist Party" in Esman and Rabinovich, eds., *Ethnicity, Pluralism, and the State*, 121–39. On Jews and Arabs in Mapam, see Yael Yishai, "Integration of Arabs in an Israeli Party: The Case of Mapam, 1948–54" in Kedourie and Haim, eds., *Zionism and Arabism in Palestine and Israel*, 240–55.
47. A cadre of these lawyers later became central figures in the military courts, defending those arrested in the occupied territories. See George Emile Bisharat, *Palestinian Lawyers and Israeli Rule: Law and Disorder in the West Bank* (Austin: University of Texas Press, 1989), pp. 92–95.
48. Mark Tessler, "Arabs in Israel" in Ann Mosely Lesch and Mark Tessler, *Israel, Egypt, and the Palestinians: From Camp David to Intifada* (Bloomington: Indiana University Press, 1989), p. 101.
49. Al-Haj, *Social Change and Family Processes*, 66–72.
50. Rosenfeld, "Men and Women in Arab Peasant to Proletariat Transformation," 200, 205.
51. One survey showed that by the 1980s as many as 85 percent of Arab households consisted of nuclear families. See Al-Haj, *Social Change and Family Processes*, 93. In the 1970s surveys showed the figure to be about 55 percent. See Smooha, *Arabs and Jews in Israel* 1: 37.
52. Henry Rosenfeld, "The Class Situation of the Arab National Minority in Israel," *Comparative Studies in Society and History* 20 (1978): 395.
53. Ibid. On the move to wage labor starting in the earliest years of the state, see Amihoud Israely, "The Employment Revolution Among Non-Jewish Minorities of Israel," *Hamizrah Hehadash* 26 (1976): 232–39 [Hebrew].
54. Khalidi, *The Arab Economy in Israel*, 172.
55. Ibid., 191.
56. Arnon and Raviv, *From Fellah to Farmer*, 23–25.

57. Aziz Haidar, *The Arab Population in the Israeli Economy* (Tel-Aviv: International Center for Peace in the Middle East, 1990), and Ruth Klinov, "Arabs and Jews in the Israeli Labor Force" (Jerusalem: Department of Economics, Hebrew University, 1989 [Working Paper No. 214]).

58. As Khalidi, *The Arab Economy in Israel*, 182, has put it, that economy has been "subservient to the interests and capacities of national capital. . . ."

59. Kimmerling, *Zionism and Economy*, 189–204.

60. Haidar, *The Arab Population in the Israeli Economy*, 131.

61. Aziz Haidar, *The Emergence of the Arab Bourgeoisie in Israel* (Jerusalem: Arab Thought Forum, 1986), ch. 1 [Arabic].

62. Al-Haj, *Social Change and Family Processes*, 111.

63. Ibid., ch. 5.

64. Lustick, *Arabs in the Jewish State*, 258.

65. See Zureik, *The Palestinians in Israel*, 175. In 1979, the Arab students at the five Israeli universities called a day of protest to express their indignation at the discrimination they said they faced.

66. Even local organizations such as the League for Jaffa Arabs and the Nazareth Heritage Society furthered this process. See Tessler, "Arabs in Israel," 115.

67. Control over local municipalities was the only autonomous focus of power for the Israeli Arabs and, especially, for the Communist party. However, the party failed to manage the municipalities effectively. They were not only discriminated against by the Israeli authorities, but they neglected local problems such as unpopular tax collection to deal with "high politics." See Majid al-Haj and Henry Rosenfeld, *Arab Local Government in Israel* (Boulder: Westview, 1990), pp. 66–68.

68. Smooha, *Arabs and Jews in Israel*, xvi. See also K. Nakleh, "Cultural Determinants of Palestinian Collective Identity: The Case of the Arabs in Israel," *New Outlook* 18 (1975): 54–57.

69. The survey was of 427 male Arab adults, commissioned by the newspaper, *Davar*, and executed by Dahaf, a professional polling institute. *Davar*, September 22, 1968. Haidar, "The Different Levels of Palestinian Ethnicity," pp. 109–10, found that Arabs in Israel felt superior in some ways and inferior in others (for instance, socioculturally). See also Sharif Kanaana, *Change and Continuity: Studies on the Effect of the Occupation on Arab Palestinian Society* (Jerusalem: Arab Studies Society, 1983) [Arabic].

70. Smooha, *Arabs and Jews in Israel*, 209.

71. Smooha, *The Orientation and Politicization of the Arab Minority in Israel*, 34, 39; and *Arabs and Jews in Israel*, 54, 137.

72. Ibid., xvii.

73. See Elie Rekhes, "Israeli Arabs and the Arabs of the West Bank and Gaza: Political Affinity and National Solidarity," *Asian and African Studies* 23 (1989): 119–54; Haidar, "The Different Levels of Palestinian Identity," in Esman and Rabinovich, eds., *Ethnicity, Pluralism, and the State*, 95–121. See also Aharon Layish, ed., Special Issue on "The Arabs in Israel: Between Religious Revival and National Awakening," *HaMizrah HeHadash* 32 (1989) [Hebrew]. From this issue, see specifically the articles of Thomas Mayer, "The Muslim Youth in Israel," pp. 10–20; Elie Rekhes, "Israeli Arabs and the Arabs of the West Bank and Gaza Strip: Political Ties and National Identification," pp. 165–91; George Kanazi, "Ideologies in Palestinian Literature in Israel," pp. 129–38. In the 1992 Israeli elections, up to 50 percent of Arab voters went for Jewish parties, attempting to re-enter the Jewish-dominated Israeli political arena. They were a major factor in the victory of the left bloc, contributing about five seats to it (in addition to five seats for the Arab parties, which constitute an integral, but unofficial, part of the Israeli left parliamentary bloc).

74. Sample surveys indicated that the proportion of Israeli Arabs who identified themselves in Palestinian terms was 57.5 percent in 1976, 54.5 percent in 1980, 68 percent in 1985, and 67 percent in 1988. The endorsement of general strikes as a means of Arab struggle was 63 percent in 1976, 55 percent in 1980, 61 percent in 1985, and 74 percent in 1988. Support of the Committee of the Heads of Arab Local Councils was 48 percent in 1976, 55 percent in 1980, 63 percent in 1985, and 71 percent in 1988. The data are from Sammy Smooha, "The Divergent Fate of the Palestinians on Both Sides of the Green Line: The Intifada as a Test," paper presented at the International Sociological Association, 12th World Congress of Sociology, Madrid, July 12, 1990.

75. According to Israeli officials, sabotage committed by Arabs in Israel increased from 69 incidences in 1987 to 238 in 1988, but then decreased to 187 the following year. Of these 187 incidents, there were 91 acts of arson, 28 thrown Molotov cocktails, 17 uses of explosives, 8 stabbings, 8 violent assaults, 6 shootings, and 3 hand grenade attacks. More frequent were "subversive nationalistic incidents"—in 1989 they included 119 stone throwings, 104 instances of writing anti-Israeli or pro-PLO slogans, 92 of hoisting the Palestinian flag, 15 road blockings, 14 acts of destruction of state emblems, 4 incidents of laying false explosives, etc. Idem, 19–20.

76. Asad Ghanim and Sara Osetzki-Lasar, *Green Line, Red Lines and the Israeli Arabs Face the Intifada* (Givat Haviva: Institute of Arab Studies, 1990), pp. 4–14 [Hebrew]; also Smooha, "The Divergent Fate of the Palestinians," 5.

77. Suleiman Shakur, cited in ibid., 12.

78. David Libai cited in Thea Buxbaum and Marla Brettschneider, "Amendment No. 3: Protector of Israeli National Security or Threat to Israeli Arabs?" *Israel Horizons* 37 (1989) and 38 (1990): 9.

79. Mar'i, *Arab Education in Israel*, xi.

80. Cited in A.L. Tibawi, "Visions of the Return: The Palestinian Arab Refugees in Arab Poetry and Art," *Middle East Journal* 17 (1963): 517.

81. Shammas, *Arabesques* (New York: Harper & Row, 1988), p. 91. In 1992 the prestigious Israel Prize for Literature went to Emile Habibi, the first time it was awarded to an Arab (in protest, the leader of the Tehiya party, Yuval Ne'eman, returned his own prize in physics).

82. Cited in Yochanan Peres and Nira Yuval-Davis, "Some Observations on National Identity of the Israeli Arab," *Human Relations* 22 (1969): 219.

83. Cited in Zureik, *The Palestinians in Israel*, 178.

7. DISPERSAL, 1948–1967

1. Turki, *The Disinherited*, 29.

2. See Elisha Efrat, "Changes in the Settlement Pattern of Judea and Samaria during Jordanian Rule," in Kedourie and Haim, eds., *Palestine and Israel in the 19th and 20th Centuries*, 207; Avi Plascov, "The Palestinians of Jordan's Border" in Owen, ed., *Studies in the Economic and Social History of Palestine*, 209. Palestinians did fruitlessly demand that the Jordanians revive and restore Jerusalem and make it the country's second capital. The Jordanians systematically moved its administrative functions to Amman. Arab Jerusalem faced some economic revival in the 1960s, connected mostly with the tourist trade.

3. See Pamela Ann Smith, "The Palestinian Diaspora, 1948–1985," *Journal of Palestine Studies* 15 (1986): 96–98.

4. The *Palestinian Statistical Abstract, 1980* (Damascus: PLO Central Bureau of Statistics, 1981), puts the figure at nearly 4.5 million Palestinians (up from 1.3 million in 1947), of whom 58.8 percent lived outside Palestine.

5. See Smith, "The Palestinian Diaspora," 90–108; Tibawi, "Visions of the Return," 507–26; Rubinstein, *The Fig Tree Embrace*, 23–26.

6. Antoine Mansour, "The West Bank Economy: 1948–1984" in T. Abed, ed., *The Palestinian Economy*, p. 71, estimates the increase in population of the West Bank in 1948–49 at 59.4 percent, or a gain of 276,500. He also estimates the yearly rate of population growth from 1952 to 1967 at 0.54 percent.

7. A smaller percentage actually started out in the camps, but some drifted there when they found no other means of sustenance.

8. The rural population growth was over 100 percent for the two-decade period (more than twice the rate for the urban areas). See Efrat, "Changes in the Settlement Pattern of Judea and Samaria," in Kedourie and Haim, eds., *Palestine and Israel in the 19th and 20th Centuries*, 197ff.

9. See Elia T. Zureik, "Reflections on Twentieth-Century Palestinian Class Structure," in Nakleh and Zureik, eds., *The Sociology of the Palestinians*, 47–63. In a study of Lebanese refugees published in 1977, it was found that 68 percent of the respondents' grandfathers had worked in agriculture while only 17 percent of the sample did so now, about three-quarters working in the service sector. The study was conducted by Samir Ayoub and is quoted in Sayigh, *Palestinians: From Peasants to Revolutionaries*, 121.

10. For the general historical, sociopolitical, and economic development of Transjordan, see Manib al-Madi and Saliman Musa, *The History of Jordan in the Twentieth Century* (Amman: 1959) [Arabic]; Aqil Abidi Hyder Hasan, *Jordan: A Political Study, 1948–1957* (London: Asia Publishing House, 1965); A. Konikoff, *Transjordan: An Economic Survey* (Jerusalem: Economic Research Institute, the Jewish Agency for Palestine, 1946); George Harris, *Jordan—Its People, Its Society, Its Culture* (New Haven: Human Relations Area Files, 1958); Frederick Gerard Peak, *A History of Jordan and Its Tribes* (Coral Gables: University of Miami Press, 1958); Benjamin Swadran, *Jordan: A State of Tension* (New York: Council for Middle Eastern Affairs Press, 1959); Paul A. Jureidini and R. D. McLaurin, *Jordan: The Impact of Social Change on the Role of the Tribes* (New York: Praeger, 1984). Also see Anis Saigh, *The Hashemites and the Palestine Question* (Beirut, 1966) [Arabic]; Yosef Nevo, *Abdullah and the Palestinian Arabs* (Tel-Aviv: Shiloach Institute, Tel-Aviv University, 1975), pp. 37–119 [Hebrew]. For Abdallah's own account, see *Mudhakkirat al-Malik Bin al-Husayn* (Jerusalem, 1946) [Arabic]; *My Memoirs Completed* (Washington: American Council of Learned Societies, 1954) [English].

11. See Shaul Mishal, *West Bank/East Bank: The Palestinians in Jordan, 1949–1967* (New Haven: Yale University Press, 1978), pp. 1–12; Avi Plascov, *The Palestinian Refugees in Jordan, 1948–1957* (London: Frank Cass, 1981), pp. 16–19; Brand, *Palestinians in the Arab World*, 161–62.

12. For this view, see Naseer H. Aruri, *Jordan: A Study in Political Development* (The Hague: Martinus Nijhoff, 1972). An opposing view is of Jordan as a polity dominated by its Bedouin minority, seeking control over (but not cultural integration with) other groups. See, for example, Clinton Bailey, *Jordan's Palestinian Challenge, 1948–1983: A Political History* (Boulder: Westview Press, 1984), pp. 3–4; and Arthur R. Day, *East Bank/West Bank: Jordan and Prospects for Peace* (New York: Council on Foreign Relations, 1986), pp. 62–67.

13. Cited in Roger N. Baldwin, "The Palestine Refugees," *Current History* (November 1957): 296.

14. There was no shortage of resettlement schemes tabled by various parties. See, for example, S. G. Thicknesse, *Arab Refugees: A Survey of Resettlement Possibilities* (London: Royal Institue of International Affairs, 1949), pp. 17–19, 41–44.

15. Brand, *Palestinians in the Arab World*, 165.

16. Mishal, *West Bank/East Bank*, 9.
17. Aruri, *Jordan*, 35–36.
18. A. K. Abu-Hilal and I. Othman, "Jordan" in C. A. O. Van Nieuwenhuijze, ed., *Commoners, Climbers and Notables: A Sampler of Studies on Social Ranking in the Middle East*, in *Social, Economic and Political Studies of the Middle East*, vol. 12 (Leiden: E. J. Brill, 1977), p. 140.
19. The urban Palestinian population was around 37 percent vs. 23 percent for Transjordanians. See Amnon Kartin, *Changes in Settlement Patterns in Transjordan on the Background of the Palestinian Migration, 1948–1967* (unpublished M.A. thesis, Tel-Aviv University, 1987), pp. 58–59 [Hebrew].
20. Mishal, *West Bank/East Bank*, 40–46. Kartin indicates that 34 percent of Palestinian youngsters through age 15 were students in different schools, against 18 percent in Transjordan. In Arab Palestine there had been a physician for each 3,333 persons, in Transjordan, for each 10,000. One daily newspaper was published in the kingdom in 1944, against 3 dailies, 10 weeklies and 5 quarterlies in Arab Palestine. The employment structure of the kingdom was fairly homogeneous, as the vast majority were fellaheen or nomads. As noted in chapters 2 and 3, the Palestinian economic structure was changing rapidly.
21. For a description of the biggest refugee camp on the West Bank, Jelazun camp (near Ramallah), see Shimon Shamir, "West Bank Refugees—Between Camp and Society," in Migdal, ed., *Palestinian Society and Politics*, 146–68; see also Yoram Ben-Porath, Emmanuel Marx, and Shimon Shamir, *A Refugee Camp in the West Bank: An Interim Report*, Jerusalem, April 1968 [Hebrew, mimeo].
22. For some basic statistical data and socio-economic indicators see Hashemite Kingdom of Jordan, *First Census of Population and Housing*, vol. 3 (Amman: Department of Statistics, 1961); International Bank for Reconstruction and Development, Economic Mission to Jordan, *The Economic Development of Jordan* (Baltimore: The Johns Hopkins University Press, 1957); A. Thavirajah, S. Akel and H. M. Abugarah, "Mid-Decade Demographic Parameters of Jordan and Population Growth," in *Demographic Measures and Population Growth in Arab Countries* (Cairo: Cairo Demographic Center, 1970). See also R. Patai, ed., *The Hashemite Kingdom of Jordan* (New Haven: Yale University Press, 1957), pp. 45–77; Kartin, *Changes in Settlement Patterns in Transjordan*, 56–57. For political reasons, Jordan's official statistics do not use Palestinian nationality in its census and demographic surveys. Aruri, *Jordan*, 45–48, estimates that the Palestinians constitute about two-thirds of East-Jordan. See also A. Sinai and Allen Pollack, eds., *The Hashemite Kingdom of Jordan and the West Bank—A Handbook* (New York: American Academic Association for Peace in Middle East, 1977), p. 121. The same estimate is made in "Divorce First, Then Cohabitation," *The Economist*, June 1, 1974.
23. There were 53 camps total in Lebanon, Gaza, Syria, and Jordan.
24. Sarah Graham-Brown, "Agriculture and Labour Transformation in Palestine" in Glavanis and Glavanis, eds., *The Rural Middle East*, 57.
25. This project diverted water by gravity flow from the Yarmouk River into a 44-mile canal in the Jordan Valley running parallel to the east side of the Jordan River. It added about 30,000 acres of irrigated land, as well as labor-intensive fruit and vegetable cultivation, mostly by the much more skilled Palestinian fellaheen. Michael P. Mazur, *Economic Growth and Development in Jordan* (Boulder: Westview Press, 1979), pp. 145–47.
26. Mansour, "The West Bank Economy," 74.
27. The Clapp Commission (formally, the United Nations Economic Survey Mission) recommended the establishment of a UN organization to handle refugee assistance after it calculated that over 650,000 were in need of help. Resolution 302 of the General Assembly on December 8, 1949, created the United Nations Relief

and Works Agency for Palestine Refugees in the Near East. UNRWA began operations on May 1, 1950. It was preceded briefly by the United Nations Relief for Palestine Refugees (UNRPR).

28. UNRWA became one of the major sources of indirect income and capital influx for all Jordan—approximately half of total external transfers in the early 1950s. See Issa Naman Fakhoury, *An Analytical Study of Jordan's Balance of Payments, 1950–1968* (Amman: Central Bank of Jordan, 1974), p. 75. In 1951, UNRWA helped the Jordanian government establish the Jordanian Development Bank. The Jordanian economy was also eventually bolstered by the private capital of wealthy Palestinians—Arab banks had released about £2.5 million of it at the end of 1955, with about 60 percent going to Jordan. See Palestine Arab Delegation, *Report of the United Nations Conciliation Commission for Palestine, 1948–1961* (New York, n.d.), p. 64. These deposits improved the situation of the old wealthy Palestinian families and reinforced class differences.

29. Aruri, *Jordan*, 48.

30. Plascov, *The Palestinian Refugees in Jordan*, 16–26.

31. Ibid., 23.

32. Plascov, "The Palestinians of Jordan's Border," 212.

33. Rosemary Sayigh, "The Palestinian Identity Among Camp Residents," *Journal of Palestine Studies* 6 (1977): 3–22.

34. The Mufti saw pan-Arabism as a threat to his own waning leadership. He broke with Nasser and moved from Cairo to Beirut in 1959, living there until his death 15 years later. See Mattar, *The Mufti of Jerusalem*, 113–14.

35. A Palestinian identified as Yasser, cited in Paul Cossali and Clive Robson, *Stateless in Gaza* (New Jersey: Zed Books, 1986), pp. 21–22.

36. Musa Alami, "The Lesson of Palestine," *The Middle East Journal* 3 (1949): 373–405.

37. *Gumhuriyyah*, April 14, 1963. Cited in Bailey, *Jordan's Palestinian Challenge*, 16.

38. Ibid., 13. Other crises were the assassination of the king in 1951 and of the prime minister in 1960.

39. See Ammon Cohen, *Political Parties in the West Bank Under the Jordanian Regime, 1949–1967* (Ithaca: Cornell University Press, 1982), pp. 15–26, 239–51.

40. Malcolm Kerr, *The Arab Cold War—1958–1964: A Study of Ideology in Politics* (New York: Oxford University Press, 1965), pp. 59–101.

41. Cohen, *Political Parties in the West Bank*, 26.

42. Muhammad Ali Khulusi, *Economic Growth in the Palestinian Gaza Strip, 1948–1961* (Cairo: United Commercial Press, 1967), pp. 42–43 [Arabic].

43. Ziad Abu-Amr, "The Gaza Economy: 1948–1984" in Abed, ed., *The Palestinian Economy*, 101.

44. Gaza's original population was in the city of Gaza itself, the town of Khan Yunis, and 15 villages.

45. The formal head of the government was Ahmad Hilmi Pasha, and Jamal al-Husseini was foreign minister. The Mufti, in fact, spent only a bit more than a week in Gaza before the British pressured the Egyptian government to have him return to Cairo.

46. Abu-Amr, "The Gaza Economy," in Abed, ed., *The Palestinian Economy*, 103.

47. See Eric Cohen, "Report on a Comparative Research of Two Towns: Chan Yunes in Gaza Strip and Nablus in the West Bank" (Department of Sociology, Hebrew University, April 1968 [Hebrew, mimeographed]).

48. Similar sentiments against resettlement were found in Syria. See Fred C. Bruhns, "A Study of Arab Refugee Attitudes," *Middle East Journal* 9 (1955): 130–38.

49. Turki, *The Disinherited*, 49.

50. Cossali and Robson, *Stateless in Gaza*, 20.

51. Beryl I. Cheal, "Refugees in the Gaza Strip, December 1948–May 1950" (unpublished M.A. thesis, University of Washington, 1985), p. 8.

52. See H. Mundus, *The Labor and the Laborers in Camp Palestine* (Beirut: Palestine Research Center, 1974), pp. 34–51 [Arabic]. Fewer than 3 percent of the refugees held work papers in 1969.

53. For a vivid description of the Rashidiyah camp over four decades, see Zvi Lanir and Elles Dobronsky, *Appointments in Rashidiya* (Tel-Aviv: Dvir, 1983) [Hebrew].

54. "Palestinian Refugee Camp Life in Lebanon," *Journal of Palestine Studies* 4 (1975): 91. A complete analysis of the camps in Lebanon in the 1960s and early 1970s, arguing for a basic similarity between them, may be found in Bassem Sirhan, "The Refugee Camps—A Sociological View," *Shu'un Filastiniyya* (1974): 47–72 [Arabic].

55. Turki, *The Disinherited*, 58.

56. Quoted in Bruhns, "A Study of Arab Refugee Attitudes," 134.

57. Cheal, "Refugees in the Gaza Strip," 48. For some of the same conclusions, see Sirhan, "Palestinian Refugee Camp Life in Lebanon," 102.

58. Cheal, "Refugees in the Gaza Strip," 39.

59. Turki, *The Disinherited*, 39.

60. *New York Herald Tribune*, November 25, 1951; March 15, 1952.

61. Bruhns, "A Study of Arab Refugee Attitudes," 130–38.

62. Sayigh, *Palestinians: From Peasants to Revolutionaries*, 10, quotes the common Palestinian refrain, "We lived in Paradise."

63. Turki, *The Disinherited*, 47, 56.

64. Cheal, "Refugees in the Gaza Strip," 54.

65. Heinz R. Hink and Kent L. Pillsbury, *The UNRWA School System and the Palestine Arab Refugee Problem* (Tempe: Bureau of Government Research, University of Arizona, 1962), p. 10.

66. Brand, *Palestinians in the Arab World*, 13.

67. Badran, *Education and Modernization in Arab Palestinian Society*, 1–14; see also Ibrahim Abu-Lughod, "Educating a Community in Exile: The Palestinian Experience," *Journal of Palestine Studies* 2 (1973): 94–111.

68. Cited in Cossali and Robson, *Stateless in Gaza*, 11.

69. Quoted in Sayigh, *Palestinians*, 118.

70. Ibid., 120.

71. Brand, *Palestinians in the Arab World*, 13.

72. Shafeeq N. Ghabra, *Palestinians in Kuwait: The Family and the Politics of Survival* (Boulder: Westview Press, 1987), pp. 33–35, 63–77.

73. See Riyad Mansur, "The Palestinian Immigrant Community in the United States and its Demographic Condition," *Shu'un Filistiniyya* (February 1980): 84–106 [Arabic]. Mansur argues that the American authorities have recently encouraged the migration of Palestinians to the U.S. as part of an Israeli-American conspiracy to defeat the Palestinian struggle.

74. Ghabra, *Palestinians in Kuwait*, 81ff.

75. I. Stockman, "Changing Social Values of the Palestinians—The New Outlook of the Arab Peasant," *New Middle East* (June, 1969): 18–31.

76. See Moshe Shemesh, *The Palestinian Entity, 1959–1974: Arab Politics and the PLO* (London: Frank Cass, 1988), chs. 1 and 2.

77. Ibid., 8ff.

78. Khalidi, "The PLO as Representative of the Palestinian People" in Augustus Richard Norton and Martin H. Greenberg, eds., *The International Relations of the Palestine Liberation Organization* (Carbondale: Southern Illinois University Press, 1989), p. 59.

8. THE FEDAY: REBIRTH AND RESISTANCE

1. See State of Israel, *Census of Population 1967: West Bank of Jordan, Gaza Strip, Northern Sinai and the Golan Heights* (Jerusalem: Central Bureau of Statistics and Israel Defense Forces, 1967).

2. Samih al-Qasim, "Resignation from the Death Insurance Company (About those who started thinking after June 5, 1967)" in Issa J. Boullata, ed., *Modern Arab Poets, 1950–1975* (Washington, D.C.: Three Continents Press, 1976), p. 117.

3. Janet Wallach and John Wallach, *Arafat: In the Eyes of the Beholder* (New York: Lyle Stuart, 1990), p. 11. See also Alan Hart, *Arafat: Terrorist or Peacemaker?* (London: Sidgwick and Jackson, 1984), p. 30.

4. Arafat's organization eventually united with one in Syria in 1959 to form the General Union of Palestinian Students (GUPS), which would become a potent source of Palestinian activism in the following decades. It formed branches in Europe and the United States.

5. See Helena Cobban, *The Palestinian Liberation Organisation: People, Power and Politics* (New York: Cambridge University Press, 1984), p. 24; and Rashid Hamid, "What Is the PLO?" *Journal of Palestine Studies* (Summer 1975): 90–109.

6. Cited in Cobban, *The Palestinian Liberation Organisation*, 21–22.

7. Hart, *Arafat: Terrorist or Peacemaker?*, 120.

8. Wallach and Wallach, *Arafat*, 106, claim that the Mufti was an early and substantial supporter of Arafat and his magazine. Their claim is based on the report of the Mufti's son-in-law, Muheideen al Husseini.

9. For more on Abu Jihad see chapter 9, p. 262. A survey of the publication's contents can be found in Naji Alush, *The March to Palestine* (Beirut: Dar al-Talia, 1964), pp. 37–42. Alush was one of the first rebels against Arafat's leadership in the late 1970s. Al-Wazir, the editor of the magazine, was born in Ramleh. In the early 1950s, he initiated raids of vengeance against Israel from Egyptian territory. Finally, he was arrested by the authorities and expelled from Egypt. Before moving to Kuwait, he was a teacher in Saudi Arabia for a short time. Later, he was the deputy commander-in-chief of the Palestinian military forces, responsible for guerrilla actions. In the late 1980s, he was killed in a special Israeli commando operation. Another central figure of this circle was Farouk Khaddumi, later in charge of external and political affairs. Other members of the inner circle, who were also members of GUPS were Salim al-Zaaun and Zuhair al-Alami. In one issue, the magazine published excerpts from the "The Protocols of the Elders of Zion."

10. Quoted in Cobban, *The Palestinian Liberation Organisation*, 24.

11. Hart, *Arafat: Terrorist or Peacemaker?*, 164–65.

12. Wallach and Wallach, *Arafat*, 110.

13. Both the Covenant and the later Charter can be found in Yehoshafat Harkabi, *The Palestinian Covenant and its Meaning* (London: Vallentine Mitchell, 1979). The section cited here is on page 110.

14. Hart, *Arafat: Terrorist or Peacemaker?*, 168, estimates that Fatah lost between 80 and 90 percent of its membership.

15. Ibid., 171.

16. Fanon (1925–61), born in Martinique, was a psychiatrist in a public hospital in Algiers when, in 1956, he joined the FLN and became one of its main ideologues.

17. Ehud Yaari, *Strike Terror: The Story of Fatah* (New York: Sabra, 1970), p. 60.

18. Ibid., 40–43

19. *Middle East Record—1969–1970* (London, 1971), p. 789. See also, Arie Yodfat and Yuval Arnon-Ohana, *PLO Strategy and Tactics* (London: Croom Helm, 1981), p. 118; and Yehoshafat Harkabi, *Fedayeen Action and Arab Strategy*, Adelphi Papers, No. 53 (London: Institute of Strategic Studies, 1968). According to Harkabi's

account, 14 Israelis were killed, but the impact on Israeli society was considerable. When the author conducted a survey among military officers, politicians, students, and kibbutz members, the estimated number of those killed was between 40 and 300.

20. Hamid, "What is the PLO?," 93.

21. According to several sources, the CIA warned the Jordanians about the planned attack. The Jordanian chief-of-staff passed the information to Fatah, advising it to evacuate the camp. Fatah refused and prepared the local resistance. See Cobban, *The Palestinian Liberation Organisation*, 41–42.

22. Shlomo Aronson and Dan Horowitz, "The Strategy of Controlled Retaliation—The Israeli Case," *Medina U'Mimshal* (Summer 1971): 92–93 [Hebrew].

23. "As for terrorism, I announced it yesterday in no uncertain terms, and yet, I repeat it for the record that we totally and absolutely renounce all forms of terrorism, including individual, group, and state terrorism" (Arafat in his December 14, 1988, press conference in Geneva). Joshua Teitelbaum has noted that "the official Arabic translation of Arafat's press conference statement quoted him as saying that the PLO 'rejects' terrorism (*narfuduhu*) not 'renounces.' A few days after the press conference, he told Vienna Television: 'I did not mean to renounce.' " See "The Palestine Liberation Organization" in Ami Ayalon and Haim Shaked, eds., *Middle East Contemporary Survey*, vol. 12 (Boulder: Westview Press, 1988), pp. 256–57.

24. Alain Gresh, *The PLO, The Struggle Within: Towards an Independent Palestinian State* (Atlantic Highlands, N.J.: Zed Books, 1988), pp. 124–26.

25. See Yaari, *Strike Terror*, 163ff.

26. See Teitelbaum, "The Palestine Liberation Organization," 252–53.

27. Jillian Becker, *The PLO: The Rise and Fall of the Palestine Liberation Organization* (London: Weidenfeld and Nicolson, 1984), ch. 33.

28. One of these heroes was a woman, Leila Khaled, who participated in two hijackings and wrote the book *My People Shall Live: An Autobiography of a Revolutionary* (London: Hodder and Stoughton, 1973).

29. The Israelis claimed that Black September was a secret wing of Fatah. Eliezer Ben-Rafael has argued that Black September was directly under the command of Salah Khalaf (p. 38), in *Israel Palestine: A Guerrilla Conflict in International Politics* (Westport: Greenwood Press, 1987)—a book based mainly on Israeli intelligence and military sources. Fatah has consistently denied this charge. No doubt the organization's roots were in Fatah, but its direct control of Black September is not clear. Salah Khalaf (Abu Iyad) claimed that the group was formed spontaneously by guerrilla fighters from several organizations, including Fatah, following the frustration of a clash between the Jordanians and the Palestinians in 1970. See Eric Rouleau, *My Home, My Land* (New York: Times Books, 1981), pp. 131–32. According to Cobban, *The Palestinian Liberation Organisation*, 55, Fatah decided to cut its relations with Black September and then lost all control over it, especially after the defection of the Iraqi-supported Sabra al-Banna ("Abu Nidal"), who formed the "Black June" guerrilla group.

30. See Shemesh, *The Palestinian Entity, 1959–1974*, 106–8.

31. Don Peretz, "Palestinian Social Stratification—The Political Implications" in Ben-Dor, ed., *The Palestinians and the Middle East Conflict*, 423.

32. Cited in Cobban, *The Palestinian Liberation Organisation*, 49.

33. Brand, *Palestinians in the Arab World*, 120.

34. Cobban, *The Palestinian Liberation Organisation*, 48–53; Brand, *Palestinians in the Arab World*, 166–72.

35. See Emile F. Sahliyeh, *The PLO After the Lebanon War* (Boulder: Westview Press, 1986), pp. 115–38, 205–44.

36. The "Jordanization" of the East Bank's Palestinian population continues to be substantial. See Harkabi, *The Palestinian Covenant*, 35.

37. Rex Brynen, *Sanctuary and Survival: The PLO in Lebanon* (Boulder: Westview Press, 1990), pp. 27–28.

38. Lanir and Dobronsky, *Appointments in Rashidiya*, 59.

39. Sayigh, *Palestinians: From Peasants to Revolutionaries*, 164–65.

40. Brynen, *Sanctuary and Survival*, 140.

41. Ibid.

42. Khalidi, *Under Siege: PLO Decisionmaking during the 1982 War* (New York: Columbia University Press, 1985), p. 59. Khalidi's claim of effective rule over Palestinians "everywhere" is greatly exaggerated.

43. "Auditing the PLO," in Norton and Greenberg, eds., *The International Relations of the Palestine Liberation Organization*, 197–98. It is almost impossible to estimate the scope of the PLO's economic activities, its sources, kinds of investments, and criteria for use and distribution of funds. From the late 1960s until its annexation by Iraq in August, 1990, Kuwait collected 5 percent of its Palestinian employees' income as a "liberation tax," which was given annually to the Palestine National Fund under Fatah control. In December, 1977, Kuwait established the "Sunduk al-Sumud," a fund to support the resistance and Palestinian culture in the occupied territories. See Brand, *Palestinians in the Arab World*, 122–25. In the late 1960s, Saudi Arabia also introduced the liberation tax (see Cobban, *The Palestinian Liberation Organisation*, 45), and similar arrangements were made by other traditional Arab regimes. Khalid al-Hassan has lauded Kuwait, Saudi Arabia, Qatar, Morocco, the Sudan, Tunisia, and others in this respect: "We never had to remind them to send what they have promised." See Cobban, 199. The PLO, according to Neil C. Livingstone and David Halevy, *Inside the PLO: Covert Units, Secret Funds and the War against Israel and the United States* (New York: William Morrow, 1989), has controlled a $2 billion budget, as well as large investments. Some have claimed this fortune has led to institutional and personal corruption in the organization's rank and file. Arafat remains one of the few figures in the movement around whom no rumors of corruption circulate.

44. Bishra Sirhan, *Palestinian Children: The Generation of Liberation* (Beirut: Palestinian Research Center, 1970), pp. 76–78.

45. Mai Sayigh, "Lament" in Salma Khadra Jayyusi, ed., *Modern Arabic Poetry: An Anthology* (New York: Columbia University Press, 1987), p. 416.

46. See Matti Steinberg, *Trends in Palestinian National Thought* (Jerusalem: Leonard Davis Institute, The Hebrew University, 1988), pp. 30–31 [Hebrew].

47. For different perspectives on the "territorialization" of the Palestinian guerrilla movement, see Brynen, *Sanctuary and Survival*, 161–80; Khalidi, *Under Siege*, 17–42; Sayigh, *Palestinians: From Peasants to Revolutionaries*, 156–87; Yaari, *Strike Terror*, 328–49; Lanir and Dobronsky, *Appointments in Rashidiya*, 55–102. For the decomposition of the Lebanese state in general, see D. C. Gordon, *The Republic of Lebanon: Nation in Jeopardy* (Boulder: Westview, 1983); Edward P. Haley and Lewis Snider (eds.), *Lebanon in Crisis* (Syracuse: Syracuse University Press, 1979).

48. Sayigh, *Palestinians: From Peasants to Revolutionaries*, 168.

49. See Meir Zamir, *The Formation of Modern Lebanon* (Ithaca: Cornell University Press, 1985), esp. ch. 2, pp. 38–96.

50. On the revolt inside the PLO see Yezid Sayigh, "Struggle Within, Struggle Without: The Transformation of the PLO Since 1982," *International Affairs* 65 (1985): 245–71. For the description of the ideological dimension of the struggle, see Muhammed al-Shuquair, "The History of the Split inside Fatah," *al-Safir* (Beirut), June 26 and 27, 1983 [Arabic]. For English excerpts, see *Journal of Palestine Stud-*

ies 13 (1983): 167–83; Eric Rouleau, "The Mutiny Against Arafat," *MERIP Reports* No. 119 (November–December 1983); Sahliyeh, *The PLO After the Lebanon War*, 139–204.

51. "The PLO as Representative of the Palestinian People" in Norton and Greenberg, eds., *The International Relations of the Palestine Liberation Organization*, 60.

52. The data given by Israeli intelligence to the Kahan Commission of Inquiry were 700–800 dead. The Lebanese Commission estimated 460 victims, and the Palestinian Red Crescent 2,000–3,000. Lebanese death certificates were issued for 1,200 people. See Zeev Schiff and Ehud Yaari, *Israel's Lebanon War* (New York: Simon and Schuster, 1984), p. 282. As is well known, the events caused a political storm in Israel, as people tried to deal with the army's—and Ariel Sharon's— complicity.

53. Cited in Khalidi, "The PLO as Representative of the Palestinian People" in Norton and Greenberg, eds., *The International Relations of the Palestine Liberation Organization*, 64–67.

54. Dahbur, "In Memory of 'Izziddin al-Qalaq" in Jayyusi, ed., *Modern Arabic Poetry*, 196.

55. Harkabi, *The Palestinian Covenant*, 39.

56. John W. Amos, *Palestinian Resistance: Organization of a Nationalist Movement* (New York: Pergamon Press, 1980), p. 45. Amos notes the ideological and personal ties between Fatah's founders and the Muslim Brotherhood. See also Emile F. Sahliyeh, "The West Bank and the Gaza Strip" in Shireen T. Hunter, ed., *The Politics of Islamic Revivalism: Diversity and Unity* (Bloomington: Indiana University Press, 1988), pp. 94–99.

57. Cresh, *The PLO*, 42.

9. STEERING A PATH UNDER OCCUPATION

1. Cited in Alan Hart, *Arafat: A Political Biography* (Bloomington: Indiana University Press, 1984), p. 235.

2. Ibid.

3. See Ariel Sharon (with David Chanoff), *Warrior—An Autobiography of Ariel Sharon* (New York: Simon and Schuster, 1989), pp. 248–60.

4. For a vivid description of the first period of Israeli occupation see Rafiq Halabi, *The West Bank Story* (New York: Harcourt Brace Jovanovich, 1982).

5. Shlomo Gazit, *The Stick and the Carrot: The Israeli Administration in Judea and Samaria* (Tel-Aviv: Zmora, Bitan, 1985), pp. 21–35 [Hebrew].

6. This amounted to two-fifths of the work force. See Fawzi A. Gharaibeh, *The Economies of the West Bank and Gaza Strip* (Boulder: Westview Press, 1985), pp. 21–23, 59. See also *Statistical Abstract of Israel—1978*, no. 29 (Jerusalem: Central Bureau of Statistics, 1979). The data in this chapter, unless otherwise noted, are from *Judea, Samaria and Gaza Area Statistics*, vol. 17 (Jerusalem: Central Bureau of Statistics, 1987), p. 412, as well as previous publications of the CBS, and various publications of the Bank of Israel, e.g., A. Bergman, *The Economic Growth of the Administered Areas, 1968–1973* (Jerusalem: Bank of Israel, 1974) [Hebrew]; and Raphael Meron, *Economic Development in Judea-Samaria and Gaza District* (Jerusalem: Bank of Israel, Research Department, 1988), pp. 7–19 [Hebrew]. (Note the shift of the terms in which the occupied territories are officially defined.) Other sources for data are Meron Benvenisti, *The West Bank Project: A Survey of Israel's Policies* (Washington, D.C.: American Enterprise Institute for Public Policy Research, 1984); and Sara Roy, *The Gaza Strip Survey* (Jerusalem: The West Bank Data Base Project, The Jerusalem Post, 1986). For an early analysis of the political implications of the absorption of these territories into Israel see B. Van

Arkadie, *Benefits and Burdens: A Report on the West Bank and Gaza Strip Economies Since 1967* (Washington, D.C.: Carnegie Endowment for Peace, 1977).

7. Shaul Mishal begins his *West Bank/East Bank: The Palestinians in Jordan, 1949–1967* (New Haven: Yale University Press, 1978) with the following incident: "In February 1971, Qadri Tuqan, a Palestinian Arab from Nablus . . . who served as a minister in Jordan's government during the 1960s, died while on a visit to Beirut. His body was returned to Nablus through the East Bank of Jordan. There, his coffin was wrapped with a Jordanian flag. But when it crossed the river into the West Bank, a Palestinian flag replaced the Jordanian one" (p. 1). Several local designs competed to be the official Palestinian national flag. Finally, in 1964, the PLO decided on the ancient flag of the Sharif of Mecca, a white, green, and black striped design with a red triangle. This flag was one of several carried by Palestinians in the 1936–39 Arab Revolt. See Mahdi Abd al-Hadi, *The Development of the Arab Banner* (Jerusalem: Author's Publication, 1986) [Arabic].

8. "The Gaza Strip: Critical Effects of the Occupation" in Naseer Aruri, ed., *Occupation: Israel Over Palestine* (Belmont, Mass.: Association of Arab-American University Graduates, 1989), p. 339.

9. Shmuel Sandler and Hillel Frisch, *Israel, the Palestinians, and the West Bank: A Study in Intercommunal Conflict* (Lexington, Mass.: Lexington Books, 1984), p. 97. They speak of the PLO as a charismatic ideological center.

10. An earlier attempt at establishing such a coordinating body was made by reconstituting the Supreme Muslim Council. It advocated returning the West Bank to Jordan. After Israel deported Council members, the first effort at creating a National Guidance Committee followed. See Halabi, *The West Bank Story*, 37–40.

11. Helena Cobban, *The Palestinian Liberation Organisation*, 173.

12. Cited in Emile Sahliyeh, *In Search of Leadership* (Washington, D.C.: Brookings Institution, 1988), p. 52. The same picture emerges from a colloquium held by the Front at the Institute of Palestine Studies on July 3, 1981, and partially published in *Shu'un Filistiniyya*, (1981): 45–77 [Arabic].

13. Ibrahim Dakkak, "Back to Square One: A Study in the Re-Emergence of the Palestinian Identity in the West Bank, 1967–1980" in Alexander Scholch, ed., *Palestinians over the Green Line: Studies in the Relations between Palestinians on Both Sides of the 1949 Armistice Line Since 1967* (London: Ithaca Press, 1983), p. 90. Dakkak was himself one of the leading figures in the Front.

14. See Joshua Teitelbaum and Joseph Kostiner, "The West Bank and Gaza: The PLO and the *Intifada*" in Jack A. Goldstone, Ted Robert Gurr, and Farrokh Moshiri, eds., *Revolutions of the Late Twentieth Century* (Boulder: Westview Press, 1991), pp. 298–323.

15. Hillel Frisch, "The Building of Palestinian Institutions in the Occupied Territories, 1967–1985" (unpublished Ph.D. dissertation, Hebrew University, 1989), p. 97 [Hebrew].

16. One source puts Shabiba membership at 40,000. See Yezid Sayigh, "The Intifada Continues: Legacy, Dynamics and Challenges," *Third World Quarterly* 11 (1989): 36.

17. Ibid., 230–31.

18. The new National Front included members of the Popular Front for the Liberation of Palestine, which joined the PLO in 1980. The left-wingers used the Front as a means to limit Fatah control. See Frisch, "The Building of Palestinian Institutions," 70–78.

19. For some echoes of this controversy, see Ibrahim Dakkak, "Development from Within: A Strategy for Survival," in Abed, ed., *The Palestinian Economy*, 287–310. For a literary expression of the ideology of sumud see Raja Shehadeh, *The Third Way: A Journal of Life in the West Bank* (Jerusalem: Adam, 1982), pp. 4–7.

20. Lesch and Tessler, "The West Bank and Gaza: Political and Ideological Responses to Occupation," *Israel, Egypt and the Palestinians*, 269.
21. For an intensive study of such changes see Marisa Escribano and Nazmi El-Joubeh, "Migration and Change in a West Bank Village: The Case of Deir Dibwan," *Journal of Palestine Studies* 11 (1981): 150–60.
22. Salim Tamari, "The Palestinians in the West Bank and Gaza: The Sociology of Dependence" in Nakhleh and Zureik, eds., *The Sociology of The Palestinians*, 84–111.
23. Sandler and Frisch, *Israel, the Palestinians, and the West Bank*, 50.
24. Fertilizer use per acre more than quadrupled from 1968 to the early 1980s, with the use of six times as many tractors. In the years after 1968, agricultural productivity doubled.
25. It went from producing more than a third of the wealth on the West Bank immediately after the war to producing only a quarter by the mid-1980s.
26. Growth averaged 6 percent annually in the West Bank and 5 percent in Gaza into the late 1970s.
27. The agricultural labor force fell from 39 percent of the total work force in 1968 to nearly half that figure, 22 percent, in 1985. By 1986, more than 50 percent of West Bank land and 30 percent of Gaza land were under Israeli control. See Meron Benvenisti, Ziad Abu-Zayed, and Danny Rubinstein, *The West Bank Handbook: A Political Lexicon* (Jerusalem: Jerusalem Post, 1986). On Israeli land-use policies, see Rami S. Abdulhadi, "Land Use Planning in the Occupied Territories," *Journal of Palestine Studies* 19 (1990): 46–63. See also Sabri Jiryis, "Domination by the Law," *Journal of Palestine Studies* 11 (1981): 83ff, and other articles in that issue. On Israel's water crisis and its implications for water use in the occupied territories, see Uri Davis, Antonia E. L. Maks, and John Richardson, "Israel's Water Policies," *Journal of Palestine Studies* 9 (1980): 3–31. On the preferential access to water for Israeli settlers and the crisis for West Bank agriculture and cities, see Sarah Graham-Brown, "The Economic Consequences of the Occupation" in Aruri, ed., *Occupation*, 300–25.
28. Bakr Abu-Kishk, *Arab Industry in the Occupied Territories* (Jerusalem: al-Multaqa al-Fikri al-Arabi, 1981), p. 8 [Arabic]. Less than 10 percent of the wealth and less than 15 percent of the labor force of the territories were accounted for by the 4,000 or so workshops, most with fewer than 10 workers, that constituted the industrial sector. See Simcha Bahiri, *Industrialization in the West Bank and Gaza* (Boulder: Westview Press [the West Bank Data Base Project], 1987); Van Arkadie, *Benefits and Burdens*, 123–25; Graham-Brown, "The Economic Consequences of the Occupation" in Aruri, ed., *Occupation*, 326–32.
29. On the territories' integration into the Israeli economy, see Tamari, "The Palestinians in the West Bank and Gaza" in Nakhleh and Zureik, eds., *The Sociology of the Palestinans*, 85.
30. "Building Other People's Homes: The Palestinian Peasant's Household and Work in Israel," *Journal of Palestine Studies* 11 (1981): 31–66.
31. These data were collected about two to three months before the beginning of the uprising, which considerably decreased the number of laborers from the territories employed in Israel. See *Judea, Samaria and Gaza Area Statistics* (Jerusalem: Central Bureau of Statistics, November 1987), pp. 34–35. The real number seems to be higher, because the statistics referred mainly to "authorized" employment. To this, we have to add persons (mainly young women and girls) working in their homes or neighborhood centers, producing semifinished products for Israeli manufacturers from pieces distributed by local subcontractors. Tamari (ibid, 97) estimates that about *half* of all wage earners of the occupied region were dependent on employment in Israel. To this, we may add the local employees of the various Israeli military and civilian authorities and, later,

those employed by the Jewish settlers. The Palestinians constituted about 8 percent of the total Israeli labor force during the late 1970s and 1980s. For the implications for Israeli society see Moshe Semyonov and Noah Levin-Epstein, *Hewers of Wood and Drawers of Water: Noncitizen Arabs in the Israeli Labor Market* (New York School of Industrial and Labor Relations, Cornell University, Ithaca, 1987), pp. 9–12, 48–51, 62–64.

32. It totaled 70–80 percent of the territories' total exports and imports, far ahead of commerce with Jordan, which was the next largest trading partner. Unofficially, some Palestinians served as go-betweens for the Jordanian and Israeli economies.

33. Israeli attempts after 1982 to control distribution of those proceeds seem to have failed. At first the capital that came in through the Fund was used to finance municipal governments, education, and housing, but after the outbreak of the Intifada it poured into welfare relief for those who lost family members or homes in the fighting.

34. Meron Benvenisti, *US Government Funded Projects in the West Bank and Gaza Strip* (Jerusalem: The West Bank Data Base Project, 1984) See also Mansour, "The West Bank Economy" in Abed, ed., *The Palestinian Economy*, 77; Gideon M. Kressel, "Consumption Patterns in the Administered Territories after a Decade of Israeli Rule" in Raphael Israeli, ed., *Ten Years of Israeli Rule in Judea and Samaria* (Jerusalem: Truman Institute and Magnes Press, 1980), pp. 84–106 [Hebrew]; D. Zakai, *Economic Developments in Judea-Samaria and the Gaza District, 1985–86* (Jerusalem: Bank of Israel, 1988), 35.

35. Sara Roy, "The Gaza Strip: A Case of Economic De-Development," *Journal of Palestine Studies* 17 (1987): 56. Roy continues: "De-development is defined as a process which undermines or weakens the ability of an economy to grow and expand by preventing it from accessing and utilizing critical inputs needed to promote internal growth beyond a specific structural level. In Gaza, the de-development of the economic sector has, over two decades of Israeli rule, transformed that economy into an auxiliary of the state of Israel."

36. Ziad Abu-Amr, "The Gaza Economy: 1948–1984" in Abed, *The Palestinian Economy*, 117.

37. Yerucham Cohen, *The Allon Plan* (Tel Aviv: Hakibbutz Hameuchad, 1969), pp. 171–89 [Hebrew]. See also, Yishai, *Land of Peace*, pp. 67–70.

38. For the development of the political and theological positions of Gush Emunim, see Gideon Aran, *From Religious Zionism to a Zionist Religion: The Origins of Gush Emunim as a Messianic Movement in Contemporary Israel* (unpublished Ph.D. dissertation, Hebrew University, 1987) [Hebrew]; Myron J. Aronoff, "The Institutionalization and Cooptation of a Charismatic-Messianic Religious-Political Movement" in David Newman, ed., *The Impact of Gush Emunim: Politics and Settlement in the West Bank* (London: Croom Helm, 1985), pp. 45–69; Ian Lustick, *For the Land of the Lord: Jewish Fundamentalism in Israel* (New York: Council on Foreign Relations, 1988); David Weisburd, *Jewish Settlers Violence: Deviance as Social Reaction* (University Park: The Pennsylvania State University Press, 1989). See also Gush Emunim, *Master Plan for Settlement of Judea/Samaria* (Jerusalem, March 1978), p. 23 [Hebrew]. The plan (known as the Drobless Plan) was redrafted and adopted by the Settlement Division of the World Zionist Organization in October, 1978 and again in 1981. See World Zionist Organization, *The One-Hundred-Thousand Plan for Year 1985 for Settlement Development in Samaria and Judea* (Jerusalem: Settlement Division, 1981) [Hebrew].

39. The Israeli legal system equalizes "the status of Jews in the territories with that of other Israelis, without changing the legal status of the territories or that of the indigenous Arab population, and without shattering the myth of a military government that complies with international law." Eyal Benvenisti, *Legal Dualism:*

The Absorption of the Occupied Territories into Israel (Boulder: Westview Press [the West Bank Data Base Project], 1990), p. 3; see also Moshe Drori, "The Israeli Settlements in Judea and Samaria: Legal Aspects" in Daniel J. Elazar, ed., *Judea, Samaria, and Gaza: Views on the Present and Future* (Washington, D.C.: American Enterprise Institute, 1982), pp. 44–80.

40. See Ehud Sprinzak, "The Iceberg Model of Political Extremism" in Newman, ed., *The Impact of Gush Emunim*, 27–45; Ian Lustick, "Israeli State Building in the West Bank and the Gaza Strip: Theory and Practice," *International Organization* 4 (1987): 151–71; Kimmerling, "Between the Primordial and the Civil Definitions of the Collective Identity" in Cohen, Lissak and Almagor, eds., *Comparative Social Dynamics*, 262–83.

41. See *The Jerusalem Post*, August 19, 1988 (based on data of the Guttman Institute of Applied Social Research) and *Davar*, August 3, 1984. The first political group that openly demanded mass expulsion by force was Rabbi Meir Kahane's party, Kach. The party won one of the 120 seats of the Israeli parliament. In the 1988 elections, the party was not allowed to run, because the Israeli Supreme Court ruled that it had a racist platform. Another party, Moledet, headed by retired General R. Zeevi, ran under the slogan of "transfer." The platform called for voluntary transfer, that is, persuading the Palestinians to leave by giving them some material incentives. Moledet won two seats in 1988 and no seats in 1992. See Asher Arian, *Politics in Israel: The Second Generation*, revised ed. (Chatham, N.J.: Chatham House, 1989), p. 92.

42. For the internal struggle and changing policy of Israel towards the 1967 occupied territories, see Yael Yishai, *Land or Peace: Whither Israel?* (Stanford: Hoover Institution Press, 1987). For analysis of the changes in the Israeli socio-political system see Dan Horowitz and Moshe Lissak, *Trouble in Utopia: The Overburdened Polity of Israel* (Albany: State University of New York Press, 1989).

43. See Hanan Mikhail Ashrawi, "The Contemporary Palestinian Poetry of Occupation," *Journal of Palestinian Studies* 7 (1978): 77–111; A. M. Elmessiri, "The Palestinian Wedding: Major Themes in Contemporary Palestinian Poetry," *Journal of Palestine Studies* 10 (1981): 77–99; Ann Mosely Lesch, "Closed Borders, Divided Lives: Palestinian Writings," UFSI Reports, No. 28, 1985; Shinar, *Palestinian Voices*, pp. 14–17, 61–66.

44. The two pro-Jordanian newspapers are *al-Quds* and *An-Nahar*. The two pro-PLO newspapers are *al-Fajr* and *Shaab*. For more on the Palestinian press under occupation see Dov Shinar and Danny Rubinstein, *Palestinian Press in the West Bank: The Political Dimension* (Jerusalem: The West Bank Data Base Project and Jerusalem Post, 1987).

45. See Aryeh Shalev, *The Intifada: Causes and Effects* (Tel-Aviv: Papyrus, 1990), pp. 28ff [Hebrew]. Israeli Arabs were part of this process of Palestinization. See Sammy Smooha, "The Divergent Fate of the Palestinians on Both Sides of the Green Line: The Intifada as a Test" (paper presented at the session on State, Nation and Ethnic Violence, International Sociological Association, XII World Congress of Sociology, Madrid, July 12, 1990).

46. The figure is from the Palestinian Academic Educational Council in Jerusalem. The Council, which was founded in September 1977, was one of the major meeting points for the local elite. Frisch, "The Building of Palestinian Institutions," 124–49, argues that professionally it failed, not having enough power to impose any real coordination among the institutions. Concerning the number of students, see Hamada Faraana, "The Aims of Higher Education in the West Bank and the Gaza Strip," *Samid al-Iqtisadi* 7 (1985) [Arabic]. The number increased until December, 1987, when all the institutions were closed as one of the Israeli responses to the uprising.

47. *Palestinian Voices*, 105; see also *Al-Bilad al-Arab*, 13 May, 1984. The "national-istic character" of Bir Zeit was also reflected in its student union's struggle to change the teaching language from English to Arabic—and in the deportation of its head, Hanna Nasser.

48. Frisch, "The Building of Palestinian Institutions", 207–12.

49. From an address to the Sixth Voluntary Work Camp in Nazareth, 1980. See Dak-kak, "Development from Within" in Abed, *The Arab Economy*, 305.

50. For a detailed description of the internal struggles within the Palestinian labor movement, see Joost R. Hiltermann, "Before the Uprising: The Organization and Mobilization of Palestinian Workers and Women in the Israeli-Occupied West Bank" (unpublished Ph.D. dissertation, University of California at Santa Cruz, 1988), ch. 3.

51. The cited data are from the Arab Thought Forum (1981), an intellectual, semi-academic research and cultural institution founded in 1977 in Jerusalem.

52. Frisch, *The Building of Palestinian Institutions*, 197–215.

53. See Hamida Kazi, "Palestinian Women and the National Liberation Movement: A Social Perspective" in Khamsin Collective, *Women in the Middle East* (London: Zed Books, 1987), p. 27. Women also protested the Balfour Declaration. See Soraya Antonius, "Fighting on Two Fronts: Conversations with Palestinian Women" in Miranda Davis, ed., *Third World—Second Sex* (London: Zed Books, 1983), p. 63.

54. See Julie Peteet, "Women and the Palestinian Movement: No Going Back?" *MERIP Report* No. 138 (January–February, 1986): 20.

55. "When a girl begins to earn money," the founder is quoted as saying, "she may begin to impose conditions on her family. We don't encourage such a spirit in our girls." Quoted in Rosemary Sayigh, "Encounters with Palestinian Women under Occupation," *Journal of Palestine Studies* 10 (1981): 12.

56. See for example Mustafa Barghouthi and Rita Giacaman, "The Emergence of an Infrastructure of Resistance: The Case of Health" in Jamal R. Nassar and Roger Heacock, eds., *Intifada: Palestine at the Crossroads* (New York: Praeger, 1990), pp. 73–87.

57. Ziad Abu-Amr, "Class Structure and the Political Elite in the Gaza Strip: 1948–1988" in Aruri, ed., *Occupation*, 94.

58. The progress of women has actually been uneven: Certainly education and new forms of wage labor have been emancipatory, but in at least one rural West Bank village there are signs of increased domestication. See Analiese Moors, "Gender Hierarchy in Palestinian Village: The Case of Al-Balad" in Glavanis and Glavanis, eds., *The Rural Middle East*, 195–207.

59. Ann M. Lesch, "Gaza: Forgotten Corner of Palestine," *Journal of Palestine Studies* 15 (1985): 45.

60. *Statistical Abstract of Israel—1985*, no. 36 (Jerusalem, Central Bureau of Statistics, 1985).

61. In fact, the story of the Israeli economy is made up of two separate histories. From 1948 to 1973, Israel averaged 10 percent growth annually in its national product, a figure among the highest in the world; from 1974 to 1988, the pace slowed to just over 3 percent with wealth per capita rising less than 2 percent annually.

62. Graham-Brown, "The Economic Consequences of the Occupation" in Aruri, ed., *Occupation*, 341, 347–49.

63. Ibid., 349–50. About three-quarters of that figure was from the West Bank, where Palestinians benefited from the ease with which they could obtain a Jordanian passport for fairly easy travel.

64. The average was 5.5 percent a year, according to the World Bank, although numbers on the Jordanian economy for that period should be seen more as orders of magnitude than exact representations.

65. They slipped 8 percent, in the first half of 1987 alone, and grant aid fell by 30 percent between 1982 and 1988. Jordanian economic growth showed some residual strength in the first half of the 1980s (about 4.1 percent), but declined rapidly in the last half of the decade. Figures are from The World Bank, *World Development Report, 1989* (New York: Oxford University Press, 1989); *The World Bank Atlas, 1989* (Washington, D.C.: The World Bank, 1989); *Trends in Developing Economies, 1989* (Washington, D.C.: The World Bank, 1989); United Nations Industrial Development Organization, Industrial Development Review Series, *Jordan: Stimulating Manufacturing Employment and Exports*, prepared by Regional and Country Studies' Branch, December 24, 1987.

66. See Tamari, "From the Fruits of Their Labour" in Glavanis and Glavanis, eds., *The Rural Middle East*, 70–94.

67. Israeli policymakers took some belated cognizance of this, instituting a series of policies in late 1991, designed to spur the growth of West Bank and Gaza Strip businesses. *The New York Times*, December 1, 1991, p. 8.

68. See Meron Benvenisti, *1987 Report: Demographic, Economic, Legal, Social and Political Developments in the West Bank* (Boulder: Westview Press, 1987), p. 47; Shalev, *The Intifada*, 209–10.

69. Penny Johnson and Lee O'Brien with Joost Hiltermann, "The West Bank Rises Up," *MERIP Report* No. 155 (1988): 6. This essay and others from the *MERIP Report* have been reprinted in Zachary Lockman and Joel Beinin, eds., *Intifada: The Palestinian Uprising Against Israeli Occupation* (Boston: South End Press, 1989); see also Adil Yahya, "The Role of the Refugee Camps" in Nassar and Heacock, eds., *Intifada*, 95.

70. The term was not new. Yasser Arafat used it in a 1973 speech celebrating the "8th year of the Palestinian Revolution" (the first Fatah attack in January 1965), to designate the internal resistance against the occupation. See *The Yearbook of the Palestinian Problem—1973*, n. 10 (Beirut: Institute of Palestinian Studies, 1976), p. 3. The term also appeared many times in Palestinian periodicals. In 1987, it was probably coined by Mohammed Milhem, former mayor of the West Bank town of Halhoul.

71. Excerpts from Mansur's poem "The Shrouded Face," translated by Dr. Rivka Yadlin of the Truman Institute of the Hebrew University.

72. "Stories of Daughters," *MERIP Report* No. 165 (1990): 29.

73. Ze'ev Schiff and Ehud Ya'ari, *Intifada: The Palestinian Uprising—Israel's Third Front* (New York: Simon and Schuster, 1990), p. 190.

74. A study of the leaflets was done by Shaul Mishal with Reuben Aharoni, *Speaking Stones: The Words Behind the Palestinian Intifada* (Tel Aviv: Hakibbutz Hameuchad, 1989) [Hebrew].

75. Radio Al-Quds, controlled by Syria, was used by Jibril's Popular Front for the Liberation of Palestine-General Command.

76. See Salim Tamari, "The Uprising's Dilemma: Limited Rebellion in Civil Society," *Middle East Report* 20 (1990): 7. See also the semiclandestine publication in English, FACTS Information Committee, *Towards a State of Independence: The Palestinian Uprising, December 1987–August 1988* (Jerusalem: September, 1988), and the highly biased paper by Samiah K. Farsoun and Jean M. Landis, "Structure of Resistance and the 'War of Positions': A Case Study of the Palestinian Uprising," *Arab Studies Quarterly* 11 (1989): 59–86.

77. On the "Intifada Profiters" and the familial workshops in the West Bank, see Danny Rubinstein in *Haaretz*, October 9, 1990. Unfortunately, at the time of this book's writing, no reliable economic data on the West Bank and Gaza Strip were available. Some reporting is available in Richard Toshiyuki Drury and Robert C. Winn, *Plowshares and Swords: The Economics of Occupation in the West Bank* (Boston: Beacon Press, 1992), ch. 2.

78. The poem is "Those Who Pass Between Fleeting Words," in Lockman and Beinin, eds., *Intifada*, 26. The second citation is found in Adel Samara, "The Political Economy of the West Bank 1967–1987: From Peripheralization to Development" in *Palestine: Profile of an Occupation* (Totowa, N. J.: Zed Books, 1989), p. 23.

79. Bank of Israel, *Annual Report, 1989* (Jerusalem: Government Printer, 1990), p. 83.

80. Sara Roy, "The Political Economy of Despair: Changing Political and Economic Realities in the Gaza Strip," *Journal of Palestine Studies* 20 (1991): 67.

81. B'TSELEM, *Information Sheet: June–July 1990 Update* (Jerusalem: The Israeli Information Center for Human Rights in the Occupied Territories, 1990): 34. B'TSELEM was founded in February, 1989, by Israeli intellectuals, lawyers, journalists, and parliament members in order to collect data on human rights violations, based on independent fieldwork as well as Israeli and Palestinian sources. Its findings are usually about 20 to 30 percent higher than those of Israeli official sources and 30 to 35 percent lower than those of its Palestinian counterpart, *al-Haq*, a Ramallah-based organization.

82. Shaul Mishal, " 'Paper War'—Words Behind Stones: The Intifada Leaflets," *The Jerusalem Quarterly* 51 (1989): 89.

83. Samih K. Farsoun and Jean M. Landis, "The Sociology of an Uprising: The Roots of the Intifada" in Nassar and Heacock, eds., *Intifada*, 31.

84. Roy, "The Political Economy of Despair," 68.

85. Ibid., 61–62.

86. Reported on Israeli television, August 29, 1988, and in *un-Nahar*, August 30, 1988.

87. "The Intifadah and the Arab World: Old Players, New Roles," *International Journal* 45 (1990): 501.

88. Many comparisons of the two revolts have been made. See, for example, Kenneth W. Stein, "The Intifadah and the 1936–1939 Uprising: A Comparison of the Palestinian Arab Communities," The Carter Center of Emory University, Occasional Paper Series, vol 1, no. 1 (December 1989); and Muhammad Khalid Al-Azhari, "1936 Revolt and 1987 Intifada (A Comparative View)," *Shu'un Filistiniyya* (1989): 3–26 (Arabic).

89. See Helga Baumgarten, " 'Discontented People' and 'Outside Agitators': The PLO in the Palestinian Uprising" in Nassar and Heacock, eds., *Intifada*, 207–26, and Ali Jarbawi, "Palestinian Elites in the Occupied Territories: Stability and Change through the Intifada," ibid., 288.

90. For example, Emile Saliyeh, cited in ibid., 287.

91. Teitelbaum and Kostiner, "The West Bank and Gaza," 317–21; and Hillel Frisch, "From Armed Struggle Over State Borders to Political Mobilization and Intifada Within It: The Transformation of PLO Strategy in the Territories," *Plural Societies* 19 (1991): 92–115, esp. 114–15. Frisch argues that the leadership in the West Bank and Gaza Strip used the many organizations that had developed in the territories as a basis for the Intifada but failed to create territory-wide organizations. Territorial consolidation failed because the PLO feared potential national competitors. See Frisch, "Between Diffusion and Territorial Consolidation in Rebellion: Striking at the Hard-Core of the Intifada," *Terrorism and Political Violence* 3 (1991): 39–62.

92. Helena Cobban, "The Palestinians: From the Hussein-Arafat Agreement to the Intifada" in Robert O. Freedman, ed., *The Middle East from the Iran-Contra Affair to the Intifada* (Syracuse: Syracuse University Press, 1991), p. 262.

93. Ibid.

94. Teitelbaum and Kostiner, "The West Bank and Gaza," 316.

95. See, for example, David McDowall, *Palestine and Israel: The Uprising and Beyond* (London: I. B. Tauris, 1989), p. 100: "The PLO's victory removed neither Jordan nor the traditional élite from the scene. The new mayors were summoned

to Amman and reminded of the value of good relations for marketing agricultural produce to Jordan. Each was helped to assess the balance of loyalty by the offer of financial assistance to his municipality."

96. On the Islamic groups among Palestinians, see Jean-François Legrain, "Islamistes et lutte nationale palestinienne dans les territoires occupés par Israel," *Revue française de science politique* 36 (1986): 227–47.

97. Lisa Taraki, "The Islamic Resistance Movement in the Palestinian Uprising," *MERIP Report* No. 156 (1989): 31.

98. Ibid.

99. Mishal, " 'Paper War,' " 82.

100. This was reported even before the Intifada in *The Manchester Guardian*, May 18, 1986.

101. See, for example, Dale Bishop, "Mosque and Church in the Uprising," *MERIP Report* No. 152 (1988): 41–42.

102. See Rita Giacaman and Penny Johnson, "Palestinian Women: Building Barricades and Breaking Barriers" in Lockman and Beinin, eds., *Intifada*, 155–69; Phyllis Bennis, *From Stones to Statehood: The Palestinian Uprising* (New York: Olive Branch Press, 1990), pp. 31–37; Shalev, *The Intifada*, 90–91.

103. See, for example, I. Gad, "From Salon Ladies to Popular Committees: Women in Uprising" in *Readings in Contemporary Palestinian Society*, vol. 2 (Bir Zeit: Bir Zeit University Press, 1989).

104. Rema Hammami, "Women, the Hijab and the Intifada," *MERIP Report* No. 165 (1990): 24–28.

105. Julie Peteet, *Gender in Crisis: Women and the Palestinian Resistance Movement* (New York: Columbia University Press, 1991), p. 209.

106. Sayigh, "Encounters with Palestinian Women under Occupation" in Elizabeth Warnock Fernea, ed., *Women and the Family in the Middle East: New Voices of Change* (Austin: University of Texas Press, 1985), p. 206.

107. Quoted in Maya Rosenfeld, " 'I Don't Want My Body to Be a Bridge for the State," *Challenge* 2 (1991): 25–26.

108. Geoffrey Aronson, *Israel, Palestinians and the Intifada: Creating Facts on the West Bank* (New York: Kegan Paul International, 1987), p. 324.

109. Including Elias Freij, the Christian mayor of Bethlehem; Zakaria al-Agha, chairman of the Arab Medical Association of Gaza; Mustafa Natsche, the dismissed mayor of Hebron; Haidar Abd al-Shafi, a Gazan active in the founding of the PNC and of the Palestinian Red Crescent; and Saeb Erakat, an instructor of political science in the West Bank.

Index